HOMERIC WHISPERS

AN ILLYRIAN BARD WITH HIS GUSLE

HOMERIC WHISPERS
intimations of orthodoxy in the
Iliad and *Odyssey*

ROBERTO SALINAS PRICE

SCYLAX PRESS

Derechos Reservados © 2006
Instituto de Investigaciones Homéricas
Ocotepec #40 (esq. Corregidora)
San Jerónimo Lídice
México, D. F., 10200

www.homero.com.mx

For
Marie Linda
belovèd wife, companion, and friend...

...and for
Branko Vukušić and Slobodan Čašule
to whom I owe so much,
and, not least,
the ever-cheerful and optimistic
Vesna Pešič

I also have an enormous debt of gratitude with a host of friends, all, in some way or another, collaborators towards a better understanding of the Homeric World. I know they know that they too have been instrumental in the writing of this book. Among these I cannot fail to mention Ronald Gottesman for his sober opinion and diligent help in the shaping of this book.

Contents

Preface		9
FOREWORD		15

1. The Iliad

I.	THE ILIAD AND ITS TROJAN GEOGRAPHY	43
II.	ILIOS: A BRIEF SURVEY	97
III.	THE TROJAN WAR AND FALL OF TROY	113
IV.	THE TROJAN DIASPORA	125

2. The Odyssey

V.	THE ODYSSEY AND ITS FANTASTIC GEOGRAPHY	137
VI.	ITHAKA: PRELIMINARY NOTES	179
VII.	THE TWELVE MISADVENTURES OF ODYSSEUS	191
VIII.	PELASGIAN TROJANISM AND THE NEW ILLYRIANS	217

3. Homer

IX	THE MAKINGS OF HELLAS	227
X.	THE HELLENIZATION OF HOMER	235
XI.	THE HOMERIZATION OF HELLAS	243
XII.	TROY VIII	251

A POSTSCRIPT	259
ILLUSTRATIONS	269
Bibliography	273
General Index	281

Preface:

This book is about what the words of Homer now tell *me* since that day, twenty years ago, when *Homer's Blind Audience* was published in 1984 in English, and in 1985 in the then politically correct "Serbo-Croatian". Its subtitle, "an essay on the *Iliad's* geographical prerequisites for the site of Ilios", was intended to convey to its reader two ideas, each sound on its own merits, yet, together, somewhat too hasty and ambitious: first, that there existed plausible reasons, based on several geographical arguments, and one scant literary reference, for understanding the *Iliad's* story about a siege on Ilios as the product of a Trojan culture that once existed along the length of Croatia's Dalmatian Coast; second, that understanding "Homer" beyond this geographical context could yield little more than literary nonsense. Somehow, the *Iliad's* narrative about Troy's geographical context seemed to fit the geographical realities of the Dalmatian Coast and so provide a clearer understanding of the general story line. Certain Trojan place-names were slightly modified, but, to all intents and purposes, intact, and some even existed in translation. Also, stories and legends about Troy were in place, and, above all, there existed the archaeology where archaeological evidence was necessary to clinch the argument. The natural, logical inference to the best explanation was that "Homer" (in reality a college of bards) had been Trojan, and that the *Iliad* was a Trojan work. Of course, the *Iliad* can be read and understood as it has been, for so many centuries, in its Asia Minor context, but, at a great loss to the reader. I have met translators of the *Iliad* and scholars of the *Odyssey* who put no stock in the importance of a geographical setting for these works, simply, because epic poetry is *not* tantamount to understanding the military strategy and logistics of, say, a Battle of Bastogne, but, rather, more on the plane of literary amusement, not unlike that of Don Quixote taking dark Satanic mills or Hudibras running riot through the Plaza del Sol...

What I expected —granted, in a foolhardy manner— was that those who had formal studies, were better informed, and most important, had better talent than mine, would come forward and correct, or expand upon, the fundamental premise when necessary. The response in western academia was limited (not in pettiness, but in volume), whereas in the now former Yugoslavia the topic of the day during the Summer of 1985 was "Troja", sometimes in favour, and sometimes against.

Among those who favoured the hypothesis was Dr. Olga Lukovič-Pjanovič, a linguist (and a former student of the celebrated Chantrainne brothers) who asked me to explain, if I could, *what* the original language of Homer had been, and, that, if I could not, she would do so for me. Of all Homeric Questions, *this* was precisely the one that I had not wished to broach, for —I shuddered to think about it!— the language in all likelihood will have been "Pelasgian", a primitive forerunner of Greek, coetaneous with a Mykenaian Linear B... which, alas! was some time later rendered by the mysterious forces of magic into the exquisite Greek in which we now possess these works[1]. When Dr. Lukovič-Pjanovič saw that I knew not a whit about the subject, she presented me with a brief work by a certain Gregory Dankovsky, in which, in 1829, he proposed that the original language of Homer was a Slavic dialect[2]. I went into a state of cultural shock, so to speak, but, with time, I learned to think differently. Those who dismiss this hypothesis as unlikely, if not altogether ridiculous, cannot even begin to give rational explanations on the etymologies of names like "*Iliad*", "Troy", "Hellespont", "Pygmies"... or several hundreds of them, in fact, and have no recourse but to offer meanings (where these are possible) derived from a language-base —Greek— that did not come into existence until some three, or perhaps four, centuries after the fact.

Among those against was the vociferous Dr. Djuro Basler, who pompously declared that I had purported to "change history" with a mere 150 pages, to which my answer was that lamentably, I was not as talented as Newton, otherwise I also might have done it in 36... Eventually, we met, apologized mutually for our numerous needless remarks about each other, and came to an agreement that I was not an archaeologist, nor was he a Homeric scholar. Dr. Basler later published a full retraction in the local Bosnian *Oslobodjenia*, and agreed to explore Gabela —the site I had identified as the Homeric Ilios— when, suddenly, and sadly, he departed this life. His magnificent archaeologi-

---

1. At that time I was satisfied with simply understanding Homeric etymologies, whenever these were possible, in terms of a Greek vocabulary. This I now regard as anachronistic and wide of the mark.

2. Dankovsky, Gregorius. *Homerus Slavicis dialectis cognata lingua scripsit*. Vindobona [Vienna]: J. G. Heubner; Posonium [Presbourg]: J. Landes et A. Schwaiger. 1829.

cal plan of the site of Daorson, which he gave me in a gesture of conciliation, is published here.

* * *

Since 1985 I have returned many times with my wife to those lands and peoples which have captivated my life, and it seems as though, since then, every week there has come to light some new insight or some new information or some new discovery, even unbidden whispers. Whereas in 1985 I had no idea (nor did I think it was relevant to the study of Homer, *per se*) how the Homeric poems came to Hellas and how they became Greek works, nor why the site of Hissarlik at the entrance to the Dardanelles became popularly known as the site of Homeric Troy, I have now come full circle and feel sufficiently comfortable with a better understanding of certain quirks about the texts and difficulties of historiography. The archaeology, or, at the least a presumption of some archaeological vestige, has always seemed like the definitive proof —the *corpus delicti*, as it were— of this or that suspicion about this or that place mentioned in Homer. However, the importance of archaeological evidence now merely seems to underscore simply what linguistics has asserted as incontrovertible truth.

Several discoveries have sharpened my understanding of the *Iliad* and *Odyssey*, but —I shall be clear about this— nested in the awareness that one cannot own the Truth. To own it (or purport to have a better possession of it than others) somehow demeans one and obliterates the purpose of conversing with it. As an amateur researcher (that is, I pay my own salary) I can only think of myself as a merchant of ideas. Thus, if on many occasions I have been sadly wanting in advice on this or that disquieting doubt about some Homeric trivia, it has been, perhaps, to my advantage to be somewhat distant from the consensus, familiar with the literature available to academia, yet not wholly swayed by it.

So it is that I am comfortable with the discovery of a *purpose* for the Trojan War, deftly woven into the narrative line of the *Iliad* (albeit not explicitly enunciated) which was only one of a number of devastating social and political events that occurred toward the close of the Bronze Age and beginning of the Iron Age (*c.* 1,100 BC). In particular, what is known in archaeology as the Dalmatian Agglomeration gives certain indications of perilous times for the period and the area in question. By contrast with the *Iliad*, the *Odyssey* is about reasons for a deeply-rooted *dissatisfaction* with the new world-order established by the conquering enemy. At the *core* of this conflict, which spread quickly throughout the known world and established a permanent new world-order, was the set of philosophical and economic tenets favouring a patriarchy over a matriarchy. Here, archaeological vestiges come into evidence (albeit it is the linguistics which tie up the argument), for the *Iliad* is about a siege and final destruction of a hillock and its sites in the shape of a *phallus*, but the *Odyssey* is about the long absence and final return to a palace, in the shape of a *vulva*. The texts describe both sites meticulously, the archaeological remains confirm their former existence.

As regards linguistics, the discovery that certain ethnicons have a number of synonyms (configured to cultural and temporal context) has been invaluable for unveiling *what* happened after the Trojan War and *why* there exist such strong reminiscences of a Trojan history in both the Slavic and Western European worlds —indeed, how it came to be that we possess the *Iliad* and *Odyssey*. One can easily understand that the name of the Germans is that of the Alemanni, or Deutsche, or Tedeschi, or Nemanič, which refer to one and the same people. The same is true with the name of the Dardanioi, *not* descendants of Dardanus, but, rather, a folk with a similar sounding name who were occupants of the SKAMANDROS (Neretva) river-valley, for linguistics shows the name of one and the name of the other have *two* different meanings, and show up in places like Rome, Macedonia, Poland, and even as far as Moscow.

Last, the most stunning discovery is that I can no longer distinguish between that mythical, ever-elusive "Homer", and the would-be person of "Orpheus", the presumed author of an *Argonautica*, a historically impossible precursor of the *Odyssey*. As much as can be said at this time about the names of these personages is that, simply, they are echoes of an archetypal image which come to one from different places and different periods, both names perhaps even meaning the same thing, both having a common source in the long-standing institutional framework of some hitherto unsuspected college of bards —not merely a college of itinerant *aoidoi* or *guslars*, talented performers who assemble lengthy verses in a given meter and on a given topic at a moment's notice, but bards with expertise not only in diverse fields of knoweldge, but also with expertise in their *preservation* and *transmission*.

So much for my Homeric disquisitions and disquietudes.

Still, this work is bound to incorporate a number of dubious assertions as well as factual mistakes. One might well ask the Gentle Reader (though he tends to be anything but that) to accommodate the author with a measure of Mercy and let significant mistakes pass as unimportant, yet, admittedly, my livelihood has been that of a merchant of ideas, so to speak, and thus I am well aware that if ideas are not clean and pristine, the consumer will look elsewhere for sounder ones. So, I leave the Gentle Reader to choose between one of two options—

- either the current hypothesis stands that the story-stuff of the *Iliad* and *Odyssey* was derived from diverse sources in the Mediterranean world and brought together by formative processes of oral transmission until finally cast (once and for all) as literary units of epic poetry in the Greek language,
- or The *Iliad* and the *Odyssey* can be shown to be sister compositions in a Slavic dialect of the same time and place which were taken abroad by *omirones* (Homeridai) who accompanied Paionian or Vard*j*aei emigrations into Macedonia, and thence into Asia Minor, where they became translated into units of epic poetry in the Greek language.

Mexico City R. S. P.
Autumn, 2005

Imagine that the natural sciences were to suffer the effects of a catastrophe. A series of environmental disasters are blamed by the general public on the scientists. Widespread riots occur, laboratories are burnt down, physicists are lynched, books and instruments are destroyed. Finally a Know-Nothing political movement takes power and successfully abolishes science teaching in schools and universities, imprisoning and executing the remaining scientists. Later still there is a reaction against this destructive movement and enlightened people seek to revive science, although they have largely forgotten what it was. But all they possess are fragments: a knowledge of experiments detached from any knowledge of the theoretical context which gave them significance; parts of theories unrelated either to the bits and pieces of theory which they possess or to experiment; instruments whose use has been forgotten; half-chapters from books, single pages from articles, not always fully legible because torn and charred. Nonetheless all these fragments are reembodied in a set of practices which go under the revived names of physics, chemistry, biology. Adults argue with each other about the respective merits of relativity theory, evolutionary theory, and phlogiston theory, although they possess only a very partial knowledge of each. Children learn by heart the surviving portions of the periodic table and recite as incantations some of the theorems of Euclid. Nobody, or almost nobody, realizes that what they are doing is not natural science in any proper sense at all. For everything that they do and say conforms to certain canons of consistency and coherence and those contexts which would be needed to make sense of what they are doing have been lost, perhaps irretrievably.

This imaginary possible world is very like one that some science fiction writers have constructed. We may describe it as a world in which the language of natural science, or parts of it at least, continues to be used but is in a grave state of disorder. We may notice that if in this imaginary world analytical philosophy were to flourish, it would never reveal the fact of this disorder. For the techniques of analytical philosophy are essentially descriptive and descriptive of the language of the present at that. The analytical philosopher would be able to elucidate the conceptual structures of what was taken to be scientific thinking and discourse in the imaginary world in precisely the way that he elucidates the conceptual structures of natural science as it is.

What is the point of constructing this imaginary world inhabited by fictitious pseudo-scientists and real, genuine philosophy? The hypothesis which I wish to advance is that in the actual world which we inhabit the language of morality is in the same state of grave disorder as the language of natural science in the imaginary world which I described. What we possess, if this view is true, are the fragments of a conceptual scheme, parts which now lack those contexts from which their significance derived...

Alasdair MacIntyre, *After Virtue, A study in Moral Theory*.
Notre Dame, Indiana: University of Notre Dame Press, 2nd. edition, 1984 (p. 1).

Foreword

The hypothesis which I wish to advance is that all geographical information contained in the *Iliad* and *Odyssey* reflects some credible measure of geographical reality, since, it would seem—

- the author's intention might well have been to register some reasonable semblance of factual information, rather than willfully present premeditated distortions of facts (for whatever reason one might suspect), and thus,

- to depart willfully from the notion there is a semblance of truth in the facts of a story line —a kind of narrative deconstructionalism, so to speak— would seem to defeat the purpose of story-telling, which is that of conveying an account of facts, fantastic, incredible, and factually mistaken as they may be, but, nevertheless, *intended* as a truthful account.

If, then, it could be said there seems to exist a gap of credibility between what Homer evidently states with pristine clarity regarding the geographical background of a nine-year siege on Troy and the the final days between contending armies, then, it would seem that—

- either the account of a Trojan War as given in the *Iliad* is of little historical value, such that it would seem pointless to establish a point of contact between Ilios, or Troy, and the site of Hissarlik at the entrance to the Dardanelles[1],

- or, the site of Ilios (also erroneously called Troy) is to be found in some other land that offers the necessary geographical setting.

---

1. That Homer is not a primary source of Trojan geography, a distinction that might fall more aptly, perhaps, on Demetrius of Scepsis (*fl. c.* 170 BC) is openly recognized: see *The Encyclopaedia Britannica*; 13th. Ed., 1926, Vol. 27, pp. 314, 316; J. M. Cook, *The Troad, An Archaeological and Topographical study*. Oxford: Clarendon Press, 1973, p. 91; G. S. Kirk, *The Iliad: A Commentary* ("Introduction to the Trojan catalogue"), Vol. I. Cambridge: Cambridge University Press, 1985, p. 248.

GEOGRAPHICAL ABSURDITIES

The immediate implication of moving the *Iliad* into a geographical context where its narrative line might find a suitable berth in existing geographical realities[2] at once evinces that its narrative line has been constrained, or reigned in, by an apparatus of geographical information: that is, it is not the story line which builds an apparatus of geographical information, but rather, quite the reverse, that a fixed number of toponyms and ethnicons fix the parameters of what the story-line may state or where it may go (see I. THE ILIAD AND ITS TROJAN GEOGRAPHY)[3].

The following eight examples of geographical absurdities in the *Iliad* are of two sorts, namely, those where this or that particular scene in an Asia Minor context is better suited to a Balkan setting, and in the reverse circumstance, instances where this or that particular scene in a Balkan setting simply cannot suit an Asia Minor context.

* * *

NOTA BENE
Conventions used throughout this work:

AIGAI, ZELEIA: onomastica of the ILIAD *corresponding to Balkan context*
Aiaia, Ogygia: onomastica of the **Odyssey** *corresponding to Balkan context*

Aigai, Zeleia: onomastica of ILIAD *used external to a Balkan context*
Aiaia, **Ogygia***:* onomastica of **Odyssey** *used external to a Balkan context*

All translations of cited text of the Iliad and Odyssey are those of A. T. Murray in the Loeb Classical Library (see Bibliography).

---

2. *A propos* of a paradigm-shift (or "candidature" of a new paradigm) T. S. Kuhn, in *The Structure of Scientific Revolutions*, The University of Chicago Press, 2nd ed., 1970, p. 169, notes how a new paradigm must not only possess the ability of solving a generally recognized problem, but also preserve in some measure the problem-solving ability of its predecessor.

3. I have given a brief outline of the structure of Homeric Geography in my *Atlas of Homeric Geography*, San Antonio, Scylax Press, 1992 and in its translation into Spanish, *Atlas de la geografía homérica*, México D. F., Ediciones Huicalco, 2001. These outlines were published to serve as a norm of general reference for a proposed full account in my *Elements of Homeric Geography*.

FOREWORD

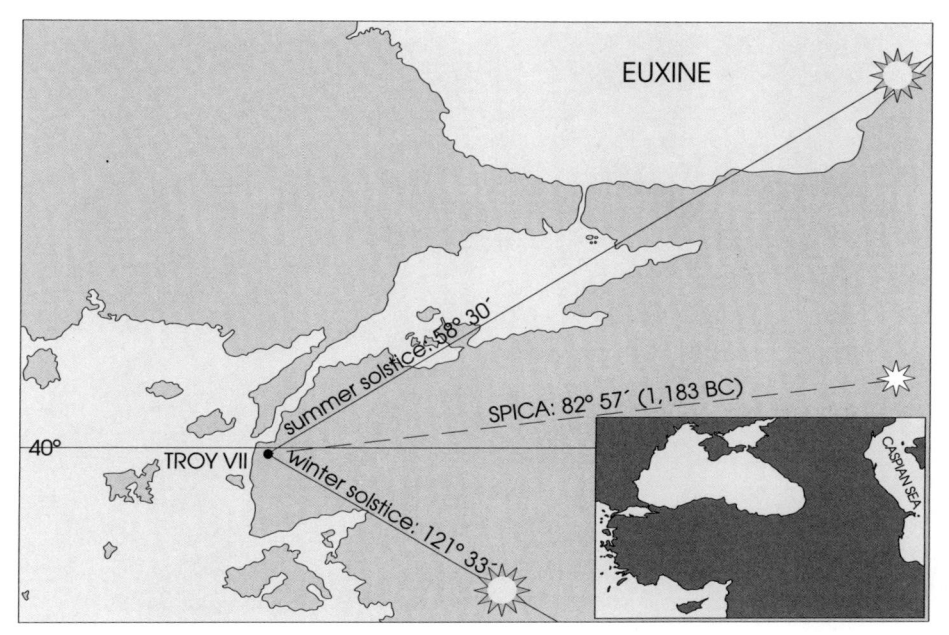

MAP 1a. NO SEA EAST OF TROY. *The only sea east of Troy are the southern waters of the Caspian Sea, which is a lake (albeit a large body of salt water).*

SEA

There are three specific (and puzzling) instances which suggest that a SEA is to be found to the east of Troy, namely:

...like the star of harvest-time [Spica] that shineth bright above all others when he hath bathed him in the stream of Ocean... (V, 6)

The sun was now just striking on the fields, as he rose from softly-gliding, deep-flowing Oceanus, and climed the heavens... (VII, 422)

Now Dawn the saffron-robed arose from the streams of Oceanus to bring light to immortals and to mortal men... (XIX, 1)

A rationalization of the foregoing instances may be found in the following (A. J. B Wace and F. H. Stubbings, *Companion To Homer*, 283):

The earth seems to be conceived as a circular plane, surrounded by the stream of Oceanus, the source of all waters, ἐξ οὗ περ πάντες ποταμοὶ καὶ πᾶσα θάλασσα / καὶ πᾶσαι κρῆναι καὶ φρείατα μακρὰ νάουσιν. (Φ 196–7) Out of Oceanus rises the sun, and sinks again into it, as do most of the stars, except for the Great Bear, which οἴη ὣ ἄμμορός ἐστι λοετρῶν Ὠκεανοῖο. (Σ 489).

On the particular brightness of the "the star of harvest-time..." (V, 6), G. S. Kirk, *Iliad: A Commentary*, II, 53 seems to suggest that the star is not rising (as, obviously, it cannot), but, rather, something different:

Here, however, washing (or bathing) implies brightness rather than setting...

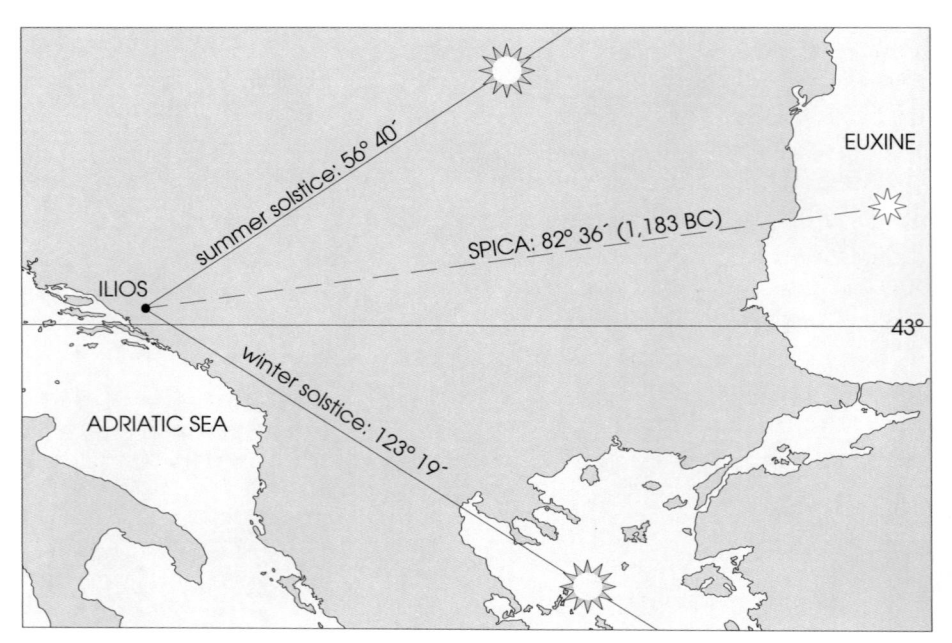

MAP 1b. A SEA IN THE EAST. *The Euxine (Black Sea) to the east of Troy answer the need of a SEA from which celestial bodies may appear to rise.*

However, the obvious oftentimes requires complex Ptolemaic explanations, as stated by M. W. Edwards, *Iliad: A Commentary*, V, 235 :

> The various one-verse and two-verse formular expressions for 'Dawn came' are discussed at 2.48–9n. Here verse 2 is the same as 11.2 and *Od.* 5.2, but verse 1, instead of bringing Dawn from Tithonos' bed ('Ἠὼς δ' ἐκ λεχέων παρ' ἀγαυοῦ Τιθωνοῖο | ..., 11.1 = *Od.* 5.1), puts together a unique combination of formulae to bring her from Ocean.

* * *

Now, there *is* no SEA —properly, OKEANOS— to the east of Troy from which Spica, "the star of harvest-time", or Sirius, as the case may be, nor the sun, nor Dawn, could have arisen (*MAP 1a*), unless the intended sea were the Euxine, the Adriatic, or the Tyrrhenian, thus placing Troy somewhere on the Balkan, Italian, or Iberian peninsulas. Granted, the Caspian Sea, albeit a lake, is, indeed, an immense body of salt water and may have been the intended sea (tinted with some measure of narrative exaggeration for popular entertainment that had no need of exact geographical knowledge), although such a likelihood seems remote, for OKEANOS was connected, as it were —forming a *stream*, as well as having currents and tides— with other parts or sections of itself (a characteristic which the Caspian cannot have), and which seems somewhat incongruous with the notion of celestial bodies setting in the sea (VIII, 485; XVIII, 240) and arising from a lake. To wit, the definition of 'Ὠκεανός, in G. Autenrieth, *Homeric Dictionary*:

> Oceanus, is distinguished from the sea (θάλασσα, πόντος, ἅλς) as a mighty stream (ποταμός, Σ 607, Υ 7; ῥόος 'Ὠκεανοῖο, Π 151) encircling the whole Earth, Σ 607.

It would seem, then, that TROIA may be situated in the Balkans, along Croatia's Adriatic Coast, between Šibenik Bay in the north and Boka Kotorska in the south, such that OKEANOS corresponds with the Euxine or Black Sea in the east, and the Adriatic in the west (*MAP 1b*), and its nature and characteristics are sufficiently satisfied.

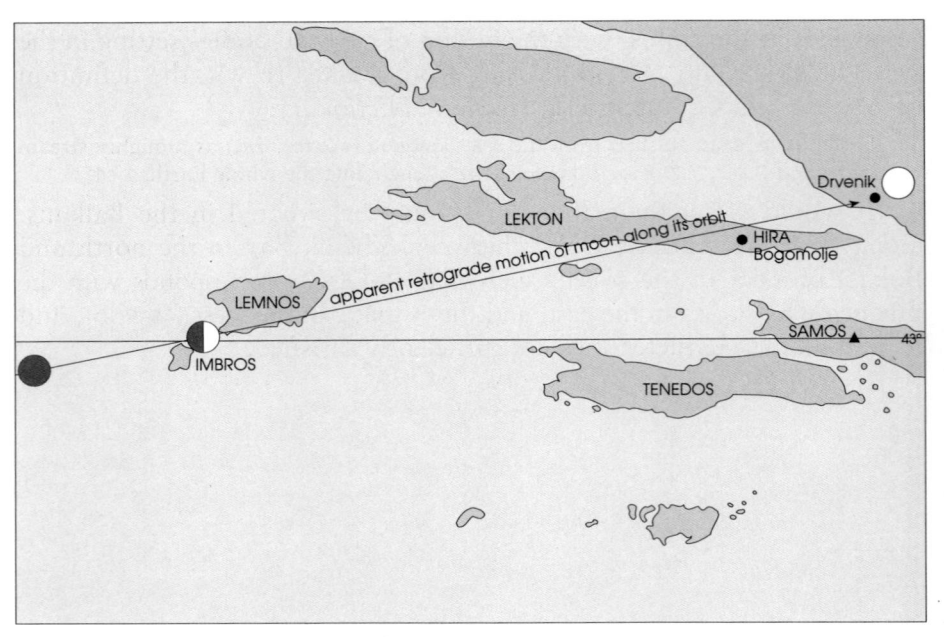

MAP 2a. DESCRIPTION OF A LUNAR CYCLE. The apparent retrograde movement of the moon (Hera) appearing as a New Moon, then in the 4th quarter, and finally as a Full Moon rising in the East at sundown.

ISLANDS

There is a passage that describes the moon's apparent retrograde movement along its orbit over a period of approximately 15 days, from a New Moon about to set in the west after sunset, to a Full Moon rising in the East, also at sunset. This description identifies the islands of IMBROS (Biševo) and LEMNOS (*Issa*, Viš), fixing their positions relative to each other and the Trojan coast (corroborated below), as well as identifying the island of LEKTON (*Lessina*, Hvar). To wit (XIV, 225 *et pas.*):

> ...but Hera darted down and left the peak of Olympus... and from Athos she stepped on the billowy sea, and so came to Lemnos, the city of godlike Thoas. There she met Sleep, the brother of Death; and she clasped him by the hand, and spake and addressed him...
>
> So spake he, and the goddess, white-armed Hera, failed not to hearken but sware as he bade... But when she had sworn and made an end of the oath, the twain left the cities of Lemnos and Imbros, and clothed about in mist went forth, speeding swiftly on their way. To many-fountained Ida they came, the mother of wild creatures, even to Lectum, where first they left the sea; and the twain fared on over the dry land, and the topmost forest quivered beneath their feet. There Sleep did halt... and mounted up on a fir-tree exceeding tall, the highest that then grew in Ida; it reached up through the mists into heaven...
>
> But Hera swiftly drew nigh to topmost Gargarus, the peak of lofty Ida, and Zeus, the cloud-gatherer, beheld her.

Hera —the New Moon on the western horizon— appears to have departed the Italian Peninsula from ATHOS (Pedaso) and some 7 days later come to LEMNOS (*Issa*, Viš), where, as a 3rd Quarter Moon, she met "Sleep, the brother of Death; and she clasped him by the hand..." (XIV, 231–2). Thence, "speeding swiftly" towards IDA (Biokovo Range) they come to LECTON (*Lessina*, Hvar) "where first they left the sea..." (XIV, 284). That Hera has come to LEMNOS *before* touching IMBROS is because the 3rd Quarter Moon (Hera and Hypnos) moves from east to west, as will a Full Moon rising in the east and throughout the night move from IDA (Biokovo Range) to LEKTON.

Towards the end of the lunar cycle of 29.5 days (that is, on the 30th day of the old cycle which is the same as the 1st of the new cycle), Hypnos and Hera are no longer joined, and so it is a question of interpretation whether it was Hypnos or Hera that "mounted up on a fir-tree exceeding tall, the highest that then grew in Ida..." (XIV, 286–88). The place where this tall fir-tree will have been located is at Drvenik ("Oakton") on the mainland, immediately opposite the eastern tip of LEKTON (*MAP 2a*). On the summit of the mountains which rise behind Drvenik are to be found the remains of some Illyrian precinct (not a burial site, or *gomila*).

* * *

The traditional location of the Trojan islands in the north Aegean for the scenario of an allegorical love-embrace between Hera and Hypnos offers nothing, as noted by W. Leaf, *The Iliad*, II, 69–73 (on XIV, 230 *et pas.*):

> Why Lemnos should have been chosen as the spot at which Sleep was to be found we cannot even guess. It is natural to suppose that there was some local cult of Hypnos there, but if so it has left no trace.

Still further, an explanation of the course taken by Hera all the way from Athos, across the sea, to Lekton, is given by R. Janko, *The Iliad, A Commentary*, IV, 186–197, 186:

> 225–79 Herē leaves for Mt Ida, but meets Sleep (Hupnos) at Lemnos en route, apparently by luck (231n.); yet his aid is vital to her plan, and she bribes him heavily to get it. This unlikely coincidence, the sole structural problem in this scene, is the small price Homer pays for the chance to surprise and amuse us with another display of her wiles.
> 225–30 The first leg of Herē's journey takes her down the N. E. foothills of Olumpos (Pieriē) and along the Macedonian coast (Emathiē) to the 'snowy mountains of the Thracians', which are neither the Rhodope range nor Mt Pangion behind Amphipolis (both too far N. E.), but Mt Athos itself to the S. E., whence she crosses the sea, in the same direction, to Lemnos (see Map, p. xxiv). Thence she will zigzag N. E. to Imbros, then S. down the coast of the Troad to Lekton, its S. W. tip

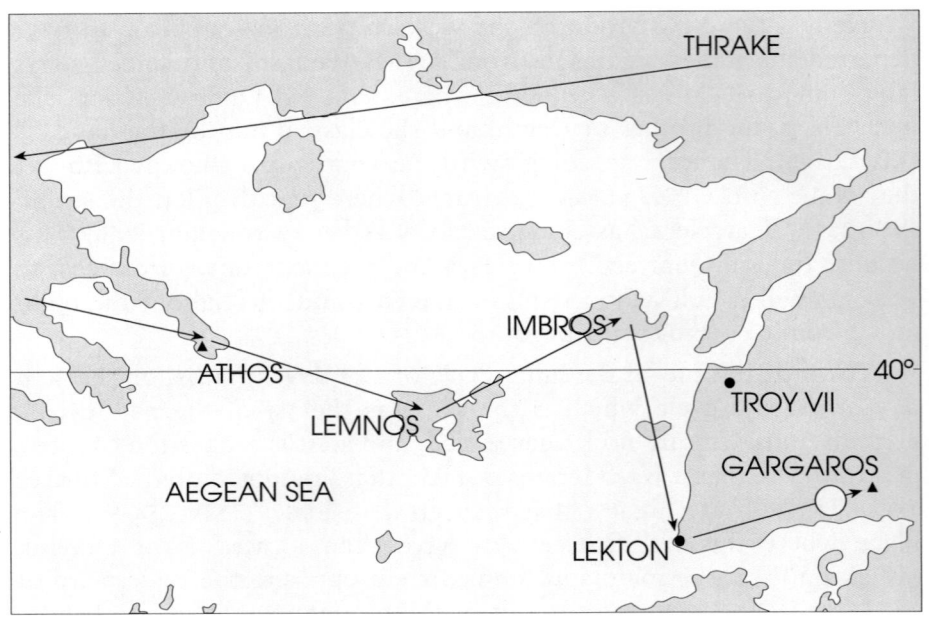

MAP 2b. A POINTLESS COURSE. Hera's (the moon) zig-zag jorney from Thrake to the summit of Gargaros seems wanting in a sense of logic or purpose.

(Strabo 13.583), now Cape Baba, before turning E. to reach Mt Ida. Had she flown in a straight line, her milage would have been halved; her itinerary is as erratic as Poseidon's at 13.10ff.

Hera's erratic course (MAP 2b) cannot seem to be anything more than, perhaps, some vague idea about the powers and whims of a deity wandering hither and thither over the face of the sea, and, being a goddess residing in the province of the irrational, need not be constrained by the rigours of geographical logic or purpose.

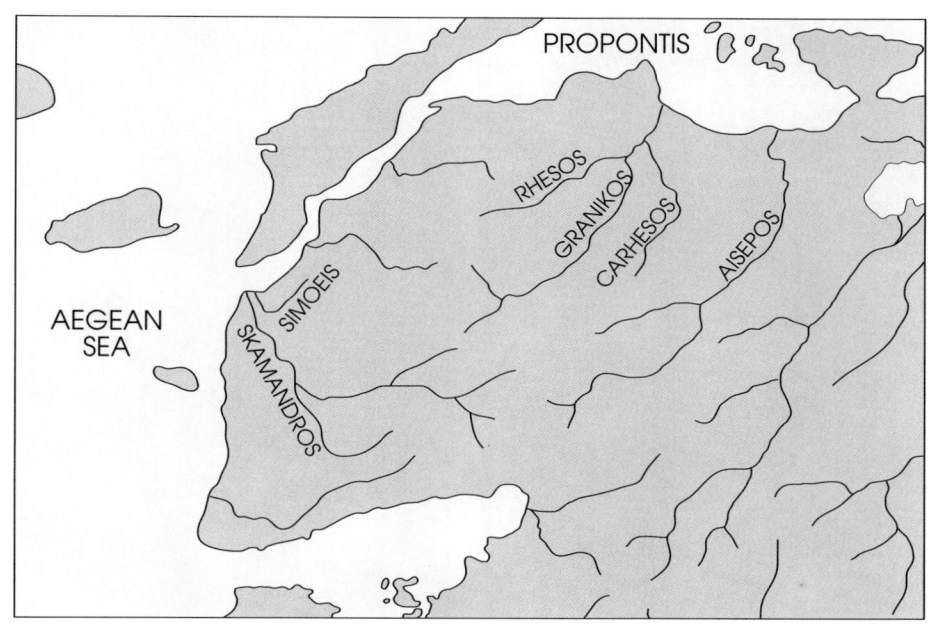

MAP 3a. NO AFFLUENTS OF SCAMANDROS. *The listed affluents of the Skamandros debouche into the Propontis (Sea of Marmara) some 100 kilometers away from the region of Troy.*

RIVERS

The description of the mighty SKAMANDROS and its affluents cannot hold up to the geographical reality of the Menderes and its only affluent, the Thymbraeus, not mentioned in Homer (XII, 17–25):

> ...then verily did Poseidon and Apollo take counsel to sweep away the wall [of the Danaans], bringing against it the might of all the rivers that flow forth from the mountains of Ida to the sea—Rhesus and Heptaporus and Caresus and Rhodius, and Granicus and Aesepus, and goodly Scamander, and Simois, by the banks whereof many shields of bull's-hide and many helms fell in the dust... —of all these did Phoebus Apollo turn the mouths together, and for nine days' space he drave their flood against the wall...

Now, the Rhesos, Granicos, Carhesos, and Aesepos debouche far away, into the Propontis, and thus, that Phoebus Apollo turned their "mouths together, and for nine days' space he drave their flood against the wall..." is perplexing, for the clear sense of a swollen river sweeping away all obstacles in its course seems defeated. This is explained by B. Hainsworth, *Iliad: A Commentary*, III, 319 (on XII, 20–25) as follows:

> 20–2 The rivers of the Troad. The Rhesos, Heptaporos, Karesos, Rhodios, and Grenikos are mentioned only here in the Iliad. That is not surprising, since together with Aisepos (which flowed past Zeleia into the Propontis, 2. 824–7) they do not flow across the Trojan plain. The names, however, form some sort of traditional list

MAP 3b. THE SKAMANDROS WATERSHED. *The SKAMANDROS and its affluents indeed lend credibility to a statement about the might of all rivers sweeping away a wall (XII, 17–25).*

for they recur (except for Karesos) in the list of rivers in Hesiod Theog. 338–45...
20 The jingle 'Ρῆσος ... Κάρησος, however handy as a mnemotic device, is uncharacteristic of Homeric/Hesiodic cataloguing style; Hesiod, loc. cit., avoided it. Heptaporos, 'seven channels' (or 'fords'), is presumably a Hellenization of an aboriginal name. The Rhesos was unidentified in classical times, 'unless it be the Rhoeites' (Demetrius of Scepsis, a would-be expert on the Troad, apud Strabo 13.1.44).

* * *

In a Balkan context the SKAMANDROS is the mighty Neretva, ample, majestic, of an inimitable soft green. It is at once obvious (MAP 3b) that, indeed, the river swollen with waters from its affluents, could easily have swept away all vestige of Danaan presence on the HELLESPONTOS (Neretva-delta).

The question about which affluent is which need be addressed elsewhere, but it suffices to mention here that the XANTHOS of VI, 4; VIII, 560; XIV, 434; and often... must be the ZANTHOS, ζα- + ἄνθος, "very flowery", as, indeed, the crytal-clear waters of the Glibuša marshes betray, for, in the *Iliad*, the same name may not be used for the same concept in two different places, as would be the case with the XANTHOS, Ξάνθος, "tawny yellow", Bradano of Lucania. Also, the ASOPOS (Mala

Neretva) is mentioned only in context with THEBE (Neum), thus as an affluent of SKAMANDROS is an inference to the best explanation since it drains HYPOPLAKIA (Jezero Kuti), one of the trefoil-shaped marshes of TROIA. The HEPTAPOROS (Ostrovača) "Seven Mouths" would seem to be so called because its waters pass the mouths of seven other affluents, with the exception of the GRANIKOS (Ugrovača), whose waters seep into the ground, yet feed the SKAMANDROS as diverse springs.

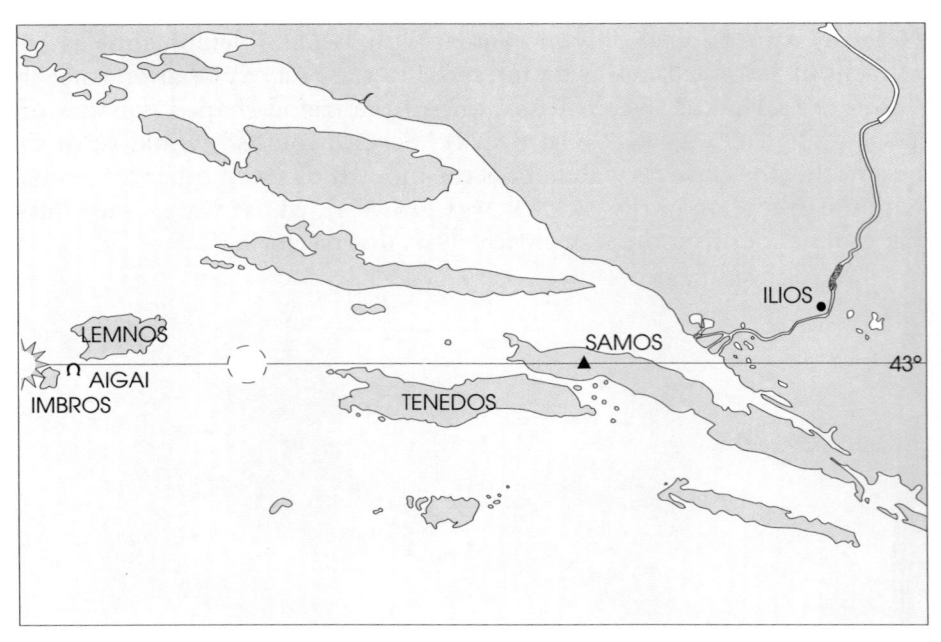

MAP 4a. AN EQUINOX SUNSET. The description of a sunset calls for a marine grotto (Palace of Poseidon) at the place where the sun disappears below the horizon.

MOUNTAINS

A metamorphosis between Zeus and Poseidon as an Autumn Equinox sunset, *exactly* due west (270°), appears to reflect a path of glimmering, golden light back to a viewer on a platform (*vinograd*) situated on the western slopes of SAMOS (Sveti Ilija/Monte Vípera, 961 mts.), the highest prominence of NERITON (Pelješac), thus (XIII, 10, *et pas*.):

> But the lord, the Shaker of Earth, kept no blind watch, for he sat marvelling at the war and the battle, high on the topmost peak of wooded Samothrace [Samos, wooded Thrace-like], from thence all Ida was plain to see; and plain to see were the city of Priam, and the ships of the Achaeans. There he sat, being come forth from the sea, and he had pity on the Achaeans that they were overcome by the Trojans...
>
> Forthwith then he went down from the rugged mount, striding forth with swift footsteps, and the high mountains trembled and the woodland beneath the immortal feet of Poseidon as he went. Thrice he strode in his course, and with the fourth stride he reached his goal, even Aegae, where was his famous palace built in the depths of the mere, golden and gleaming, imperishable for ever. Thither came he, and let harness beneath his car his two bronze-hooved horses, swift of flight...
>
> There is a wide cavern in the depths of the deep mere, midway between Tenedos and rugged Imbros. There Poseidon, the Shaker of Earth, stayed his horses, and loosed them from the car, and cast before them food ambrosial to graze upon...

FOREWORD

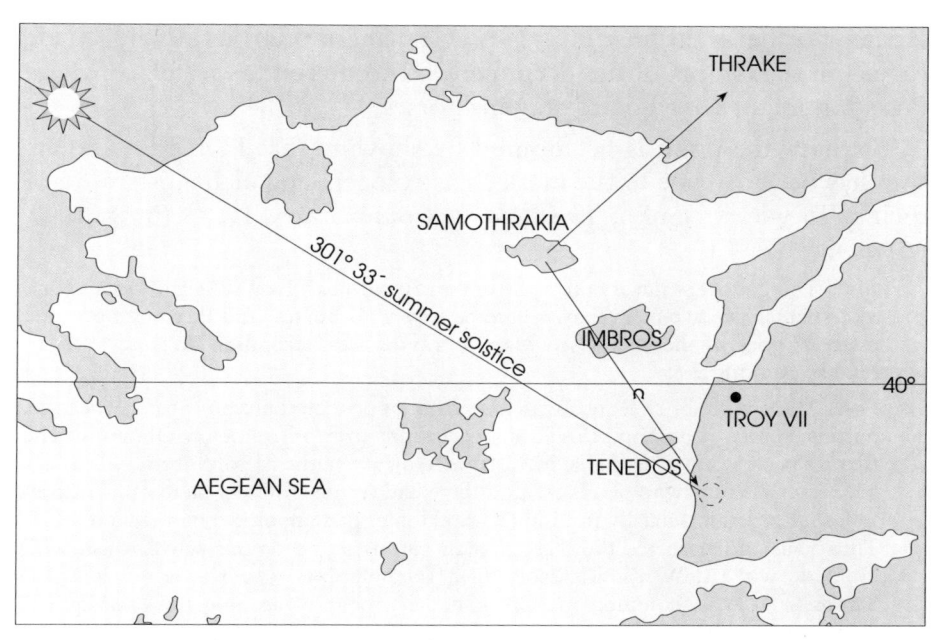

MAP 4b. AN IMPOSSIBLE SUNSET. There exists no grotto where one might expect to find it, and, furthermore, the sun cannot ever align with the islands in question.

Poseidon kept no blind watch on κορυφῆς Σάμου ὑληέσσης Θρηικίησ "Samos, wooded Thrace-like…", and "Thrice he strode…" —TENEDOS, LEMNOS, IMBROS— "…and with the fourth stride he reached his goal, even Aegae… in the depths of the mere…", which is a marine grotto (not unlike the famous one at Capri) called Modra Spilja, "Magician's Cave", in Biševo's Balun Cove.

Still, that "There is a wide cavern in the depths of the deep mere, *midway* between Tenedos and rugged Imbros…" and not at ÍMBROS itself where Modra Spilja is located (*MAP 4a*), is explained by the fact that the sun's disk, as observed from the elevation of the *vinograd* platform on SAMOS (about 750–800 mts. above sea level), appears to sink below the horizon the distance of its diameter to an apparent place "midway between Tenedos and rugged Imbros…"

* * *

In Asia Minor the foregoing alignment of islands in the description of a sunset is physically impossible, since, at latitude 40° N, the sun may only reach its maximum northern declination of 301°, 33´ during a midsummer sunset, and the alignment of the islands in question has an even greater northerly declination (MAP 4b). Furthermore, there *is* no "wide cavern in the depths of the deep mere..." to be found *any* place where Poseidon might have had to stay his horses.

Perhaps the point is belaboured by showing that Homeric scholarship has been as wide of the mark as astrologers and alchemists were of their's. To wit, R. Janko, *The Iliad: A Commentary*, IV, 45 (on XIII, 10, *et pas.*):

> 10–38 The god steps across the sea from an island near Troy to Aigai, drives back to a submarine cave near Troy, where he leaves his horses, and then (by no stated method) goes to the camp (see Map p. xxvi)... Leaf proposed deleting 11–16 to remove Samothrake.
>
> 10–12 The picture of two gods watching from opposite mountain-tops is evocative; putting Poseidon on Samothrake distances him from restraint on Olumpos. The island's peak (5,250 ft) is visible N.W. from Troy above the isle of Imbros, which lies between. The poet who places the god there had seen it from the plain of Troy himself; such a detail is hardly traditional. 'So Homer had appointed it, and so it was... Thus vain and false are the mere human surmises and doubts which clash with Homeric wit' (A. W. Kingslake, *Eothen*, London, 1844, 65). The island is called Samos at 24.78, a common pre-Greek name probably meaning 'hill'; its epithet 'Thracian' proves that Homer knew of Ionian Samos too (this distinction recurs at *HyAp* 34, 41). The variant Σάου (Did/AT) allegedly stood for Saoke, the mountain's name, but Aristarchus, who was born there, rightly equated the island with its peak (T).
>
> 21–2 There were places called Aigai in Euboea, Achaea and Macedon (now Vergina); cf. C. Imber, *CQ* 29 (1979) 222; Fowler, *Phoenix* 42 (1988) 101n. Clearly it is not on the coast of Samothrake! The fact that the god's fairy-tale palace is under the sea suggests that we should not seek its location too seriously.

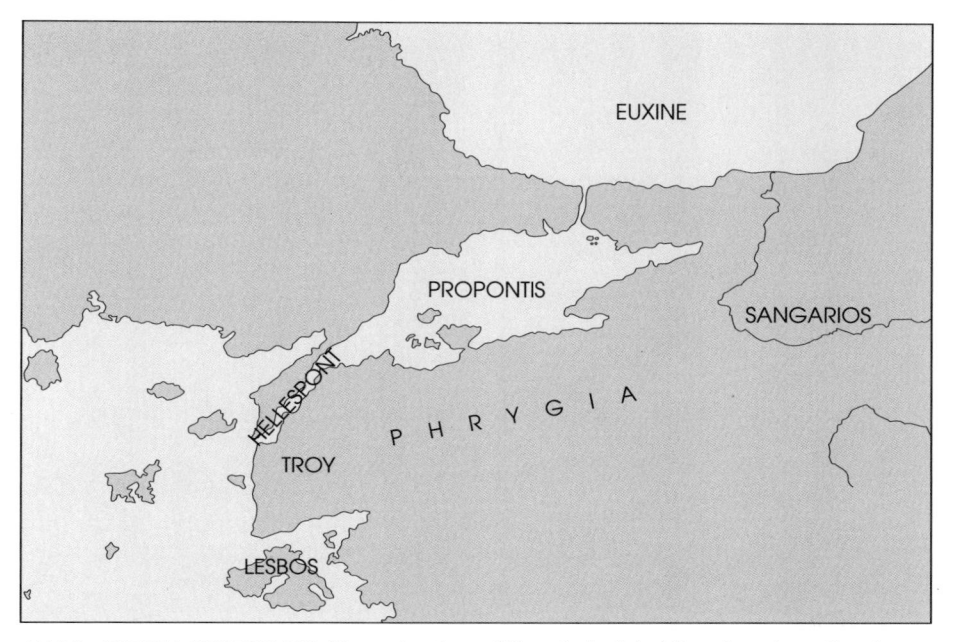

MAP 5a. PHRYGIA IN THE UPLAND. The extension of Phrygia in Asia Minor lies along the shores of the Propontis, from the Hellespont to the Sangarios.

DISTRICTS

Towards the close of the *Iliad* Priam visits Akhilleus to ransom the body of Hector, and Akhilleus describes the land over which, upon a time, but now no longer, Priam held sway (XXIV, 543–546):

> "And of thee, old sire, we hear that of old thou wast blest; how of all that toward the sea Lesbos, the seat of Macar, encloseth, and Phrygia in the upland, and the boundless Hellespont, over all these folks, men say, thou, old sire, wast preeminent by reason of thy wealth and thy sons."

The extension or boundaries of Phrygia, and how this territory relates to Troy proper is questioned by W. Leaf, *The Iliad*, II, 468:

> It is to be presumed that Phrygia and Lesbos, the boundaries themselves, are included in the space within which Priam was most blessed; it is a small thing to say that he "surpassed all men" in the Troad where he was king. Ἑλλήσποντος must evidently be taken to include the sea on the W. coast of the Troad as well as the narrower channel on the N. to which we now confine the name.

An additional explantion is offered by N. Richardson, *The Iliad: A Commentary*, VI, 333:

> Verses 544–5 define the whole area within which Priam's kingdom lies, surrounded by Lesbos to the south, Phrygia to the east, and the Hellespont to the north… Makar was a legendary colonist of Lesbos, which was called Makaria after him.

The commentaries given by both Leaf and Richardson seem reasonable (i.e., that Lesbos and Phrygia, in *addition* to Troy itself, are to be

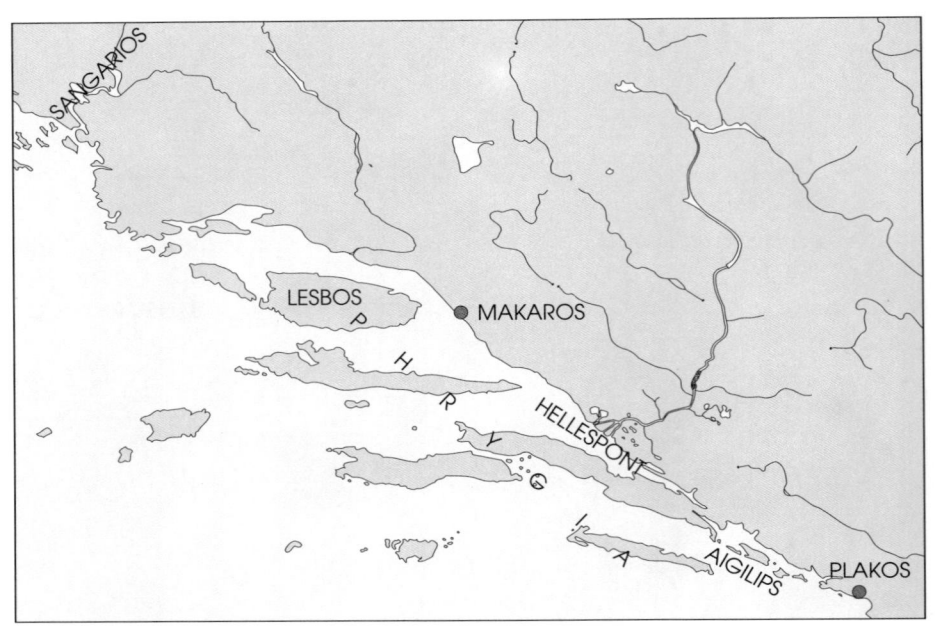

MAP 5b. PHRYGIA, THE DALMATIAN ARCHIPELAGO. *The name apparently means "brow land", apt enough for the generally elongated islands of the Dalmatian Archipelago.*

included in the lands over which Priam held sway), but, for their want of clarity as to *where* Phrygia should be situated (MAP 5a), relative to the Sangarius (XVI, 719) which debouches into the Euxine, and to Zeleia (II, 824) on the shores of the Propontis at the nether foot of Ida, occupied by Troes.

* * *

In a Balkan context, the term PHRYGIA (apparently related with ὀφρῦς, "brow") refers to the generally narrow and elongated islands of the Dalmatian Archipelago. Thus, the understanding of XXIV 543–546 above, is that the HELLESPONTOS (Neretva delta-valley) is the *only* exit from the enclosed interior out into PHRYGIA (MAP 5b), and hence a natural reference point for all that which is enclosed by the Trojan seaboard, namely, to the north, the furthest island, LESBOS (*Brattia*, Brač) opposite MAKAROS (*Mucurrum*, Makarska) on the mainland.

Now, half of the description of PHRYGIA given by Akhilleus has been wholly excised from the text, for all that which is enclosed by the Trojan seaboard *south* of the HELLESPONTOS is obviously incompatible with an Asia Minor context, since it will have included the furthest island to the south, AIGILIPS (*Elaphites*, Lafota, Lopud, and others) opposite PLAKOS

(Mlini) on the mainland, and erroneously understood as "a district, or island, under the rule of Odysseus, B 633" (Autenrieth, G. *A Homeric Dictionary*, 1979), and therefore to be found in the archipelago at the mouth of the Gulf of Patras on the western coast of Hellas.

The cruelty in the false deference of Akhilleus for the old king in the last days of the *Iliad* —perhaps the last week— is that these are proud and unfeeling words of triumph: The AKHAIOI have conquered TROIA, and established *their own* cult, at *Brattia* (LESBOS) in the north, and *Elaphites* (AIGILIPS) in the south; for the enormous significance of this act, see III. THE TROJAN WAR AND FALL OF TROY.

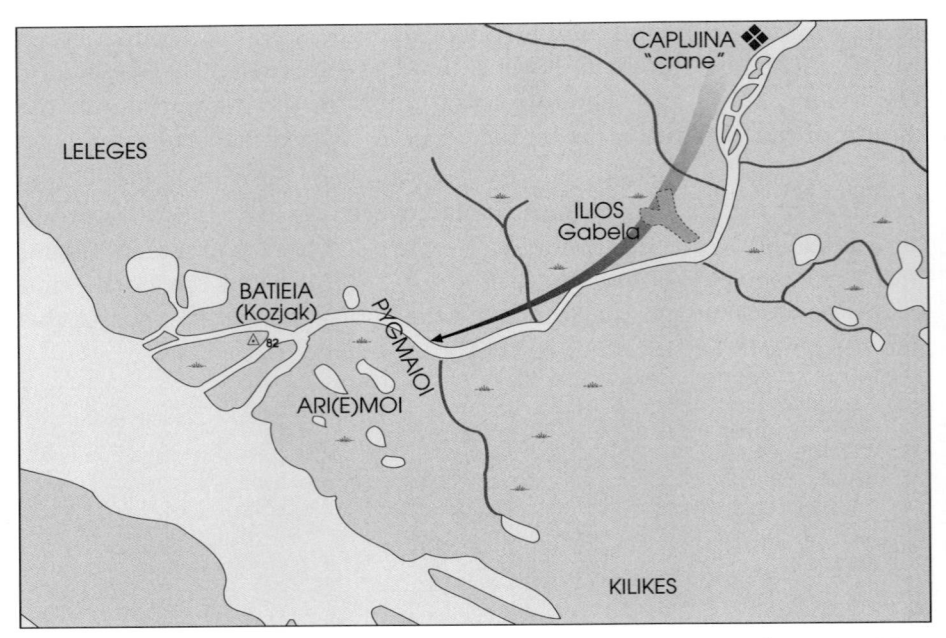

MAP 6a. ARIMOI (ARIEMOI) IDENTICAL WITH DELMATAE. *Both names mean the same thing, "ram"/ "sheep", and are (for some obscure reason) associated with marshy places.*

PEOPLES

Of the several tribal groups confederated under the collective name of TROES, perhaps the most puzzling and whimsical relationship between two peoples was that of the ARI(E)MOI and the PYGMAIOI, who seemed to have occupied the same region of the Neretva delta-valley.

That the ARI(E)MOI occupied the Neretva delta-valley is discovered early on, when invading forces disembark on the mainland proper and move forward (II, 738):

> So marched they then, as though all the land were swept with fire; and the earth groaned beneath them, as beneath Zeus that hurleth the thunderbolt in his wrath, when he scourgeth the land about Typhoeus in the country of the Arimi, where men say is the couch of Typhoeus.

Furthermore, the name of the ARI(E)MOI, akin with ἄρηεν, "ram", would seem to be answered by that of the *Delmatae*, or Dalmatians, in whose name is enclosed the Illyrian word that passed into the Albanian language as *dalmeh*, meaning "sheep". It is likely that the presence of the Delmatae in this region inspired the modern name of Kozjak, "goat hill" for BATIEIA (II, 813).

The name of the PYGMAIOI, a midget folk, also occurs early on (and appropiately so, it would seem) after the nine-year gestation of this moment when a horde of invading Danaan forces meet the Trojans head on (III, 2–7):

> ...the Trojans came on with a clamour and with a cry like birds, even as the clamour of cranes ariseth before the facce of heaven, when they flee from wintry storms and measureless rain, and with clamour fly towards the streams of Ocean, bearing slaughter and death to Pygmy men, and in the early dawn they offer evil battle.

The imagery of this simile entered the world of Greek art, then Roman, and in time even into the Renaissance, always portraying a flock of long-beaked cranes harassing a host of distressed negroid midgets. The area of the Hutovo Blato marshes opposite ILIOS (Gabela) has always been a favourite haunt of bird-hunters, a habitat to over 300 species of birds, so that the appearance of birds of all sorts —even the κύμινδις of XIV, 291— should come as no surprise. The simile, one might presume, is a recollection of pre-Trojan days —pre-Illyrian, anthropologically and archaeologically speaking— of some early folk that occupied a neolithic site on the hillsides immediately behind the town of Čapljina (which means "crane"), and who, for whatever the reason, warred against a Pygmy, or "fist"-folk.

Of cranes, these have been simply birds, and common enough in the region, but of Pygmies, scholarship has not been able to say much, to wit, G. S. Kirk, *The Iliad: A Commentary*, I, 265 (on III, 5–6):

> The war of the cranes and Pygmies ('fist-like men', from πυγμή = fist) is not elsewhere referred to by Homer, but was a popular theme later, first on the foot of the Attic black-figure François vase painted by Kleitias of about 570 B.C. (and on at least three other black-figure pots), then in Hecataeus (AbT on 6). Herodotus 3.37.2 alludes to a pygmy-like cult-statue in upper Egypt, and at 2.32.6 had heard of little men in the heart of Africa; the idea of pygmies may have been based on fact — Aristotle thought so too, and that they lived in caves (*Hist. An.* 8 597a6). The strange idea of their war with cranes was perhaps derived from a lost Egyptian folk-tale, although Willcock *ad loc.* could be right that the birds' flying in formation may have something to do with envisaging them as an army.

Now, πυγμή is the Grecized form of what was an earlier *kug-*, whence Rus. *kukla,* "puppet" (cognate with Fr. *poupee,* and akin with Sp. *muñeca,* "fist" *and* "doll"). Thus, from a story about cranes and dolls must surely be derived a later, tamer, variation of storks and babies. Moreover, Pygmies on the François vase are shown mounted on goats with clubs, hooked sticks, and slings, and Ctesias (late 5th cent. BC) and Megasthenes (*c.* 350–290 BC) have them disguised as rams, or riding on rams and goats, and sallying forth to destroy cranes' eggs.

Presumably, then, the *kug*-folk upon a time eventually yielded the verdant expanses of the Neretva delta-valley to the ARI(E)MOI, though, more likely, the *kug*-folk were never anything more than scarecrows set

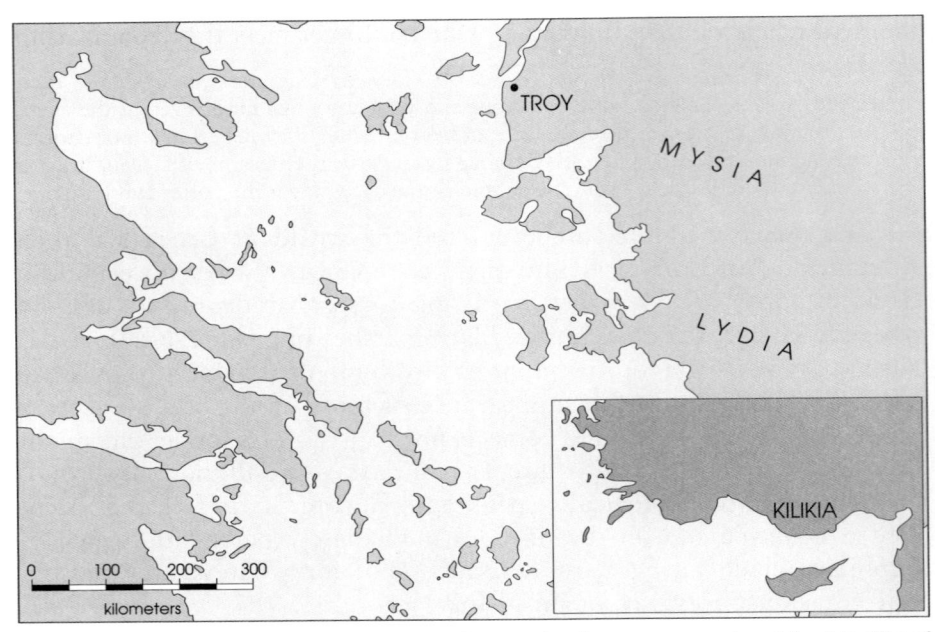

MAP 6b. ARIMOI (ARIEMOI) A PEOPLE OF KILIKIA. An academic consensus about the identity of these people is as inexistent as it is wide of the mark.

up by the ARI(E)MOI in their fields to keep all kinds of birds away from their crops.

* * *

In an Asia Minor context, there is difficulty relating the ARI(E)MOI with a territorial extension between invading Danaan forces presumably assembled on the shores of the Hellespont, and defending Trojan lines further inland, thus W. Leaf, *The Iliad*, I, 81 (on III, 281 *et pas.*) reads εἰν Ἀρίμοις, ὅθι φασὶ Τυφωέος ἔμμεναι εὐνάς:

> The connexion of Zeus τερπικέραυνοσ with the phenomena of a volcanic district has been thought to allude to the violent electrical disturbances which often accompany eruptions. Ἄριμα is said to be a volcanic region in Kilikia (according to others in Mysia, Lydia, or Syria). But A., perhaps following Ar., gives Εἰναρίμοις, and so Virgil must have read *Aen.* ix. 716, "durumque cubile Inarima Iovis imperiis imposta Typhoeo." The metaphor of lashing reappears in the story of the defeat of Typhoeus by Zeus in Hes. *Theog.* 857 where he is described as a monster with a hundred snakes' heads spitting fire, the son of Gaia and Tartaros.

Further, G. S. Kirk, *The Iliad: A Commentary*, I, 243 (on II, 281–4) states:

> For εἰν Ἀρίμοις see West on *Theog.* 304; it is clear that ancient critics did not know which particular region this signified, and that local claims were made on behalf of

several different apparently lightning-blasted or generally volcanic areas. Strabo 13.626 (perhaps partly from Apollodorus according to Erbse 1, 337 who quotes the passage) mentions various suggested locations: near Sardis, in Mysia, in Cilicia or Syria, or in the west near Mt Etna (where Pindar, *Py.* 1.15ff. placed Tuphos and the Corycian cave) or in Pithekoussai (modern Ischia).

So much for the ARI(E)MOI. Still, independently of a connection between the ARI(E)MOI (regardless of who they were or where they may have lived) and the PYGMAIOI, any understanding of PYGMAIOI in an Asia Minor context is difficult, as evinced in the quote from Kirk above.

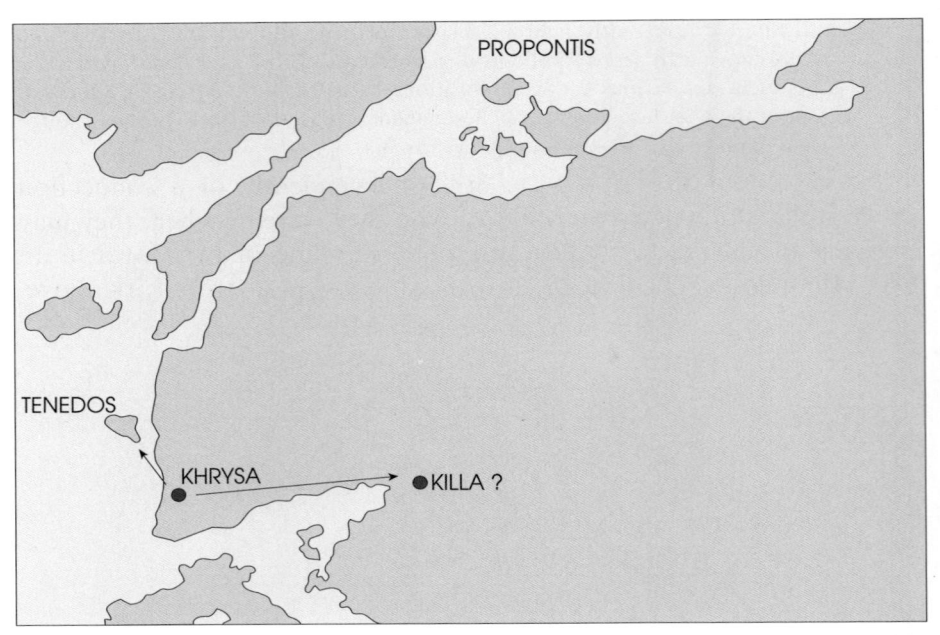

MAP 7a. SMINTHIAN APOLLO RULES OVER TENEDOS. A land-locked mouse-god is presumed to have exerted an influence on Tenedos.

TOWNS

Khrysa and Killa are two towns mentioned early on (I, 37):

> "Hear me, [Chryses] thou of the silver bow, who dost stand over Chryse and holy Cilla, and dost rule mightily over Tenedos, thou Sminthian..."

Of these towns nothing much has been ventured, and, furthermore, nothing at all is known about why the "Sminthian..." one "of the silver bow..." should have ruled "mightily over Tenedos...". G. S. Kirk, *The Iliad: A Commentary*, I, 57 (on I, 37) ventures the following:

> "Khruse... probably lay on the west coast of the Troad some five miles north of Cape Lekton, near the site of the later city of Hamaxitos, where there are slight remains of a temple of Apollo Smintheus; see Cook, *Troad* 232–5. Strabo (13. 612f) objected that this temple was too far from the sea to fit the Homeric description (cf. 34–6 and 430–41); that seems rather pedantic since the later Smintheum (surely a crucial factor in the case) is only a kilometre or so from the coast. He placed it south of Mt Ida in the plain of Adramuttion, with Thebe and Killa in the same area. Thebe at least probably did lie there (cf. Cook, *Troad* 267), and Killa may have done; in any case Khruseis must have been on a visit away from home when she was captured at Thebe, 1.366–9..."; I, 98 (on I 430–9): "At 308–12 a ship was launched for Odysseus' voyage to Khruse; now he arrives there... This description of the ship's arrival, like that of its return home at 475–87, is full of 'Odyssean' language...".

That Strabo identified Sminthian Apollo with a "mouse"-god (*Geography*, 13. 1. 64) might, perhaps, justify some association with

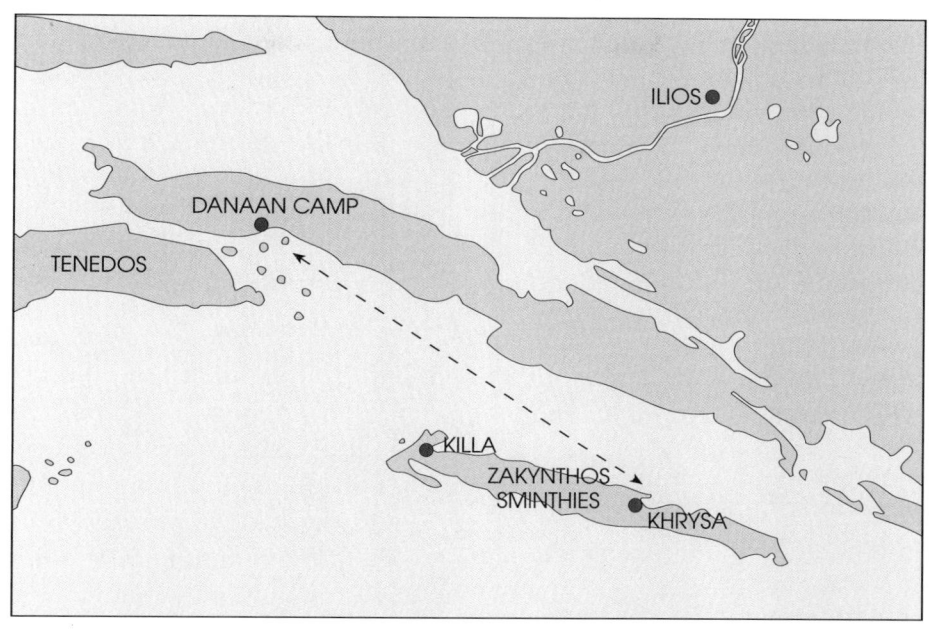

MAP 7b. APOLLO RULES OVER THE SMINTHIES. *The name of these folks seems to have been derived from an Illyrian root sminth-, a term for the local marten.*

"over Tenedos..." on a pun with τένδω, "to nibble", "gnaw", for what else can a mouse do?

* * *

In a Balkan context, KHRYSA (Sobra) and KILLA (Polače) are port-towns on the southeast and northwest of ZAKYNTHOS (*Melita*, Mljet), thus Apollo is the mighty ruler of that island and not any other. Obviously, the name of ZAKYNTHOS could not appear in the text when TROIA was replicated in Asia Minor, and hence changed to Tenedos (supported by the pun on nibbling, above), since it fell to the dominion of Odysseus (II, 634) which was understood to lie at the entrance to the Gulf of Patras. The very name of the island is connected with the *kuna*, or "marten", valuable like mink and sable for its fur (whence the current name of the Croatian unit of currency). Pliny (the Elder) recorded that the affable Maltese dog took its name from this island, but perhaps the other Malta (between Italy and North Africa) was intended. The epithet of Apollo, "Sminthian", is derived not from any attribute of the marten, but, rather, from that of the occupants of this island, the SMINTHIES.

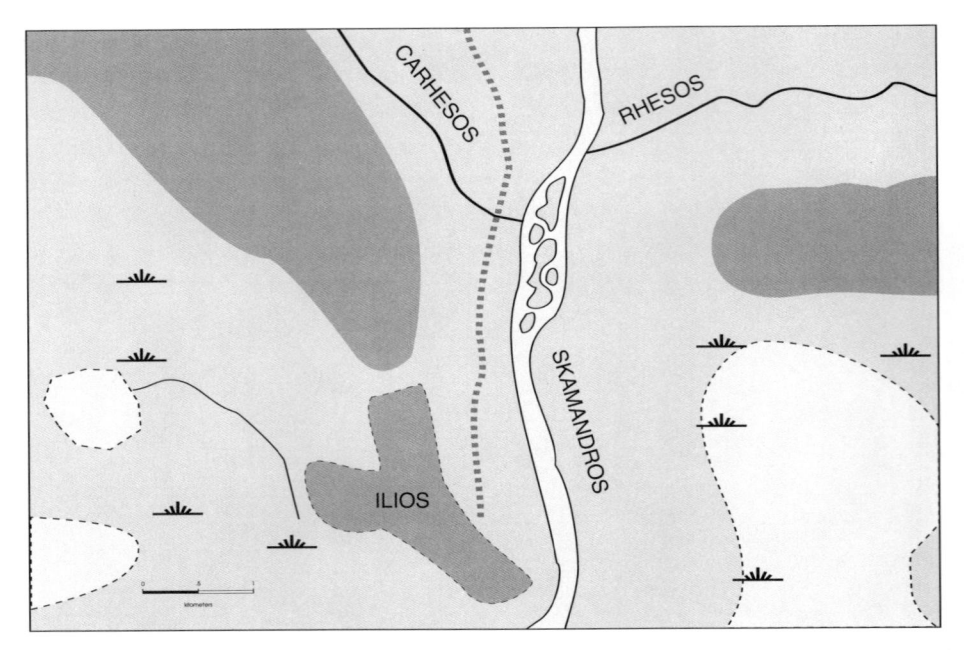

MAP 8a. FOUR GEOGRAPHICAL REFERENTS. A description of the region (XXII, 143ff) calls for (in the order enumerated, the site of 1) ILIOS, 2) a road, 3) two fountains that feed SKAMANDROS, and, 4) broad "washingtanks".

PLACES

There are a number of places in the countryside surrounding ILIOS (Drijeva/Gabela) that are remarkable for some reason or other. These are topographical features scattered schematically throughout the marshy plains, and differ from a one-word toponym or ethnicon in that they require two or more words for a description (XXII, 143, *et pas.*):

> ...and Hector fled beneath the wall of the Trojans, and plied his limbs swiftly. Past the place of watch, and the wind-waved wild fig tree they sped, ever away from under the wall along the waggon-track, and came to the two fair-flowing fountains, where well up the two springs that feed eddying Scamander. The one floweth with warm water, and round about a smoke goeth up therefrom as it were from a blazing fire, while the other even in summer floweth forth cold as hail or chill snow or ice that water formeth. And there hard by the selfsame springs are broad washing-tanks, fair and wrought with stone, where the wives and fair daughters of the Trojans were wont to wash bright raiment of old in the time of peace...

There is a place up-stream from ILIOS where the SKAMANDROS (Neretva) widens considerably, and its waters trickle in narrow streams and rivulets through islets of rounded stones and boulders, until they once again meet in a mighty flow deep enough to accomodate small cargo vessels. This is the place of "broad washing-tanks, fair and wrought with stone", and, on the right bank, where the KARHESOS

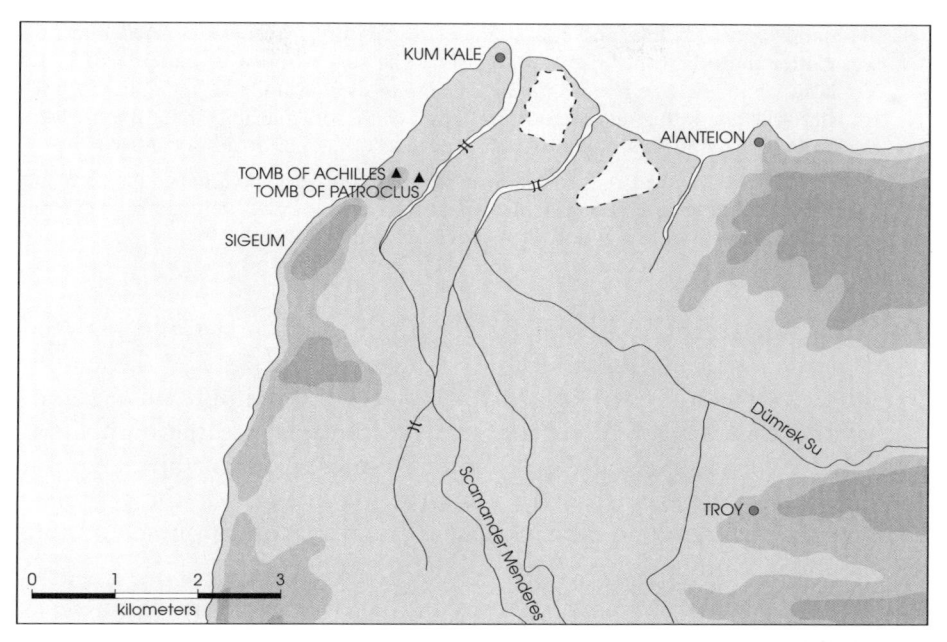

MAP 8b. GEOGRAPHICAL REFERENTS WANTING. *The necessary topographical conditions for a description given in XXII, 143ff are not present in Asia Minor, principal among these being two affluents of Skamandros.*

(Trebižat) debouches, is a place called Struge, which means "funnel", and where even today the locally woven *kilim* are washed and set out to dry. The waters of the KARHESOS are "hot", albeit they do not send up steam, but they are "hot" because, on the opposite left bank, the waters of the RHESOS (Bregava) are frigid, on account that they are seasonal, and the product of melted winter snows.

* * *

These "two fair-flowing fountains, where well up the two springs that feed eddying Scamander" cannot be found any place in the environs of Troy/Ilios (Hissarlik). Thus, N. Richardson, *The Iliad: A Commentary*, VI, 123 (on XXII, 147–56):

> 'In spite of the loving detail with which the *Iliad...* describes the double fountain under the walls of Troy, it is no longer possible to use it as evidence: no such combination of hot and cold springs now exists in the plain' (Leaf, *Troy* 48). But 'what he gives us is in fact very characteristic of the Troad at large, though not of the immediate surroundings of Troy. The hot springs of the Troad are as marked a feature as the cold which break out all over many-fountained Ida' (*ibid*. 49–50). Already in antiquity, by the time of Demetrius of Scepsis (Strabo 13.1.43, 602), there were no hot springs by the walls of Troy, whereas such were known to exist on Mt Ida (so T on 149). Two large springs, in particular, form one of the sources of the

Skamandros on Mt Ida, and some nineteenth-century travellers asserted that one was hotter than the other (Leaf, *ibid*. 50–2). The suggestion was made by R. L. K. Virchow (*Beiträge zur Landeskunde der Troas*, Berlin 1880, 33–43) that the poet transferred these in his imagination to Troy, where some springs do still exist near the walls (Leaf, ibid. 165–6). But Cook (Troad 293) has doubts about this.

Ancient scholars solved the problem of identification here by suggesting that the springs were either fed by Skamandros underground, or else were simply near the river (Arn/A148, Porph. 1.256.24, Demetrius of Scepsis in Strabo loc. cit.).

* * *

The foregoing eight examples of geographical comparisons between what would appear to be plausible realities and recognized difficulties would seem like sufficient reason to pursue a more ample understanding of the *Iliad* in a Balkan context. Certainly, a greater number of examples (two instances per geographical concept, for instance) cannot serve a better purpose, that is, be more convincing, for the objective remains the same, which is that of a sufficient reason to pursue a more ample understanding of the *Iliad* in a Balkan context.

A set of comparative examples might likewise be desirable for seeking an understanding of the *Odyssey* in a Balkan context. Still, such a proposition seems both redundant and unneccesesarily laborious for the following two reasons: first, since it is a given that the Misadventures of Odysseus begin with his visit to the KIKONES at **Ismaros**, a folk from the environs of *Tragurium*, Trogir, and end with his final arrival at **Arethousa** at the bottom of **Phorkys** fjord, the Korčulanski Canal at the eastern end of Pelješacs Peninsula, from where he walks to ITHAKA, then any reason to seek an onomastica relative to the series of misadventures that occurred between these two places in waters beyond this immediate context is artificial and superfluous; second, the story of Odysseus —his misadventures— cannot be understood, that is, related to a Balkan context, without *first* having an adequate working knowledge of a correct geography of TROIA.

1. The Iliad

CHAPTER I

THE ILIAD AND ITS TROJAN GEOGRAPHY

The world of Homeric Geography is divided into two major parts, namely, that information which concerns the Trojan Homeland in the east and that which concerns the World Abroad in the west. Thus, all geographical data found in the *Iliad* (and the *Odyssey* as well) concerns, unequivocally, one or the other division. In the *Iliad*, all geographical information is stored in four different groups, as follows:

- *Catalogue of Ships* (II, 494–759): a listing assembled by the text's authorship of peoples and places abroad that sent forces against Troy. It contains information about Troy (II, 625–637) which, properly, belongs in the TROJAN GROUP (assembled by the text's scholar).

- *Catalogue of Trojan Forces* (II, 816–877): a listing assembled by the text's authorship of peoples and places abroad which remained loyal or sympathetic to Troy. It contains information about Troy (II, 819–827, 846–847, 862–863) which, properly, belongs in the TROJAN GROUP (assembled by the text's scholar).

- DANAAN GROUP: a listing assembled by the text's scholar of peoples and places mentioned here and there throughout the text that are not listed in the *Catalogue of Ships* and that are patently non-Trojan.

- TROJAN GROUP: a listing assembled by the text's scholar of peoples and places mentioned here and there throughout the text which are not listed in the *Catalogue of Trojan Forces* but are patently Trojan.

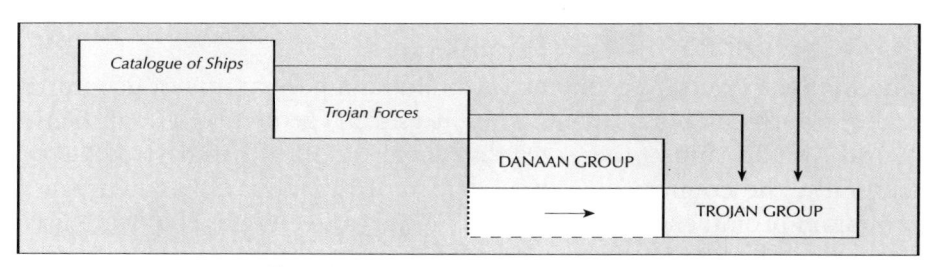

TABLE 1.1. TROJAN FORCES. The catalogue, properly, is that of Trojan allies abroad.

GEONYMS

In Homeric Geography, a toponym or an ethnicon may be called a *geonym*, that is, a *one-word* term that encloses in its linguistic structure and its meaning some geographical or historical truth. The advantage of calling a Homeric toponym or ethnicon a "geonym" is to distinguish it as genuinely Homeric from any other that might *appear* to be genuinely Homeric, but, in fact, is an interpolation. Also, the term "geonym" serves to distinguish a Homeric toponym or ethnicons as a *one-word* statement from any other term of broader meaning, such as might be "onomastica", and thus avoids confusion with names that do not convey an adequate geographical sense (such as Agamemnon, Atridai, and so on). Furthermore, with the term "geonym" is recognized an important difference between a one-word statement and the description of a "place", which, though nonetheless a geographical position, requires two or more words to describe it, such as might be the SKAIAN GATES or the TROIC PLAIN.

GEOGRAPHICAL CONCEPTS AND PARADIGMS

Geonyms are of a variety of *geographical concepts*, divided into groups of *physical* geography and *social* geography, from which it is to be understood that the geographical characteristic of this or that geonym is either a natural geographical feature, or one established by man. With this distinction is the beginning of orthodoxy in the management of neat and orderly geographical information, which prevents the scholar from falling into error (beside allowing for better inferences and arriving at better conclusions on this or that geonym).

Each group of concepts, for instance SEA (*TABLE 1.2*), which is made up of four geonyms, forms a *geographical paradigm*. Each geographical paradigm preserve a schematic distribution of geonyms relative to one another in a balanced symmetry, thus lending the paradigm a certain harmony and internal coherence (not unlike, for example, the four cardinal points, north, south, east, and west).

72 GEONYMS

The *Iliad* uses only 72 geonyms for building an apparatus of geographical information about TROIA (albeit it uses 300 geonyms to describe the World Abroad, and of these, 200 that came specifically to destroy ILIOS). Certainly, the country must have had more than, say, 19 towns, or 4 mountain prominences, but 72 is the number of geonyms that were used (even though the apparatus might be thought of as somewhat "artifi-

TROJAN GEONYMS

PHYSICAL GEOGRAPHY

SEA	ISLANDS	RIVERS	MOUNTAINS
AIGAI	AIGILIPS	AISEPOS	BATIEIA
HELLESPONTOS	EKHINAI	ASOPOS	GARGAROS
IKARIAN SEA[1]	IMBROS	GRANIKOS	IDA
OKEANOS	LEKTON	HEPTAPOROS	KALLIKOLONE
	LEMNOS	KARHESOS	NERITON
	LESBOS	RHESOS	PERGAMOS
	TENEDOS	RHODIOS	SAMOS
	ZAKYNTHOS	SANGARIOS	THROSMOS
		SATNIOEIS	
		SIMOEIS	
		SKAMANDROS	
		(ZANTHOS)	

SOCIAL GEOGRAPHY

DISTRICTS	PEOPLES	TOWNS	PLACES[2]
ASKANIA	AMAZONES	AIPEIA	FORDS
DARDANIA	ARIMOI	ANTHEIA (ANTREIA)	BATHS
HYPOPLAKIA	DARDANOI	DOULIKHION	PORTS
PHRYGIA	KADMEIOI	ENOPE	STABLES
THYMBRA	KEPHALLENES	HIRA	ROADS
TROIA	KIKONES	ILIOS	TOMBS
ZELEIA	KILIKES	ITHAKA	CAMPS
	LELEGES	KARDAMYLE	WALLS
	LESBIDES	KHRYSA	
	PHRYGES	KILLA	
	PYGMAIOI	KROKYLEIA	
	SINTIES	LYRNESSOS	
	SMINTHIES	MAKAROS	
	TROES	PEDASOS	
		PHARE	
		PLAKOS	
		SKYROS	
		THEBE	
		TROIA	

1. The name of the Ikarian Sea betrays a corruption, for it occurs in the text as the name of a place, and not as a geonym. To judge from the name HELLESPONTOS, a geonym for the Ikarian Sea might be rendered as (IKAROPONTOS) (between square brackets to signal an editorial emendation).

2. There do not exist geonyms in the text that might be classified as "places", since these are mentioned in terms of two or more words. A classification of "places" constitutes a secondary but inseparable aspect of a geographical aparatus of Troy.

TABLE 1.2. GEOGRAPHICAL STRUCTURE OF TROY. The corpus of Trojan geonyms listed according to geographical concepts (paradigms), divided into physical and social geography. PLACES is not, strictly, a part of Trojan Geography, for this concept deals, properly, with topography.

cial" or "belaboured", as distinguished from a modern scientific study). The number does not seem casual, but, rather, associated with a spiritual value, as if the Homeric poems were an end unto themselves.

A GENERAL RULE

A general rule in the *Iliad* is that no place may be known by two different geonyms, albeit the same geonym may be used for two different kinds of places. Thus, ILIOS (Drijeva/Gabela) is not also TROIA (Daorson), though the name of TROIA is that of a *city* as well as that of a *district*.

However, the reverse occurs in the *Odyssey*, where a place may go by two geonyms, a former and a current one, albeit two different places may not use the same geonym.

IDENTIFICATION OF GEONYMS

The current state of "preservation" of Homeric geonyms (374, including Trojan geonyms) is the natural result of a linguistic evolutionary process over the course of three millennia, and might be classified into four general groups (TABLE 1.3).

As regards Trojan geonymy, more or less 25% (18) geonyms remain intact, given the similarity with the original or in translation (TABLE 1.4). The remaining geonyms must meet two fundamental conditions to be identified, namely, that each geonym keep a schematic place with other geonyms of its group, and that the presumed meaning of the geonym keep some similarity —or association of ideas— with the topography in question.

ETYMOLOGIES

The *Iliad* and *Odyssey* are Greek works simply because, regardless of their pre-Greek origins, we have received these directly from a Greek cultural heritage and in the Greek language. However, not withstanding the Graecity of these works, etymologies of geonyms are elusive, if not altogether impossible or misleading, as these are, conventionally, most often derived from a Greek vocabulary. However, if, indeed, it may be safely presumed that some Greek words are direct derivations from an ancestral Mykenaian Linear B, this simply cannot be true of Homeric geonyms, since they *all* have an origin —not necessarily a Trojan one— in a language far removed in distance and time from the geographical context of Mykenaian Linear B. Furthermore, all geonyms became *recorded* by the *Iliad* and *Odyssey's* authorship some four centuries *prior* to the early formation of several Greek dialects.

It should be understood that little is known of the Illyrian language and nothing of a Language X detected in many geonyms (which could,

	INTACT NOMENCLATURE
MODIFIED GEONYMS	those so slightly modified in orthography that they may be considered still intact
TRANSLATED GEONYMS	those which in the course of time have suffered a translation into another language
	ALTERED NOMENCLATURE
EQUIVALENT GEONYMS	those whose identification is established by some association of the geonym with a local feature
INFERRED GEONYMS	those whose identification is established only by an inference to the best explanation

TABLE 1. 3. CURRENT STATE OF HOMERIC NOMENCLATURE. The "preservation" or "survival" of Homeric geonyms into the present falls into four categories.

INTACT GEONYMS		cognate	"transformed"
AMAZONES	(Ἀμαζόνες)		Liburni
ARIMOI	(Ἄριμοι)		Delmatae
DOULIKHION	(Δουλίχιον)	Žuljana	
ENOPE	(Ἐνόπη)	Epetium	
HYPOPLAKIA	(Ὑποπλάκια)		Jezero Kuti
HIRA	(Ἱρή)		Bogomolje
KEPHALLENES	(Κεφαλλῆνες)		Pleras
KILLA	(Κίλλα)	Polače	
KROKYLEIA	(Κροκύλεια)	Korčula	
LEKTON	(Λεκτόν)	Lessina	
LEMNOS	(Λῆμνος)		Issa
MAKAROS	(Μάκαρος)	Mucurrum	
NERITON	(Νήριτον)		Pelješac
PHARE	(Φάρη)	Phare	
PLAKOS	(Πλάκος)		Mlini
RHODIOS	(Ῥόδιος)		Buna
SATNIOEIS	(Σατνιόεις)	Cetina	
ZANTHOS	(Ζάνθος)		Glibuša

TABLE 1. 4. INTACT GEONYMS. are those which have suffered a slight linguistic modification or a modern translation into an equivalent meaning.

perhaps, accurately be called "Pelasgian"), but that in many cases meanings seem to have spilled into what are now Serbian and Russian languages, as well as into Greek and Latin, from which plausible meanings can be reasonably inferred.

TEXTUAL CORRUPTIONS

The question of *integrity* of information —the reliability— of the source-material need be addressed: surprisingly, it is, generally speaking, sound, with few distortions, but none that could widen a difference between a cursory first translation[1] and a final vulgate recension as to make one indistinguishable from the other.

The corruptions are of three kinds, as follows:

• OMISSION: the lesser of two evils, a geonym has fallen out of the text, but the greater is that an entire set of lines has been excised to accommodate new understanding in a new geographical context. An example of such wanton mutilation of the text is to be seen regarding the dominions of Priam given in XXIV, 543–545.

• EMENDATION: an editorial effort to make a reading suitable to its context by the substitution of one geonym for another, as in the curse of Chryses extending to TENEDOS (I, 37–39).

• ORTHOGRAPHY: alteration of spelling (that consequently has a bearing on the meaning implicit in a geonym) as in the case of Ξάνθος (tawny or muddy yellow) for Ζάνθος (very verdant, flowery).

A FINAL NOTE

The *Iliad's* 72 geonyms for a geography of Troy is, of itself, rich with nuances and *double entente*, and is be understood as a geographical photograph, so to speak, taken at some time close to the burial rites of Hektor, at the end of Book XXIV. Its life —that is, its movement, what it betrays of the human condition— is towards the past, and these facts may be ascertained not only from factual statements, but also from diverse inferences and deductions. However, what *cannot* be ascertained is that life, that movement, that which *will* occur in the future, and something about the present photograph of Troy's geography, without the information supplied by the *Odyssey's* 46 geonyms for a geography of Troy.

---

1. A first translation (or rough draft of sorts) from a Slavic language into an early Greek dialect necessarily must contemplate the question about a transposition of phonetic values of one orthography into the equivalent values of another. For example, an original NICA became Greek ΝΙΞΑ, albeit the correct orthography entered unencumbered into the Latin, *Nicaea*, whence modern Nice. Further questions of a translation from an original Slavic text into an early Greek version are addressed in X. THE HELLENIZATION OF HOMER.

I. THE ILIAD AND ITS TROJAN GEOGRAPHY

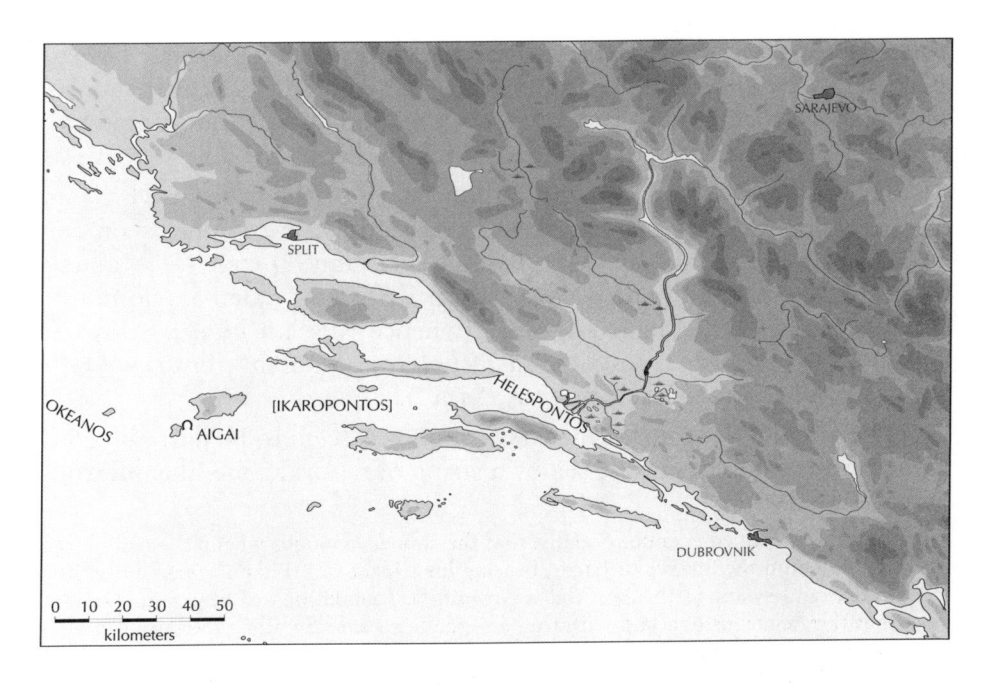

SEA

The geographical paradigm for the vast amplitude of the SEA (*thálassa* x 42, *pélagos* x 1, *póntos* x 50) is made up of four geonyms for different areas, outward and westward from TROIA.

WEST			EAST
⇦ open sea		inter-island channels	⇨
OKEANOS	**AIGAI**	**(IKAROPONTOS)**	**HELLESPONTOS**
open sea	grotto	enclosed sea	brackish marsh
cockroach?	goat	bird	ram
Og + annax*	αἴξ	Ikaros	Helle

* Og (progenitor of Magog) is probably that revolting monster recorded in Hebrew myth of a much later date, which, by the mercy of Noah, was allowed to cling to the Ark during the Deluge. It might have been the cockroach, for which reason it is said to this day that it is so difficult to eradicate it is even "ante-Diluvial".

TABLE 1.5. SEA. *Since the substance of the sea is basically the same, regardless of the place or the area described, its four geonyms bear common associations of ideas.*

HELLESPONTOS ('Ελλήσποντος), delta of the SKAMANDROS (*Naro*, Narenta, Neretva): a region marked by convoluted brackish channels and marshy islets where the Neretva spills into the Adriatic, midway between Split in the north and Dubrovnik in the south.

The name is a compounded reduplicative of the type in which its two component elements are synonymous; thus, an emphasis on the topography of the marshy delta, from a Pelasgian (?) root ϝelj, "marsh vegetation" (whence Latin *vellus* "shorn wool"), + paleo-Slavic *pont-*, "marsh", akin with English "*pond*" (whence Russian *ponizu*, "low or flat land" and *pontos*, a synonym of *balaton*, "marsh", but *not* Latin *pons*, "bridge", nor Greek πόντος, "sea").

The alluvial deposits of the HELLESPONTOS seem to be partially contained from spilling into the sea by a string of natural cone-like outcroppings, thus (XII, 25):

> ...and Zeus rained ever continually, that the sooner he might whelm the wall in the salt sea. And the Shaker of Earth, bearing his trident in his hands, was himself the leader, and swept forth upon the waves all the foundations of beams and stones, that the Achaeans had laid with toil, and made all smooth along the strong stream of Hellespont, and again covered the great beach with sand, when he had swept away the wall; and the rivers he turned back to flow in the channel, where aforetime they had been wont to pour their fair streams of water.

Later Greek lore would derive the name of the HELLESPONTOS from the story that Helle fell from the ram Frixus into the sea (πόντος) at precisely this place. The story preserves an element of truth by relating the name of Helle with this marshy area, as well as that of the ram Frixus, for both are associated with the name of the ARI(E)MOI (occupants of the Neretva delta), forerunners of the *Delmatai* or *Dalmatae* (whose name is preserved in Albanian *dalmeh*, "sheep").

[IKAROPONTOS] (['Ικάροποντος]), Korčulanski Channel: the inter-island sea contained between LEKTON (*Lessina*, Hvar) in the north and TENEDOS (*Corcyra Melaina*, Korčula) in the south.

The name for this part of the sea is associated with the marshy connotations of the HELLESPONTOS, like a "marshy sea", as it were, for all flotsam and jetsam that falls into the sea along the southern coast is quickly swept into this region by winds and swift currents (II, 144):

> And the gathering was stirred like the long sea-waves of the Icarian main, which the East Wind or the South Wind has raised, rushing upon them from the clouds of father Zeus.

The [IKAROPONTOS] (as might have been the original name, in keeping with HELLESPONTOS), will have been so named after Ikaros (son of Daidalos and father of Penelope) who flew like a kite or some bird so

I. THE ILIAD AND ITS TROJAN GEOGRAPHY

high into the sky that his waxen wings melted from the heat of the sun and he plummeted into the sea, not unlike Helle from the ram Phrixius. Iris was also seen to be going down in the same general area (XXIV, 77):

> So spake he, [Zeus] and storm-footed Iris hasted to bear his message, [to Thetis] and midway between Samos and rugged Imbros she leapt into the dark sea, and the waters sounded loud above her. Down sped she to the depths like a plummet of lead, the which, set upon the horn of an ox of the field, goeth down bearing death to the ravenous fishes.

It will be this idea of "marshiness", exaggerated as it may be, where, after the Fall of Troy, a single drowning man will seem to have many adventures, not unlike the many men had an adventure on the marshes of TROIA.

AIGAI (Αἰγαί), Modra Spilja: a marine grotto in Biševo's Balun Cove, lying exactly due west of SAMOS (Sveti Ilija, Pelješac), from where a sunset at the time of the equinoxes would appear as a shimmering path of golden light touching the islands of TENEDOS (Korčula), LEMNOS (Viš), and IMBROS (Biševo), reflected off the surface of the sea back to a viewer at a *vinograd* midway up the western side of SAMOS (XIII, 17, *et pas.*):

> Forthwith then he [Poseidon] went down from the rugged mount, [Samos wooded Thrace-like] striding forth with swift footsteps...
> Thrice he strode in his course, and with the fourth stride he reached his goal, even Aegae, where was his famous palace built in the depths of the mere, golden and gleaming, imperishable for ever.
> There is a wide cavern in the depths of the deep mere, midway between Tenedos and rugged Imbros. There, Poseidon, the Shaker of Earth, stayed his horses, and loosed them from the car, and cast before them food ambrosial to graze upon...

That the marine grotto is "...midway between Tenedos and rugged Imbros", and not in IMBROS itself, conforms to the fact that this phenomenon, as viewed from the *vinograd* —an astronomic observatory and not a vineyard or olive orchard— would appear to place the diameter of the sun's disk between IMBROS and TENEDOS the instant the upper rim sank below the horizon. On days when the sea is calm, the midday sunlight, penetrating through an opening in the grotto's vault, illuminates objects in the water with a shimmering blue glow.

The name of AIGAI appears to be cognate with Greek αἴξ, "goat" (thus, the famous Blue Grotto of Capri). The reason for the name is not immediately apparent, but, since the original reading for the Zodiac sequence begins with BULL in January[2], then March (Spring Equinox) falls in CRAB, and September (Autumn Equinox) in GOAT, or *Capricorn*.

---

2. See VII. THE TWELVE MISADVENTURES OF ODYSSEUS (p. 199).

Nobody knows for certain what *ambrosia* is, but it seems likely it is some sort of mollusk —a delicious sea-snail?— to be found at this place. The blue glow of this grotto might suggest a connection with Hindu *ambrita*, a heavenly dew from which blue sapphires are solidified. Furthermore, when Hera arrived at the confluence of the SIMOEIS (Krupa) with the SKAMANDROS (Neretva), her horses, like those of Poseidon, likewise fed on ambrosia (V, 773, *et pas.*):

> But when they were come to the land of Troy and the two flowing rivers, where the Simoïs and Scamander join their streams, there the goddess, white armed Hera, stayed her horses, and loosed them from the car, and shed thick mist about them; and Simoïs made ambrosia to spring up for them to graze upon.

Blue ambrosia —if this understanding is correct— will have come from some variety of conch, or *murex*. That it was also found at the confluence of rivers suggests ambrosia was some prized sweet-water snail, and these occasionally are to be found in the region, the shells of which are as large as one's cupped hand, and, to boot, are a gourmet's delight.

OKEANOS ('Ὠκεανός), *Mare Adriaticum*, Adriatic Sea: properly, the open sea beyond LEMNOS (*Issa*, Viš) and IMBROS (Biševo).

The sea may be thought of as common to all lands and to all peoples, but in the *Iliad* OKEANOS is exclusively that part of the Adriatic which corresponds to TROIA, and it is mentioned in geographical terms west and east of TROIA corresponding with the Adriatic and Euxine respectively (*Table 1.6.*). That there was a knowledge of a sea in the east invites speculation that TROIA, in its apogee, was a maritime nation, and, since it had important colonies abroad (spread along the length of the Italian Peninsula), it could have exerted a measure of control over maritime as well as land routes. The sad irony is that TROIA was subdued and finally conquered by the numerous contingents listed in that marvellous geographical treatise, the *Catalogue of Ships* (II, 816–877).

OKEANOS is mentioned in 19 instances, which is odd, for the number at once suggests a relationship with the Metonic Cycle[3]. Thus, it will be 19 years after the end of the *Iliad* that Odysseus will seem to be drowning in the [IKAROPONTOS].

---

3. Metonic Cycle: A period of 19 years, after which the phases of the Moon will recur on the same calendar date and within two hours of the same time, discovered by Meton of Athens in 433 B.C. It arises from the fact that 235 lunations equal 19 tropical years almost exactly, about 6939.5 days. (*Norton's Star Atlas*, 1973).

I. THE ILIAD AND ITS TROJAN GEOGRAPHY

	OKEANOS IN THE WEST
I; 423:	Zeus goes to Okeanos and Aithiopes
III; 5:	Cranes go to Pygmies and Okeanos
VIII; 485:	Sun goes to Okeanos
XIV; 311:	Hera goes to the house of deep-flowing Okeanos
XVI; 151:	Podarge and Zephyr beside the streams of Okeanos
XVIII; 240:	Sun sets in the stream of Okeanos
XXIII; 205:	Iris goes to the streams of Okeanos and Aithiopes
	OKEANOS (GENERALLY)
XVIII; 399:	Eurynome, daughter of backward flowing Okeanos
XVIII; 607:	Shield of Achilles surrounded by river Okeanos
XX; 7:	Okeanos river goes to Olympos
XXI; 195:	Okeanos source of rivers, seas, springs, wells
XVIII; 489:	Bear, also called Wain, alone has no bath in Okeanos
	OKEANOS IN THE EAST:
V; 6:	Star of harvest-time rises from the stream of Okeanos
VII; 422:	Sun arises from soft-gliding, deep-flowing Okeanos
XIV; 201:	Hera goes to the limits of earth and Okeanos
XIV; 246:	Hypnos lulls Hera, even in streams of river Okeanos
XIV; 302:	Hera goes to the limits of earth and Okeanos
XVIII; 402:	Hephaistos surrounded by the stream of Okeanos
XIX; 1:	Eos arises from streams of Okeanos

TABLE 1. 7. NINETEEN REFERENCES TO OKEANOS. The number is that of the moons's Metonic Cycle, and therefore relevant to ocean tides.

The name of OKEANOS is, perhaps, derived from that of Og (+ *annax*, PIE for "king" or "queen"), the progenitor of Magog, who is mentioned in the genealogy of Japeth —Iapetus, from whom Dardanus was descended— in the *Table of Nations* of *Genesis*, X, 2–4. He is also known as the Reem, which turns up in rabbinical commentaries[4] as an evil horned-monster which was allowed, by the mercy of Noah, to cling to the Ark.

---

4. A. E. Speicer, *The Anchor Bible Genesis, Introduction, Translation and Notes*. Garden City, New York: Doubleday & Company, Inc., 1964. pp 64–72. Also, Robert Graves and Raphael Patai, *Hebrew Myths, the Book of Genesis*. Garden City, New York: Doubleday & Company, Inc., 1964. p. 54.

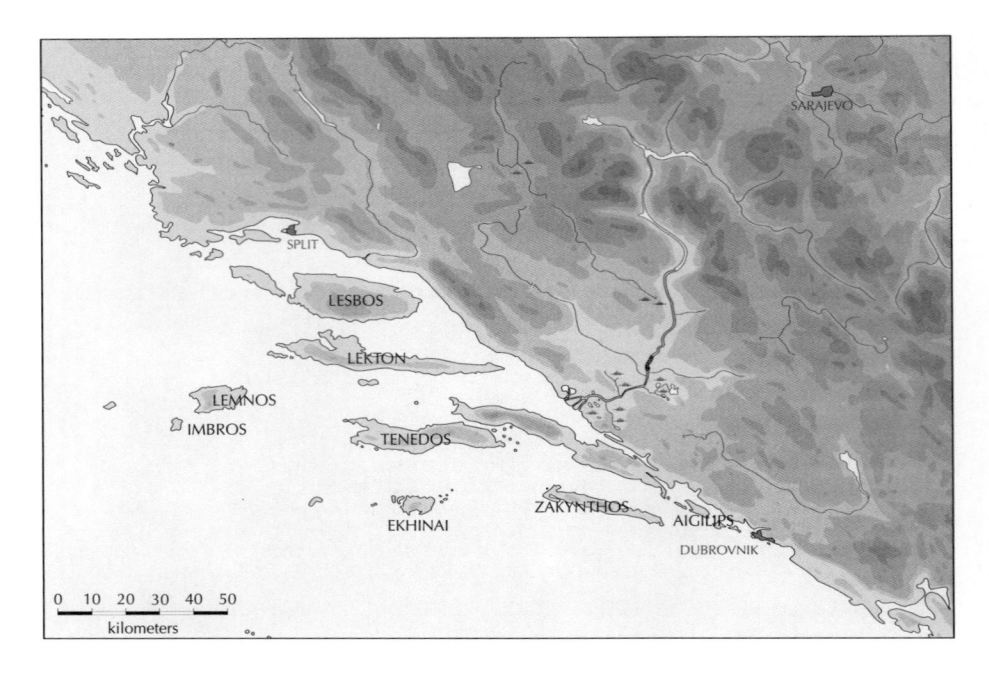

ISLANDS

Of the many islands (more than 1000) that comprise the Adriatic Archipelago, the *Iliad* only integrated eight of the most prominent in its geography of TROIA. Each possesses a unique topographical or climactic feature, and, generally, they are long and narrow, lying in a more or less east-west direction, for which reason they aptly lend the name of PHRYGIA, "brow land" (ὀφρύς) to the region in which they lie.

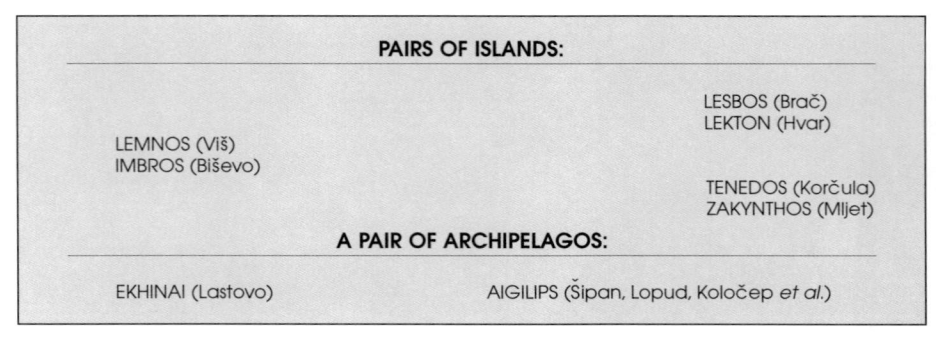

PAIRS OF ISLANDS:	
	LESBOS (Brač)
	LEKTON (Hvar)
LEMNOS (Viš)	
IMBROS (Biševo)	
	TENEDOS (Korčula)
	ZAKYNTHOS (Mljet)
A PAIR OF ARCHIPELAGOS:	
EKHINAI (Lastovo)	AIGILIPS (Šipan, Lopud, Koločep *et al.*)

TABLE 1. 9. ISLANDS. *No sense of schematic harmony can be made of the Trojan isles unless the EKHINAI and AIGILIPES are treated separately, as archipelagos, hence their name in the plural.*

ISLANDS OF THE NORTH

LESBOS (Λέσβος), *Brattia, Thauria,* Brač: the northernmost island of the Trojan Archipelago, occupied by LESBIDES (not necessarily lesbians), with the port-towns of AIPEIA (Milna) and SKYROS (Pušica) at the west and east ends, respectively.

This island was taken by Akhilleus early on, during the nine years of Danaan raiding and pillaging the Trojan Coast before the start of the Trojan War, where he settled, until, according to post-Homeric lore, he was discovered by Odysseus in SKYROS (Pušica), dressed as a woman (IX, 128):

> "And I [Agamemnon] will give [to Achilles] seven women skilled in goodly handiwork, women of Lesbos, whom on the day when himself took well-built Lesbos I chose me from out the spoil, and that in beauty surpass all women folk... And seven well-peopled cities, will I give him, Cardamyle, Enope, and grassy Hire, and sacred Pherae and Antheia with deep meadows, and fair Aepeia and vine-clad Pedasus. All are nigh to the sea, on the uttermost border of sandy Pylos..."

Another reference to LESBOS (adjusted to suit an understanding in an Asia Minor context, yet not altogether unintelligible) concerns the former dominions of Priam and the port-town of MAKAROS (*Mucurrum,* Makarska), directly opposite on the mainland (XXIV, 543):

> And of thee, old sire, we hear that of old thou wast blest; how of all that toward the sea Lesbos, the seat of Macar, encloseth, and Phrygia in the upland, and the boundless Hellespont, over all these folk, men say, thou, old sire, wast preeminent by reason of thy wealth and thy sons.

The etymology of LESBOS is, at best, obscure. However, the association of this island with women of odd habits is legion, thus, in the *Odyssey,* it is also the island of **Aiaia**, home of the sorceress Kirke.

External to Homer, of course, is the story about Akhilleus dressed as a woman already mentioned (see TOWNS: SKYROS, below), and also that of Agamemnon sacrificing his daughter Iphigenia in *Thauria* (cf. Euripides, *Iphigenia in Tauris*) which sounds as though he simply turned her over to lesbian women. Further, the story about the head of Orpheus swimming to LESBOS, singing (after being torn to shreds by the Maenads), sounds like an allusion to a tadpole, since the frog (*žaba*) in the Slavic world is synonymous with pubescent girls (hence the saying to be between "*žabe i babe*", that is, between "froggies and grannies") as echoed in the name of Sappho, the ugly, goitre-ridden, toad-poetess of exquisite lines about her girls.

LEKTON (Λεκτόν), *Lessina/Pharos,* Hvar: an island with the port-towns of PHARE (Hvar) at the west end, and HIRA (Bogomolje) at the east.

LEKTON is mentioned only once (XI, 283):

> To many-fountained Ida they [Hera and Hypnos] came, the mother of wild creatures, even to Lectum, where first they left the sea; and the twain fared on over the dry land, and the topmost forest quivered beneath their feet. There Hypnos did halt... and mounted up on a fir-tree exceeding tall, the highest that then grew in Ida; it reached up through the mists into heaven[5]...

The name of LEKTON appears to be made up of two roots, *lep-* "shell", "husk", + *ϝit-* "elongated land" (the idea aptly conveyed in Spanish *lengüeta*), which yields *leppit*(*on*), and, by gutturalization of labials, *lekkit*(*on*), from where, by sibilation, Latin *Lessina*, and by elision, Greek LEKTON. The port-town of PHARE, later Greek *Pharos*, became Hvar, the current name of the island.

ISLANDS OF THE WEST

LEMNOS (Λήμνος), *Issa* [*Pissa*], Viš: an island occupied by the SINTIES, a seemingly jolly folk despite their *sinister* associations. It was they who attended Hephaistos on the occasion of his fall from heaven (I, 590):

> "Yea, on a time ere this, when I [Hephaistos] was fain to save thee [Hera], he [Zeus] caught me by the foot and hurled me from the heavenly threshold; the whole day long was I borne headlong, and at set of sun I fell in Lemnos, and but little life was in me. There did the Sintian folk make haste to tend me for my fall."

It would seem that Hephaistos became associated with LEMNOS and the SINTIES on account of their merchandising of metal goods, which is easily understood, but also because the statement made by Hephaistos about his accident (and the reason for his permanent lameness), is that he is represented in the sky by the tiny constellation of Pleiades, the seven banished sisters (the seven stars visible to the naked eye), as if, like a premature seven-month baby, he had been expelled from his mother's womb (and somehow, consequently, his lameness). That he fell among SINTIES on LEMNOS "at set of sun" is an exact statement, for it corresponds with the sunset of a Spring Equinox at 6:38 pm on March 21, 1100 BC, as seen from the astronomical observation platform (± 700 mts.) in the area of Nakovana on the western slopes of SAMOS (Sveti Ilija, Pelješac).

The name of LEMNOS has "bleary" connotations in Greek, as might be from the watery eyes of those who tended the smoky forges of Hephaistos, albeit the name (whence modern Viš) is so called on account of a *pitch*, or natural clay, of a soft and velvety quality found *only* on this island (and well-known throughout exYugoslavia).

---

5. See *Map 2a*, pp. 18–19 for this description of the moon's apparent retrograde motion in the course of approximately 15 days.

The SINTIES also cared for Philoktetes when he was bitten on the foot by a poisonous snake at the base of Sveti Ilija (Monte Vípera) in just retribution for his hubris in being the first to jump from his ship onto Trojan soil (II, 722):

> But Philoctetes lay suffering grievous pains in an island, even in sacred Lemnos, where the sons of the Achaeans had left him in anguish with an evil wound from a deadly water-snake. There he lay suffering; yet full soon were the Argives beside their ships to bethink them of king Philoctetes.

IMBROS (Ἴμβρος), Biševo: a small island about 5 kms. south-west of LEMNOS, it was most noted as a reference point on the distant horizon for astronomical observations made from the "vinograd" astronomical observation platform on the western slopes of SAMOS (Sveti Ilija). It is here, at Balun Cove, where AIGAI (Modra Spilja) is located.

ISLANDS OF THE SOUTH

TENEDOS (Τένεδος), *Corcyra Melaina*, Korčula: an island with the port-towns of ANTHEIA [ANTREIA?] (Vela Luka) in the west, and KROKYLEIA (Korčula) in the east.

TENEDOS is, to be sure, an important island, yet it plays an almost insignificant part in the *Iliad's* narrative line (beyond the editorial non-sense about Sminthian Apollo standing over Khryse and Killa and ruling mightily over Tenedos already mentioned in pp. 34–35). It belongs to the dominion of Odysseus (II, 631 *et pas*.):

> And Odysseus led the great-souled Cephallenians that held Ithaca and Neritum, covered with waving forests, and that dwelt in Crocyleia and rugged Aegilips; and them that held Zacynthus, and that dwelt about Samos, and held the mainland and dwelt on the shores over against the isles. Of these was Odysseus captain, the peer of Zeus in counsel. And with him there followed twelve ships with vermilion prows.

That Odysseus possessed twelve vermillion-prowed ships suggests (independently of his intimate association seen later with the twelve houses of the Zodiac) their manufacture on TENEDOS, which, in later times, became associated with ships and ship-building. According to Greek lore, the name of the island was derived from that of Tenes, who, in anger against his father, cut the moorings of his ship and so came to the island which took his name (Apollodorus, *Epitome*, III, 22-25). A still more ingenious story is that of the Trojan Horse which, though purportedly mentioned for the first time in the *Odyssey* (viii, 487–535), may be shown to be a bogus account, since Odysseus —the prime informant of his own account— was already among the KIKONES by the time this event is supposed to have occurred. Still, a rationalization of the story must surely lie in the direction of a ship built and decorated in the Illyrian manner with the prow of a horse head and the stern of a horse tail as a rudder that sailed around the tip of NERITON (Pelješac), past the HELLESPONTOS (Neretva delta), up-stream the SKAMANDROS (Neretva), to the sandy banks immediately below KALLIKOLONE (Stari Grad). Everyone knows the rest of the story.

TENEDOS is likely to have been of logistical importance in the success of Agamemnon's endeavour, whose camp lay across the straight at Orebič, at the foot of SAMOS (Sveti Ilija/Monte Vípera), for it was here, one would think, that he gained a foothold on Trojan territory as well as having access to refurbishing his ships during the long wait before launching a final naval assault on the mainland proper.

The only other reference to TENEDOS is of a certain woman from here, Hekamede, who perhaps refused to treat Philoktetes? (XI, 624):

> And for them [Nestor and Makhaon] fair-tressed Hecamede mixed a potion, she that old Nestor had taken from out of Tenedos, when Achilles sacked it, the daughter of great-hearted Arsinous.

ZAKYNTHOS (Ζάκυνθος), *Melita*, Mljet: an island occupied by SMINTHIES (after whom Sminthian Apollo of I. 39 takes his epithet) with the port-towns of KILLA (Polače) and KHRYSE (Sobra) at the western and eastern ends, respectively. Like KROKYLEIA (and by extension all of TENEDOS?), this isle also fell to the dominion of Odysseus (II, 631):

> And Odysseus led the great-souled Cephallenians that held Ithaca and Neritum, covered with waving forests, and that dwelt in Crocyleia and rugged Aegilips; and them that held Zacynthus, and that dwelt about Samos and held the mainland and dwelt on the shores over against the isles.

The name of ZAKYNTHOS, presumably derived from *za-* "very" (or "with many"), + *kynth-* > Serbian *kuna*, "marten", seems closely related with that of the SMINTHIES, which, according to Strabo (*Geography*, 13. 1. 64), came from an ancient Cretan word, *sminthos*, meaning "mouse". A further association may be seen in Pliny, who records (*Natural History*, III, 26, 152) that, according to Kallimakhos, the Maltese terrier got its name from Meleda. The later name of *Melita* "sweet", "honey", is generic (and hence of great antiquity), proper to those places such as MILETOS (*Lacus Nemorensis*, Lago di Nemi) where small sources of fresh water are to be found, such as those on this island (and hence its later name).

PAIR OF ARCHIPELAGOS

EKHINAI (Ἐχῖναι), *Lagosta*, Lastovo: the collective name for a cluster of isles lying south of TENEDOS (Korčula) (II, 625):

> And those from Dulichium and the Echinae, the holy isles, that lie across the sea, over against [Elis], these again had as leader Meges, the peer of Ares, even the

son of Phyleus, dear to Zeus, begat—he that of old had gone to dwell in Dulichium in wrath against his father.

The reference to a location of these isles "over against Elis" is a crude editorial emendation for "over against Doulikhion" when these isles were sought (on cue with the close relationship of Meges with Epeians in XIII, 692 and XV, 520) considerably further south, in fact, somewhere opposite the coast of Elis, since, nowhere in the *Iliad* (excepting here), is there any reference to Trojan geographical data in terms of foreign geographical information.

The story goes that Phyleus was expelled from Elis by his father and so came to DOULIKHION (Žuljana), where he married the sister of Odysseus who bore him Meges. Perhaps Meges too was sent abroad (for whatever the reason) and thus his presence in the EKHINAI. That this set of isles was so distant from all others, yet of a certain importance, is seen not only in its epithet, "holy" —why they should have been so is not yet fully understood— but also by the distinguished participation of Meges in the Trojan War.

AIGILIPS (Αἰγίλιψ), *Elaphites* (Olipa, Jakljan, Šipan, Ruda, Lopud, and Koločep): the collective name for a string of islands of varying size that hug a stretch of mainland from NERITON (Pelješac) to Dubrovnik.

This archipelago also fell to the dominion of Odysseus (II, 631):

> And Odysseus led the great-souled Cephallenians that held Ithaca and Neritum, covered with waving forests, and that dwelt in Crocyleia and rugged Aegilips; and them that held Zacynthus, and that dwelt about Samos and held the mainland and dwelt on the shores over against the isles.

The name of AIGLIPS is connected with "goat", and why this will have been so is anybody's guess. The later Greek name of *Elaphites*, "deer isles" (whence still later *Delaphodia* and Latin *Lafota*, now Lopud) would seem to echo its earlier Trojan name, albeit, it is a name like that of *Brattia* (LESBOS), derived from an Akhaian presence along the Trojan Coast and their reason for eventual destruction of ILIOS.

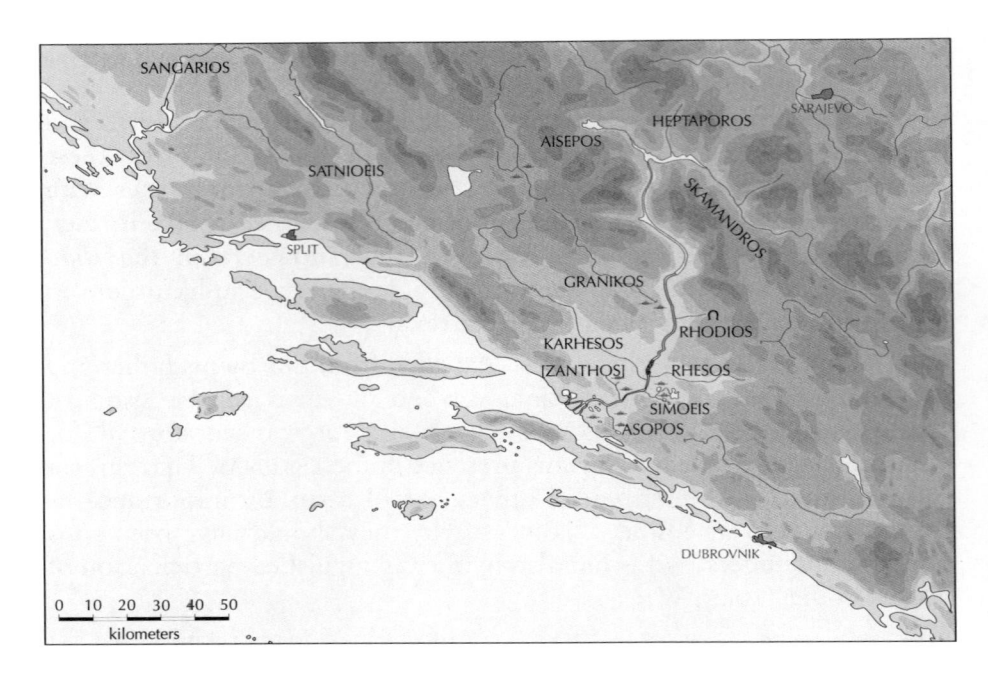

RIVERS

Three great rivers drain the territory of Troy into the Adriatic Sea and do not form part of the great Danubian watershed which drains the greater part of the Balkan Peninsula into the Euxine or Black Sea. Also, numerous underground streams —technically rivers but regarded as geological curiosities— may be seen here and there bubbling up in the sea a short distance from the shoreline.

THE THREE RIVERS OF TROY:

SANGARIOS
ample, navigable delta

SATNIOEIS
narrow, almost impenetrable delta

SKAMANDROS
ample, navigable delta

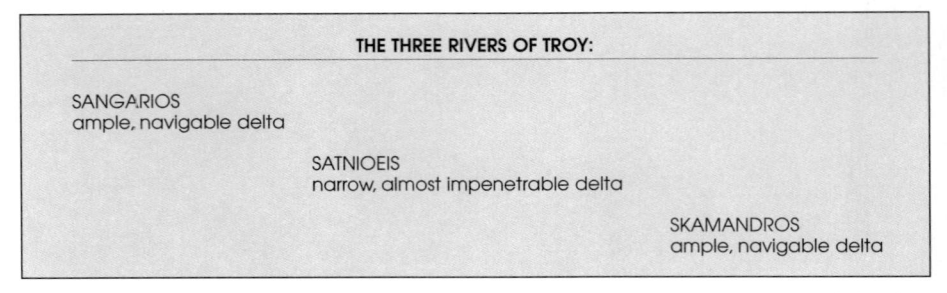

TABLE 1. 11. RIVERS. The delta-valley of the SKAMANDROS, unlike the other rivers of Troy, has always been a rich source of food supply, naturally attracting human occupation.

I. THE ILIAD AND ITS TROJAN GEOGRAPHY

THE THREE RIVERS OF TROY:

SANGARIOS (Σαγγάριος), Krka: the northernmost river of Troy, the natural border of a country which had no defined borders.

The following reference to the SANGARIOS and PHRYGIA (as if the SANGARIOS flowed through PHRYGIA) is garbled, the result of an effort to understand these lines in an Asia Minor context (III, 184):

> Ere now have I [Priam] journeyed to the land of Phrygia... and there I saw in multitudes the Phrygian warriors... that were then encamped along the banks of Sangarius. For I, too, being their ally, was numbered among them on the day when the Amazones came, the peers of men.

The sense of this passage should be understood as Priam having passed through PHRYGIA, and, in the company of PHRYGIANS (that is, diverse island folk), gone thence to the banks of the SANGARIOS, where he met the AMAZONES.

Presumably, the AMAZONES, a folk from abroad, settled in Trojan territory, and thus, Priam, with the help of PHRYGES —for without them any territorial acquisition would eventually have become meaningless— was able to contain the AMAZONES along the banks of the SANGARIOS. By way of integrating these newly arrived folks into a Trojan federation of tribes Priam took Hekabe, daughter of the lord of the AMAZONES, who bore him Hektor (XVI, 717):

> ...Asius, that was uncle to horse-taming Hector, and own brother to Hecabe, but son of Dymas, that dwelt [in Phrygia] by the streams of Sangarius.

The AMAZONES seem to have been driven across the Adriatic from their former homeland deeply ensconsed in the Maiella Massive by Bellerophonetes (VI, 185–202), who afterwards wandered about in the district of ALEION (Molise). The northern boundary of this district was the *Sa(g)grus*, today the Sangro, from which an inference of a connection with the name of the SANGARIOS (Σαγγάριος), a generic kind of toponym that simply dropped a phonemic *n*, that is, the letter γ.

SATNIOEIS (Σατνιόεις), *Titio* ? (= Tsitsio = Cicio?), Cetina: a river which rises from the marshy plain (now Perucko Lake) at the foot of mount Dinara (1,831 mts.), and cuts a deep gash across the Biokovo range to debouch suddenly at PEDASOS (*Oneum*, Omiš) from a deep and narrow gorge flanked by high, sheer cliffs (VI, 34):

> ...and the king of men, Agamemnon, slew Elatus that dwelt in steep Pedasos by the banks of fair-flowing Satnioeis.

That a certain Naiad nymph bore Satnius to Oleus as he tended his herd by the banks of SATNIOEIS (XIV, 445) will have been somewhere in the interior, in the region where the SATNIOEIS rises, for doing so elsewhere will have been physically impossible. It would seem there is a parallel between the name of Satnius, derived from that of the SATNIOEIS, with the name of Simoeisius, born under similar circumstances by the banks of the SIMOEIS (IV, 474–477).

SKAMANDROS (Σκάμανδρος), *Naro/Narenta, Vissena*, Neretva: the southernmost river of Troy, it cuts transversally through the mountains of IDA (Biokovo Range) and debouches into the Adriatic between Split in the north and Dubrovnik in the south.

The meaning of SKAMANDROS is anybody's guess (for hardly is the second element, *-andros*, "man", part of the linguistic equation). The Greeks told the story that the river took its name from a Cretan prince who jumped into its waters[6], and, also, that women who bathed in the river could (or would) become pregnant, a story which could be interpreted to account for its many conger eels. Both stories have a shred of truth, even if tenuous. It will have been Teucros —again, according to Greek lore— the youthful companion of Skamandros, who will have taken the name of KRETE to the environs of Rome (cf. Cretone), and the fertility of its waters, as if impregnating the womb of Mother Earth, surely accounts for an *autochthonous* folk, the DARDANIOI, who occupied the banks of the SKAMANDROS river-valley and are identical with the *Narensi* of later times, occupants of *Narona* (whose suffix *-ona* denotes a social group).

A partial description of the affluents of SKAMANDROS (listed in a schematic order, *Table. 1. 12.*) is given as follows (XII, 17–33):

> ...then verily did Poseidon and Apollo take counsel to sweep away the wall, [of the Danaans] bringing against it the might of all the rivers that flow forth from the mountains of Ida to the sea—Rhesus and Heptaporus and Caresus and Rhodius, and Granicus and Aesepus, and goodly Scamander, and Simois, by the banks whereof many shields of bull's-hide and many helms fell in the dust... —of all these did Phoebus Apollo turn the mouths together, and for nine days' space he drave their flood against the wall...

AFFLUENTS OF SKAMANDROS, FROM NORTH TO SOUTH

HEPTAPOROS (Επταπορος), Ostrovača: one of the two sources of the SKAMANDROS (Neretva), the other being the SKAMANDROS itself, so called because its waters, or those of the SKAMANDROS with which they have mingled, pass the mouths, or "pores", of *seven* affluents (for the

---

6. Prof. Radoslav Matič, of Čapljina, as long ago as 1985, held to the idea that eponymy is not sound linguistics, such that the SKAMANDROS (Neretva) did not acquire a name simply because a man of the same name jumped into it, and that, in any case, it could have been the other way about, that a man (a presumed Cretan prince) simply took the name of a river called SKAMANDROS.

I. THE ILIAD AND ITS TROJAN GEOGRAPHY

THE AFFLUENTS OF SKAMANDROS IN THE ORDER OF THEIR LISTING (XII, 17):	
RHESOS	like KARHESOS (Trebižat), it flows but then dries
HEPTAPOROS	with SKAMANDROS passes 'seven mouths'
KARHESOS	like RHESOS (Bregava), it flows in cascades
RHODIOS	emerges from depths of a chasm
GRANIKOS	disappears into crags in the ground
AISEPOS	like SIMOEIS (Krka), it drains two mountain lakes
SKAMANDROS	mingles with waters of HEPTAPOROS (Ostrovača)
SIMOEIS	like AISEPOS (Rama), it drains two marshes

TABLE 1.12. LISTED AFFLUENTS. The particular order of listing pairs affluents with similar features such that the SKAMANDROS might be thought of as synonymous with the HEPTAPOROS.

ALL AFFLUENTS OF THE SKAMANDROS, FROM NORTH TO SOUTH:			
	HEPTAPOROS – SKAMANDROS		
	(Ostrovača) (Neretva)		
AISEPOS (Rama)		RHODIOS	(Buna)
GRANIKOS (Ugrovača)		RHESOS	(Bregava)
KARHESOS (Trebižat)		SIMOEIS	(Krupa)
ZANTHOS (Norin)		ASOPOS	(Mala Neretva)
	HELLESPONTOS		
	(Neretva delta)		

TABLE 1.13. ALL AFFLUENTS. A diagramme of their location relative to SKAMANDROS and to each other establishes paired sets of intrinsic features in each as well as an association of ideas in their names.

GRANIKOS (Ugrovača) never reaches the SKAMANDROS but, rather, disappears into the porous ground).

AISEPOS (Αἴσηπος), Rama: this affluent seems to have had a generic type name like ASOPOS, "with deep reeds, that coucheth in grass" (below), since, like the SIMOEIS, it drained two marshy valleys (II, 824):

> And they that dwelt in Zeleia beneath the nethermost foot of Ida, mean of wealth, that drink the dark water of Aesepus, even the Troes, these again were led by the glorious son of Lycaon, Pandarus...

GRANICOS (Γρήνικος), Ugrovača: this affluent seeps into the porous ground before reaching the SKAMANDROS, albeit its waters may be seen in the river welling up at different places from different underwater sources.

RHODIOS ('Ροδίος), Buna: it emerges, flowing softly, majestically, from the depths of a chasm at the base of a sheer cliff. In its name is the Slavic root *rod-* "to emerge, spring up (from the earth)", whence *rodina*, Mother Earth, *narodna*, "national".

RHESOS ('Ρῆσος), Bregava: this affluent flows below and along the length of Ošanici, the hill on which TROIA (the city) is perched, thus its name, from the Slavic root *res-*, whence Latin *rex*, "king", recalls the burial site of Tros. The modern name, cognate with *berg-* "hill", "mountain", would seem to betray a point of contact with the original name.

KARHESOS (Κάρησος), Trebižat: the name of this affluent would seem to allude to its four curtain-like falls, thus *kar(t)-* "card" (the idea of a flat surface) + *-es(s)os*, in Greek, a qualitative type-ending.

SIMOEIS (Σιμόεις), Krupa: this affluent drains the two marshy areas of the ILEIAN PLAIN (Hutovo Blato) and flows into the SKAMANDROS opposite KALLIKOLONE (Gabela, Stari Grad) (XX, 51):

> And over against her [Athene] shouted Ares, dread as a dark whirlwind, calling with shrill tones to the Trojans from the topmost citadel, [Pergamos] and now again as he sped by the shore of Simoïs over Callicolone.

The Greek understanding of the name is "snub-nosed", which seems topographically apt since it drains two separate murky areas, thus SKAMANDROS calls on the SIMOEIS (XXI, 307):

> "Dear brother [Simoïs], the might of this man let us stay... fill thy streams with water from thy springs, and arouse all thy torrents..."

Presumably, SKAMANDROS will have also called on the [ZANTHOS] (Norin) which drains the TROIC PLAIN (Glibuša) on the opposite side, and thus the name would seem to have a bearing on that of the Norin, and perhaps even that of Narona (Vid) situated on the western hillsides.

XANTHOS [ZANTHOS] (Ξάνθος [Ζάνθος]), Norin: the last tributary on the right bank of the SKAMANDROS, it drains the TROIC PLAIN (Glibuša) over which many episodes of the Trojan War occurred, to wit (VI, 1; XXI, 1; XXI, 328):

> So was dread strife of the Trojans and Achaeans left to itself... as they aimed one at the other their bronze-tipped spears between the Simois and the streams of Xanthus.

> But when they were now come to the ford of the fair-flowing river, even eddying Xanthus that immortal Zeus begat, there Achilles cleft them [the Trojans] asunder, and the one part he drave to the plain toward the city... but the half of them were pent into the deep-flowing river with its silver eddies.

> But Hera called aloud, seized with fear for Achilles, lest the great deep-eddying River should sweep him away. And forthwith she spake unto Hephaestus, her dear son: "Rouse thee, Crook-foot, my child! for it was against thee that we deemed eddying Xanthus to be matched in fight. Nay, bear thou aid with speed... do thou along the banks of Xanthus burn up his trees, and beset him about with fire... ".

The name of ZANTHOS, "very flowery", indeed describes the dense marsh vegetation of bulrushes and reeds in the region. However, in an

Asia Minor context, an understanding of the relationship between this affluent and the SKAMANDROS itself becomes lost, and so ZANTHOS became Xanthos, conventionally meaning "tawny yellow", albeit there existed the XANTHOS (Bradano) in LYKIA (*Lucania*).

ASOPOS (Ἀσωπός), Mala Neretva: this affluent drains the marshes of HYPOPLAKIA (Jezero Kuti) and debouches relatively nearby, at Opuzen (IV, 376–390):

> "Once verily [says Agamemnon] he [Tydeus] came to Mycenae, not as an enemy, but as a guest, in company with godlike Polyneices, to gather a host; for in that day they were waging a war against the sacred walls of Thebe, and earnestly did they make prayer that glorious allies be granted them... So when they had departed and were got forth upon their way, and had come to Asopus with deep reeds, that coucheth in the grass, there did the Achaeans send forth Tydeus on an embassage. And he went his way, and found the many sons of Cadmus feasting in the house of mighty Eteocles. Then, for all he was a stranger, the horseman Tydeus feared not, all alone though he was amid the many Cadmeians, but challenged them all to feats of strength, and in every one vanquished he them full easily..."

The ASOPOS, with the ZANTHOS (Norin) and SIMOEIS (Krupa) completes the trefoiled complex of marshes, a natural geological feature which gave TROIA its name (see below, DISTRICTS).

MOUNTAINS

The mountains of Troy might be thought of as a letter Y, the arms of which represent IDA (Biokovo Range) which is "unrestricted", so to speak, for it extends as far inland as ZELEIA (Jabalnica Gorges), and NERITON (Pelješac Peninsula) which is "contained", as it were, by the peninsula itself[7]. Both ranges are tipped with an important summit. The foot of the letter Y represents all elevated ground of the SKAMANDROS delta-valley, likewise, all proportion kept, tipped with an important summit, and, further inland, the most important set of elevations, the hillock of ILIOS (Drijeva/Gabela).

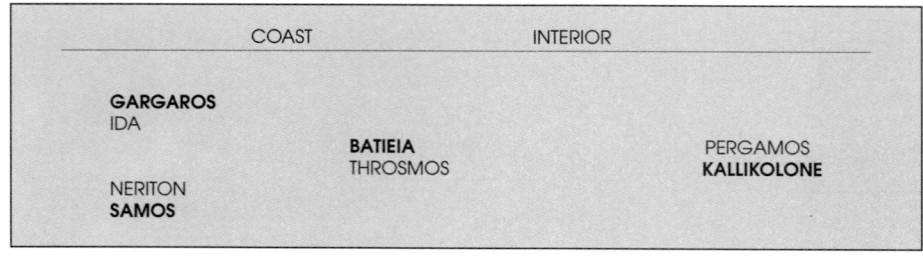

COAST		INTERIOR
GARGAROS IDA		
	BATIEIA THROSMOS	PERGAMOS **KALLIKOLONE**
NERITON **SAMOS**		

TABLE 1. 15. MOUNTAINS. A prominence (bold) is an inseparable feature of a mountain, thus BATIEIA is inseparable from the flat, elevated ground of the delta-valley, and KALLIKOLONE, though lower than PERGAMOS, is the most important feature of ILIOS.

7. "Balkan" is a Turkish term which means "mountainous".

I. THE ILIAD AND ITS TROJAN GEOGRAPHY

IDA ("Ιδα), Biokovo Range: the name, generally, for all mountains and hills, though, specifically, one might think of the name as that of the wall-like range which runs parallel with the coast. Thus, IDA is used for mountains in the distant district of ZELEIA (Jabalnica Gorges) (II, 824):

> And they that dwelt in Zeleia beneath the nethermost foot of Ida, mean of wealth, that drink the dark water of Aesepus, even the Troes, these again were led by the glorious son of Lycaon, Pandarus...

Also, for those mountains within the SKAMANDROS (Neretva) delta-valley (XII, 17):

> ...then verily did Poseidon and Apollo take counsel to sweep away the wall, [of the Achaeans] bringing against it the might of all the rivers that flow forth from the mountains of Ida to the sea...

GARGAROS (Γάργαρος), the twin peaks of Sveti Jure, 1762 mts. and Sveti Ilija, 1640 mts.: these are situated at the latitude of LESBOS (Brač).

The name of GARGAROS suggests a "throat", as of a volcano, albeit this range is Karstic limestone. However, near the summits of both Sveti Ilija and Sveti Jure are numerous caves packed with perennial snows, oddly, a topographical feature not to be found elsewhere. The reduplicative sense in the name of GARGAROS is carried in the name of another Sveti Ilija, 770 mts., some 45 kilometers to the south along the same range, near the HELLESPONTOS (Neretva delta) (VIII, 47):

> To Ida he [Zeus] fared, the many-fountained, mother of wild beasts, even to Gargarus, where is the demesne and his fragrant altar. There did the father of men and gods stay his horses, and loose them from the car, and shed thick mist upon them; and himself sat amid the mountain peaks exulting in his glory, looking upon the city of the Trojans and the ships of the Achaeans.

BATIEIA (Βατίεια), Kozjak, 82 mts.: the location of Batieia within the HELLESPONTOS (Neretva delta) corresponds with that of Kozjak, the most prominent of several outcroppings (II, 811):

> Now there is before the city a steep mound afar out in the plain, with a clear space about it on this side and on that; this do men verily call Batieia, but the immortals call it the barrow of Myrine, light of step. There on this day did the Trojans and their allies separate their companies.

Kosjak means "goat" or "goatlike", in keeping with the name of the ARI[E]MOI (occupants of the HELLESPONTOS), later called *Delmatae* or Dalmatians, after whom this coast is so called, and whose name became Albanian *dalmeh*, "sheep".

Several of these outcroppings dot the HELLESPONTOS here and there, but a curious geological phenomenon is that several of these seem aligned, like posts, as it were, containing the alluvial silt that prevents the HELLESPONTOS from spilling out into the sea (such as the Po delta has done). These outcroppings served, upon a time, as burial sites (a fact which has been archaeologically substantiated, and, for as much as BATIEIA was once the barrow of Myrine, the site was now destined for Akhilleus (VII, 84):

> "...his [Achilles'] corpse will I render back to the well-benched ships, that the long-haired Achaeans may give him burial, and heap up for him a barrow by the wide Hellespont. And some one shall some day say even of men that are yet to be, as he saileth in his many benched ship over the wine-dark sea: 'This is a barrow of a man that died in olden days, whom on a time in the midst of his prowess glorious Hector slew'."

THROSMOS (Θρωσμός), all elevated ground in the Neretva delta-valley: though the flat expanses of high ground contained within the Neretva delta-valley can hardly be thought of as a "mountain", or "mountainous", it is nevertheless higher than the marshy level of the environs, and thus, topographically, a height (X, 159):

> "Awake [says Nestor], son of Tydeus, why slumberest thou the whole night through in sleep? Knowest thou not that the Trojans on the Throsmos in the plain are camped hard by the ships, and but scant space still holdeth them off?"

NERITON (Νήριτον), Sabbioncello/Pelješac Peninsula: a long (65 kms.) and narrow peninsula, almost an island, connected to the mainland by a narrow neck of land some 500 mts. wide (II, 631):

> And Odysseus led the great-souled Cephallenians that held Ithaca and Neritum, covered with waving forests, and that dwelt in Crocyleia and rugged Aegilips; and them that held Zacynthus, and that dwelt about Samos and held the mainland and dwelt on the shores over against the isles.

The name is derived from *ner-* "murky (area)" (cognate with Latin *nares*, "nostrils") inspired on the Korčulanski and Stonski Channels (fjords) which flank the eastern end of the peninsula where it is attached to the mainland, + ϝit- "promontory", conferred in the names of PYTHO (*Portus Delphinus*, Portofino) and ITON (Cilento).

SAMOS (Σάμος), Sveti Ilija/Monte Vípera, 961 mts.: the highest prominence of NERITON (Pelješac), situated at its western end.

On the western slopes of SAMOS, in the region of Nakovana, at ± 700 mts., are the remains of an astronomical observation platform from which the following description of an equinox sunset takes place (already mentioned in the *Foreword*, p. 26) (XIII, 17):

> Forthwith then he went down from the rugged mount, striding forth with swift footsteps, and the high mountains trembled and the woodland beneath the immortal feet of Poseidon as he went. Thrice he strode in his course, and with the fourth stride he reached his goal, even Aegae, where was his famous palace built in the depths of the mere, golden and gleaming, imperishable for ever. Thither came he, and let harness beneath his car his two bronze-hooved horses, swift of flight...

Independently of the importance evinced in the archaeological remains of ILIOS and ITHAKA, perhaps SAMOS —its summit— holds the most fascinating answers to specific questions about the authorship of the *Iliad* and *Odyssey*. The names of Homer and Orpheus seem inextricable from the composition of these works, yet their identity as that of the same individual becomes fused, blurred, and, eventually, a historical improbability. Who, then, was their author, their prime creative force? How did these sublime Upanishads come into being?[8] Perhaps the question of *who* is less important than understanding something about the structure and mechanics of an institutional framework that created these epics —certainly, not an intellectual endeavour that suddenly came into being as a result of a Trojan War or Misadventures of Odysseus, or a literary tradition that evolved over a period of time as a result of these events, but an institutional framework that already existed long before they occurred.

PERGAMOS (Πέργαμος), the collective name for the hills of Avala (63 mts. above sea level) and Djerzeles: these form the adjacent heights of ILIOS (Drijeva/Gabela). See II. ILIOS: A BRIEF SURVEY.

KALLIKOLONE (Καλλικολώνη), Stari Grad: the southeastern promontory of ILIOS (Drijeva/Gabela). See II. ILIOS: A BRIEF SURVEY.

---

8. An initial *response* to the question, helter-skelter and short of the mark as it may be, but already *oriented* in the right direction, is still premature, since it is important to understand that the authorship of the *Odyssey* offers supplementary information about peoples and places not mentioned in the *Iliad*, some of which is pertinent to this area of Nakovana.

DISTRICTS

TROIA (Τροίη): the name of a region, without precise frontiers, limited in the north by Šibenik Bay and in the south by Boka Kotorska, and inland as far east as the upper reaches of the SKAMANDROS (*Naro*, Neretva). The name of TROIA, following later Greek tradition, would remit its origins to that of Tros, after whom, presumably, the TROES (Trojans) were so called, and from whom, in turn, that of TROIA was derived. However, a Slavic understanding of the name calls for the idea of *tro-* "three", inspired on the trefoiled set of marshes in the Neretva delta-valley[9] (see map, PLACES), and thus for a revision in the name of Tros, who will have been so called for having been born in the region, and whence the name of TROIA, and that of the TROES.

	TROIA:	
islands	seaboard	interior
PHRYGIA	ASKANIA	DARDANIA

TABLE 1. 17. DISTRICTS. *The district of DARDANIA comprises two lesser districts north and south of the SKAMANDROS delta-valley, and a third, upstream, at the river's head-waters.*

9. The fundamental notion of "three" is found in stories about the foundation of *Trinoventum*, the city of the *Trinovantes*, by Brut the Trojan, today called London, and the French city of Troyes, the city of the *Tricases*.

THE ISLANDS AND SEABOARD

PHRYGIA (Φρυγίη), Dalmatian Archipelago: the islands, including the peninsula of NERITON (Pelješac), are generally long and narrow, and lie horizontally in a "brow-like" manner, suggesting, perhaps, the name of this district —its meaning and origin unknown— evolved into later Greek *ophrys*, "brow"[10].

PHRYGIA was occupied by PHRYGES (one of the two phyla of TROES, the other being the landbound DARDANIOI, for which see PEOPLES, below). This district was understood to be that through which the Sangarios of Asia Minor flowed when Troy became associated with the region at the entrance to the Dardanelles (III, 184):

> Ere now have I [Priam] journeyed to the land of Phrygia... and there I saw in multitudes the Phrygian warriors... that were then encamped along the banks of Sangarius. For I, too, being their ally, was numbered among them on the day when the Amazones came, the peers of men.

Presumably, the intention of this statement is nothing more than diverse PHRYGIAN folks having accompanied Priam (for whatever the reason) to the banks of the SANGARIOS (Krka), where they met newly arrived AMAZONES.

ASKANIA (Ἀσκανίη), Dalmatian Coast: the length of the Trojan coast, it could be said to have extended from Šibenik Bay in the north to Boka Kotorska in the south (II, 862):

> And Phorcys and godlike Ascanius led the Phrygians from afar, from Ascania, and were eager to fight in the press of battle.

The meaning of this name eludes all reasonable assumptions, from which an inference, perhaps, that the root *ask(a)-* may mean different things in different languages. However, if this root conveys nothing more than the idea of "coast" or "seaboard", as here (thus Ascanius, son of Aineias, settled the coast of *Latium*), or an "edge", as it were, then the name of the PELASAGOI (a folk of LYKIA) may, perhaps, be remitted to those folks, who, upon a time, in the distant past, occupied the receding edges of the last polar ice-cap and fled into the Mediterranean Basin from the devastating perennial floodings of northern Europe and Asia.

---

10. There are stories about a certain Kyknos, evidently upon a time conflated but later separated into two different accounts of a personage with the same name, and the story of Tenes, a son of Kyknos, coming to the island of Leukophrys and subsequently naming it Tenedos, after his own name. Again, the Greek invention of eponymy yields nothing, other than a quaint story, but, since Kyknos is both a Ligurian king as well as a personage associated with the Po, there would seem to be a tint, or insinuation, of an early (pre-Trojan?) Venetic immigration into the region, evinced in the presence of Tenes in the region.

THE INTERIOR

DARDANIA (Δαρδανίη), the inland country, without definite borders, but, in a more specific way, the SKAMANDROS delta-valley: the Greek perception (and scholarship ever since, cf. M. W. Edwards, *The Iliad: A Commentary*, vol. V, p. 316) is that the name is derived from that of Dardanus (XX, 215):

> At the first Zeus, the cloud-gatherer, begat Dardanus, and he founded [κτίσσε] Dardania, for not yet was sacred Ilios builded in the plain to be a city of mortal men...

Here, the verb κτίζω, as understood in *classical* Greek, is clear about conveying the idea *to people* or *occupy* a country, or of a city, *to found, plant, build*, whence the inescapable eponymous tradition. Still, the sense of this verb (3rd pers. sing. aorist) in Homeric Greek is not more than "he occupied", which is not altogether anything near "peopling" a district or "founding" a city. From this, then, an easy understanding that Dardanus and Dardania have different meanings, in different languages, the one of "dart" in the totemic identity of a wasp-man, and the other, of "fig", natural to the SKAMANDROS delta-valley (cf. Albanian-Illyrian *dardhe*, "pear").

DARDANIA comprised three unique regions of the SKAMANDROS delta-valley THYMBRA, on the right bank, and HYPOPLAKIA, opposite, on the left bank, and, away from the coast, in the interior, where the SKAMANDROS turns to flow in a general southerly direction, the district of ZELEIA.

SUB-DISTRICTS OF DARDANIA

THYMBRA (Θύμβρη), Baćinsko Jezero: this subdistrict is heard of only once, in the babbling words of the terrified Dolon, before being put to death (X, 430):

> "Towards the sea lie the Carians and the Paeonians, with curved bows, and the Leleges [read LELEXOI] and Caucones, and the goodly Pelasgi. And towards Thymbre fell the lot of the Lycians and the lordly Mysians, and the Phrygians that fight from chariots and the Maeonians, lords of chariots. But why is it that ye question me closely regarding all these things?"

The information, although intended as a calculated lie, is, in fact, garbled, the result of editorial tampering to suit an Asia Minor context. Nevertheless, the importance of the statement is that "Lycians... lordly, Mysians... and Maeonians, lords of chariots...", Trojan allies listed in the *Catalogue of Trojan Forces [Abroad]* (II, 816–876), are contained within THYMBRA, an inland district already taken by AKHAIAN forces beached on the SKAMANDROS right bank.

The etymology of THYMBRA is difficult (if not impossible?), but most likely obeys to its curious topography of small pockets of fresh water (one, where Diomedes bathed after having killed Dolon, mentioned below, in PLACES).

HYPOPLAKIA [SIPOPLAKIA] (Ὑποπλακίη [Σιποπλακίη]), Jezero Kuti: one of three marshes which contributes to the name of TROIA, drained by the ASOPOS (Mala Neretva). The name, with that of PLAKOS (Mlini), occurs in a garbled reference to THEBE (Klek) (VI, 395):

> ...Andromache, daughter of great-hearted Eëtion, Eëtion that dwelt beneath wooded Placus [ὑπὸ Πλάκῳ ὑληέσσῃ], in Thebe under Placus [Ὑποπλακίη], and was lord over the men Cilicia; for it was his daughter that bronze-harnessed Hector had to wife.

Placus [ὑπὸ Πλάκῳ ὑληέσσῃ] and Hypoplakia [Ὑποπλακίη] are two different places, but, because of an erroneous understanding of Trojan geography in an Asia Minor context, Placus is presumed to have been the name of a southern spur of Ida (cf. G. S. Kirk, *The Iliad: A Commentary*, vol. II, p. 211). The original orthography, [SIPOPLAKIA], means "wetland marshland", from the root *sipo-* "wetland" (cf. marshes of *Sipontum*), + *plak-* "cake" (by extension a "flattened islet", "marshland"), indeed, an apt name for this district. The modern name of Kuti is derived from Greek πύθω, "to rot", "corrode" (whence *putrid*). Thus, the relationship of HYPOPLAKIA [SIPOPLAKIA] with Placus and Thebe, above, can only be speculative.

ZELEIA (Ζέλεια), Jablanica Gorges: the most distant region of TROIA in the hinterland, where the SKAMANDROS turns from a general northwestern flow southward towards the sea. The region was perhaps once a marshland (II, 824):

> And they that dwelt in Zeleia beneath the nethermost foot of Ida, men of wealth, that drink the dark water of Aesepus, even the Troes, these again were led by the glorious son of Lycaon, Pandarus, to whom Apollo himself gave the bow.

That these TROES of ZELEIA were "men of wealth" is surely because of the many gold and silver deposits found in the region.

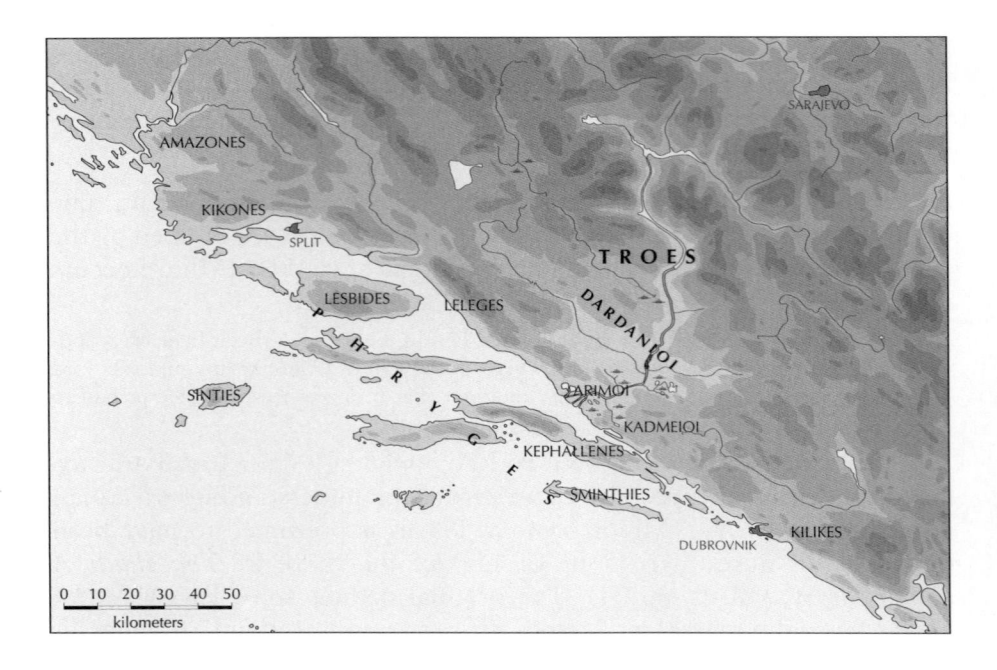

PEOPLES

Homeric ethnological theory is succinct: it understands the history of humankind, its own and abroad, as that of an autochthonous folk which, rather than passing through phases of intellectual development —Stone Ages, Bronze and Iron Ages— simply became covered, because of certain socio-political conveniences (or economic advantages), by the blanket of a new cultural heritage, itself having its unique history, which, in time, agglutinated the local understanding of a world-order with the novel import of spiritual values and approaches to life. Thus, "autochthony" was nothing more than the semen-stuff in the mighty strength of a river's waters fertilizing the ever-thirsty womb of Mother Earth of the grand Danubian Basin. This explained Lepenski Vir, the *oldest civilization* in Europe (*c.* 8,000 BC) which later became dimmed by the unique discovery of writing (one squiggle, one sound) by the Vinča Culture, which, in time, again was blanketed by a Pelasgian cultural stratum. It was the Greek intelligentsia which, for want of an adequate instruction in these matters, came up with the perverse invention of "eponymy", the practice of ascribing the name of anything to that of some make-believe ancestor... thus, Dardanus was the eponymous ancestor of the DARDANIOI, and from this simple, self-evident observation, the beginning of a grand misunderstanding of everything.

	TROES:	
PHRYGES		DARDANIOI
islands	**seaboard**	**interior**
	AMAZONES	
	KIKONES	
	LELEGES	
LESBIDES		
SINTIES		(PYGMIES) ARI(E)MOI
SMINTHIES		
	KADMEIOI	
	KEPHALLENES	
	KILIKES	

TABLE 1.19. PEOPLES. The SINTIES, an emminently merchant folk, would seem to be of foreign stock, as are the AMAZONES and KADMEIOI. The DARDANIOI and ARI(E)MOI are synonymous.

TROES (Τρῶες), Trojans: a collective ethnicon for a number of folks of diverse cultural (rather than ethnic) characteristics. The term would seem to convey political connotations, derived from that of TROIA (the country, *not* the city), so called from the *tro-* (three) natural, marshy districts near the end of the SKAMANDROS (*Naro*, Neretva) river. Thus, Hektor was supreme commander of *all* defensive forces (II, 816):

> The Trojans were led by great Hector of the flashing helm, the son of Priam, and with him were marshalled the greatest host by far and goodliest, raging with the spear.

TWO MAJOR PHYLA

The TROES were divided into two phyla, these being the sea-faring PHRYGES, occupants of ASKANIA (the coast) and PHRYGIA (the islands), and the land-bound DARDANIOI, occupants of DARDANIA (the interior hinterland).

PHRYGES (Φρύγες), occupants of the coast and islands (II, 862):

> And Phorcys and godlike Ascanius led the Phrygians from afar, from Ascania, and were eager to fight in the press of battle.

DARDANIOI (Δαρδάνιοι), occupants of the hinterland (by contrast with the sea-faring PHRYGES), but, properly, of DARDANIA, the lower portion of the SKAMANDROS (Neretva) river (II, 819):

> Of the Dardanians again the valiant son of Anchises was captain, even Aeneas, whom fair Aphrodite conceived to Anchises amid the spurs of Ida, a goddess couched with a mortal man.

The exquisite beauty of the above lines —unexploited until Virgil's *Aeneid*— lies in the understanding that Aineias, a Dardanid as well as a Dardanian, born on the hillsides "amid the spurs of Ida", will have been a vehicle for the direct transmission of a fig-totem and its underlying connotations, as in the story about the *Rumalia*, or "fig-orchard", where Romulus and Remus were suckled by a she-wolf.

ISLAND FOLK (PHRYGES)

LESBIDES (Λεσβίδες), inhabitants of LESBOS (Brač): of these folk it may be said they were, like most folks of the world, of a generally pious nature, for there exists no obvious reason why the females of this island —in particular this island and nowhere else— chose odd habits. However, the reverse argument is that females of odd habits were especially famous on LESBOS for some particular reason (which will not become relevant until after a geography of the *Odyssey* has been established). Otherwise, the women of LESBOS will have been nothing more than what good women should be (industrious and obedient) (IX, 128):

> "And I [Agamemnon] will give [to Achilles] seven women skilled in goodly handiwork, women of Lesbos, whom on the day when himself took well-built Lesbos I chose me from out the spoil, and that in beauty surpass all women folk."

SINTIES (Σίντιες), inhabitants of LEMNOS Viš): the *sinister* reputation of these folks might be thought of as that of a money-loving, metallized clan of merchants —perhaps of diverse ethnic origins?— who, because of the advantageous situation of their island, not only caught the sea-traffic of Adriatic trade routes but also traded with copper goods from ARISBE (*Arretium*, Arezzo) in central Italy, as well as iron wares from Troy itself. Several references to LEMNOS mention commercial goods and services (wine, women, and slaves) available on the island (VII, 465; VIII, 221; XXI, 40; XXIV, 751).

It was the SINTIES who cared for Hephaistos when he was thrust from heaven (I, 590):

> "Yea, on a time ere this, when I [Hephaistos] was fain to save thee [Hera], he [Zeus] caught me by the foot and hurled me from the heavenly threshold; the whole day long was I borne headlong, and at set of sun I fell in Lemnos, and but little life was in me. There did the Sintian folk make haste to tend me for my fall."

The SINTIES also cared for Philoktetes when he was bitten on the foot by a poisonous snake at the base of Sveti Ilija (Monte Vípera), in just retribution for his hubris in being the first to jump from his ship, and not Agamemnon, onto Trojan soil (II, 722):

> But Philoctetes lay suffering grievous pains in an island, even in sacred Lemnos, where the sons of the Achaeans had left him in anguish with an evil wound from a deadly water-snake. There he lay suffering; yet full soon were the Argives beside their ships to bethink them of king Philoctetes.

SMINTHIES (Σμινθιες), inhabitants of ZAKYNTHOS (Mljet): the name of these islanders is inferred from a plea made to a sympathetic Phoebus

Apollo (who is likewise "Lesbid", or "Sintian", for there is no reason why he should not favour other folks as well) (I, 37):

> "Hear me [Chryses], thou of the silver bow [Phoebus Apollo], who dost stand over Chryse and holy Cilla, and dost rule mightily over Tenedos [Zakynthos], thou Sminthian..."

Certain females of ZAKYNTHOS, like those of LESBOS, were distinguished from the norm by some trait peculiar to them. At the outset of the *Iliad* it is Khryseis, daughter of Khryses, who is the object of contention, but, again, as with the LESBIDES, her *rôle* will not become relevant until after a geography of the *Odyssey* has been established.

PEOPLES OF THE NORTHERN COAST (ASKANIA)

AMAZONES ('Αμαζόνες), a folk who occupied the banks of the SANGARIOS (Krka) in the northern borders of Troy: they seem to have come from abroad (VI, 186) and are presumably the most recent addition to the Trojan confederation of tribal identities, perhaps at first repulsed from the diverse islands of PHRYGIA but finally settling in the northernmost borders of TROIA (hence their presence in Asia Minor) (III, 184):

> Ere now have I [Priam] journeyed to the land of Phrygia... and there I saw in multitudes the Phrygian warriors... that were then encamped along the banks of Sangarius. For I, too, being their ally, was numbered among them on the day when the Amazones came, the peers of men.

Evidently, Priam negotiated successfully with the AMAZONES, for he took Hekabe, mother of Hektor, as wife (XVI, 719):

> ...Asius, that was uncle to horse-taming Hector, and own brother to Hecabe, but son of Dymas, that dwelt [in Phrygia] by the streams of Sangarius.

Later Greek lore brought the AMAZONES into the Trojan War, but this sounds like a good reason to connect the totemic identity and uncouth behaviour of Akhilleus with an equally odd Penthesilea, leader of the would-be breastless female Amazons, by making him fall in love with her after her death, an act of necrophilia, proper to birds of carrion. That the AMAZONES were presumed to have been breastless is surely an echo of males practicing partial or total emasculation for the purpose of spiritual purification after a period of reproduction. Such a practice is likely to bring on feminoid sexual characteristics, albeit these have nothing to do with softening of the manly attributes of valour or ferocity.

KIKONES [SIPONES] (Κίκονες [Σίπονες]), a folk from the marshy environs of *Tragurium* (Trogir) and *Salona* (II, 846):

> And Euphemus was captain of the Ciconian spearmen, the son of Ceas' son Troezenus, nurtured of Zeus.

The original name [SIPONES] means "marsh-folk (< *sipo-* "marsh", cf. the marshes of *Sipontum*, and [SIPOPLAKIA], + *-ones*, suffix denoting a people), meaningless to a Greek-speaking folk, and so became emended to read KIKONES, "stork people".

LELEGES (Λέλεγες), occupants of the region between PEDASOS (Omiš) in the north and LYRNESSOS (Ploče/Kardeljevo) in the south: the simple reduplicative *le-le-* in the name of these folks identifies them as natural to the upper, relatively level stretches of IDA, the Biokovo Range, tipped by the twin peaks of GARGAROS, Sveti Ilija and Sveti Jure (XX, 89):

> "Not now for the first time shall I [Aeneas] stand forth against swift-footed Achilles; nay, once ere now he drave me with his spear from Ida, when he had come forth against our kine, and laid Lyrnessos waste and Pedasos withal; howbeit Zeus saved me, who roused my strength and made swift my knees. Else had I been slain beneath the hands of Achilles and of Athene, who ever went before him... and bade him slay Leleges and Trojans with spear of bronze."

These folks are mentioned again, in relation to PEDASOS (Omiš) on the SATNIOEIS (Cetina), (XXI, 86):

> "—Altes that is lord over the war-loving Leleges, holding steep Pedasos on the Satnioeis."

PEOPLES OF THE SOUTHERN COAST (ASKANIA)

KADMEIOI (Καδμεῖοι), descendants of Kadmos: presumably, the exclusive occupants of THEBE (Klek) (IV, 376–390):

> "Once verily [says Agamemnon] he [Tydeus] came to Mycenae, not as an enemy, but as a guest, in company with godlike Polyneices, to gather a host; for in that day they were waging a war against the sacred walls of Thebe, and earnestly did they make prayer that glorious allies be granted them... So when they had departed and were got forth upon their way, and had come to Asopus [that is, HYPOPLAKIA (Jezero Kuti), where the ASOPOS (Mala Neretva) rises] with deep reeds, that coucheth in the grass, there did the Achaeans send forth Tydeus on an embassage. And he went his way, and found the many sons of Cadmus feasting in the house of mighty Eteocles. Then, for all he was a stranger, the horseman Tydeus feared not, all alone though he was amid the many Cadmeians, but challenged them all to feats of strength, and in every one vanquished he them full easily..."

The exploits of Kadmos are many, but it suffices to mention only that his Etruscan counterpart seems to have been that of a certain Tages, who born among the Tyrsenoi or Tyrrhenoi, but settled in the region of TEGEA (environs of MANTINEA, *Mantua*), where he instituted the practice of writing letters on *cloth*. Otherwise, Kadmos was the son of Agenor, founder of AMYKLAI (*Patavium*, Padova/Padua), and sent abroad in search of his lost sister Europa. He came to Illyria, where he settled peacefully with Harmonia among the Encheleïs.

The two singular Greek misconceptions about Kadmos are that he was credited with the invention of Greek letters (thought to have been an import of North Semitic script into Hellas), and that a putative son Illyrus was the eponymous ancestor of the Illyrians. As regards Greek letters, Kadmos is likely only to have brought back a much simplified form of the Vinča script (which earlier had passed into the Rasena (Etruscans) without much problem. As for the descent of Kadmos, these will have been the KADMEIOI, as above, for Illyrians were simply those who practiced the cult of Illyrism.

KEPHALLENES (Κεφαλλῆνες), occupants of the long and narrow peninsula of NERITON (Pelješac), they became known later as the Illyrian *Plerai* (II, 631):

> And Odysseus led the great-souled Cephallenians that held Ithaca and Neritum, covered with waving forests, and that dwelt in Crocyleia and rugged Aegilips; and them that held Zacynthus, and that dwelt about Samos and held the mainland and dwelt on the shores over against the isles.

KILIKES (Κίλικες), the southernmost folk of Troy, from the environs of PLAKOS (Mlini) and KARDAMYLE (Cavtat) (VI, 414):

> "My father [Andromache] verily godly Achilles slew, for utterly laid he waste the well-peopled city of the Cilicians, even Thebe of lofty gates. He slew Eetion, yet he despoiled him not... but he burnt him in his armour, richly dight, and heaped over him a barrow; and all about were elm-trees planted by nymphs of the mountain... And my mother, that was queen beneath wooded Placus, her brought he hither with the rest of the spoil, but thereafter set her free, when he had taken ransom past counting; and in her father's halls Artemis the archer slew her."

The understanding of the above is that THEBE was the city of Eetion, a Kadmeian, albeit he was lord of the KILIKES who held PLAKOS (Mlini) and KARDAMYLE (Cavtat).

LANDBOUND FOLK

ARIMOI [ARIEMOI] (Ἄριμοι [Ἀριεμοι]), occupants of the HELLESPONTOS (Neretva delta), a folk later known as *Delmatae* or Dalmatians (II, 783):

> ...and the earth groaned beneath them, [the Danaans] as beneath Zeus that hurleth the thunderbolt in his wrath, when he scourgeth the land about Typhoeus in the country of the Arimoi, where men say is the couch of Typhoeus.

The above reference to Typhoeus alludes the periodic *smoky* brushfires that ravish the surrounding hillsides towards the end of the dry summer months, apparently, for some unknown reason, only in this region of the Balkans.

PYGMAIOI (Πυγμαῖοι), occupants of the HELLESPONTOS (Neretva delta) together with the ARIMOI [ARIEMOI] or *Delmatae* (III, 1):

> Now when they were marshalled, the several companies with their captains, the Trojans came on with clamour and with a cry like birds, even as the clamour of cranes ariseth before the face of heaven, when they flee from wintry storms and measureless rain, and with clamour fly toward the streams of Ocean, bearing slaughter and death to Pigmy men, and in the early dawn they offer evil battle. But the Achaeans came on in silence, breathing fury...

Now, since it is unlikely that two different folks will have occupied the same district, then the required inference is that the PYGMAIOI were a fictitious folk. Thus, in the light of an identification of cranes and scarecrows already established in the *Foreword*, the foregoing simile might be nothing more than just that, but, since the town of Čapljina, a short distance north of where the Trebižat enters the Neretva means "crane", and archaeological vestiges on the hillside behind the town apparently date from a pre-Trojan period (perhaps Late Neolithic–Early Bronze?), then it would be likely the simile reflects consistent efforts by foreign folks wishing to settle in the region.

I. THE ILIAD AND ITS TROJAN GEOGRAPHY

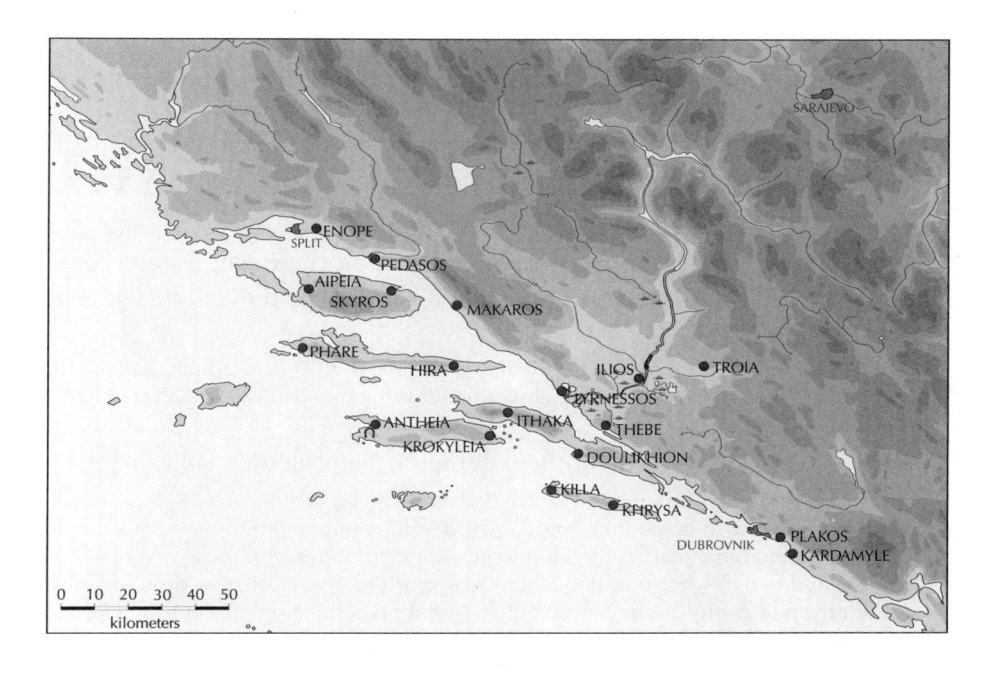

TOWNS

Of the many large towns and villages of smaller size that TROIA must have had in its day, only nineteen were selected for a geographical paradigm. Of these, eight are island port-towns equally distributed north and south of NERITON (Pelješac) and situated approximately at opposite ends of the larger islands, and eight are mainland port-towns, also equally distributed north and south of the SKAMANDROS (*Naro*, Neretva). The remaining three "towns" may be thought of as "cities", at some distance and some elevation from the sea.

ISLAND PORTS	MAINLAND PORTS	"CITIES"
AIPEIA	ENOPE	ILION
SKYROS	PEDASOS	ITHAKA
PHARE	MAKAROS	TROIA
HIRA	LYRNESSOS	
- - - - - NERITON (Pelješac)	- - - - - SKAMANDROS (Neretva)	
ANTHEIA	THEBES	
KROKYLEIA	DOULIKHION	
KILLA	PLAKOS	
KHRYSE	KARDAMYLE	

TABLE 1.21. TOWNS. All Trojan port-towns are occupied today by modern urban settlements, with the exception of ITHAKA and TROIA, which are archaeological sites.

ISLAND PORT-TOWNS NORTH OF NERITON:

AIPEIA (Αἴπεια), Milna: port-town situated at the western end of LESBOS (Brač). This was one of the seven towns offered by Agamemnon to Akhilleus (IX, 149–153; 292–295; see PEDASOS below, TABLE 1. 22.) which, presumably, he had already sacked at the onset of the Trojan War (ie., at the arrival of Danaan forces in the region).

SKYROS (Σκῦρος), Pučišća: port-town situated on the northeastern coast of LESBOS (Brač). For some yet unknown reason, Akhilleus, in particular, is associated with SKYROS (IX, 666):

> And Patroclus laid him down on the opposite side, and by him in like manner lay fair-girdled Iphis, whom goodly Achilles had given him when he took steep Scyros, the city of Enyeus.

It was in SKYROS that Akhilleus fathered Neptolemus (XIX, 326):

> "...nay, nor though it were he that in Skyros is reared for me [Akhilleus], my son well-beloved—if so be godlike Neoptolemus still liveth. For until now the heart in my breast had hope that I alone should perish far from horse-pasturing Argos, here in the land of Troy, but that thou shouldest return to Phthia, that so thou mightest take my child in thy swift, black ship from Skyros, and show him all things—my possessions, my slaves, and my great high-roofed house."

According to Greek lore, it is here that Odysseus found Akhilleus dressed as a woman (Apollodorus, *Library*, III, xiii, 8).

PHARE (Φαρή), *Pharos*, Hvar: port-town situated at the western end of LEKTON (Hvar), nestled within a small bay. *Pharos* means "light house" (< φάω, *to give light, shine*), but perhaps originally "haven", because of the safety afforded to vessels anchored within the bay protected at its mouth by the Pakleni Isles, a string of low-lying barren rocks that form a natural breakwater. This was one of the seven towns offered by Agamemnon to Akhilleus (IX, 149–153; 292–295; see PEDASOS below, TABLE 1. 22.).

HIRA (Ἱρή), Bogomolje: port-town situated at the eastern end of LEKTON (Hvar). HIRA means "divine" or "wonderful" (and by extension "holy"), a meaning survived in that of Bogomolj, "God-prayer". This town, for some obscure reason, is associated with Drvenik, "Oakland", on the mainland, opposite (XIV, 283):

> To many-fountained Ida they [Hera and Hypnos] came, the mother of wild creatures, even to Lectum, where first they left the sea; and the twain fared on over the dry land, and the topmost forest quivered beneath their feet. There Hypnos did halt, or ever the eyes of Zeus beheld him, and mounted up on a fir-tree exceeding tall, the highest that then grew in Ida; and it reached up through the mists into heaven. Thereon he perched, thick-hidden by the branches of the fir, in the likeness of a clear-voiced mountain bird, that the gods call Chalcis, and men Cymindis.

ISLAND PORT-TOWNS SOUTH OF NERITON:
ANTHEIA ("Άνθεια), Vela Luka: port-town situated at the western end of TENEDOS (Korčula). The name would seem to have been inspired on the marshy area of Blato immediately behind the port-town. This was one of the seven towns offered by Agamemnon to Akhilleus (IX, 152–000; 294–000). It bears the same relationship to AIPEIA as KILLA to PHARE (see PEDASOS below, *TABLE 1. 22.*).

When a Greek presence was established in the region (6th cent. BC), the bay of Vela Luka became the *Sinus Hyllicus*, after Hyllas, the youthful companion of Herakles, who wandered too far from the ship *Argo* in search of fresh water, and, falling into a well —or snatched by nymphs from the cave of Vela Spilja close by— was never again seen. Though the story about the *Argo* being present in the region is anachronic and utterly untenable, the name of Hyllas is important in an Illyrian context (it occurs also as *Peninsula Hyllica*, west of *Tragurium*, Trogir), as it is fundamental to an understanding of later Greek stories about the arrival of **Dories** in Hellas and the cultural bridge for the transmission of the *Iliad* and *Odyssey* from an Adriatic into an Aegean context.

KROKYLEIA [KORKYLEIA] (Κροκύλεια [Κορκύλεια]), *Corcyra Melaina*, Korčula: port-town situated at the eastern end of TENEDOS (Korčula), it fell to the dominion of Odysseus (II, 631):

> And Odysseus led the great-souled Cephallenians that held Ithaca and Neritum, covered with waving forests, and that dwelt in Crocyleia and rugged Aegilips; and them that held Zacynthus, and that dwelt about Samos and held the mainland and dwelt on the shores over against the isles.

Krokyleia is a metathesis of Korkyleia, whence the classical and modern forms of the name. The root *kor-* connotes "corky", in a negative context, or "rocky", in a positive context. The name became extensive to the island itself, surely because of the oddity of the cork-tree found on this isle alone of the many in the Adriatic Archipelago, but, also, perhaps, on the importance of Blato, an Illyrian settlement situated towards the western end, a name likewise connoting "sponginess".

KILLA (Κιλλα), Polače: port-town within a deep and narrow cove situated at the western end of ZAKYNTHOS (I, 37):

> "Hear me, [Chryses] thou of the silver bow, who dost stand over Chryse and holly Cilla, and dost rule mightily over Tenedos [ZAKYNTHOS], thou Sminthian..."

The inclusion of TENEDOS (Korčula) in Chryse's mighty invocation of Sminthian Apollo is an emendation for ZAKYNTHOS, since it is impossible to account for the name of this island in an Asia Minor context.

KILLA was one of the seven towns offered by Agamemnon to Akhilleus (IX, 149–153; 292–295). It bears the same relationship to PHARE, as ANTHEIA to AIPEIA (see PEDASOS below, TABLE 1.22).

KHRYSE (Χρύση), Sobra: port-town situated towards the northeastern end of ZAKYNTHOS, within a cove of the same name ideally suited for anchorage (I, 430):

> And meanwhile Odysseus came to Chryse bringing the holy hecatomb. When they were now got within the deep harbour, they furled the sail, and stowed it in the black ship, and the mast they lowered by the forestays and brought it to the crutch with speed, and rowed her with oars to the place of anchorage. Then they cast out the mooring stones and made fast the stern cables, and themselves went forth upon the shore of the sea. Forth they brought the hecatomb for Apollo, that smiteth afar, and forth stepped also the daughter of Chryses from the sea-faring ship. Her then did Odysseus of many wiles lead to the altar, and place in the arms of her dear father...

MAINLAND PORT-TOWNS NORTH OF THE SKAMANDROS:

ENOPE [EPONE] ('Ενόπη ['Επόνη]), *Epetium*, Stobrec: the northernmost mainland port-town, situated a few kilometers east of Split. This was one of the seven towns offered by Agamemnon to Akhilleus (IX, 149–153; 292–295; see PEDASOS below, TABLE 1.22).

On a cue with the topographic and semantic relationships of KILLA with PHARE and of ANTHEIA with AIPEIA, it would seem that a similar relationship might exist between ENOPE [EPONE], the northernmost mainland port-town, and KARDAMYLE, the southernmost mainland port-town. Thus, the name of ENOPE may be discarded as either a metathesis of [EPONE] (which contains the Illyrian type-ending *-one* denoting a social gathering), or an educated correction by some Alexandrine editor to make this the place where Enops came from (XIV, 444), for [EPONE] became *Epetium*, perhaps akin with Latin *appetitus*, "appetite", and would thus bear a semantic relationship with KARDAMYLE, whence "cardamon", a spice.

PEDASOS (Πήδασος), *Oneum*, Omiš: port-town situated at the mouth of the SATNIOEIS (VI, 33):

> ...and the king of men, Agamemnon, slew Elatus that dwelt in steep Pedasos by the banks of fair-flowing Satnioeis.

PEDASOS is not only "steep" (on account of being mounted on the hillside at the mouth of the deep gorge through which the SATNIOEIS flows), it is also distinguished by the epithet αμπελόεσσαν, "vine-clad", which would seem to be used *exclusively* in allusion to *vinograd* sites found *only* in the region of Troy (IX, 149–153):

I. THE ILIAD AND ITS TROJAN GEOGRAPHY

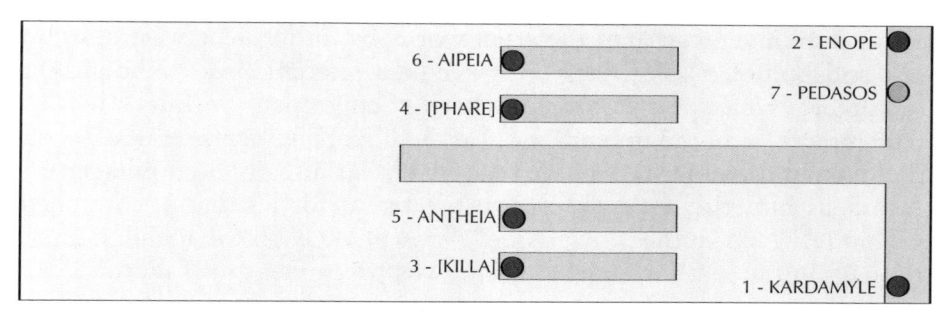

TABLE 1. 22. SIX WELL-PEOPLED CITIES. The gift-package that Agamemnon offered Akhilleus is, to all intents and purposes, the strategic controll of all PHRYGIA and ASKANIA, such that, the inclusion of PEDASOS as part of the gift is redundant (and perhaps an interpolation).

> "And seven well-peopled cities will I [Agamemnon] give him [Achilles], Cardamyle, Enope, and grassy Hire [read KILLA] and sacred Pherae [Phare] and Antheia with deep meadows and fair Aepeia and vine-clad Pedasos. All are nigh to the sea on the nethermost borders of sandy [?] Pylos [that is, "bay"]..."

However, that this city was the seventh, somewhat superfluous city that sets an otherwise schematically neat gift-package out of kilter[10], as well as the redundant explanation about the location of the cities in question relative to "...the sea on the nethermost borders of sandy Pylos", indeed suggests a tampering with the text (for what reason is anybody's guess, but most likely to avoid ambiguity about towns in Asia Minor with those of mainland Hellas).

Once restored, the editorial intrusion and intention of the original offer become self-evident (see *TABLE 1. 22*), since, Akhilleus, to all intents and purposes, is already master of the mainland shore and islands north of NERITON (Pelješac), having lived for a time on LESBOS where his son was born (XIX, 327), sacked LYRNESSOS and PEDASOS (XX, 92), and finally established his own camp at THEBE after sacking it (I, 366). The remainder of the offer, south of NERITON (Pelješac), seemed of no interest.

MAKAROS (Μάκαρος), *Mucurrum*, Makarska: port-town situated under the heights of IDA (Biokovo Range) opposite the eastern tip of LESBOS (Brač) (XXIV, 543):

> "And of thee [Priam], old sire, we hear [says Akhilleus] that of old thou wast blest; how of all that toward the sea Lesbos, the seat of Macar, encloseth, and Phrygia in the upland, and the boundless Hellespont, over all these folk, men say, thou, old sire, wast preeminent by reason of thy wealth and thy sons."

---

10. The ever-present trinity in Homer, where two parts or elements are identical or similar to each other, albeit the third is closely related and inseparable, but different from the other two.

A dubious integrity of the cruel words by an insolent wastrel to an old and humbled king rests on a needless referent of a "...boundless (ἀπείρων) Hellespont" for all that is contained within PHRYGIA (καθύπερθε) "...in the upland" or "on the upperside" with MAKAROS on the mainland and LESBOS in the sea (which has already been pillaged by Akhilleus himself), *unless* it is also a referent for all that is contained within PHRYGIA in the "lower side", with PLAKOS on the mainland and AIGILIPS in the sea, for, indeed, Priam was preeminent over *all* folk.

The justification for the inference of an editorial excision is not only that such a reading would be otherwise meaningless in an Asia Minor context, but, also, that by the time Priam goes to Akhilleus for the body of Hektor, the invading AKHAIOI have already vanquished Troy, and, to all intents and purposes, established a new World Order by giving new names to LESBOS and AIGILIPS. The new names have come down to us as *Brattia* (from Illyrian *brentos*, "stag"), whence Brač, and *Elaphites* ("Deer Isles"), whence *Lafota*, Lapad.

LYRNESSOS (Λυρνησσός), Ploče (now Kardaljevo): port-town located in THYMBRA (Neretva delta's right bank), it bears the same relationship to this sub-district as THEBE to HYPOPLAKIA (Neretva delta's left bank). It is the first of the four port-towns north of the SKAMANDROS (II, 688):

> For he lay in idleness among the ships, the swift-footed, goodly Achilles, in wrath because of the fair-haired girl Brises, whom he had taken out of Lyrnessus after sore toil, when he wasted Lyrnessus and the walls of Thebe, and laid low Mynes and Epistrophus, warriors that raged with the spear...

MAINLAND PORT-TOWNS SOUTH OF THE SKAMANDROS:

THEBE (Θῆβαι), Klek: port-town ensconced in a cove at the mouth of the Klek-Neum Bay, it bears the same relationship to the sub-district of HYPOPLAKIA (Neretva delta's left bank) as LYRNESSOS to THYMBRE (Neretva delta's right bank). It is the first of the four port-towns south of the SKAMANDROS (IV, 376–390):

> "Once verily [says Agamemnon] he [Tydeus] came to Mycenae, not as an enemy, but as a guest, in company with godlike Polyneices, to gather a host; for in that day they were waging a war against the sacred walls of Thebe, and earnestly did they make prayer that glorious allies be granted them... So when they had departed and were got forth upon their way, and had come to Asopus [that is, HYPOPLAKIA (Jezero Kuti), where the ASOPOS (Mala Neretva) rises] with deep reeds, that coucheth in the grass, there did the Achaeans send forth Tydeus on an embassage. And he went his way, and found the many sons of Cadmus feasting in the house of mighty Eteocles. Then, for all he was a stranger, the horseman Tydeus feared not, all alone though he was amid the many Cadmeians, but challenged them all to feats of strength, and in every one vanquished he them full easily..."

I. THE ILIAD AND ITS TROJAN GEOGRAPHY

The relationship of THEBE with HYPOPLAKIA (which is drained by the ASOPOS) would seem clear from the above, still, a relationship with PLAKOS is garbled (VI, 395) because ὑπὸ Πλάκῳ ὑληέσσῃ... "beneath wooded Plakos..." was confused with Θήβῃ Ὑποπλακίη "Thebe (close to) Hypoplakia...".

DOULICHION (Δουλίχιον), Žuljana: port-town is marked by a prominent complex of *vinograd* structures located opposite the modern sea-side village in the cove of the same name on the southern shore of NERITON (Pelješac). This is the place that Phyleus came to, across the sea from ELIS, on that occasion of his expulsion from the land (II, 625):

> And those from Dulichium and the Echinae, the holy isles, that lie across the sea, over against Elis [Neriton], these again had as leader Meges, the peer of Ares, even the son of Phyleus, dear to Zeus, begat—he that of old had gone to dwell in Dulichium in wrath against his father.

Presumably, modern *žulj-* is a phonetic derivation from δzουλj-, likely in association with the hard work of slavery (*žuljana* means "callus"). Oddly, this sea-side town and cove mimic the sea-side town and cove of Brijesta on the north side of NERITON (Pelješac), dotted with rocks and islets, "keys", or Spanish *callos* (Latin *callus*), which recalls *brijesta*, a hard word, like oak, whence the name of the "brigantine").

PLAKOS (Πλάκος), Mlini: port-town situated south of Dubrovnik, on the north side of the Bay of Zaton. The meaning of the modern name is "mill" (VI, 395):

> ...Andromache, daughter of great-hearted Eëtion, Eëtion that dwelt beneath wooded Placus, in Thebe under Placus [ÑUpoplakḥ], and was lor d over the men Cilicia; for it was his daughter that bronze-harnessed Hector had to wife.

That Eëtion will have been a Kadmeian does not preclude him from being lord of KILIKES, not unlike Odysseus, a Kephallenian, being lord of the SMINTHIES. Thus (VI, 414):

> "My father verily goodly Achilles slew, for utterly laid he waste the well-peopled city of the Cilicians, even Thebe of lofty gates. He slew Eëtion, yet he despoiled him not... but he burnt him in his armour, richly dight, and heaped over him a barrow; and all about were elm-trees planted by nymphs of the mountain... And my mother, that was queen beneath wooded Placus, her brought he hither with the rest of the spoil, but thereafter set her free, when he had taken ransom past counting; and in her father's halls Artemis the archer slew her."

KARDAMYLE (Καρδαμυλη): *Epidaurum*, Cavtat: southernmost of the mainland port-towns, situated south of Dubrovnik, on the south side of the Bay of Zaton. This was the first of seven towns offered by Agamemnon to Akhilleus (IX, 149–153; 292–295; see *TABLE 1.22*):

"And seven well-peopled cities will I [Agamemnon] give him [Achilles], Cardamyle, Enope, and grassy Hire [Killa] and sacred Pherae [Phare] and Antheia with deep meadows and fair Aepeia and vine-clad Pedasos. All are nigh to the sea on the nethermost borders of sandy [?] Pylos [that is, "bay"]..."

The hillsides of Troy are rich throughout the summer months with the aromas of many spices, cardamon among them. That KARDAMYLE should have been so-called, obeys, perhaps, to its value, second only to that of saffron (until vanilla was discovered in the New World).

"CITIES"

A feature which the three cities of TROIA share that distinguishes them from mainland port-towns (ASKANIA) and island port-towns (PHRYGIA) is that they are situated at some elevation and at some distance from the sea. Thus—

ILIOS (Ἴλιος), Drijeva/Gabela: see II. ILIOS: A BRIEF SURVEY.

ITHAKA (Ἰθάκη), Donja Vručica: see VI. ITHAKA: A BRIEF SURVEY.

TROIA (TROY) (Τροίη), Daorson: a necropolis set on the edge of a plateau overlooking the RHESOS (Bregava) in the vicinity of Ošanici, about 3 km. from the town of Stolac.

The site is approached from its base along a well-trodden path, about 1 km. or so past a few farmhouses, and here and there among the stone walls of animal pens, are the remains of ancient masonry against the hillside. At the top, towards the western end of a flat, earthy field, may be seen the monumental limestone walls of TROIA, behind which was the "city", precariously perched in several levels —some 260–280 mts.— on a spur affording it a measure of natural protection, one side overlooking the Radimlja, a tributary of the RHESOS (Bregava), and the other, the open valley of Stolac.

DESCRIPTION OF TROIA

The name of Daorson is derived from that of the Daorsi, not unlike Narona is derived from that of the Narensi (both clans or *gens* being Vard*j*aei, who were synonymous with the DARDANIOI). Daorson, by metathesis Daroson, would seem to echo the name of Taruisa found in Hittite documents.

The story of the foundation of TROIA is told in context with the story about the foundation of ILIOS (see below, II. ILIOS: A BRIEF SURVEY). The site seems to have been a necropolis of the Vinča Culture, later taken over by the Pelasgian occupation of these lands. Though the massive wall at once suggests a defensive artifice of a civilian population,

I. THE ILIAD AND ITS TROJAN GEOGRAPHY

oddly, there exist no remains of human habitation on the inside, behind the walls, but, rather, on the outside. Furthermore, several architectonic features betray an esoteric function of the site rather than a pragmatic one. However, though human habitation cannot be precluded from having been present on the site, it is an awkward location, and even possibly anachronic of an Illyrian folk of the Early Iron Age.

The *Iliad* seems remarkably sparse about descriptions of TROIA (as it is about ITHAKA). This would seem correct, in the understanding that ILIOS was the strategic goal of an Akhaian Campaign, albeit TROIA was ancillary to the spiritual values incorporated in ILIOS, and therefore, in a way, inseparable.

Obviously, a distinction should be made between what is evidently the post-Trojan archaeology of the ACROPOLIS, which incorporates a STOA, a NECROPOLIS, and an AGORA, and that which merely concerns the nature of the site during the period of the Trojan War.

> **GENERAL DESCRIPTION OF TROIA (ONLY THREE EPITHETS)**
>
> εὐτείχεος, "well-walled":
>
> I, 129: Agamemnon will be compensated if they sack **well-walled** (city of ?) Troy
> VII, 71: Hector warns Akhaioi to take **well-walled** Troy or be vanquished beside ships
> VIII, 241: Agamemnon made sacrifice in eagerness to lay waste **well-walled** Troy
>
> εὐρυάγυιος, "with wide streets":
>
> II, 140: Agamemnon suggests leaving for no hope they shall take **broad-wayed Troy**
> XXIV, 774: Helen says she now has no one beside her in **broad Troy**
>
> ὑψίπυλος, "with high gates":
>
> XVI, 698: Achaeans might have taken **high-gated Troy**
> XXI; 544: Achaeans would have taken **high-gated Troy**

TABLE 1.23. EPITHETS OF TROIA. The site of TROIA seems to have been only of incidental importance in the destruction of ILIOS, the goal of the entire Akhaian Campaigne. Line VII, 71, may be either an emendation or an interpolation.

1. CITY WALL: Of cyclopaean masonry, with huge, squared, mortar-bound limestone blocks, some 3 mts. long. It runs for 63 mts., about 2.50 mts. wide, and in places is more than 4 mts. high.

2. TOWERS: Two square towers positioned at the ends of the wall. One, immediately overlooking the CITY GATE, the other, distant, lying in rubble, was perhaps an addition of a much later date (3rd to 1st century BC).

3. CITY GATE: About 2 mts. wide, it pierces the wall beside one of the towers. The masonry is so grooved and notched as to betray the use of a door.

4. CISTERN: Perhaps related with the Temple of Athene on ILIOS (also a cistern) it seems to have been serviced by a set of stairs running to the valley below, thus lending some meaning to Hector's words about Andromache's certain fate (VI, 456):

> "Then haply in Argos shalt thou ply the loom at another's bidding, or bear water from Messes or Hypereia, sorely against thy will..."

5. STAIRS: A set of long, narrow steps hewn into the cliff-side, leading from the CISTERN to the base of the hill. Their only function seems to have been that of servicing the CISTERN, for the main access to the site from the plain below will have been the usual way up.

I. THE ILIAD AND ITS TROJAN GEOGRAPHY

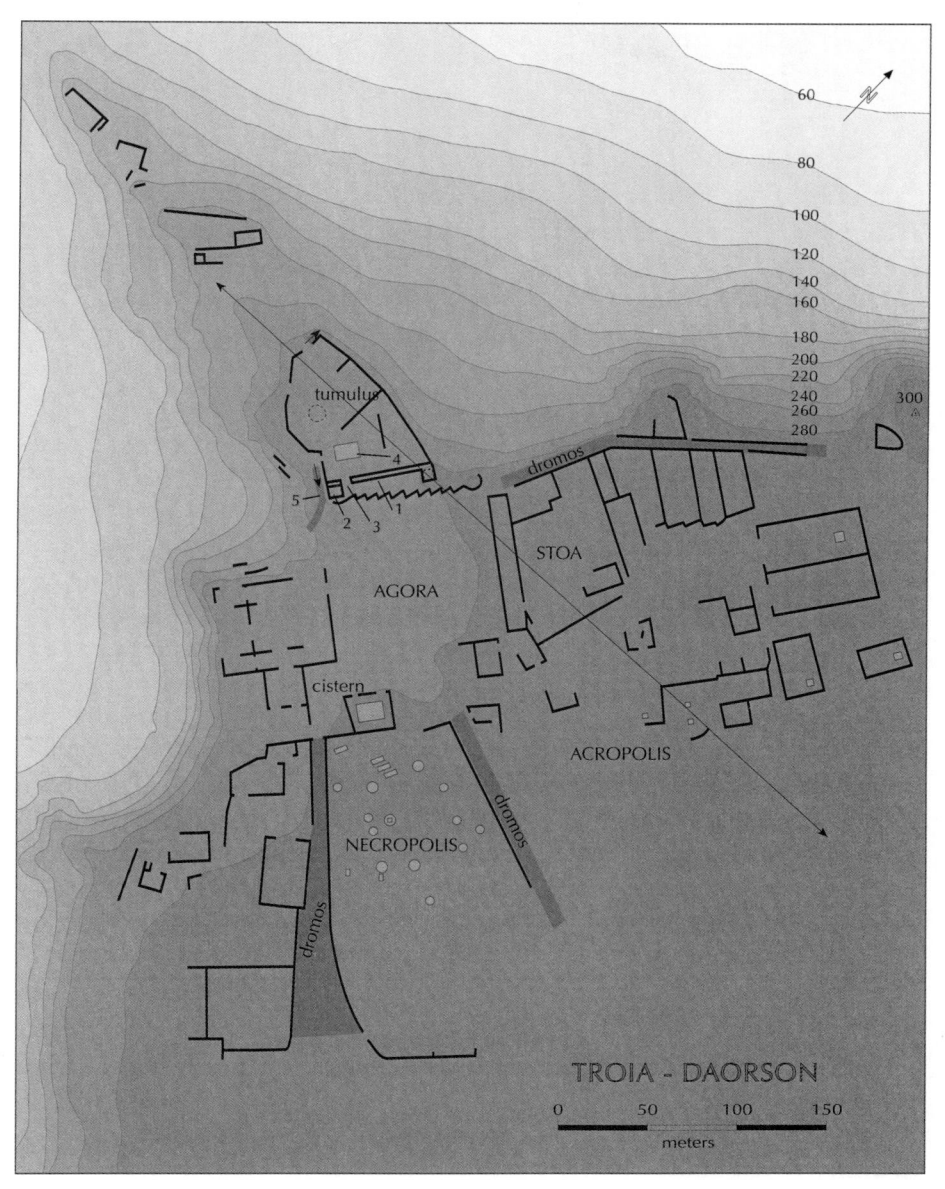

Map 1. 24. DAORSON (OŠANICI). A massive "defensive" wall, otherwise useless, and a stairway hewn into rock on the precarious southwestern edge, confer an esotric architecture to a site otherwise unsuitable for urban setlement. The site was used as a necropolis, and overlooks a later Bogomil burial ground marked by several hewn stecci.

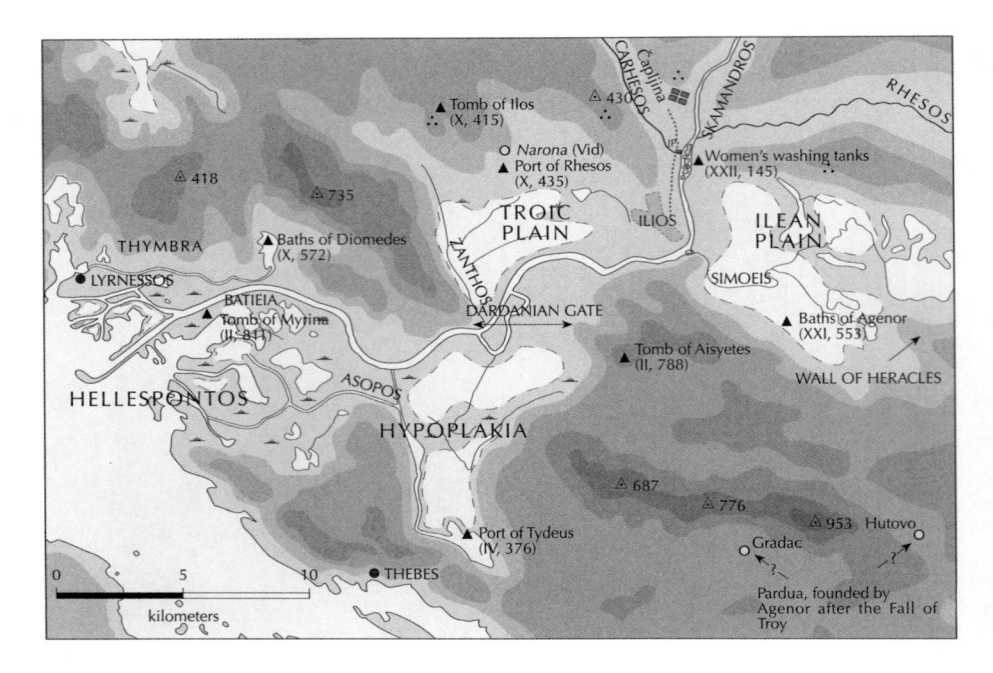

PLACES

Of the eight geographical concepts that make up the geographical apparatus of a Trojan Geography (four physical and four social), the eighth, a "marsh", is the place where many scenes of the Trojan War have been staged. One might think a marsh is, properly, a physical concept of geography since, like a "lake", it possesses distinct physical characteristics (with the exception that its boundaries are ill-defined). However, a marsh is no different than a district (whose borders are likewise ill-defined), and, thus, properly, should be thought of as a social concept of geography. Perhaps this distinction is tantamount to splitting hairs, still, it is important for the sake of orthodoxy.

All the places of different scenes in the narrative line of the *Iliad* are precise geographical locations, but, since they can only be described in terms of two or more words, do not qualify as geonyms. An attempt to quantify and qualify these different places might look something like *Table 1. 0* (which does not purport to be definitive and merely serves to show an intrinsic difference in their nature). Perhaps the only important observation which can be made is that some places are ancient geological curiosities, and of a permanent nature, while others are the product of human endeavour, and of a temporal nature.

DESCRIPTION OF THE SKAMANDROS DELTA-VALLEY

The transversal cut of the the ample SKAMANDROS (*Naro*, Neretva) river through the mass of IDA (Biokovo Range) forms three wide, eminently marshy, *treble*-shaped plains which are permanently fed by a great number of underground sources that well up here and there. It was this natural trefoil of the SKAMANDROS delta-valley formed by the TROIC PLAIN (Glibuša), ILEIAN PLAIN (Hutovo Blato), and HYPOPLAKIA (Jezero Kuti) that that gave its name to TROIA (< *tro-* Slavic "three"), and not that of Tros, father of Ilos, after whom the city of TROIA (Daorson), a necropolis, was named.

In the names of these three distinct geographical units is to be seen a recurrent treble-format throughout the *Iliad* and *Odyssey*, in which two elements are the same, almost indistinguishable the one from the other, while the third, though an intimate and inseparable part of the three-part unit, is of a unique characteristic. Thus, the TROIC PLAIN and ILEIAN PLAIN are intimately associated (as are the names of Tros and Ilos, albeit this is not as much as to infer that the name of Tros is derived from that of the TROIC PLAIN as that of Ilos from the ILEIAN PLAIN), while the third, likewise a marsh, is a geonym classified as a district.

It is from the goings to and fro of Danaans and Trojans over these eminently muddy plains that the *Iliad* takes its name (whence *ilo*, Serbian "mud") and not so from a siege and war to take Ilios (or Troy, hitherto another name for the objective in question).

TROIC PLAIN (πεδίον τὸ Τρωϊκὸν), Glibuša: the marshland to the west of ILIOS (Drijeva/Gabela) drained by the [ZANTHOS] *Norin*, Norino—

> X, 1 *et pas.*:
> Now beside their ships all the other chieftains of the host of the Achaeans were slumbering the whole night through, overcome of soft sleep, but Agamemnon, son of Atreus, shepherd of the host, was not holden of sweet sleep... So often as he gazed toward the Trojan plain, he marvelled at the many fires that burned before the face of Ilios, and at the sound of flutes and pipes, and the din of men...

How much is "many"? If the fires that Agamemnon saw could be thought of as an allegory of the abundant fireflies in these marshes, then, roughly, what he saw, at the rate of 1 firefly x 5 mts^3., within an area of some 1,120,000 mts^2., or so, flying with the wind, like cinders swirling hither and thither, then, with a margin of error of 25%, will have been something like 850,000 fireflies. Such are the exigencies of allegories.

Another reference —equally dubious?— is when Idomeneus sees how the chariot-race fares, in the distance (XXIII, 457 *et pas.*):

> "My friends, leaders and rulers of the Argives, is it I alone that discern the horses, or do ye as well? Other are they, meseemeth, that be now in front, and other is the charioteer that appeareth; and the mares will have come to harm out yonder on the plain, they that were in front on the outward course. For in truth I marked them sweeping first about the turning-post, but now can I nowhere spy them, though mine eyes glance everywhither over the Trojan plain, as I gaze. Did the reins haply slip from the charioteer, and was he unable to guide the course aright about the post, and did he fail in the turn? Even there, methinks, must he have been hurled to earth, and have wrecked his car [ἅρμα], and the mares must have swerved from the course in wild terror of heart."

There can be no horse-drawn chariots running over the swampy TROIC PLAIN, thus the question about Idomeneus spying horses in the distance is a tongue-in-cheek question, for the real issue is a charioteer falling from his "car", which necessarily refers to a *drijeva*, a smallish, flat-bottomed boat still used in the region for getting about from one place to another. The Greek ἅρμα, "chariot", connotes, properly, the idea of "(something) assembled", as clearly understood in the Spanish verb *armar*, "to assemble" (and alternately, "to supply with arms").

ILEIAN PLAIN (πεδίον Ἰλήϊον), Hutovo Blato: the marshes to the east of ILIOS (Drijeva/Gabela) drained by the SIMOIS (Krupa) (XXI, 553 *et pas.*):

> "Ah, woe is me [Agenor]; if I flee before mighty Achilles, there where the rest are being driven in rout, even so shall he overtake and butcher me in my cowardice. But what if I leave these to be driven before Achilles, son of Peleus, and with my feet flee from the wall elsewhither, toward the Ilean plain, until I be come to the glens and the spurs of Ida, and hide me in the thickets? Then at even, when I have bathed me in the river and cooled me of my sweat, I might get me back to Ilios".

Agenor was son of Antenor (XI, 59), one of the Elders of Troy whom later Greek lore credited with the foundation of *Patavium* (Padua), and Agenor with the foundation of *Pardua*.[11] Thus, he is likely to have fled either to Hutovo, or its neighbour, Gradac "...in the glens and spurs of Ida", and "...then at even", come down to bathe in Hutovo Blato before getting back to ILIOS.

The irony of Agenor seeking safety from Akhilleus in the thickets of the ILEIAN PLAIN, a natural sanctuary for over 300 species of birds, or up "...in the glens and spurs of IDA", in Hutovo or Gradac, is that he is not any safer from the merciless onslaught of a totemic bird-man whose name means "eagle", until after sunset.

---

11. There is confusion about Agenor and Antenor with the Agenor the Elder, founder of AMYKLAI *Patavium* (Padua) and father of Kadmos, with the foundation of *Pardua* (the site not yet adequately identified) by Agenor and the presumed foundation of Padua by Antenor after the Trojan War.

I. THE ILIAD AND ITS TROJAN GEOGRAPHY

FEATURES OF THE SKAMANDROS DELTA-VALLEY:	
permanent	**temporal**
FORDS	ROADS
POOLS	TOMBS
PENS	CAMPS
GATES	WALLS

TABLE 1.26. TOPOGRAPHICAL DETAILS. Features which are the result of accidents of nature are echoed by others which are the result of human initiative.

PLACES OF INTEREST WITHIN DARDANIA

The design of some general scheme for a methodological description of this or that place relevant to the diverse activities of Danaan and Trojan within the SKAMANDROS delta-valley might turn up a classified list of notable places such as that proposed in *TABLE 1.26*. However, whatever the scheme, arbitrary as it might seem, its corresponding set of descriptions properly concerns *topography*, and the places relevant to the *activities* of Danaans and Trojans within the SKAMANDROS delta-valley.

Of the many places of interest there is one in particular which is of singular importance, the DANAAN DEFENSIVE WALL (VII, 331–343; VII, 433–441):

> "...were it well [says Nestor to Agamemnon] that thou make the battle of the Achaeans to cease at daybreak, and we will gather to hale hither on carts the corpses with oxen and mules; and we will burn them a little way from the ships that each man may bear their bones home to their children, whenso we return again to our native land. And about the pyre let us heap a single barrow, rearing it from the plain for all alike, and thereby build with speed a lofty wall, a defence for our ships and for ourselves. And therein let us build gates close-fastening, that through them may be a way for the driving of chariots; and without let us dig a deep ditch hard by, which shall intervene and keep back chariots and footmen, lest ever the battle of the lordly Trojans press heavily upon us."
>
> Now when dawn was not yet, but night was still 'twixt light and dark, then was there gathered about the pyre the chosen host of the Achaeans, and they made about it a single barrow, rearing it from the plain for all alike; and thereby they built a wall and a lofty rampart, a defence for their ships and for themselves. And therein they made gates, close-fastening, that through them might be a way for the driving of chariots. And without they dug a deep ditch hard by, wide and great, and therein they planted stakes.

The location of this wall will have been at the western end of the TROIC PLAIN —else Helen could not have identified the enemy for Priam (III, 161–244)— such that the ditch or moat outside the wall, facing the plain, will have been the ZANTHOS right bank, running N–S for a considerable number of meters. The proposed funeral pyre for the Danaan dead scarcely seems to have been situated at the south end of the wall, where the ZANTHOS flowed into SKAMANDROS, but, rather, at the north end (at a prudent distance from the main hub of the camp).

Now, the DANAAN DEFENSIVE WALL will have been erected already at the end of one third of the thirty six month period of Danaan presence in the SKAMANDROS delta-valley (that is, the duration of the Trojan War). Its strategic function seems obvious, to pen Trojan forces within the TROIC PLAIN, albeit Hector was able to break out and breached it (XII, 442 *et pas.*). Still, the wall's function as a prop in the landscape for the narrative line, is, symbolically, that of the meridian, hence the funeral pyre at the north end will have corresponded with the sun's most northerly position at mid-summer, in keeping with the *purpose* of the Trojan War, not the return of Helen and compensation for damages, but, rather, the establishment of a patriarchy (see III. THE TROJAN WAR AND FALL OF TROY).

CHAPTER II

ILIOS: A BRIEF SURVEY

ILIOS (Drijeva/Gabela), is the *only polis* in the *Iliad* dressed with buildings and streets, perched along the length of an oddly phallus-shaped hillock beside the Neretva river.

Nothing of archaeological relevance is known with certainty about the site, other than being grouped with forty-odd other Illyrian *gomile* or burial sites in the region, as yet undated. However, there still remain a number of superficial archaeological vestiges, scant as they are, from which to draw important inferences about the site. Thus, despite the ravages of time, and the need of a population to live someplace above the hazardous marshy surroundings, this hillock has been continuously occupied, ever since losing its sacred status after its methodical desecration and the destruction of its various precincts.

THE FOUNDATION OF ILIOS

The *Iliad* gives an account of the Royal House of Troy up to the Trojan War, which brought the Late Bronze Age to a sudden close *c.* 1,200 BC (XX, 215–240[1]):

> "... at the first Zeus, the cloud-gatherer, begat Dardanus, and he founded Dardania, for not yet was sacred Ilios builded in the plain to be a city of mortal men, but they still dwelt upon the slopes of many-fountained Ida. And Dardanus in turn begat a son, king Erichthonius, who became richest of mortal men. Three thousand steeds had he that pastured in the marsh-land; mares were they, rejoicing in their tender foals. Of these as they grazed the North Wind became enamoured, and he likened himself to a dark-maned stallion and covered them; and they conceived, and bare twelve fillies... And Erichthonius begat Tros to be king among the Trojans, and from Tros again three peerless sons were born, Ilus, and Assaracus, and godlike Ganymedes that was born the fairest of mortal men; wherefore the gods caught him

---

1. Two facts may be ascertained about this genealogy: first, that Greek lore made Dardanus a descendant of Iapetos, the Biblical Japheth; second, that the Royal House of Troy is exactly that genealogy of Japheth which appears in the "Table of Nations", *Genesis*, X, 1–5. This point of contact between the *Iliad* and *Genesis* (further enhancing Cyrus H. Gordon's *Homer and Bible*, 1967) is an invaluable hint for reading a Homeric genealogy with the same rigour of orthodoxy as reading *Genesis*. How this point of contact might have been established will be addressed later.

up on high to be cupbearer to Zeus by reason of his beauty, that he might dwell with the immortals. And Ilus again begat a son, peerless Laomedon, and Laomedon begat Tithonus and Priam and Clytius, and Hicetaon, scion of Ares. And Assaracus begat Capys, and he Anchises; but Anchises begat me [Aeneas] and Priam goodly Hector".

The common understanding about the name of ILIOS is that it is derived from that of Ilos, just as the TROES derive theirs from that of Tros, as noted by M. W. Edwards, *The Iliad: A Commentary*, Vol. V, p. 319 (on XX, 230–2):

> Tros is of course the eponymous founder of the Trojan race, as the poet suggests by the figura etymologica in this line... He [Ilos] is of course the eponymous founder of Ilion; the tale is told in Apollodorus, Library, 3. 12. 3.

Now, eponymy, the practice of ascribing the name of a people, a place, or an institution to that of an "ancestor", is a Greek invention devised to substitute for inadequate etymological information of this or that particular name (of course, with the unavoidable subsequent inferences which detract from any measure of acceptable historical thinking). Thus, there is no quarrel with the statement that Dardanus "founded Dardania, for not yet was sacred Ilios built in the plain...", though the inference that the first name is merely an eponym of the second is hasty, for Dardanus will have had a totemic identity, perhaps that of the most disagreeable wasp (*stršljen*) plentiful (and respected) in the Neretva delta-valley, and whose name would convey that of "dart" + *annax*, "king"[2], and Dardania (the district) will have been so called for the abundance of wild figs in the region (hence the Dardani were an Illyrian folk that moved into the region of western Macedonia and eastern Albania, whose name is derived from Albanian *dhard*, "pear"). In any case, Erikhthonios, whose name translates into "wool of the earth" and whose totemic identity will have been the wooly tarantula, will have been evicted from the region by hostile DARDANIOI, who acquired a totemic wasp identity —that is, a local "pear-identity" folk who expressly sided with Dardanus— which is the natural enemy of the tarantula[3]. That Erikhthonios should have acquired an arachnid totemic identity, out of context with the remainder of the illustrious line of

---

2. Unknown to me until shortly before publication of this work is that I have been anticipated by my late friend, Radivoje Pešič, of Belgrade: *On the scent of Slavic autochtony in the Balkans.* "Zavicaj". Casopis Matice Iseljenika Srbije. Godina XXXVI. Maj-August 1989. 344–347. p. 77–79:

> In pre-Greek, or to be more precise in Pelasgic, *darda*, means "bee". But, it is only the first level of identification... In Sanskrit *dārdhya* means "consistency", "firmness", "strength", "power"...

3. Erikhthonios will have emigrated to Apulia, which name is cognate with πῶλος, "foal", and founded ATHENAI (*Taras/Tarentum*), whence the name of the *tarantula*, natural to the region. It will have been with this inmigration from TROIA —certainly an important cultural and economic event— that the Daunian, Iapygian and Messapic peoples of Apulia became Illyrized.

descent from Dardanus, reads oddly and could, perhaps, be interpreted as reflecting some local discontent, for whatever the reason[4]. Further, along the same line, Tros will most assuredly *not* have been the founder of the Trojan race (as stated above), for the TROES took their name from TROIA (the district, not the city), so called from the *three* (Slavic *tro-*) treble-shaped marshes of the region (see pp. 86–7). Tros will have had a son Ilos and then built a city which he called ILIOS, or, alternately, first he built a city and then he had a son. Whatever the order is immaterial, for the name of ILIOS has no linguistic bearing with that of Ilos: on the one hand ILIOS is a λι-type name that, for want of some convincingly explained reason, was not conventionally transposed to Greek λλ (as in Ἁλίαρτος, classical *Bilitio*, later Bellinzona), and thus a theoretic original ιλλ- would relate "Illios" (perhaps meaning "phallus", as the shape of this hillock betrays) with a name of the Illyrii. Then, on the other hand, the name of Ilos, in keeping with the name of Tros, might, in like manner, be thought to have been derived from the abundant *ilo*, Slavic "mud" in the region. However, the unique totemic characteristic of Ilos is that he possessed a natural fire, or light, and thus the name begs a derivation from PIE **luq*, whence Latin *lux*, and *lupus*, λύκος, "wolf", and its association with light. Furthermore, if one could presume that Tros was engendered in the TROIC PLAIN (πεδίον τὸ Τρωϊκὸν), then, it follows that Ilos came from the ILEIAN PLAIN (πεδίον Ἰλήϊον) and thus his fiery associations are enhanced by the occurrence of occasional, spontaneous marsh-fires (due to several natural causes, among them lightning and methane gas).

Here, a digression is necessary, for the account in Apollodorus, *Library*, 3. 12. 3 (*fl.* 140 BC), mentioned above, preserves shreds of truth about the foundations of TROIA and ILIOS, and the difference between these names, albeit muddled. It will have been Ilos who followed a Dalmatian hound (white, with black penny-like spots), and not a dappled cow, that found its way to a necropolis, Ate, "Fate", which he thereafter named TROIA (Daorson, p. 107), after the name of his father. Why it was that Ilos sought a necropolis in particular for his father, that is to say, refurbished an already-established necropolis with esoteric architectural features, seems to have a direct bearing on the totemic identity of Tros, that of the amazingly long-lived cicada which matures underground as a nymph for seventeen years before emerging from its chrysalis to chirrup shrill music all summer long. Still later, Ilos will have

---

4. A vivid example of switching loyalties, as in this instance of a pear-folk siding with a wasp-folk, may be seen in the loyalty of Odysseus, a Trojan, siding with the invading AKHAIOI.

gone to ILIOS (which was already founded, meaning, that Tros had already designed some preliminary form of priestly habitation and cult-precinct), and established a TEMPLE OF ATHENE, or pond, or reservoir, or sacred well, on KALLIKOLONE (Stari Grad), analogous with the marshy surroundings where Ilos was born, as well as homologous with the male urinary meatus. The common denominator between TROIA (Daorson) and the TEMPLE OF ATHENE is that the one is a fetid place, a necropolis (hence discovered by a Dalmatian hound), and the other likewise fetid, as might be by analogy with marshes and homology with the urinary meatus. Later lore explained that a lightning bolt, or a meteor —or even a palladium, of all things— had fallen from heaven (and hence the associations with Ilos, the totemic fire-fly, in a way likewise fallen from heaven), for which reason the name for such a kind of place passed into the Latin as a *puteus*, a "well" or "trench", cognate with that which is "*putrid*".

Laomedon inherited the kingdom. It was he who built the WALLS OF ILIOS (p. 108), and, again, one wonders why it was that he built walls, in particular, with no practical sense of defense from the onslaught of an attacking enemy. The answer would seem to lie, as with his ancestors, in the destiny of his totemic identity, that of a caterpillar that weaves the walls of a cocoon from which it eventually emerges as a butterfly. This presumed totemic identity connects -*med*, the second element in his name, with that of Gany*med*es, from which the inference that, since Greek lore claimed that Ganymedes, the transvestite brother of Ilus, was wafted up to heaven to serve the gods, then -*med* is an Illyrian root meaning, or associated with, that which flies through the air[5].

THE PHALLUS-SHAPE OF ILIOS

It is, precisely, the geological phallus-shape of this hillock that yields an understanding of its three parts, and the relationship the places on these parts bear with each other (MAP 2.2).

I. PERGAMOS

PERGAMOS is the collective name for the western hill of Avala (from the Arabic *havalah*, "hill"), and the adjacent northern hill of Djerzeles (so-called in memory of a local folk-hero). The classification of the number of times that PERGAMOS occurs in the text reveals that this place com-

---

5. The root *med*- in MEDEON (*Comum*), *Mediolanum* (Milano), *Med*ea, *Med*usa, connotes "hair", and is most likely of Pelasgian origin, whereas -*med*, in Gany*med*es and Lao*med*on connotes "flying", and may be of Illyrian origin.

II. ILIOS: A BRIEF SURVEY

AVALA (WESTERN HILL): PALACE OF PRIAM (ALSO, SANCTUARY OF APOLLO)	
V; 508:	Apollo looks **down** on Trojans from PERGAMOS
V; 446:	Apollo places Aeneas **up** in his sanctuary on PERGAMOS
V; 460:	Phoebos Apollo goes **up** on PERGAMOS
VII; 21:	Apollo goes forward looking **down** from PERGAMOS
DJERZELES (NORTHERN HILL): ROOMS OF ALEXANDER	
VI; 512:	Paris comes **down** in shining armour from high PERGAMOS
XXIV; 700:	Cassandra goes **up** to observe Priam from PERGAMOS

TABLE 2. 1. REFERENCES TO PERGAMOS. The presence of Apollo on Avala seems self-evident, and that of Cassandra on Djerzeles seem justified by the root cas- in her name, connecting her with "cloth" (> cassok), and the rooms where Helen broidered her peplos.

prised two different parts (TABLE 2. 1). Thus, the two hills of PERGAMOS are homologous with the testicles, and, from this, perhaps, might be understood a meaning of "scrotum", akin with πήρα, "sack" and γέμος, "load". So it is that PERGAMOS has an easy, natural association of ideas with the sense of "progeny", hence of "the future", as may be adduced from the idea of forecasting predictable astronomical phenomena at the Palace of Priam, and the foretelling by Helen of the likewise predictable actions and fates of the Trojan War participants in the Rooms of Alexander.

II. [SKAIA]

[SKAIA] is the name of the southeastern spur along which the town of Gabela proper is situated. Though the name is nowhere mentioned in the text of the *Iliad*, it may be inferred from the name of the Scaian Gates at the bottom of this spur (hence so written in square brackets to denote an editorial comment). It is homologous with the shaft of the penis, and the name appears to be derived from an Illyrian root *ska-* connoting "unwanted", "undesirable", and perhaps denoting "expunge", "expurgate" whence Serbian *skidati*, "peel off", "to rip out (a page from a book)", associated with the "circumcision" of the prepuce with which the SKAIAN GATES are homologous. Perhaps such an etymology could account for Priam and Hecabe's THALAMOS TREASURE CHAMBER (see below), "excavated", as it were, under [SKAIA], somewhere in the vicinity of the SKAIAN GATES.

II. KALLIKOLONE

The tip of the southeastern spur, at the distal end of "the topmost citadel" of PERGAMOS (Avala and Djerzeles), today is the site of a Turkish fortress in ruins called Stari Grad ("Old City") (XX, 51):

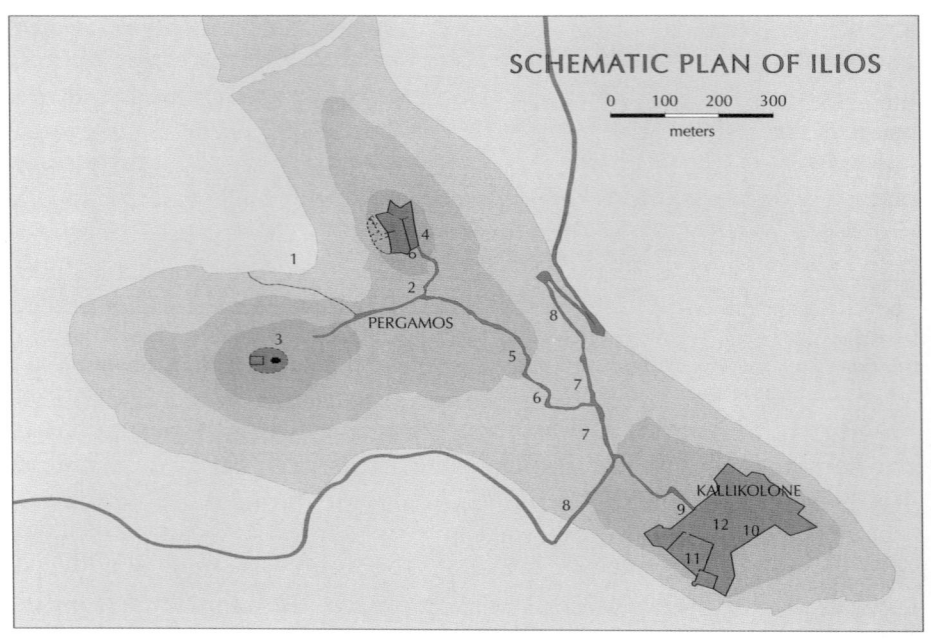

MAP 2. 2. THREE PARTS OF ILIOS. *That ILIOS was configured in the shape of a phallus from its inception conforms to the precept of a triad associated with light, in which two of its parts are the same, while the third is different but nevertheless a part of the whole.*

And over against her [Athene] shouted Ares, dread as a dark whirlwind, calling with shrill tones to the Trojans from the topmost citadel, and now again as he sped by the shore of Simois over Callicolone.

The hill of KALLIKOLONE is homologous with the glans, and together with [SKAIA] and PERGAMOS, completes the unmistakable phallus-shape of ILIOS. The name, in Illyrian, is a compound-type word that accentuates its topography, and means "callus-hill" (that is, "hill rough like a callus"), albeit the Greek departs far from the original sense, and is rendered as "Beauty Hill". Upon a time KALLIKOLONE was enclosed by the famous WALLS OF ILIOS, erected under the aegis of Laomedon to house within them the TEMPLE OF ATHENE.

PLACES ON ILIOS

The goal of the Trojan War was the desecration and destruction of ILIOS. Though the site was naturally defended on all sides by marshes, access could be gained with a modicum of ease onto any part of the hillock, with the exception of the walled TEMPLE OF ATHENE (Stari Grad). Thus, the long siege by hostile forces, and the period of the war itself, has the ring of a destruction for some specific reason other than the return of Helen or the death of Hektor (as will be seen later).

II. ILIOS: A BRIEF SURVEY

I. PERGAMOS
1. PRIAM'S STABLES
2. PROTHYRON
3. PALACE OF PRIAM (SANCTUARY OF APOLLO)
4. ROOMS OF ALEXANDER

II. (SKAIA)
5. HOUSE OF HECTOR AND ANDROMACHE
6. CITY AND CENTRAL AVENUE
7. THALAMOS TREASURE CHAMBER
8. SKAIAN GATES

III. KALLIKOLONE
9. PLANK-DOORS
10. WALLS OF ILIOS
11. PRIAM'S BELVEDERE
12. TEMPLE OF ATHENE

TABLE 2. 3. TWELVE SITES ON ILIOS. *The various descriptions of places on ILIOS are not the result of random poetic whim, but, rather, descriptions of a fixed number of places according to a preconceived, orderly plan.*

Though it would seem that the hillock of ILIOS has seen continuous occupation since its destruction —a period of three millennia— some inferences to the best explanation can be made about this or that place, and their relationship with other places on the hillock better understood, until that time when adequate archaeological investigation can yield precise information.

1. PRIAM'S STABLES: the plain at the intersection of the adjacent western and northern spurs of PERGAMOS (Avala and Djerzeles, respectively) is a V-shaped pen naturally suited for containing animals, from which there led up a lane along either side of the slopes (XXIV, 263):

> "Will ye not make me ready a waggon, and that with speed, and lay all these things therein, that we may get forward on our way?"
>
> So spake he, and they, seized with fear... brought forth the light-running waggon drawn of mules... And for Priam they led beneath the yoke horses that the old king kept for his own and reared at the polished stall.

It would seem that these horses and stables were inherited from Erikhthonios, who, upon a time, was owner of three thousand mares (XX, 221). Another niche or "stable" similar to this one is found on the left bank of the SIMOEIS (Krupa), a short distance before it debouches into the SKAMANDROS (Neretva), where Simoeisius was born on the day his mother went there to tend her sheep (IV, 488), and where Hera stabled her horses to feed on "ambrosian fodder" (V, 773–777).

2. THE PROTHYRON AND ECHOING PORTICO: The landing at the intersection of Avala (the western spur) and Djerzeles (the northern spur), at the convergence of a short lane and a long trail leading up from Priam's

Stables, opens the way to the Palace of Priam, the Rooms of Alexander, and to the City and Central Avenue along the length of [SKAIA] (the southeastern spur). The site, which might be said to be the axis on which the *trinacria* shape of Ilios spins, was like a vestibule (XXIV, 322):

> Then the old man made haste and stepped upon his car, and drave forth from the gateway and the echoing portico... But when they had gone down from the city and were come to the plain, back then to Ilios turned his sons and daughters' husbands...

The "echoing portico" is a reference to the convex, amphitheater-like intersecting of the spurs, which would seem to have captured all sounds from Priam's Stables below, perhaps even magnifying them.

3. **THE PALACE OF PRIAM (SANCTUARY OF APOLLO)**: On the summit of Avala is the (once) intact oval platform of a megalithic observatory, with its major axis aligned east-west. In the center is the small chapel of Sveti Stephan, and a short distance behind the chapel are the remains of a rectangular construction —most likely a look-out post (of the Venetian era?)— and, up until some decades ago (mid-20th century), were twelve Bogomil *stecci* —large limestone blocks, almost always hewn into the shape of a V-roofed house— surrounding the chapel. These have since been removed and replaced with contemporary graves which now surround the platform[6]. Here was the site of the Palace of Priam, also called the Sanctuary of Apollo (V, 446):

> Aeneas then did Apollo set apart from the throng in sacred Pergamos where was his temple builded. There Leto and the archer Artemis healed him in the great sanctuary, and glorified him...

The description of this sanctuary as the Palace of Priam is given with considerable detail, as follows (VI, 242):

> ...the beauteous palace of Priam, adorned with polished sun halls and in it were fifty chambers of polished stone, built each hard by the other; therein the sons of Priam were wont to sleep beside their wedded wives; and for his daughters over against them on the opposite side within the court were twelve roofed chambers of polished stone, built each hard by the other; therein slept Priam's sons-in-law beside their chaste wives...

The "polished sun halls..." (αἰθούσῃσι τετυγμένον) is a reference to the area between an outer and inner ring of stones aligned in such a manner as to fix a set of points on the horizon (sunrises and sunsets) and

---

6. Between 1976 when I first visited Gabela and 1985 when attention was brought to the importance of the site, graves for the local population were accommodated outwards from the oval platform which was, until then, intact (see *Homer's Blind Audience*, 1984). However, since 1985, The Roman Catholic Church, in particular the perverse local factotum of the Franciscan Order, has seen fit to excercise its endemic no-accountability policy and wantonly dug into and destroyed the platform by building a complex of rent-seeking concrete crypts. Alas, anything for the Faith...

II. ILIOS: A BRIEF SURVEY

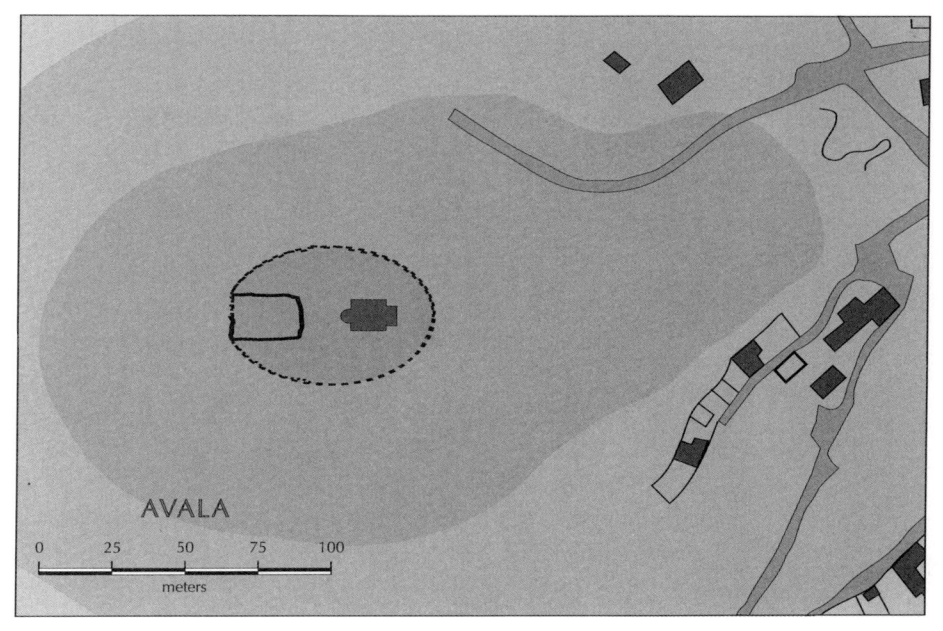

MAP 2.4. AVALA. *The site functioned as a megalithic observatory, whose purpose was that of measuring time-periods, thus, the prediction of certain celestial phenomena (such as determining the occurrence of solstices and equinoxes).*

so-called because they "catch" the warmth of sunlight. That there were "fifty chambers of polished stone..." for the sons of Priam in an outer ring suggests the Aubrey Circle at Stonehenge, albeit in Homer, 50 is always the number of (unwanted or uncared for?) progeny, but may be construed to have an association with 4-year lunar cycles (50 x 29.5 = 1,475 days, almost the same as 4 x 365 = 1,460 days). The inner ring of "twelve roofed chambers (τέγεοι θάλαμοι) of polished stone..." for Priam's daughters was perhaps in the shape of an elongated letter C, or horseshoe, aligned on the east-west axis in the direction of the equinoxes, and seems like an obvious allusion to the twelve houses of the Zodiac[7].

4. ROOMS OF ALEXANDROS: On the summit of Djerzeles (the northern hill) are the remains of an angular building dating from the Ottoman Empire, superimposed on the remains of an earlier building. The complex, unlike the oval platform of an astronomic observatory on Avala,

---

7. The closest archaeological equivalent of this megalithic observatory is at Sarmizegetusa, near Gradište, in Roumania. Megalithic monuments, which are of a great variety, have been known to mankind since remote antiquity —since Tyrins and Mycenae received their Homeric names— but their purpose has never been fully understood beyond that of being a palacial residence, a funerary precinct, or an astronomic observatory.

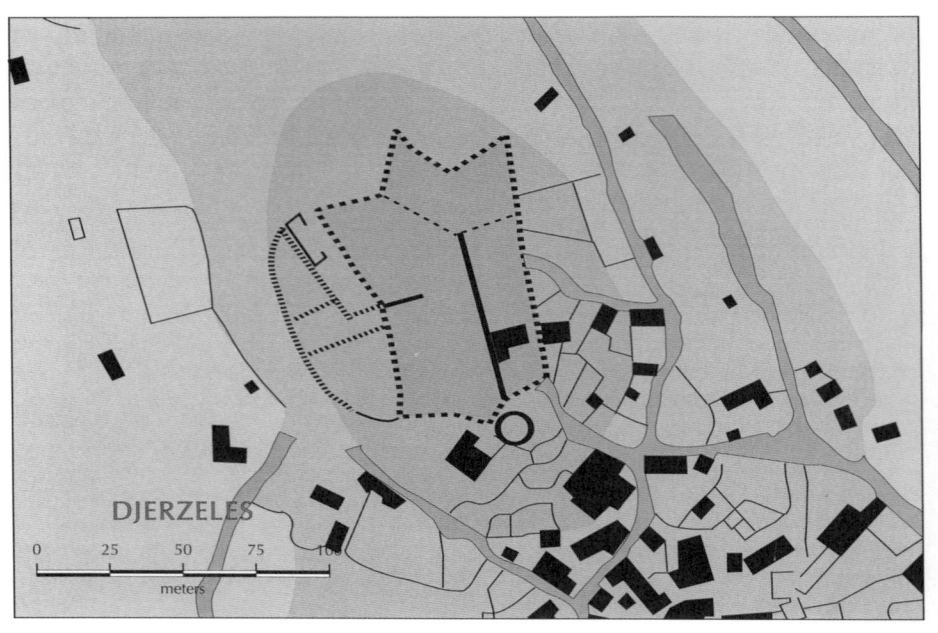

MAP 2.5. DJERZELES. *The mixed remains of Ottoman and "Illyrian" constructions betray the former existence of a complex of rooms on several levels. The angular features of the wall are an indication of the site's later function as a fortress, as at Stari Grad (below).*

betrays the former existence of several rooms. Beside these ruins stand the remains of the Venetian Torre di San Antonio. The site corresponds with the location for the Rooms of Alexandros (VI, 313):

> ...but Hector went his way to the palace of Alexander, the fair palace that himself had built with the men that were in that day the best builders in deep-soiled Troy; these had made him a chamber [θάλαμος] and hall [δῶμα] and court [αὐλή] hard by the palaces of Priam and Hector in the citadel.

The location of these rooms on Djerzeles, opposite those on Avala, seems corroborated by the following (VI, 503):

> Nor did Paris tarry long in his lofty house, but did on his glorious armour, dight with bronze, and hastened through the city... even so, Paris, son of Priam, strode down from high Pergamos...

The rooms comprised three units, a chamber (θάλαμος), a hall (δoμα), and a court (αυλα), albeit Helen was to be found in still another place (III, 125):

> She [Iris] found Helen in the hall (μέγαρον) where she was weaving a great purple web of double fold, and thereon was broidering many battles of the horse-taming Trojans and brazen-coated Achaeans...

It was in these rooms where an initial draft of the *Iliad* was set up (presumably from information about *future* events, collected at the Palace of Priam).

II. ILIOS: A BRIEF SURVEY

5. HOUSES OF HEKTOR AND ANDROMAKHE: A set of royal dwellings, situated on the border of [SKAIA] with PERGAMOS. No vestige of these dwellings is immediately visible, and so may be regarded as symbolic of other similar but less important dwellings scattered along the length of the southeastern spur of ILIOS (VI, 369):

> ...Hector of the flashing helm departed [from the Rooms of Alexander] and came speedily to his well-built house. But he found not white-armed Andromache in his halls... So Hector, when he found not his peerless wife within, went and stood upon the threshold, and spake amid the serving women...

6. THE 'CITY' AND CENTRAL AVENUE: The dwellings on [SKAIA] will have been of an undetermined number and of an unspecified sort (perhaps of mud-bricks?) which most likely were allotted to the priestly elite of King Priam's family (VI, 390):

> ...and Hector hastened from the house back onto the same way along the well-built streets. When now he was come to the gates, as he passed through the great city, the Scaian, whereby he was minded to go forth to the plain...

Common folk will have been relegated to live elsewhere, anywhere, excepting ILIOS. The enormous number of Trojans seeking refuge from the Danaans' onslaught may well have been temporarily accommodated within the Walls of Ilios, though uncomfortably so, but certainly not in the "city" dwellings on a permanent basis.

7. THE THALAMOS TREASURE CHAMBER: One might imagine the former existence of an underground labyrinthine passage located *below* the heights of PERGAMOS, in the vicinity of the SKAIAN GATES, inferred from the following instances (VI, 288, *et pas.*):

> But the queen herself went down [καταβήσετο, from her hall and the city] to the vaulted treasure-chamber wherein were her robes, richly broidered... Of these Hecabe took one... Then she went her way.

The Thalamos Treasure Chamber seems to have been fitted with a pair of swinging doors (or, alternately, it had two entrances fitted with only one door) hinged at a slant such that they might swing but never remain open, as adduced from the following allusion (XXIV, 315):

> Forthwith he [Zeus] sent an eagle, surest of omen among winged birds, the dusky eagle, even the hunter, that men call also the black eagle. Wide as is the door of some rich man's high-roofed treasure-chamber, a door well fitted with bolts, even so wide spread his wings to this side and to that; and he appeared to them on the right, darting across the city. And at sight of him they waxed glad, and the hearts in the breasts of all were cheered.

The eagle is surely the constellation Aquila, its opened wings tipped with the stars Alshain and Tarazed flanking Altair, whence the inference of two swinging doors, perhaps situated on either side of the Central Avenue.

No such chamber or labyrinthine passage is known to exist under the town of Gabela, though it is a fact that the curious "proteus fish", blind salamanders living in underground recesses and common to the Yugoslavian Adriatic coast, have occasionally been brought up by townspeople drilling wells. However, it should be noted that in this vicinity of Gabela —where the SKAIAN GATES will have been located, and where today one passes from one side of the hillock to the other— there exists a deposit of tuffa which is incompatible with Karstic geology, and must therefore be assumed to be an artificial deposit.

8. SKAIAN GATES: Access from the plain onto the hillock of ILIOS is gained at the base of [SKAIA] from either the northern or southern sides, which lead up to a point more or less midway, from where one way leads either up to PERGAMOS through a Central Avenue, or, in the opposite direction, to KALLIKOLONE (VI, 237):

> But when Hector was come to the Scaian gates and the oak tree, round about him came running the wives and daughters of the Trojans...

On his way out, back into the fray, he uses the same route (VI, 392):

> ...now he [Hector] was come to the gates, as he passed through the great city, the Scaian, whereby he was minded to go forth to the plain...

9. PLANK-DOORS: The walls overlooking the SKAIAN GATES were broken at the middle, opposite the CENTRAL AVENUE, by a gate to the enclosure within (not to be confused with THEANO'S GATE, below) (XVIII, 274):

> "...the city [height] shall be guarded by the walls and the high gates and the plank-doors fastened together, large, well-smoothed, fixed-fast, bolted shut."

10. WALLS OF ILIOS: The walls of the Ottoman fort of Stari Grad now run along the perimeter of Gabela's southeastern promontory (albeit these may have been rebuilt according to European fortification standards during the Venetian occupation). It was within this ample fort that the walls which Laomedon built also traced a circuit along the perimeter of KALLIKOLONE. It was in keeping with his totemic identity as a cocoon-weaving caterpillar (see p. 100) to have built walls, but to have hired Poseidon and Apollo to carry out the project is a puzzle (XXI, 442):

> ...we came at the bidding of Zeus and served the lordly Laomedon for a year's space at a fixed wage, and he was our taskmaster and laid on us his commands. I verily built for the Trojans round about their city a wall, wide and exceedingly fair, that the city might never be broken; and there, Phoebus, didst herd the sleek kine of shambling gait amid the spurs of Ida, the many ridged.

To think of Poseidon and Apollo as two personages, noted for whatever building skills may have distinguished them, and who acquired a divine stature at some time between Laomedon's reign and the Trojan War, does not ring true. Instead, these divinities may represent nothing

II. ILIOS: A BRIEF SURVEY

more than alluvial silt brought up from the plain to fill in and level off the enclosure.

11. PRIAM'S BELVEDERE: At the western corner of the walls, overlooking the SKAIAN GATES, is a belvedere which offers an unrestricted view of the TROIC and ILEIAN PLAINS in the distance. It was here, at the onset of the Trojan War, where the Elders of Troy sat (III, 149):

> ...they that were about Priam... sat as elders of the people over the Scaian Gates... like unto cicadas that in a forest sit upon a tree and pour forth their lily-like voices, even in such wise sat the leaders of the Trojans upon the wall.

It was to this place that Helen was called forth from her quarters on PERGAMOS (Djerzelez), and asked to sit with King Priam and the Elders (the Τειχοσκοπία, III, 161–244) and identify the host assembled on the nether side of the TROIC PLAIN (Glibuša Marshes) (III, 162):

> "...sit before me [Priam], that thou mayest see thy former lord and thy kinsfolk and thy people..."

It was also from this belvedere, that, still later, King Priam and the Elders watched, aghast, horrified, the chase that Achilles gave after Hector (XXII, 131, *et pas.*):

> So he [Hector] pondered as he abode, and nigh to him came Achilles...
> But trembling gat hold of Hector when he was aware of him, neither dared he any more abide where he was, but left the gates behind him, and fled in fear; and the son of Peleus rushed after him... Past the place of watch, and the wind-waved wild fig-tree they sped, ever away from under the wall along the waggon track...
> But hard upon Hector pressed swift Achilles in ceaseless pursuit... Oft as he strove to rush straight for the Dardanian gates [read πύλαι σανίδες, "plank doors"] to gain the shelter of the well-built walls, if so be his fellows from above might succor him with missiles, so oft would Achilles be beforehand with him and turn him back toward the plain, but himself sped on by the city's walls.

12. TEMPLE OF ATHENE: Nothing now remains of the precinct within the Walls of Ilios, excepting what looks like a rectangular watering trough, long-filled with rubble (VI, 297):

> Now when they were come to the enclosure of Athene on the city height, the doors were opened for them by fair-cheeked Theano... for her had the Trojans made priestess of Athene... Then with sacred cries they all lifted up their hands to Athene; and fair-cheeked Theano took the robe and laid it upon the knees of fair-haired Athene...

Given the general associations of Athene with watery places such as marshes, sources of rivers, springs, wells, and the like, and the homology of KALLIKOLONE with the glans and of her precinct with the urinary meatus, one easily adduces that her temple will have been a sacred well, or reservoir of sorts, tended, precisely, by Theano. Thus, the understanding of the passage above must be that Hecabe and her retinue, once

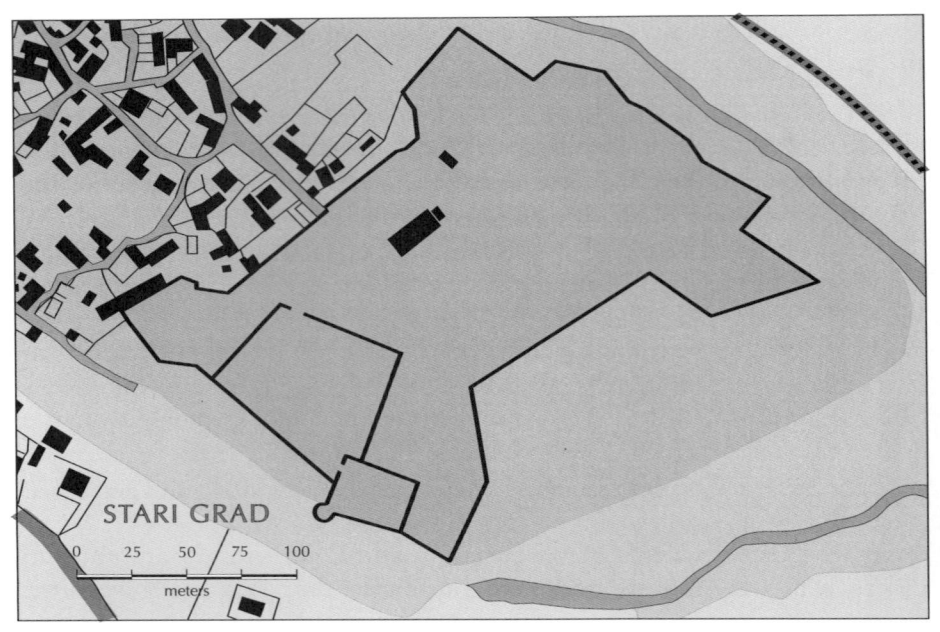

MAP 2. 6. STARI GRAD. *The wall now visible dates from the period of the Ottoman domination of the area. A wall from the Trojan period (Laomedon), now covered, perhaps had no significant defensive purpose and may have rsembled that of Daorson.*

inside "the enclosure of Athene in the city height..." had "the doors opened for them by fair-cheeked Theano..." that is, some sort of sluice gates to drain the well or reservoir, and thus be able to lay Hecabe's robe "upon the knees of fair-haired Athene..."

What sort of image was *in* this presumed sacred well or reservoir? The *rebus* of Athena (ever inseparable from her aegis) will have been the tortoise, and her epithet ἠυκόμοιο, "fair-haired", would seem to play on her natural *alopecia* and slimy strands of green algae. That Theano will have draped Hecabe's votive offering on the (four) "knees" of a tortoise makes sense, and so does the fact that it denied the prayer that accompanied the votive offering (VI, 311), for, indeed, the tortoise will have had its head retracted within its shell.

This robe (perhaps the one brought to Hecabe by Paris from SIDON (*Lanuvium*) on his return to TROIA with Helen?) will have been to a queen what an aegis is to a goddess and a shell to a tortoise. Perhaps it will have been specially decorated with certain designs, or images, or even letters (as in the Etruscan manner of writing on cloth). However, votive offerings of lesser importance, and far more common than a precious robe, are rounded, ovoid river-stones, variously decorated with

II. ILIOS: A BRIEF SURVEY

sets of criss-cross lines in the manner of a tortoise shell, usually found in the immediate periphery of sacred wells.

It is at the TEMPLE OF ATHENE that an important point of contact can be established between an earlier autochthonous Vinča stratum in the region that became overlayed with a new Pelasgian Trojanism (see VIII. PELASGIAN TROJANISM AND THE NEW ILLYRIANS). The many Vinča dolls representative of the Mother Goddess will, of course, have an association with the natural moisture of her sex and of humidity in general, hence her later Pelasgian identity as Athena and of her particular associations with humid places. Furthermore, the Vinča script around these figurines will have been transferred onto Athena's aegis, or, in a symbolic manner, directly onto a tortoise shell.

Stories preserved in Greek lore about the Aiantes connect them with Athena and her rebus: the one, Aias (the taller), came to TROIA from SALAMIS/**Gyrai** (Isole Chéradi) at the entrance to ATHENAI (*Taras/ Terentum*, Taranto); he was distinguished for possessing a formidable shield (VII, 219–223), and while some say he went mad and committed suicide by burying his sword in the ground and thrusting himself upon the upright blade (which is the only way of killing a tortoise), others say that he was drowned in mud thrown at him by Trojans; the other Aias (the shorter) came to TROIA with the LOKROI from *Bruttium*, the tip of the Italian Boot; ironically, he met his death at **Gyrai**/SALAMIS, where the other Aias (the Taller) was from, when the "rock" (isle) split as the result of an earthquake, and the half that he was on went into the sea (V, 500–511, see *MAP 9.3*); oddly, the root *chere-* in Chéradi is also present in Russian *tcherepaha*, "turtle"; also, the root *sal-* is associated with later expressions or remembrances of Athena and letters on her aegis (see IV. THE TROJAN DIASPORA).

THE NAMES OF DRIJEVA AND GABELA

ILIOS is likely to have become known as "Kapela", a name conveying the idea of both "chapel" and "head", as a "capital", or seat of authority, on a cue with the phallic homology of KALLIKOLONE with the glans (cf., Italian *capezzolo*, "nipple", "teat"). Presumably, the name of Kapela became Illyrized as Gabela, for Mavro Orbini recorded in his *Regni dei gli Slavi*, of 1661, that Gabela was the name given to a section of Risan, in Boka Kotorska, from where the Illyrian Queen Teuta reigned, that is, from the then "capital" of the Illyrian queendom.

A millennium-and-a-half later, the port facilities at Gabela became known as Drijeva, after the name of a small cargo vessel much used in this area, a word derived from *drvo*, "oak" (cf. *brigesta*, "a hard wood", whence "brigantine"). Then, under the Turks, the name of Gabela became closely associated with the Arabic *kabalah*, a term for the rationalization of diverse taxes and duties which at that time levied on salt and slaves traded at this place, from whence is derived the current Italian word *gabella*, a "tax" or "duty".

Today, there seems little reason to visit Gabela other than to see the remains of an Ottoman fortress later used by the Venetian Republic (Stari Grad), or, perhaps, to contemplate the surrounding fields below from the place where the spiritual stuff of our Western Civilization emanated.

CHAPTER III

THE TROJAN WAR AND FALL OF TROY

According to the *Iliad*, the cause of the Trojan War was the abduction of Helen, wife of Menelaos, by Alexander, alias Paris, son of King Priam of Troy. This act was present in the mind of Hector as he considered, in a fleeting moment, extricating himself from a doom, for which he had naught to do, by returning Helen and all the stolen wealth in addition to paying a considerable penalty (XXII, 111–121), an act which had previously been proposed by the very Agamemnon himself, but was turned down (III, 456–460). However, the *Iliad* is mute about the *circumstances* of Helen's abduction that culminated with the eventual destruction of Troy, but can be reconstructed in the following: towards the end of the *Iliad*, when the cremation of Hector is underway, Helen states she has been in Troy now the twentieth year (εἰκοστὸν ἔτος) since she left her native land (XXIV, 763–767); *if* it could be assumed that she was now in her fortieth year, even though at the peak of her sexuality an unwanted and an "unclean" woman (as after childbirth), then, it could be calculated that the AKHAIOI took possession of ARGOS (*Cajeta*, Gaeta), a Pelasgian enclave (II, 681), when Helen was in her twentieth year of life, and that during the subsequent six years she was taken by Menelaos to LAKEDAIMON (*Venetia*, Venezia Giulia) where he consolidated his power, while Agamemnon did likewise, moving her sister Klytemnestra to the district of ARGOS (*Apulia, Arpi/Argyrippa*, Fóggia) where he became firmly established; the union of Menelaos and Helen did not go beyond six years, for in the seventh (when Helen was in her twenty-seventh year), Alexander visited any one of the PAPHLAGONES (II, 851-855) in the environs of the Po delta, set in the very midst of LAKEDAIMON, and forthwith abducted Helen (who, as a Pelasgian escaping the clutches of an evil Akhaian, will have gone willingly) and, to boot, also took the local treasury with him; Alexander and Helen will have traveled upstream the ALPHEIOS (*Padus*, Po), exited the Piemont through the natural route of the later *Via Aemilia Scauri*, passing KRISA (*Crixia*, Piana Crixia), and entered into Tyrrhenian waters at *Vada Sabatia* on the Ligurian Coast; thence they came to KRANAI, **Khios** (*Ilva/Aethalia*, Elba) where they had dalliance with each other (III, 443–445); in due time they continued to Helen's native ARGOS (*Cajeta*, Gaeta), where Paris found precious robes among neighbouring Sidonian women (**Kydones** of the *Odyssey*, xix, 172–180) inhabitants of *Lanuvium*) as a gift for his mother (VI, 289–292); in the following year, the eighth year after the taking of Pelasgian Argos (Helen is now in her twenty-eighth year), there was a meeting called at AULIS (*Pedone*, Cuneo) to which no one came because of its distant and ill-suited location; however, a second meeting was called at DAULIS *Rubra*/*Aulla*), in the Apuan hills behind the modern naval port of La Spezia; finally, the couple rounded the Italian Peninsula and entered Adriatic waters, headed for Troy.

THE AKHAIAN PINCER

The Akhaian Pincer established by Menelaos and Agamemnon at the Adriatic headwaters and Straights of Otranto, respectively, was short-lived —since there were no ancestral roots that justified the acquisition of these new territories— but, strategically, in the short term, they were effective. These new territories were, to be sure, aggressive encroachments on Illyrian populations, both in the north as well as the south. However, some short time after the Fall of Troy —by the time of the Ionian Migrations *c.*1,150 BC— those artificial territories ceased to exist, their new occupants now moving to new lands in Hellas.

It could be reasonably presumed that the purpose of such a geographical pincer was to curtail Trojan commerce. Perhaps some other reason might have been the need of acquiring iron-smelting technology and the control of iron-bearing sites to which Troy, as a political entity, was a hindrance. Still another reason, to which the authorship of the *Iliad* and *Odyssey* subscribed, and which is, indeed, a *most* subtle point of contact between one epic and the other, will be seen below with an understanding of *how* the *Catalogue of Ships* (II, 494–759) worked, and, still later, with the acts of Odysseus, on two islands that he visited.

THE DANAAN ARRIVALS

Eventually, Danaan forces began arriving at a place today occupied by the port of Orebič, on the south side of NERITON (Pelješac Peninsula), opposite TENEDOS (*Corcyra Melaina*, Korčula). The site would seem to have been strategically well-suited for an invasion of the Trojan mainland, since the long and narrow peninsula of NERITON (Pelješac), though technically the mainland, seemed more like an island and a logical stepping-stone before a final naval assault on the HELLESPONTOS

III. THE TROJAN WAR AND FALL OF TROY

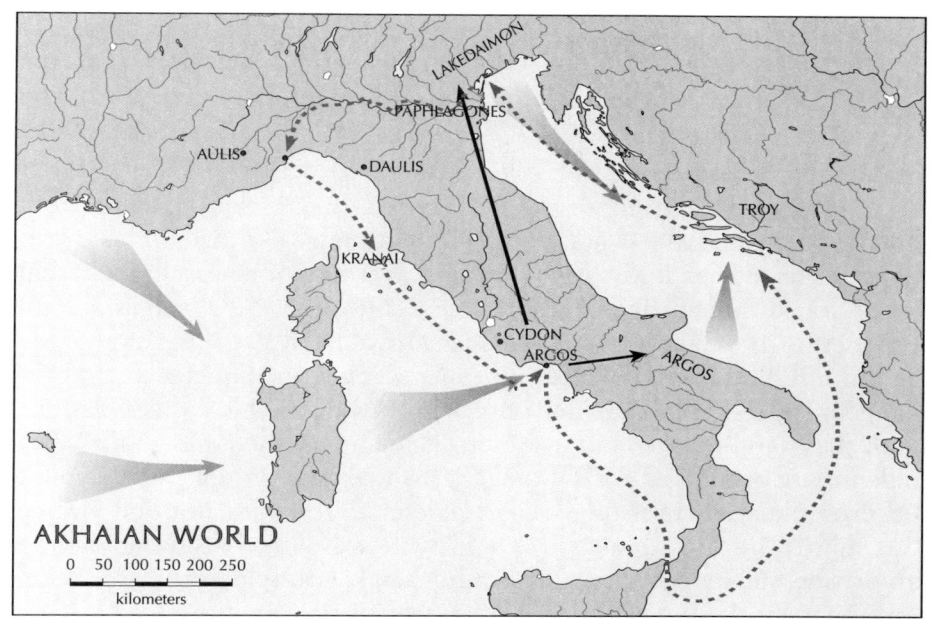

MAP 3.1. AKHAIAN EXPANSIONISM. A folk calling themselves AKHAIOI, possibly of Western Mediterranean origins, took ARGOS, pillaged it, and then moved into places in opposite directions in a concerted effort to establish a strategic pincer on Troy.

(Neretva delta) itself. Furthermore, the logistics seemed viable, with periodic servicing to vessels from TENEDOS (*Corcyra Melaina*, Korčula) an island apparently connected with ship-building (on account of its woods) from remotest times[1] (and which some two-and-a-half millennia later lent its name to the famous "Corsair"), as well as supplying the invading forces with sundry goods and special services from LEMNOS (*Issa*, Viš).

As for the arrival of the "Greek" forces (a term for a people who did not become historical reality until some four to five centuries later), there is some confusion about a certain Philoktetes and one Protesilaos, both of whom seem to have been first to step on Trojan soil:[2] of Philoktetes, he brought a contingent to Troy from MELIBOIA (*Lacus Fucinus*, Lago di Celano) and was bitten on the toe by a venomous snake when he jumped from his vessel onto the shores below SAMOS (Sveti Ilija/Monte Vípera), perhaps in just retribution for anticipating

---

1. There seems to lurk a subtle hint of ship-building in the Greek story about the origin of the name of Tenedos (Apollodorus, *Epitome*, III, 23–25), reputedly derived from that of Tenes, who, accused of improprieties by his step-mother, was set afloat in an ark which washed ashore on this island, where he became king.

2 See G. S. Kirk, *The Iliad: A Commentary*, I, p. 232–34.

Agamemnon, and, because of the stench of his festering wound, he was sent to LEMNOS (*Issa*, Viš), where he remained for the duration of the war (II, 716–728); of Protesilaos, who also brought a contingent to Troy from ITON (Cilento), he was the first to be slain by a Dardanian as he jumped from his ship (II, 695–710).

The tragicomic irony of the Philoktetes story is that he came from the region around MELIBOIA whose population was known, in historical times, to have been knowledgeable with a variety of magical and herbal cures for different ills, and that near METHONE (*Marruvium*, San Benedetto) the snake was held in *sacred* awe (as it is to this day). That he did not cure his own snake bite suggests his incompetence, and his banishment to LEMNOS is not only *à propos* of the bleary associations with the island's name, but also with Hephaistos, the lame god, having fallen there and cared for by the SINTIES (an otherwise a *sinister* folk). Of Protesilaos, there is likewise a tragicomic irony, for not only did he die, smitten by a Dardanian arrow, his wife was likewise smitten, not by an arrow, but by the image of her husband with which she was so in love, that she died of grief when her father finally saw fit to take it from her and throw it into the fire. Alas!

THE CATALOGUE OF SHIPS

The *Catalogue of Ships* (II, 494–759) is a long and tedious list of who came from where on how many ships to fight against Troy.[3] As a census, it seems hardly germane to the story of the goings to and fro of Danaans and Trojans over the Trojan marshes. Modern scholarship considers it a descriptive catalogue of a Mykenaian Age Hellas that survived into the time of the composition of the *Iliad*, and was, like many other would-be independent units of the *Iliad*, brought together within a comprehensive whole, by who knows whom, but generally called "Homer".

However, the *Iliad* can hardly function as any sort of testament of a Trojan War without the *Catalogue of Ships*, since, the value of the *Iliad's* geographical information, and the historical inferences adduced from this information, are derived from that data contained in the *Catalogue of Ships*. Simply, the *Catalogue of Ships* is an invaluable part of the *Iliad*, indeed, as important to the *raison d'être* of the narrative line as any other part. Thus, it is definitely *not* a patch external to the authorship of the *Iliad* (and *Odyssey*), stitched onto a convenient place within

---

3. An estimate is anywhere from 35,000 to 40,000 men on 1,174 ships. One can imagine the difficulties in the logistics of such a campaign, as well as its devastating effects on the local economy.

III. THE TROJAN WAR AND FALL OF TROY 117

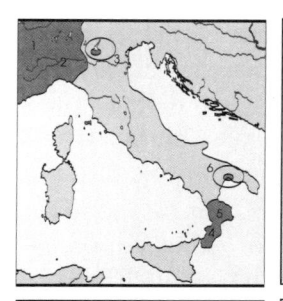

¶	peoples	§ I places	Bk. II
1	BOIOTOI	—	494–510
2	PHOKES	—	517–526
3	MINYAI	ASPLEDON	511–516
4	LOKROI	—	527–535
5	ABANTES	EUBOIA	536–545
6	ATHENAIOI	ATHENAI	546–558

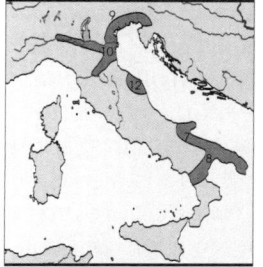

¶	peoples	§ II places	Bk. II
7	AKHAIOI	ARGOS	559–568
8	—	AIGIALOS	569–580
9	—	LAKEDAIMON	581–590
10	GERENES	—	591–602
11	ARKADES	ARKADIA	603–614
12	EPEIOI	ELIDA	615–624

¶	peoples	§ III places	Bk. II
13	—	EKHINAI	625–630
14	KEPHALLENES	—	631–637
15	AITOLOI	—	638–644
16	KRETES	—	645–652
17	RHODIOI	—	653–670
18	—	SYME	671–675

¶	peoples	§ IV places	Bk. II
19	—	KALYDNAI	676–680
20	HELLENES	HELLAS	681–694
21	—	ITON	695–710
22	—	BOIBE	711–715
23	(THAUMAKES?)	OLIZON	716–728
24	—	OIKHALIA	729–733

¶	peoples	§ V places	Bk. II
25	—	ASTERION & TITANOS	734–737
26	—	ELONE	738–747
27	ENIENES & PERHAIBOI	DODONA	748–755
28	MAGNETES & AITHIKES	PELION	756–759

the narrative line, but, rather, occurs where it does because that is where it was intended to be. It seems likely the *Catalogue* may have been inspired by an independent Trojan inventory, or catalogue, of a schematic distribution (for mnemonic purposes) of Trojan allies abroad.

The *Catalogue of Ships* has been edited, most certainly by any one or all of the celebrated Alexandrine editors, Aristarchus, Zenodotus, and Aristophanes, and, by who knows what host of other editors. A case in point is bringing an otherwise linguistically sound Ἴλην καὶ Πετεῶνα... HILE and PETEON (*Fidentia*, Fidenza and *Florentiola*, Firenzuola d'Arda) into a better sounding (but incorrect) Ὕλην καὶ Πετεῶνα... (II, 500). Also, from an earlier date, perhaps from the *Iliad* and *Odyssey's* Pisistratean recensions of about 550 BC, come corrections as regard an *order* of enumeration, as may be seen with the first three contingents (previous page). Furthermore, not least of all, as a master-recension passed from hand to hand for copying, a natural corruption through error of transcription, or a loss of lines, rendered a garbled conflation of ¶15 and ¶18 (as well as elsewhere, but in lesser degrees).

It is true, the *Catalogue of Ships* is not a scientific treatise of the geography of the Italian Peninsula, for it consigns unabashedly selective and therefore biased information, albeit invaluable for an understanding of peoples and places according to *someone*, *c.*1000 BC. Furthermore, what seems like unique information about those to whom the authorship of the *Iliad* and *Odyssey* is ascribed, is that they specifically assigned to those awful brothers, Agamemnon and Menelaos, districts in the shape of a *trinacria*, the sun-faced, three-legged rebus for the sun's equinoxes and solstices (the spring equinox being the same as the autumn equinox, hence represented by one leg). This would seem to suggest that a sun-ritual of some sort, and not the abduction of Helen, nor the looting of Argos, was at the core of the Danaan Invasions of Troy.

TRINACRIAS AGAINST ILIOS
Clearly, the *trinacria*-districts in the south and the north, represented by Agamemnon and Menelaos respectively, betray a preconceived effort of suppressing ILIOS (Drijeva/Gabela). However, ILIOS was not a trinacria, it only *seemed* to look like one, for its shape was that of a phallus. Thus, the sun-symbol trinacrias represented by Agamemnon and Menelaos would seem to suggest the ulterior purpose of AKHAIOI overrunning an Illyrian Messapic peoples in the south, and an Illyrian Venetic peoples in the north, was the eventual establishment in the entire Balkan

III. THE TROJAN WAR AND FALL OF TROY

Peninsula of a sun-worshipping cult, or, if it please the Gentle Reader, the suppression of a matriarchal society in favour of a patriarchal world-order. Now, the discerning eye will notice that the trinacria corresponding to Menelaos is not as smooth and well-defined as that of Agamemnon, for it is surmounted with a "crook", so to speak, corresponding with the district of the ARKADES, ¶11. However, this protrusion, as it were, is clearly *not* part of the intended trinacria, for these peoples "... with matters of seafaring had they naught to do" (II, 614) and therefore are not to be taken into consideration... Clever folk, these Illyrian bards...

The Danaan forces raided and pillaged the Trojan coast for nine years (II, 134), taking goods and the comeliest of women captive. It was during this period, prior to the appointed time when a final naval assault on the Trojan HELLESPONTOS (Neretva delta) would be made, that Odysseus discovered Akhilleus regaling himself dressed as a woman at SKYROS (Pušica), a port-town situated at the eastern end of the island of LESBOS (*Brattia*, Brač). This event, whose correct geographical background was so badly misunderstood by the Greek intelligentsia, is recorded by Sir James George Frazer (Apollodorus III. xiii. 8. The Loeb Classical Library) as follows:

> As to Achilles disguised as a girl at the court of Lycomedes in Scyros, see Bion, ii. 5 sqq.; Philostratus Junior, Imag. 1; Scholiast on Homer, Il. ix. 668; Hyginus, Fab. 96; Statius, Achill. i. 207 sqq. The subject was painted by Polygnotus in a chamber at the entrance to the acropolis of Athens (Pausanias i. 22. 6). Euripides wrote a play called The Scyrians on the same theme. See Tragicorum Graecorum Fragmenta, ed. Nauck 2, pp. 574 sq. Sophocles composed a tragedy under the same title, which has sometimes been thought to have dealt with the same subject, but more probably it was concerned with Neoptolemus in Scyros and the mission of Ulysses and Phoenix to carry him off to Troy. See The Fragments of Sophocles, ed. A.C. Pearson, vol. ii. pp 191 sqq. The youthful Dionysus, like the youthful Achilles, is said to have been brought up as a maiden. See above, iii. 4. 3, with the note. One of the questions which the emperor Tiberius used solemnly to propound to the antiquaries of his court was: What was the name of Achilles when he lived as a girl among girls? See Suetonius, Tiberius, 70. The question was solemnly answered by learned men in various ways: some said that the stripling's female name was Cercysera, others that it was Issa, and others that it was Pyrrha. See Ptolemy Haphaestionis, Nov. Hist. i. in Westermann's Mythography Graeci, p. 183.
>
> 1. The usual story was that the crafty Ulysses spread out baskets and women's gear, mingled with arms, before the disguised Achilles and his girlish companions in Scyros; and that while the real girls pounced eagerly on the feminine gauds, Achilles betrayed his sex by snatching at the arms. See Philostratus Junior, Imagines, i; Scholiast on Homer, Il. xix. 326; Ovid, Metamorph. xiii. 162 sqq. Apollodorus tells us that Achilles was detected by the sound of a trumpet. This is explained by Hyginus (Fab. 96), who says that while Achilles was surveying the mingled

trumpery and weapons, Ulysses caused a bugle to sound and a clash of arms to be heard, whereupon Achilles, imagining that an enemy was at hand, tore off his maidenly attire and seized spear and shield. Statius gives a similar account of the detection (Achill. ii. 167 sqq.).

THE DURATION OF THE TROJAN WAR

It would seem, perhaps, that some Danaan or Pelasgian account of the Trojan War, that is to say, some report of a foreign event in a distant land —an *ex post facto* account, as it were, and, indeed, as the *Iliad* has usually been regarded— might have been structured in this or that particular manner. As it is, scholarship has always been at odds with regard to the time-period the *Iliad* occupies, since, it has failed to recognize that the presence of divinities, principally of Athena, among the affairs of us mortals, are celestial bodies —Hera, the moon, for instance— which give a meticulously detailed account, an ephemerides, of day-by-day events. From this, the inference that Athena, as the planet Venus, which precedes and follows sunrises and sunsets, necessarily yields a considerably greater number of days and nights than hitherto suspected. Furthermore, on a cue with the nine years the invading Danaans have already spent on Trojan territory, it is an easy inference to adduce that three more years —the very account of the *Iliad*— occupies the span of the Trojan War, a period of twelve years, which is a nice number for having an almost unavoidable association with the twelve Houses of the Zodiac. The *Iliad*, then, occupies a period of thirty six months, but these appear to be lunar and not solar months, from Full Moon to Full Moon, a period of 29.5 days (that is, a Full Moon on every 30th day, which is the end of the previous cycle and beginning of the next).

Now, the division of the text into lunar "chapters", so to speak, is an arduous task, since the *Iliad's* current division into twenty four books implies that, if in Book I it is relatively easy to detect one lunation, this leaves thirty five lunations in twenty three books. In Book II perhaps three lunations may be detected, such that the *Catalogue of Ships* may have covered the space of one lunation. Thus the BOIOTOI ¶1 are the first to leave on the evening of a Full Moon (II, 494–510), such that by the fifteenth day, the evening of a New Moon (II, 000), the twelve vermillion-prowed ships of Odysseus —the only ones so distinguished in the entire text— listed exactly at the middle of the *Catalogue of Ships*, are barely rounding the western tip of NERITON (Pelješac), the midpoint between AGAMEMNON'S CAMP at Orebič and the HELLESPONTOS, and that by the time the MAGNETES (II, 756–759) leave, it is the end of one lunar cycle and the beginning of the next.

III. THE TROJAN WAR AND FALL OF TROY

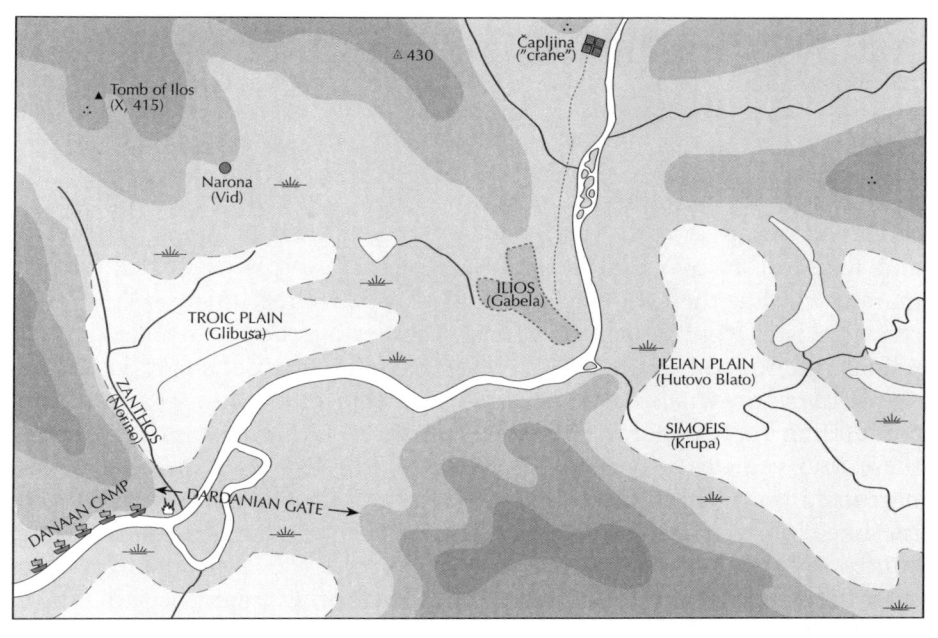

MAP 3.3. TROIC AND ILEIAN PLAINS. *The foundation of* ILIOS *in the midst of marshes was not for some defensive reason, but, rather, because the site was a precinct of Athena, who was associated with all humid places (as was, also, the site of* ATHENAI*).*

THE DANAAN CAMP AND WALLS

A sense of military strategy might suggest that an invading army go no further up the SKAMANDROS (Neretva) than the DARDANIAN GATE, that gate or pass behind which lie the TROIC and ILEIAN PLAINS and through which the SKAMANDROS flows (see *Map 3.2* TROIC AND ILEIAN PLAINS). Furthermore, since physical access onto ILIOS (Gabela) could be gained only from the side of the TROIC PLAIN on the right bank of the SKAMANDROS, it is likely, then, that a DANAAN CAMP will have been established at the confluence of the ZANTHOS (Norino) with the SKAMANDROS (Neretva) (VII, 333 *et pas.*):

> "... we will gather to hale hither on carts the corpses with oxen and mules; and we will burn them a little way from the ships that each man may bear their bones home to their children... And about the pyre let us heap a single barrow, rearing it from the plain for all alike, and thereby build with speed a lofty wall, a defence for our ships and for ourselves. And therein let us build gates close-fastening, that through them may be a way for the driving of chariots; and without let us dig a deep ditch hard by, which shall intervene and keep back chariots and footmen, lest ever the battle of the lordly Trojans press heavily upon us."
>
> ... then was there gathered about the pyre the chosen host of the Achaeans, and they made about it a single barrow, rearing it from the plain for all alike; and thereby they built a wall and a lofty rampart, a defence for their ships and for themselves.

And therein they made gates, close-fastening, that through them might be a way for the driving of chariots. And without they dug a deep ditch hard by, wide and great, and therein they planted stakes.

NAVAL ENGAGEMENTS

An inescapable fact about the Trojan War, specifically, the many deeds of Danaans and Trojans going back and forth over the TROIC (Glibuša) and ILEIAN (Hutovo Blato) PLAINS, is that these plains are eminently marshy, even as their modern names betray. It is their intrinsic "muddy" characteristic from which the "*Iliad*" (cf. Serbian *ilo*, "mud"), takes its name, and not so from ILIOS (Gabela), the citadel under siege. Thus, the use of horse-drawn cars (δίφρος, x 69) and chariots (ἅρμα, x 62) between contending forces necessarily calls on a need of understanding one of these two vehicles —perhaps ἅρμα, "armature"— as a *drijeva*, a flat-bottomed boat still in use for punting in the waters among ever-shifting isle-like clumps of bulrushes and reeds. In a sense, then, the innumerable confrontations between mortal enemies on these marshy fields casting their "long-shadowed" punting poles at each other might be thought of as miniature naval engagements, each enclosing some poetic secret yet to be unravelled.

That a yet undetermined (and unclassified) number of "naval engagements" or "iliads", so to speak, over terrain which looks sound enough from a distance, but in fact is an intricate swampland, is a subtle point of contact with the *Iliad's* sister composition, the *Odyssey*, an account about one man (by contrast with diverse accounts of many participants in the *Iliad*) who gets caught up in the treacherous waters of the IKAROPONTOS (inter island sea-channel), which, like a marsh, as it were, is thick with flotsam and jetsam that is swept up by swift currents coming in from the south.

Presumably, the self-evident numerical superiority of invading Danaans (evinced in the number of vessels and men listed in the *Catalogue of Ships*) over defending Trojans was a deciding factor in the outcome of a conventional understanding of the Trojan War. Still, the Fall of Troy, as in the sense of final capitulation, cannot, properly, be ascribed to the single factor of numerical superiority and the inevitable vanquishing of defending forces, yet, at what point Trojans are no longer able to stave off a definitive assault and an inevitable destruction of ILIOS is not narrated in the *Iliad*. Nevertheless, inferences of a continued conflict may be drawn from knowledge about the ruse of a Trojan Horse devised by the enemy to gain access into ILIOS, mentioned in the *Odyssey* (vii; 487–498). However, this information may be shown to be

BIRD-MAN *VERSUS* BULL-MAN RITUAL		
AKHILLEUS *VS* HEKTOR	**MELEAGROS *VS* GIANT BOAR**	**THESSEUS *VS* MINOTAUR**
Hektor, unrestrained, runs wild and wreaks havoc in the plains and ships of Akhaioi	Giant Boar, on the loose, runs wild and wreaks havoc over the fields of Kalydon	Minotaur terrorizes Athenians and obtains yearly tribute of lads and maidens
Akhilleus finally agrees to enter the Trojan War and avenge the death of Patroklos	Meleagros invites many famous heroes to participate in a hunt for the Giant Boar	Thesseus contracted to slay Minotaur by Athenians who no longer wish to pay tribute
Akhilleus dresses in splendid armour fashioned for him by Hephaistos	Meleagros and his guests arm as if going forth to war	Thesseus collects a number of accoutrements, among them a ball of string and a mirror
Akhilleus chases after Hektor who runs three times under the walls of Ilios	Meleagros and a party of famous heroes give chase to the Giant Boar	Thesseus enters the Labyrinth and cautiously seeks out the Minotaur
Akhilleus confronts and slays Hektor	Meleagros confronts and slays the Giant Boar	Thesseus confronts and slays the Minotaur
Akhilleus falls in love with Penthesilea and makes love to her (albeit she is dead)	Meleagros and Atalanta retire to Olenos and indulge in bout of wild love	Thesseus and Ariadne retire to the isle of Kranas and indulge in bout of wild love

TABLE 3. 4. SIX STAGES OF A RITUAL. The celebration of this ritual, with variations according to the persons and place in question, evidently recollects a memory of a sedentary farmer community plagued by the pillaging whims of nomadic societies, not unlike a bird flying into a farmer's orchard and picking at fruit indiscriminately.

an interpolation, for, no sooner does the *Iliad* come to a close, than Odysseus shows up among the KIKONES, and, since he is the prime informant of the *Odyssey*, it will have been impossible for him to have been aware of the duplicity of Greeks bearing gifts.

RITUAL DEATH OF HECTOR

The climax of the *Iliad* is the final confrontation between Akhilleus and Hektor. True, the confrontation and dismal outcome for Hector was in revenge for his slaying of Patroklos. Still, blameless of all fault, and even of a responsibility in dissuading the AKHAIOI from their purpose of substituting a matriarchy for that of a patriarchy, he was the designated guardian of TROY: οἶος γὰρ ἐρύετο Ἴλιον Ἕκτορ. (VI, 403).

That a totemic bird-man (Akhilleus) assails and vanquishes a totemic bull-man (Hektor) is seen almost exactly in the stories of Meleagros (partridge-man) and the giant boar of Kalydonia (literally, a miniature European rhinoceros, now extinct), and Theseus (meaning uncertain) and the Minotaur (cave bull-man). In these stories are preserved the ritual steps taken by a bird-man who prepares himself, enters the dominion of a bull-man, finds and slays him, and then leaves with a beloved one for a bout of love-making (*TABLE 3. 4.*).

It would seem that this ritual is symbolic of a lawless bird-man invading and freely partaking of a bull-man's well-tended orchard, and, perhaps, representative of a natural, mutual antipathy between the nomadic AKHAIOI, and a settled, farming folk such as the PELASGOI.

A RETROSPECT: THE LOCAL EFFECT OF AN AKHAIAN PRESENCE

The story about a Trojan War told by the *Iliad* has an external literal sense, that is, the "Anger of Akhilleus", or the "Death of Hector", and a recondite, internal sense, which is about the causes and effects of Akhaian incursions on Pelasgian dominions on the Italian Peninsula and Trojan dominions on the Balkan Peninsula.

Certainly, the Akhaian presence on Trojan territory, accompanied by a host of Danaan "loyalists", so to speak, was the cause of local permanent changes of political and cultural structures (and, presumably, also of economic and social standards). Oddly, the AKHAIOI seem to have left scant evidence of their presence, and, furthermore, to judge from information in the *Odyssey*, as well as later Greek writers, to have vanished from existence altogether, for Agamemnon left no progeny to speak of, nor did Menelaos. The names of AKHAIIS and of the AKHAIOI eventually became established in Greece, most likely taken thence by additional migrations *after* to the Ionian Migrations (but, then again, perhaps the name was simply assigned to the Peloponnese at a much later date, when a Homeric understanding of Hellas was sought). However, the notion of a powerful geo-political Akhaian Pincer against Troy, not only economically strong, but also accompanied by a powerful religious tenet that supplanted an esoteric matriarchal society for a pragmatic approach to daily life under a patriarchal society, simply vanished, or, alternately, *transformed* into another society.

The Fall of Troy would presage the close of the Heroic Age, followed by a new age —new states, new languages, new technologies, a new intellectual world— that touched all sectors of all societies within the Mediterranean Basin. Apparently, the common denominator of other political and social disturbances more or less coetaneous with the Trojan War was the rapid spread of an idea, of a way of life, that of a patriarchal society.

CHAPTER IV

THE TROJAN DIASPORA

After the Fall of Troy there went with the Trojan Diaspora into the four winds two fundamental contributing factors in the development of our Western Civilization, the one, material, and the other, spiritual: the one, a *peoples* who emigrated to diverse places and would, in the first generation, tint the cultural features of a new society with their own traits; the other, the transmission of a *pamjat* or "remembrance" of memories and knowledges, albeit oftentimes altered and modified according to circumstances[1].

ROME, THE DAUGHTER OF TROY

The best known story about the Foundation of Rome is the one told by Virgil in the *Aeneid* (30–19 BC) about Aineias, who left his ravaged country carrying his old and sickly father on his back, and, eventually, after many travails, arrived at the shores of *Latium* on the Tyrrhenian side of Italy. The reason this story in particular is so well-known is because, according to the *Iliad*, the line of descent of Aineias from Tros is eminently chthonic (XX, 215 *et pas.*): the three children of Tros were Ilos, Ganymedes, and Assarakos; Ilos, the totemic fire-fly, went up into the atmosphere, not unlike his later counterpart, the Prophet Elijah would do in a flaming horse and chariot; Ganymedes was such a beautiful androgynous youth that he also was wafted off into thin air and became cup-bearer (but more likely *sommelière*) to the gods; only Assarakos was the one to remain in Troy, and from him was born Kapys, and from him Ankhises, the father of Aineias. So it is that after all eminent Trojan personages also disappeared into the four winds after the Fall of Troy, only Aineias left a trail of founding cities and visiting different places[2].

---

1. A fuller account of the subject-matter of this chapter is to be given at a later date in a work to be call *Gesta trojanorum* ("Deeds of the Trojans").

2. The question regarding an approximate date for a local historical memory of a story about Aineias —in essence, an historical connection between Rome and Troy— can be seen later, in VIII. PELASGIAN TROJANISM AND THE NEW ILLYRIANS.

Eventually, erudite knowledges, rumours of his whereabouts, and old-wives tales were handed down from one generation to another (*The Oxford Classical Dictionary*. 1999):

> The list of Aineias' westward wanderings towards Italy is already long and contradictory by the 1st cent. BC (cf. Dion. Hal. 1. 44–64), including cities and cults supposedly named after him in Thrace, Chalcidice, Epirus, and Sicily, and visits to Delos, and Crete. A visit to Carthage, possibly involving a meeting with Dido, is certainly part of the itinerary by the time of Naevius' *Bellum Punicum* (3rd cent. BC), where it is seen as an ancestral cause of the enmity between Rome and Carthage. As Rome confronted a Greek-speaking Mediterranean world in the 3rd cent. BC, it found it politically and culturally useful to claim as its founder Aineias, famous through his appearance in Homer, but also an enemy of the Greeks; a particular stimulus was the invasion of Italy by Pyrrhus of Epirus (280 BC), who claimed descent from Achilles and saw Rome as a second Troy (Paus. 1. 12. 2). In consequence, Roman poets (e.g. Ennius), historians (e.g. Cato (Censorius), and antiquarians (e.g. Varro) stressed the Trojan origins of Rome; considerations of chronology eventually lead to the view that Aineias founded not Rome, but a preceding city, Lavinium, and that Rome's eponymous founder Romulus was his distant descendant.

One of the places presumably founded by Aineias was *Aenona*, today Nin (though the environs evince human habitation from much earlier times), some 17 kilometers northwest of Zadar. To the east rises the stark *Mons Albius* (Velebit Range), a sight that cannot be separated from the quaint aspect of the modern town[3]. Another place visited by Aineias before he left Adriatic waters was *Bouthrotum*[4], now Butrinto, on the southern border of Albania with Epirus. Virgil makes Aineias stop here for a short stay (*Aeneid*, III, 344, *et pas.*):

> "Such words she [Andromache] poured forth weeping, and was idly awaking a long lament, when the hero Helenus, Priam's son, draws near from the city with a great company. He knows us for his kin, joyfully leads us to the gate, and freely pours forth tears at every word. I advance, and recognize a little Troy, with a copy of great Pergamus, and a dry brook that takes its name from Xanthus, and embrace the portals of a Scaean gate.

Aineias eventually reached RHYTION (*Lavinium*, Pratica de Mare) on the shores of *Latium*, where he was met with enmity by the Rutuli, an ancient people of the region[5], but his son Ascanius eventually moved the

---

3. *Mons Albius* should read *Mons Albus* or *Albanus*, for there is a marked difference between *albi-* and *alba-* place names: Albion, Elbe, and related names like *Lusitania*, Lucerne, are probably of Celtic origin and associated with an early date now lost in the mist of myth when Giants wandered over the face of Europe, prior to the Deluge. Names like Albania and *Alba Longa* are post-Trojan, for which reason the association of Aineas with *Albius* reads oddly, anachronistically, since it is difficult to relate ante-Diluvian Celts with this area (but not impossible).

4. *Bouthrotum*, like *Bosphoros* ("Oxford") seems likewise associated with things Trojan, albeit it is likely a generic-type toponym.

seat of a new government to *Alba Longa*, on the slopes of LYKTOS (*Lacus Albanus*) and LYKASTOS (*Albanum*) in the Alban Hills, south-east of Rome.

Now, the *tour de force* in the story of Aineias is that his genealogy goes back to Dardanus (XX, 215), whose birthplace is a matter of some confusion as a result of many places changing names as new states, new frontiers, and new languages blossomed here and there after the Fall of Troy: GORTYNA (or Gortynaia) was thought to have become Cortona, where, according to Lycophron (*Alexandra*, 208, early 3rd cent. BC), Ulysses (*alias* Etruscan Vlixes/Uluxe, and most certainly *not* to be confused with Odysseus) was buried[6]. Later, Virgil (*Aeneid*, vii, 207) made Dardanus come from the Tuscan town of Cortona which his father Corythus founded (ibid. ix, 10); thus, the inference to the best explanation is that Corythus will have founded GORTYNA (Γόρτυν), one of the cities of KRETE mentioned in the *Catalogue of Ships* (II, 646), which became Rome. The meaning of the name is "city" (conveying, of course, the grand effort and accomplishment of building one), derived from a root **grd-* from which words such as *gorod* and *grad,* also meaning "city". Furthermore, an early link between this area and Troy is to be found in the many stories about Skamandros, a Cretan prince, and his youthful companion, Teucros (whose name, it seems, is akin with that of the KRETES).

(V)ENETIAN DISPLACEMENTS AND PANNONIAN ARRIVALS

The arrival of Menelaos with Helen into the area of LAKEDAIMON (the Veneto; *Catalogue of Ships* ¶7) displaced a number of folks, among them

---

5. The names of RHYTION and *Lavinium* would appear to coincide in association of ideas, and that of the Rutuli is certainly more than a phonetic coincidence, albeit the meaning of the name connotes the root **ru-*, whence *ruber* and *rufus*. That the seat of the Rutuli was regarded as the nearby town of (V)*Ardea* is incorrect, for this place fell to the PAIONES.

6. Classical academicians of old and of the present seem to derive much glee from the would-be contrapuntal positions of a Greek Ulysses (whom Homer calls Odysseus) sojouring in the same beaches as his former Trojan enemy Aineias. The *deus ex machina* is delightfully jejune: the one gains a son, Telegonos, while the other loses a father, Anchises; the deceitful conqueror becomes lost in Latium, the pious vanquished-one goes on to found Rome, and so on. See François Hartog (trad. Horacio Pons), *Memorias de Ulises, Relatos sobre la frontera en la antigua Grecia*. México, Argentina: Fondo de Cultura Económica, 1999, p. 221 ff and fn.: Dionisio de Halicarnaso, *Les antiquites romaines*, I, 72, 2, traducción de Valérie Fromentin y Jacques Schnäbele, París, Les Belles Lettres, 1990. Un manuscrito dice *después* de y no *con* Ulises. C. Ampolo, "Enea ed Ulisse nel Lazio da Hellanico a Festo", en *Parola del passato*, 47, 1992, pp. 321–341; F. Solmsen, "Aeneas Founded Rome with Odysseus", en *Harvard Studies in Classical Philology*, 90, 1986, pp. 93–110. Sobre Eneas como figura de reconciliación entre griegos y troyanos, y por lo tanto también romanos, véase A. Momigliano, "How to Reconcile Greeks and Trojans", en *Settimo contributo alla storia degli studi classici e del mondo antico*, Storia e Letteratura, Roma, 1984, pp. 437–461. E. Bickerman, "Origines gentium", en *Classical Philology*, 47, 1952, pp. 65–81.

the ENETI (*Venetii*; *Catalogue Trojan Forces*, ¶7), who migrated eastward (in the direction of least resistance) and settled in the general area of Pannonia (Hungary and Slovenia). It was, perhaps, news about the recent displacements of these folks that took Paris to that general area of the Veneto to survey the gravity of the damage done by AKHAIAN invasions which gave place to the abduction of Helen, a Pelasgian woman, and therefore, culturally, a Trojan.

After the Fall of Troy another band of Trojans, the ruling elite or sires (pana) of Troy, emigrated and settled among kin, displaced Eneti. With these folks there also emigrated DARDANIOI —or perhaps the reverse is the case, that it was an elite DARDANIOI or *panas* who emigrated— and also a folk from the Neretva delta known as *Vardaei* or *Vardjaei*[7]. The general area became known as Pannonia (*pana*, "sires" + *-ones*, Illyrian suffix denoting social agglomeration).

In time, the Greek perception of these two migratory movements of ENETI and TROES now occupying a new territory —its causes and effects never really understood— gave rise to a belief that a certain Antenor, an Elder of Ilios, had led a band of Eneti, from Paphlagonia on the Euxine, and stopped in Korčula (where his house is candidly pointed out by eager tourist guides), from whence he went on to the marshy delta of the Po, where the Eneti settled, and, eventually, became the founder of *Patavium*, Padua[8].

Pannonia became the point of departure for two major migrations, in opposite directions. The one, went up-stream the Danube, across the Raetian Alps, into the headwaters of the Rhine, and thence downstream into the North Atlantic, where the name of the Veneti became established on the coast of Brittany (a folk that Julius Caesar met in 50–49 BC). The other went northeast, into the Baltic region, where the name of the Vends (Eneti) became established[9], and, further, in an arc, as far into Russia as Moscow.

7. Why these Trojan folk are *not* mentioned in Homer is a conundrum: the fact is, they have been accounted for under a different name, that of the DARDANIOI, who are *not* the progeny of Dardanus, but, rather, the offspring of the river SKAMANDROS (that is, a folk common to the river-valley, and thus synonymous with the PAIONES, whose name means, simply, "river folk"). The corollary to this identity is that the name of Dardanus has one meaning, but the inference that the name of the DARDANIOI means the same as that of their (would-be) eponymous ancestor is a gross mistake in logical thinking, and means something entirely different —probably "fig" or "wild pear", abundant in the region— from which the deduction that in the linguistic investigations of the *Iliad* and *Odyssey* there are *two* languages in play.

8. Other convoluted stories, of a far later date, derived from Frankish sources (below), purport to explain origins of names (Germanic Sugambri, Pannonian Sycambria; the name of the Franks from that of Francio, a son of Hector) and establish a genealogy, if not directly from King Priam, certainly from Antenor himself.

WESTERN EUROPEAN TROY LEGENDS

Now, conventional scholarship is aware of stories about a Trojan heritage in the evolution of a Western European culture: on the one hand, the Trojan ancestry in the history of the Franks until it comes into full bloom in the direct genealogical descent of the great Charlemagne from King Priam of Troy; on the other hand, the arrival of Brut, a grandson of Aineias, in England, where he founded New Troy which later became London.

One might be prone to seek a justification for these legends, not so much to learn about *why* they came to be, nor *when,* but *where* they came from —as if somehow they were legitimized by some sort of umbilical memory— for one could likewise ask, why specifically Trojan origins, and not, say, some descent from Vedic sources or Tartaric migrations?

THE PANNONIAN ORIGIN OF THE FRANKS

Gregory, Bishop of Tours (538–594 AD), wrote in his *Historia Francorum* (II, 9):

> The historians whose works we still have give us all this information about the Franks, but they never record the names of their kings. It is commonly said that the Franks came originally from Pannonia [Hungary] and first colonized the banks of the Rhine. Then they crossed the river, marched through Thuringia, and set up in each country district and each city long-haired kings chosen from the foremost and most noble family of their race.

Subsequently, three manuscripts compiled between 658–661 AD as a *Chronica*, recapitulate the first six books of Gregory's *Historia Francorum* but added that Trojans escaping the Sack of Troy were led westward by Frigia, and that Francion, later called Francus, brought them to the Rhine. All the extant manuscripts of this chronicle are anonymous, and its ascription to a certain Fredegarius, presumed to have been a Burgundian monk, dates from an edition by Claude Fauchet (Paris) in 1579. This Fredegarius drew for early Merovingian times on information derived from the *Historia Francorum* of Gregory of Tours, which ends with the year 591, three years before Gregory's death, and chronicles events among the Franks between 584 and 642. The manuscript is important —albeit said to be written in a barbarous Latin— because the events mentioned are contemporary, and hence a unique source of information for this period.

9. Matej Bor, with Josko Savli, and Ivan Tomazic, in their work on pre-Greek Balkan paleography have assembled a list of thirty words current in Britanny, Poland, and Slovenia of identical or similar meaning, given in their *Veneti, First Builders of European Community*. Canada, British Columbia: Anton Skerbinc, 1996.

Still later, a century after Fredegarius, another anonymous *Liber historiae Francorum* makes Aineias reign in Troy during a ten-year siege, while Priam and Antenor led refugees to Pannonia. There they built a city which they called Sicambria, and some time later, when these Trojans helped subdue the Alans, Valentinian I (321–375 AD), a native of Cibalae, in Pannonia, called them Franks, on account of their ferocity. However, still later, when tax-collectors were sent to collect their due they were killed by the Franks, whereupon Roman forces were sent to seek revenge. The Franks then moved away to the farthest reaches of the Rhine, where German strongholds were located, and in time they chose from among the decent of Priam a certain Faramund, who begat Clodio, who begat Merovech, who begat Childeric...

BRUT AND THE FOUNDATION OF TRINOVANTUM
According to the *Historia regum Britanniae* of Geoffrey of Monmouth († 1155), a Welsh monk, Brutus, or Brut, a grandson of Aineias, arrived in England in 1074 BC, 109 years after the traditional Fall of Troy. His account is steeped in Trojan lore (Aaron Thompson, *The British History, Translated into English from the Latin of Jeffrey of Monmouth*, London, 1718:

> CHAP. XVI Albion divided between Brutus and Corineus.
> The Island was then called *Albion*, and was inhabited by none but a few Giants. Not withstanding the pleasant Situation of Places, the Plenty of Rivers abounding with Fish, and the engaging Prospect of Woods, made *Brutus* and his Company very desirous to fix their Habitation in it...
>
> CHAP. XVII The Building of *New Troy* by *Brutus* upon the River *Thames*.
> ... Here [along the shore of the River Thames] therefore he built a City, which he called *New Troy*; under which name it continued a long Time after, till at last by the Corruption of the Original Word, it came to be called *Trinovantum*. But Afterwards when *Lud*, the Brother of *Cassibellaun*, who made War against *Julius Caesar*...

In the reference to Lud, above, there is mention of his brother, a certain Nennius, of the 8th century, a would-be author of an *Historia Britonum*, who objected changing the name of *Trinovantum* to that of *Caer Lud* (from where eventually the name of London), but Thompson minces words and cautiously avoids this issue, leaving one at odds about what Nennius had to say, if anything, regarding the foundations of *Trinovantum* by Brutus. Thompson prefaces his translation of Monmouth with a criticism of those in England who were opposed to this history:

> ...John of Westhamstede, an obscure writer of the fifteenth Century... [and] indeed the famous Polydore Virgils [sic] contempt of it has been shewn to proceed from his

IV. THE TROJAN DIASPORA

Vanity in extolling his countrymen the Romans, whom he would by no means allow the Britains to rival either in Valour or Nobility of Descent.

The origin of the Brut story appears to be steeped in European lore, rather than in any plausible memory of an historical event (R. Garnett and E. Gosse, *English Literature, An Illustrated Record*, I, p. 79–80):

> ... [Layamon's] *Brut* is the fabulous history of the settlement in Britain of Brutus and his Trojans... it is professedly a paraphrase of the *Brut* of the French poet Wace, author of the *Roman de Rou*. The French *Brut* was written in 1155... Wace himself derived his tale from the Latin *Historia Britonum* of Geoffrey of Monmouth, written about 1147... in so far as his history did not follow Nennius, it was derived from a book of Breton legends, now lost. Among them was the tale of the Trojan colonisation of Britain, which could not have arisen either among Celts or Teutons until they had come under Latin influence; but, once invented, was soon accepted as an unquestionable fact.

The appearance of any sort of Trojan legend among Celts or Teutons until after their exposure to Latin literature (and *thence* taken to England) is an inference to the best explanation, for, certainly, there is no other reasonable explanation.

The "New Troy" of Geoffrey of Monmouth which became "Trinovantum" reads in the wrong order, for the *Trinovantes*, a peoples residing on the shores of the Thames, will have built *Trinoventum*, whose meaning could, conceivably, be understood as that of "New Troy" on a cue of *tri-* and *tro-* with "three". There *is* no earlier reference to the *Trinobantes* than that found in Julius Caesar's *De Bello Gallicum*, V, 20–22, and, so, how these peoples acquired their name is anybody's guess.

According to Geoffrey of Monmouth, Cassibelaunus routed Julius Caesar from England. However, Julius Caesar describes having stood on the right bank of the Thames, opposite the city of the *Trinovantes* (more or less at the place where Shakespeare's *Julius Caesar* was performed at the Globe Theatre some 16 centuries later) and had little to say of the sight, and nothing whatsoever about being routed from the place. Geoffrey goes on to mention, with some regret, how Lud, brother of Cassibelaunus, changed the name of "*Trinovantum*" to Caer Lud or "City" of Lud, whence *Caerlond, Lugdunum, Londinium*, London.

So it is, then, that stories about the Trojan origins of London are not in Nennius, or Gildas, or some lost book of Breton legends (albeit a possibility), nor can they be ascribed to contact with the Graeco-Roman tradition, but, rather, to an import of Saxon stories about a Trojan paternity.

EASTERN EUROPEAN CONNECTIONS WITH TROY

By contrast with Western European Troy legends which seem to have been taken abroad only by TROES, and hence an emphasis on a Trojan genealogical descent, as well as an association with *tro-/tri-* "three" place names, the Eastern European Troy legends seem to have evolved from a population of migrating DARDANIOI, which is as much as to say *Vardjaei* or *Vardaei*, who left their alias in new settlements. The following quote regarding DARDANIOI seems *à propos* (Lengyel, A. and Radan, G. T. B. (eds.), *The Archaeology of Roman Pannonia*. p. 22:

> Nevertheless, some tribes of the pre-Roman middle Danube area remain the subject of controversy. Let's take, for example, the Dardanians, whose troublesome existence in the Ancient World is matched by the troubles they have created in modern research.

An adequate understanding of how the apparently unrelated names of DARDANIOI and *Vardjaei* are juggled and how the name of the PAIONES fits into this equation is important to an understanding of how these people were responsible for the success of the Dorian Invasions into Hellas, and, as such, for laying the geographical and cultural bridge-work for the transference of the *Iliad* and *Odyssey* into a new Hellenic context (see below, IX. THE MAKINGS OF HELLAS).

THE FOUNDATION OF WARSAW

The Vardzaei (the Ar*dz*awa of Hittite documents) went in a northeastern direction —sometime in the early Iron Age?— and settled at a place on the Vista or Vistula a few miles upstream from where this river is fed by the Narev, and founded Warszawa/Warsaw. The similarity of the Narev with that of the *Narenta*, Neretva, seems obvious, and, further, the Neretva is registered as the *Vissena* in the *Theatrum Orbis Terrarum* of the Flemish geographer, Abraham Ortelius (1527–1598). The symbol of this city is, aptly, an ondine, one of the fifty daughters of Neleus.

Evidently, the migration of ENETI/Vends and DARDANIOI/Var*j*aei into the Baltic region brought with them a vast cornucopia of pagan myth, little of which, if any, today, has a meaning beyond "the crazy ideas and ugly figures that those people (Slavs) believed in…", unless this body of knowledges can be understood in the context of its *source*, as follows below.

THE FOUNDATION OF MOSCOW

The folks who had come into the plains (*polje*) of Poland and founded Warsaw, went on even further, far into Russia, and came to the site of Moscow.

Now, something about the relationship between Tros and Ilos, and the cities of ILIOS (Drijeva/Gabela) and TROIA (Daorson), is already understood (pp. 98–99), and it is from this relationship that the figure of Ilos, the totemic fire-fly, emerges as a self-evident magical phenomenon, an ember-spark, a wisp of light, born from the spontaneous combustion of marsh gases or from lightning bolts. In time, the identity of Ilos became that of Perun, a divinity of fire and lightning known throughout the Slavic World. Still later, Perun became Christianized, and his identity taken by that of Elijah, of whom it is said that he arose into heaven in a flaming quadriga. He is heard to this day thundering through the clouds whenever there is a lightning storm.

Another local identity of Ilos was that of Mosk, and his cheerful brother Radgost, who was murdered by the Rom[10]. A title for Radgost was Svetiarilo, whose name is not quite "santo cabrón", but, rather, more on the order of "visibly goatlike", sexually unrestrained, the equivalent of the Greek Pan. A connection between Ilos and Mosk is seen in the identity of Ilos as Meschech in the *Table of Nations* (*Genesis*, X, 22–22), whom Greeks identified as Moschos. According to later Greek lore, the (twin?) brother of Ilos, Ganymedes, was removed from sight on account of his androgynous beauty, albeit Radgost, who will have been "gay" (in that unhappy use of the word), was murdered by the Rom, *another* name for the DARDANIOI.

Mosk became the founder of Moskva/Moscow. Be that as it may, the arrival from Rome (Constantinople/Istanbul) in Moscow during the 12th century AD of the first Tzarist presence among Russian peoples brought not only political innovations (and their subsequent social consequences), but a host of "Roman" lore, that is, recollections about this or that event or personage of former times, and variant versions of these, of when Troy was an empire.

So it is that Moscow is also known as the Third Rome. Oddly (but understandably?) there was a movement afoot in Mexico City towards the end of the 1700s sponsored by the Jesuit order to dub this city as the Fourth Rome, on the premise that the conquest of (almost all) America by Spain (that is, in fact, the spiritual police of Rome over the souls of uneducated heathen) represented a secondary phase of Western

---

10. Radivoje Pešic (ed.), *Velesova Kniga*, Fr. 33. Beograd: Pešic i Sinovi, 1999. This work contains invaluable information on early Slavic myth and history, compiled from earliest sources and assembled in Novgorod between the 7th and 9th centuries AD. A Russian version of this work exists, albeit differing in format (and perhaps not as reliable).

Civilization. The effort failed. Vast tracts of former Spanish territory fell into the incompetent management of know-nothing Free Masons who soon lost it to those who were conversant with what had, by now, become unalienable and universal principles of Law.

2. The Odyssey

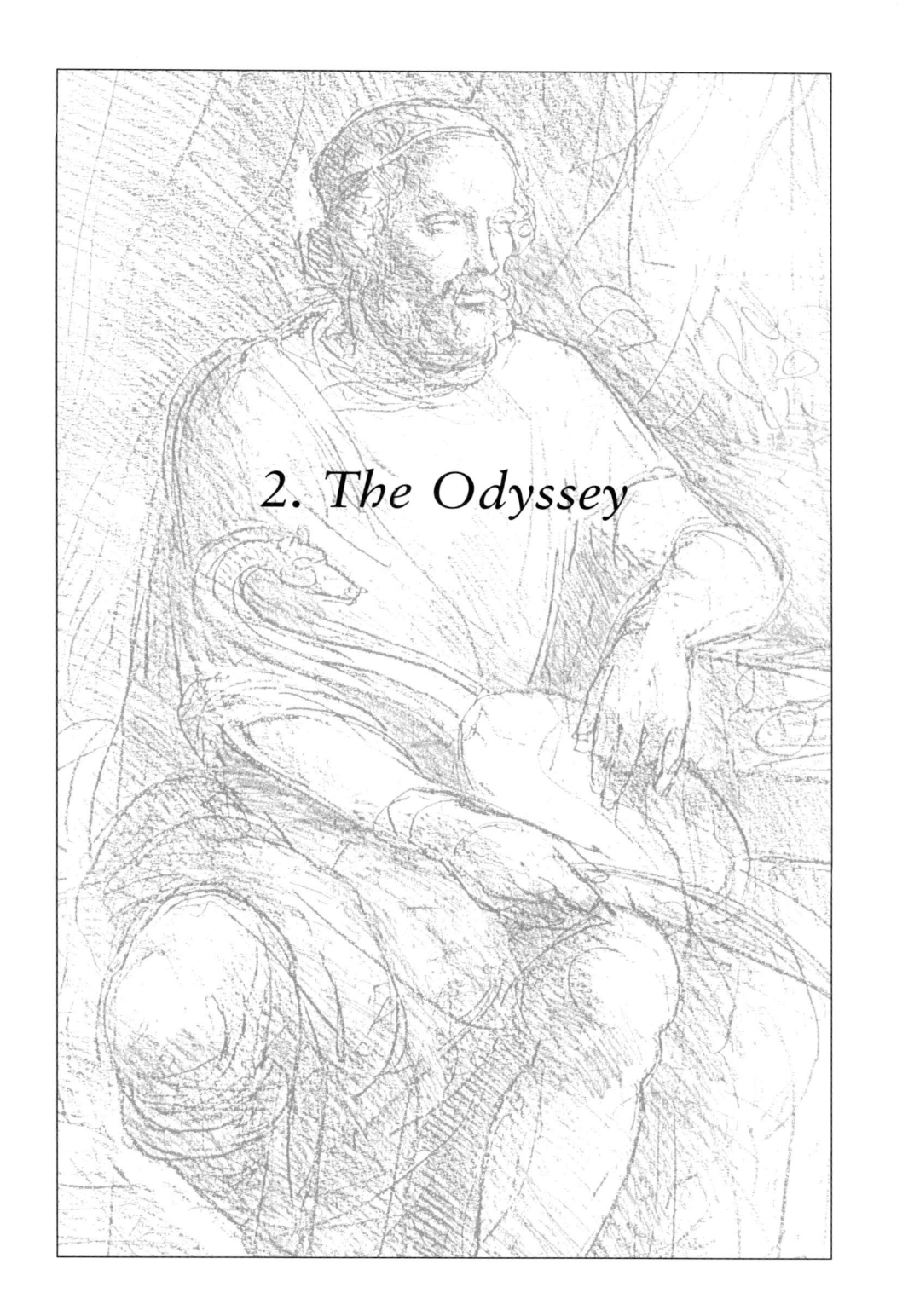

CHAPTER V

THE ODYSSEY AND ITS FANTASTIC GEOGRAPHY

The methodology used in the *Odyssey* for the structure of an apparatus of geographical information is the same as that used in the *Iliad*, though it differs in format and detail. Its information depends, in a measure, on the geography already established in the *Iliad* (and so, *à priori*, it may not vary from it), and is divided into two major units of geographical information, THE WORLD ABROAD and THE ILLYRIAN HOMELAND. Each of these units in turn is made up of three different kinds of information, each of which, again, comprises groups of physical and social concepts of geography (TABLE 5.1).

KNOWN GEOGRAPHY

Information about peoples and places already known through the *Iliad's* apparatus of geographical information may be thought of as common knowledge. This information, though first acquired through the *Iliad*, in the *Odyssey* is often expanded on with sundry details.

SUPPLEMENTARY GEOGRAPHY

Additional information about peoples and places to what to has already been established in the *Iliad's* apparatus of geographical information.

THE WORLD ABROAD	THE ILLYRIAN HOMELAND
KNOWN GEOGRAPHY physical concepts social concepts	KNOWN GEOGRAPHY physical concepts social concepts
SUPPLEMENTARY GEOGRAPHY physical concepts social concepts	SUPPLEMENTARY GEOGRAPHY physical concepts social concepts
FICTITIOUS GEOGRAPHY physical concepts social concepts	FICTITIOUS GEOGRAPHY physical concepts social concepts

TABLE 5.1. BASIC DIVISION OF THE ODYSSEY'S GEOGRAPHY. *The stark division into two distinct groups of geographical data, as in the Iliad, relates to the shaping of a novel world-order.*

KNOWN GEOGRAPHY

PHYSICAL CONCEPTS

SEA	ISLANDS	MOUNTAINS
AIGAI	LEMNOS	NERITON
HELLESPONTOS	LESBOS	SAMOS
OKEANOS	TENEDOS	
	ZAKYNTHOS	
	(LEKTON)[1] Same	

SOCIAL CONCEPTS

DISTRICTS	PEOPLES	TOWNS
TROIA	KEPHALLENES	DOULIKHION
	KIKONES	ILIOS
	SINTIES	ITHAKA
	TROES	THEBE
	(KILIKES)[2] Kadmeiones	Skyros[3]

SUPPLEMENTARY GEOGRAPHY

PHYSICAL CONCEPTS

SPRINGS	ISLANDS	MOUNTAINS
Arethousa	Asteris	Hermaios
		Korax
		Neion

SOCIAL CONCEPTS

HARBOURS	PEOPLES	CAPES
Nerikos	Harpyiai	Leukas
Phorkys		
Rheithron		

FICTITIOUS GEOGRAPHY

PHYSICAL CONCEPTS

SPRINGS	ISLANDS	STRAIGHTS
Artakia	Aiaia	Kharybdis
	Aiolia	
	Ogygia	
	Planktai	
	Skheria	
	Thrinakia	

SOCIAL CONCEPTS

HARBOURS	PEOPLES	TOWNS
Telepylos	Kyklopes	Ismaros
	Laistrygones	
	Lotophagoi	
	Phaiakes	
	Seirenes	
	Skylla	

TABLE 5. 2. THE ODYSSEY'S GEOGRAPHY OF THE ILLYRIAN HOMELAND. The Odyssey's apparatus of geographical information. 1. LECTON emended to read Same; 2. KILIKES emended to read Kadmeioi. 3. Skyros is an interpolation, superfluous to an apparatus of geographical information.

V. THE ODYSSEY AND ITS FANTASTIC GEOGRAPHY

This information, albeit sparce, relates to NERITON (Pelješac Peninsula), which was occupied by KEPHALLENES, but also establishes the presence of the **Harpyiai** as a people, and not any sort of demiurge.

FICTITIOUS GEOGRAPHY

Information about monstrous creatures and strange places in the Land of Nevernever visited by Odysseus (while in a drunken stupor?). This information is of an allegorical nature, albeit, nevertheless, subject to classification according to geographical concepts.

GEONYMS AND A GENERAL RULE

A geonym in the *Odyssey* functions in the same manner as it does in the *Iliad* (that is, it is a one-word geographical statement). However, the rule observed in the *Odyssey* is the reverse of that in the *Iliad*, namely, that *a place* may have two names, a former and a latter, albeit *different places* may not have the same name.

CONCEPTS AND GEOGRAPHICAL PARADIGMS

Four new geographical concepts have been introduced into a geography of the ILLYRIAN HOMELAND, namely, 1) springs and 2) straights, which are physical concepts, and 3) harbours and 4) capes, which are social concepts. It would seem that capes should be reckoned as a social rather than as a physical concept. However, for as much as there exist many prominent capes on the highly indented islands and coastline, only one cape has been singled out for its characteristics, therefore making it a social concept.

Again, as with the *Iliad*, each concept (with two or more geonyms) forms a geographical paradigm, that is, the schematic distribution of geonyms to a specific region. The symmetry of a geographical paradigm is central to an understanding of Homeric Geography.

PHYSICAL CONCEPTS		SOCIAL CONCEPTS	
SEA	3	DISTRICTS	1
ISLANDS	12	PEOPLES	12
SPRINGS	2	HARBOURS	4
MOUNTAINS	5	TOWNS	5
STRAIGHTS	1	CAPES	1
total:	23		23

TABLE 5. 3. GEOGRAPHICAL CONCEPTS OF THE ODYSSEY. There are five concepts of physical geography and five concepts of social geography.

RATIOS OF PHYSICAL CONCEPTS TO SOCIAL CONCEPTS		
KNOWN GEOGRAPHY	SUPPLEMENTARY GEOGRAPHY	FICTITIOUS GEOGRAPHY
1 : 1	1 : 1	1 : 1

TABLE 5.4. RATIOS. The ratio of concepts in KNOWN GEOGRAPHY cannot be 1:1 if, for instance, Skyros is to be regarded as a genuine geonym.

RATIO OF PHYSICAL CONCEPTS TO SOCIAL CONCEPTS

The net ratios of physical concepts to social concepts is an important mechanism of internal control in Homeric Geography, that helps keep geographical data from falling out of kilter.

CORRUPTIONS AND EMENDATIONS

In the course of time the text has suffered a deterioration. Thus, under the concept of islands, the name of Same reads oddly, wanting a sense of geographical reality, and should be understood as a substitution for LEKTON (*Pharos/Lessina*, Hvar). Again, under the concept of peoples, the name of the Kadmeioi likewise reads oddly, geographically out of schematic balance with the list of other peoples, perhaps to be thought of as a restoration —to the best understanding of an editor— for the name of the KILIKES (the southernmost peoples of Troy).

IDENTIFICATIONS*

The identification of Odyssean geonyms with toponyms and ethnicons along the length of Croatia's Dalmatian Coast may be said to fall into three general categories, thus—

- first, those which may be said to be still intact
- second, those which may be said to be intact albeit in translation
- third, those whose identification is adduced from a geographical sense enclosed in the geonym, or from some indication in the text

---

*. I owe the shaping of my understanding of the *Odyssey* to the late Aristid S. Vučetić, of 4 Kuničeva Ul., Dubrovnik, who, in the Summer of 1967, and later in subsequent correspondence, taught me much about the many, many places along the Dalmatian Coast visited by Odysseus. To him, once again, I give full credit for the discovery that the Wanderings of Odysseus occured in these waters.

V. THE ODYSSEY AND ITS FANTASTIC GEOGRAPHY

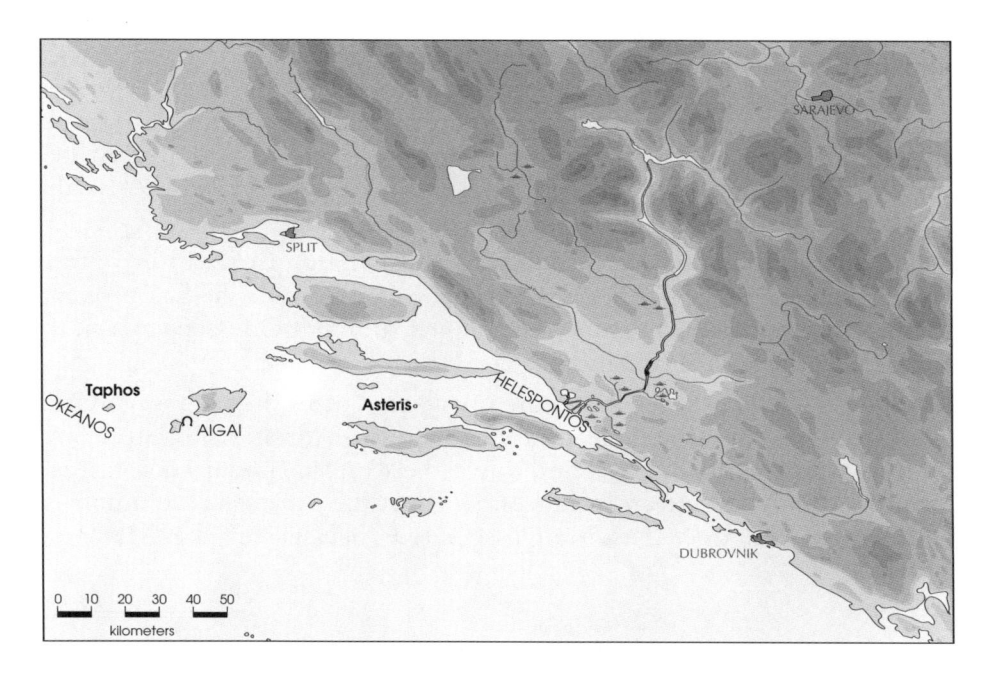

SEA

The nomenclature for the paradigm of the SEA has changed: the name of [IKAROPONTOS], in whose very waters Odysseus bobbed like the flotsam and jetsam that originally inspired this geonym before reaching **Skheria** (Sčedro), is noticeably absent. However, two other geonyms have appeared, which, although strictly not names of the SEA, are best understood in the context of this paradigm, namely, the small island of **Taphos** (Svetac) (which, like KYTHERA, **Kythereia** (Palagruza), is not properly a part of Trojan Geography), and the even smaller island of **Asteris** (Pločica).

"FOREIGN" GEOGRAPHY		"DOMESTIC" GEOGRAPHY
OKEANOS	AIGAI	HELLESPONTOS
(Taphos) place of death	Asteris place of murder	

TABLE 5. 6. GEONYMS FOR THE SEA. The location of geonyms for SEA relative to each other would suggest their increasing importance outwards from the mainland. Ironically, the geonym for the waters in which the Misadventures of Odysseus occurs (that is, his narration about his woes) is absent.

KNOWN GEOGRAPHY

HELLESPONTOS (Ἑλλήσποντος), the marshy delta of the SKAMANDROS (*Naro*, Neretva): a place where a barrow for Akhilleus, Patroklos, and Antilokhos may be erected that may be seen by all (xxiv, 82), must be the very same place as BATIEIA (Kozjak, 82 mts.), also called the Tomb of Myrine (II, 811).

AIGAI (Αἰγαί), the marine grotto Modra Spilja (Balun Cove, Biševo): the glorious palace that Poseidon goes to (v, 380) as soon as he has broken up the raft of Odysseus, scattered its planks, and sent Odysseus to a similar palace, the palace of Alkinoos (vii, 81).

OKEANOS (Ὠκεανός), generally, the open sea, but in the *Odyssey* more identified with the strong maritime current of the Adriatic Sea that flows up the eastern (Balkan) coast and down the western (Italian) coast: it is mentioned only in sixteen instances, short of the nineteen, the number with which OKEANOS has been associated (because of the Metonic Cycle).

		OKEANOS IN THE WEST
x,	508:	cross OKEANOS and come to grove of Persephone...
x,	511:	at grove of Persephone beach ship by OKEANOS...
xi,	13:	ships came to furthest marge of deep-flowing OKEANOS
xi,	21:	beached our ships and went beside stream of OKEANOS
		LOCAL FACTS ABOUT OKEANOS
iv,	568:	OKEANOS sends the Zephyr to Elysian Plain
v,	275:	Bear or Wain does not bathe in OKEANOS
x,	139:	Kirke and Aeetes born from Perse, whom OKEANOS begot
xi,	158:	Between world and Hades two rivers and streams, OKEANOS is first
xi,	639:	ships borne down stream of OKEANOS...
xii,	1:	ships left stream of river OKEANOS and come to sea and Aiaian isle
xx,	65:	cast forth at mouth of backward-flowing OKEANOS
xxiv,	11:	Hermes leads souls past (rock of Leukas and streams of OKEANOS)
		OKEANOS IN THE EAST
xix,	434:	the sun rising from soft-gliding, deep-flowing OKEANOS
xxii,	197:	early Dawn comes forth from streams of OKEANOS
xxiii,	244,:	Athene stayed Dawn at streams of OKEANOS
xxiii,	347:	Athene rouses Dawn from OKEANOS

TABLE 5. 7. REFERENCES TO OKEANOS. The general misunderstanding about the Odyssey's correct geographical context frequently called for the editorial emendation of otherwise sound text, as in xxiv 11 (and perhaps other instances where clarity is wanting).

V. THE ODYSSEY AND ITS FANTASTIC GEOGRAPHY

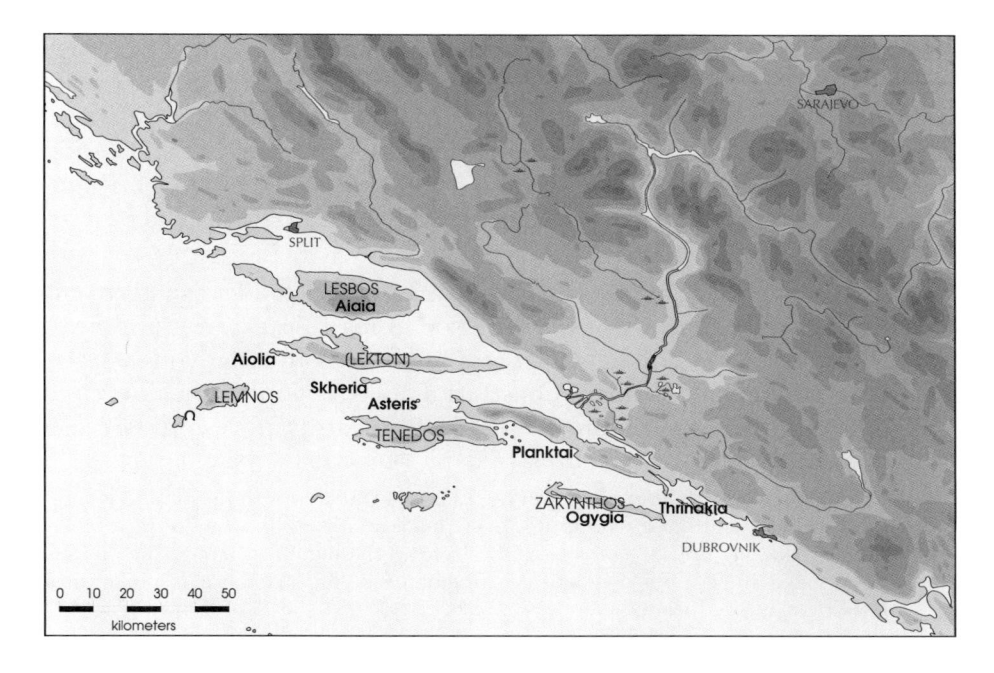

ISLANDS

Of ISLANDS, the names of some are already known from the *Iliad*, while the double identity of others is revealed. Also, a number of small islets, hitherto ignored, now take on an identity.

KNOWN ISLANDS

The former control of the coast exerted by Troy has been reduced, under the new political order, to include only those islands that have a relevance to the affairs of NERITON (Pelješac).

LESBOS (Λέσβος), *Tauria/Brattia*, Brač: the island is mentioned by old Nestor as the place where Menelaos overtook him on their respective returns to PYLOS and SPARTA after the Fall of Troy (iii, 169), and twice again (iv, 342; xvii, 133) as the place where Odysseus upon a time wres-

	LESBOS	
	(LECTON) Same	
LEMNOS	----------------	NERITON (Pelješac)
	TENEDOS	
	ZAKYNTHOS	

TABLE 5. 9. GEONYMS OF KNOWN ISLANDS. The name of Same (inspired on that of SAMOS?) replaced the name of LEKTON, which read out of kilter with the presumed location of the Odyssean homeland in the Ionian Isles of the western coast of Hellas.

tled and bested a certain Philomeleides (much to the glee of the AKHAIOI present). The name of Philomeleides, depending on whether the name is to be read with ε or η, means either "honey lover" or "sheep lover", and may be the cue, perhaps, on account of his sweetness, to the story (not originally in Homer) told in Apollodorus, *Library*, III, xiii, 8 about Akhilleus being discovered by Odysseus at SKYROS (Pušica), dressed as a girl.

[LEKTON] (Λεκτόν), Pharos, Hvar: the name of this island was altered by (pre-Alexandrine?) editors of the Odyssey to read Σάμη (an island near that of Ithaka), to suit the new geography of Troy in Asia Minor, since Lecton (a site on the southern coast) in a context with Dulichium and Zacynthos (islands at the mouth of the Gulf of Patras in western Greece) would make no sense whatsoever, thus (i, 245; xvi, 123; xix, 131):

> "...all the princes who hold sway over the islands—Dulichium and Same and wooded Zacynthus—and those who lord it over rocky Ithaca, all these woo my mother and lay waste my house. And she neither refuses the hateful marriage, nor is she able to make an end; but they with feasting consume my substance: ere long they will bring me, too, to ruin".

The above, then, should read as "aristoi from Doulikhion, and the wooded isles of Lekton and Zakynthos..." on the basis that this reading makes for a sounder triad (where two elements are similar, and the third is different but an inseparable part of the whole) since it is already known that DOULIKHION is not an island, but a port-town, and that SAMOS is not an island, but a mountain (*Table 5.3*). Thus, the reading of xvi, 250, "aristoi from Dulichium (52), [Lekton] (24), Zacynthos (24) (which woo Penelope...)" seems to have a smoother understanding. Still again, elsewhere, the context of geonyms with ITHAKA made necessary the substitution of [Lekton], a presumed place on the Troad, for Same (ix, 24):

> But I [Odysseus] dwell in clear-seen Ithaca, wherein is a mountain, Neriton, covered with waving forests, conspicuous from afar; and round it lie many isles, hard by one another, Dulichium, and Same [Lekton], and wooded Zacynthus. Ithaca itself lies close to the mainland (χθαμαλή, that is, on the peninsula which is part of the mainland) the furthest toward the gloom, but the others lie apart, towards the Dawn and the sun...

LEMNOS (Λῆμνος), *Issa*, Vis: the island is inhabited by SINITIES, indeed a *sinister* folk, and so their language is ἀγριοφώνους, "harsh" (viii, 294).

TENEDOS (Τενεδος), *Corcyra Melaina*, Korčula: according to senile Nestor, the first port of call of the Akhaioi returning home upon leaving the Camp of Agamemnon, across the narrow straights (iii, 159).

ZAKYNTHOS (Ζάκυνθος), *Melite*, Mljet: it is odd, indeed, that wooers (*aristoi*) of Penelope came from Dulichium (town), [Lecton] (island),

and Zacynthus (island) (xvi, 250), yet there was no knowledge in ITHA-KA about the nine-year sojourn of Odysseus on ZAKYNTHOS (**Ogygia**).

SUPPLEMENTARY GEOGRAPHY

Asteris ('Ἀστερίς), Pločica: this islet, little more than a rock in the [IKAROPONTOS] (Korčulanski Canal), is the place where the destruction of Telemakhos awaits him xii, 1 et pas.):

> But the wooers embarked, and sailed over the watery ways, pondering in their hearts utter murder for Telemachos. There is a rocky isle in the midst of the sea, midway between Ithaka [read Lemnos] and rugged Samos, Asteris, of no great size, but therein is a harbour where ships may lie, with an entrance on either side. There it was that Achaeans tarried, lying in wait for Telemachos.

Obviously, the name of LEMNOS (*Issa*, Vis) could not remain in the text if Troy was to be identified with the northwestern corner of Asia Minor and Ithaka with an island of the same name at the mouth of the Gulf of Patras, and was emended to read, simply, Ithaka.

Asteris is not mentioned in the *Iliad*, but the isle lies more or less at the place where Iris plummets into the sea to bring death to fishes (XXIV, 77):

> So spake he [Zeus], and storm-footed Iris hasted to bear his message, and midway between Samos and rugged Imbros she leapt into the dark sea, and the waters sounded loud above her. Down she sped to the depths like a plummet of lead, the which, set upon the horn of an ox of the field, goeth down bearing death to the ravenous fishes.

FICTITIOUS GEOGRAPHY

Of the six islands which Odysseus claimed to have visited, three lay north of NERITON (Pelješac), and three to the south. Of these, three are islands that also go by other, earlier names, and three are new to the geography of the *Odyssey*.

Aiaia			
	Aiolia	Skheria	
	Planktai		NERITON (Pelješac)
		Ogygia	Thrinakia

TABLE 5. 10. GEONYMS OF FICTITIOUS ISLANDS. The schematic allocation of geonyms is not only a balance between those sitiated north and south of NERITON, but also a balance between those with a prior identity, and those which are new.

ISLANDS WITH A PRIOR IDENTITY

Aiaia (Αἰαίη), LESBOS, *Thauria/Brattia*, Brač: the dominion of Kirke, a sorceress, the first within the Homeric canon to confirm the traditionally bizarre behaviour of female (and presumably also male?) LESBIDES (x, 135 *et pas.*; xii, 1 *et pas.*):

> "...and we came to the island of Aeaea, where dwell fair-tressed Circe, a dread goddess of human speech, own sister of Aeetes of baneful mind; and both are sprung from Helios, who gives light to mortals, and from Perse, their mother, whom Oceanus begot."

> "Now after our ship had left the streams of Oceanus and had come to the wave of the broad sea, and the Aeaean isle, where is the dwelling of early Dawn and her dancing-lawns, and the risings of the sun, there on our coming we beached our ship on the sands, and ourselves went forth..."

That the location of the "Aeaean isle" should be understood as lying towards the east "where is the dwelling of early Dawn" is correct, since this statement is given by Odysseus on his return trip to Aiaia from the Netherworld (situated at the furthest shores in the west, on the Italian coast).

The "dancing lawns..." (of Dawn) suggest some sort of megalithic observatory on Brač. Indeed, there exist numerous *vinograd* structures on the island (albeit yet uncatalogued), all betraying esoteric features, and perhaps one of these might have had some function as a solar observatory. However, that such an observatory would be so exquisitely described as a ϛερτθυ "dancing lawn" seems like an allusion to Kirke's *circular* web, in whose trap all hapless victims attempt to extricate themselves, as if in a dance of death.

The name Aiaia maybe an onomatopoeic, presumably derived from the wailings of Kirke's happy(?) victims, though some would seek a more likely derivation, from Aia (Αἶα), whence that of Aetes, brother of Kirke (S. West, *Com. Hom. Od.* 52), albeit such an etymology gains nothing. The name, then, must be of the type of a simple reduplicative geonym like GARGAROS (Sveti Ilija and Sveti Jure), or DODONA (Corno Grande and Corno Piccolo), or LELEGES (occupants of hillsides below GARGAROS), that denotes twin mountain peaks, such as those of Vidova Gora (778 m. and 730 m.), the two highest elevations of *all* the islands in the region that rise behind the port-town of Bol, on the island's southern shores.

The name of Vidova Gora, "Vid's Mountain" (that is, Svetovid), at once seems to conjure remains of an unconscious collective memory, as it were: this Slavic deity, according to Saxo Grammaticus, is the paganized version of Saint Vitus (though, in fact, it is the other way about). Svetovid possessed four heads (or alternately four faces) each oriented to the cardinal points; he was credited for being the most accurate of the Slavic pantheon in foretelling the future, in which there appears to have existed a drinking ritual of a brew imbibed from a horn, always mounted during his exhausting nightly travails on a white stallion. The Christianized Saint Vitus, the patron saint of young people and, of all creatures, dogs —one is reminded of the Nordic name Sven, "hound", cognate with "swine" and an association with youth, as in the linguistic connection of Latin *porcus*, "pig" with *puer* "boy"— is closely associated with a malady of the central nervous system known as Sydenham's Chorea.

That Odysseus kills a stag —Illyrian *brentos*, whence Latinized *Brattia* and Graecized *Thauria*— and takes it to the boats for his men to feast on (xxii, 000), is symbolic of a conscious disdain, if not an overt revulsion, of the new patriarchal order established by the invading Akhaioi represented by the stag, in whose antlers is borne a solar disk. **Aiaia** is the northernmost of the Trojan islands, and this event will be repeated in **Thrinakia**, the southernmost of the islands.

Ogygia ('Ὠγυγίη) ZAKYNTHOS, *Melita*, Mljet: home of Kalypso (vii, 244):

> "There is an isle [says Odysseus to Arete], Ogygia, which lies far off in the sea. Therein dwells the fair-tressed daughter of Atlas, guileful Calypso, a dread goddess, and with her no one either of gods or mortals hath aught to do; but me in my wretchedness did fate bring to her hearth alone, for Zeus had smitten my swift ship with his bright thunderbolt, and had shattered it in the midst of the wine-dark sea. There all the rest of my trusty comrades perished, but I clasped in my arms the keel of my curved ship and was borne drifting for nine days, and on the tenth black night the gods brought me to the isle, Ogygia, where the fair-tressed Calypso dwells, a dread goddess. She took me to her home with kindly welcome, and gave me food, and said that she would make me immortal and ageless all my days; but she could never persuade the heart in my breast. There for seven years' space I remained continually, and ever with my tears would I wet the immortal raiment which Calypso gave me. But when the eighth year came in circling course, then she roused me and bade me go, either because of some message from Zeus, or because her own mind was turned. And she sent me on my way on a raft, stoutly bound, and gave me abundant store of bread and sweet wine, and clad me in immortal raiment, and sent forth a gentle wind and warm."

There would seem to be some connection between the girl Khryseis taken from Agamemnon and delivered by Odysseus to her father Khryses at KHRYSA (Sobra) in the days before the Trojan War (I, 430), and Kalypso, "fair tressed...", and "dread goddess...". That a female possessing certain knowledges and powers —whose nature and purpose is not yet adequately understood— was associated with this island may be seen in the modern name of Babino Polje, "Grannie's Field", situated on the island's southern shores. At best, the girl Khryseis represents nothing more than a wench to an otherwise uncouth invader, while the real function of such a female is, perhaps, to be ascertained (if not discovered) in a sister account of the days following the Fall of Troy, the *Odyssey*. Such as this may be, it is the fact that post-Homeric lore thought of this girl as a Khryseid —a generic name— and so identified her as Astynome, "city guardian" (I. Malalas, *Chronographia*, 100, 15; Eustathius, *Commentarii ad Homeri Iliadem*, I, 123, 10; G. Cedrenus, *Compendium historiarum*, I, 28, 22; I, 221, 19). The choice of name is not altogether anhistorical, since, an Illyrian understanding —long before the Greek language came into being— may by found in *asti-* (with an *iota* rather than an *upsilon*), perhaps meaning "keel", whence Latin *hasta*, "spear", "javelin", Spanish *asta*, "(flag) pole", and *astillero*, "ship yard", and thus "keel-planner", that is, the inspiration for the building of a boat (hence, quite *à propos*, the tradition of fixing an image of a young maiden at the head of a keel). Her connection with Kalypso, then, might be seen in Kalypso's instructions to Odysseus to build himself a boat, even a raft, if need be.

Odysseus (safe from the common miscarriage of a seven-year term), will have assembled a raft in the eighth year of his stay on **Ogygia** at KILLA (Polače), situated at the western end of the island. This inference is derived on a cue with a $p = q$ linguistic equivalent, thus KILLA would seem akin with PYLOS (*Classis*) and *Pula* (Pola), and, indeed, whence modern Polače. Now, since the inhabitants of PYLOS should be called, properly, Pyloes (cf. TROIA, TROES (*not* Troies nor Troioi, "Trojans"), then the name of the PYLIOI (Πύλιοι [< πυλj-, < πυλλ-]) would seem cognate with the Spanish *quilla*, English *keel*, and therefore to be understood as "keel men" or "ship-builders", rather than as mere inhabitants of PYLOS (VII, 134; XI, 753; XXIII, 633).

A remnant of the name of **Ogygia** is found in that of Ogiran, a tiny islet off the southern coast of this island.

Thrinakia (Θρινακίη), AIGILIPS, *Elpahites*, Šipan, Lopud, Koločep: the name is a collective one and therefore that of an archipelago (as, indeed, both its earlier and later identities betray), as well as that of a unique symbol, the three-legged sun-faced disk representing the sun's three positions on the meridian during mid-summer, the spring and autumn equinoxes, and mid-winter (xii; 127):

> [says Kirke to Odysseus] "'And thou wilt come to the isle Thrinacia. There in great numbers feed the kine of Helios and his goodly flocks, seven herds of kine and as many fair flocks of sheep, and fifty in each. These bear no young, nor do they ever

die, and goddesses are their shepherds, fair-tressed nymphs, Phaethusa and Lampetie, whom beautiful Neaera bore to Helios Hyperion. These their honoured mother, when she had borne and reared them, sent to the isle Thrinakia to dwell afar, and keep the flocks of their father and his sleek kine. If thou leavest these unharmed and heedst thy homeward way, verily ye may yet reach Ithaca, though in evil plight...'"

That the kine of Helios (males, for "these bear no young...") occupy **Thrinakia**, and that the men of Odysseus will later feast on these (xxx, 000–000), means whatever mystical meaning one may wish to lend the fact, until a connection is made with the later name of *Elaphites*, or "Deer Isles": the kine of Helios will have been the stag[1] with antlers of fire, the new symbol of a new world-order, the patriarchy, established by the AKHAIOI.

HITHERTO UNKNOWN ISLANDS

Aiolia (Αἰολίη), Pakleni Islets: the home of Aiolos, King of the Winds, this small and barren archipelago serves as a breakwater at the mouth of PHARE (*Pharos*, Hvar), protecting vessels anchored in its bay from the seasonal harsh *bura* winds.

Skheria (Σχερίη), Sčedro: a small isle anchored on the southern coast of LEKTON (*Pharos / Lessina*, Hvar), home of the **Phaiakes**, an amiable folk (but distantly related with the savage and cruel **Kyklopes** of LEKTON).

Here, Odysseus visits the beautiful palace of Alkinous (vii, 81):

> ... but Odysseus went to the glorious palace of Alcinous. Of bronze were the walls that stretched this way and that from the threshold to the innermost chamber, and around was a cornice of cyanus [a blue enamel, or glass paste, imitating lapis lazuli]. Golden were the doors that shut in the well-built house, and doorposts of silver were set in a threshold of bronze. Of silver was the lintel above, and of gold the handle. On either side of the door there stood gold and silver dogs, which Hephaestus had fashioned with cunning skill to guard the palace of great-hearted Alcinous; immortal were they and ageless all their days. Within, seats were fixed along the wall on either hand, from the threshold to the innermost chamber, and on them were thrown robes of soft fabric, cunningly woven, the handiwork of women. On these the leaders of the Phaeacians were wont to sit drinking and eating, for they had unfailing store. And golden youths stood on well-built pedestals, holding lighted torches in their hands to give light by night to banqueters in the hall.

This description is that of the Milky Way, the band of suffused light across the night-sky stretching from one side of the horizon to the other,

---

1. The stag with antlers of fire has become synonymous with the Skythian folk which occupied Eastern Europe some time after the Fall of Troy, roughly from the Danube to the Don, Caucasus and Volga, and thought of by Greeks and Romans as a barbarous nation. Indeed, Akhaiism —to coin a term— was short-lived, three decades or so, and vanished... or became transformed.

with blotches of black at one end, and the first magnitude stars *Sirius* and *Procyon* at the other.

Planktai (Πλαγκταί), Planjak, *et al*: a cluster of rocks and inhospitable islets scattered in the channel between TENEDOS (Korčula) and NERITON (Pelješac), likely only occupied by the Dalmatian seal, now extinct (xii; 37):

> "'To the Sirens first shalt thou come, who beguile all men whosoever comes to them. Whoso in ignorance draws near to them and hears the Sirens' voice, he nevermore returns, that his wife and little children may stand at his side rejoicing, but the Sirens beguile him with their clear-toned song, as they sit in a meadow, and about them is a great heap of bones of mouldering men, and round the bones the skin is shrivelling. But do thou row past them, and anoint the ears of thy comrades with sweet wax, which thou hast kneaded, lest any of the rest may hear. But if thou thyself hast a will to listen, let them bind thee in the swift ship hand and foot upright in the step of the mast, and let the ropes be made fast at the ends to the mast itself, that with delight thou mayest listen to the voice of the two Sirens. And if thou shalt implore and bid thy comrades to loose thee, then let them bind thee with yet more bonds. But when thy comrades shall have rowed past these, thereafter I shall not fully say on which side thy course is to lie, but do thou thyself ponder it in mind, and I will tell thee of both ways. For on the one hand are beetling crags, and against them roars the great wave of dark-eyed Amphitrite; the Planctae do the blessed gods call these.'"

The name of the **Planktai** puns on their elusive nature, some barely submerged below sea level, and is likely Graecized early on from an original *plak-* "millstone" (as in the names of HYPOPLAKIA and PLAKOS which convey a sense of a flattened mass). That Jason and the Argo barely escaped being crushed by these rocks (xii, 70–00) is clearly an interpolation, for the presence of Orpheus in the region, from whose *Argonautica* (now non-existent, *if* it ever existed) the authorship of the *Odyssey* will have to have taken the account, cannot be attested to (nor his presumed historicity accounted for until *after* the *Iliad* and *Odyssey* were taken abroad and translated).

V. THE ODYSSEY AND ITS FANTASTIC GEOGRAPHY

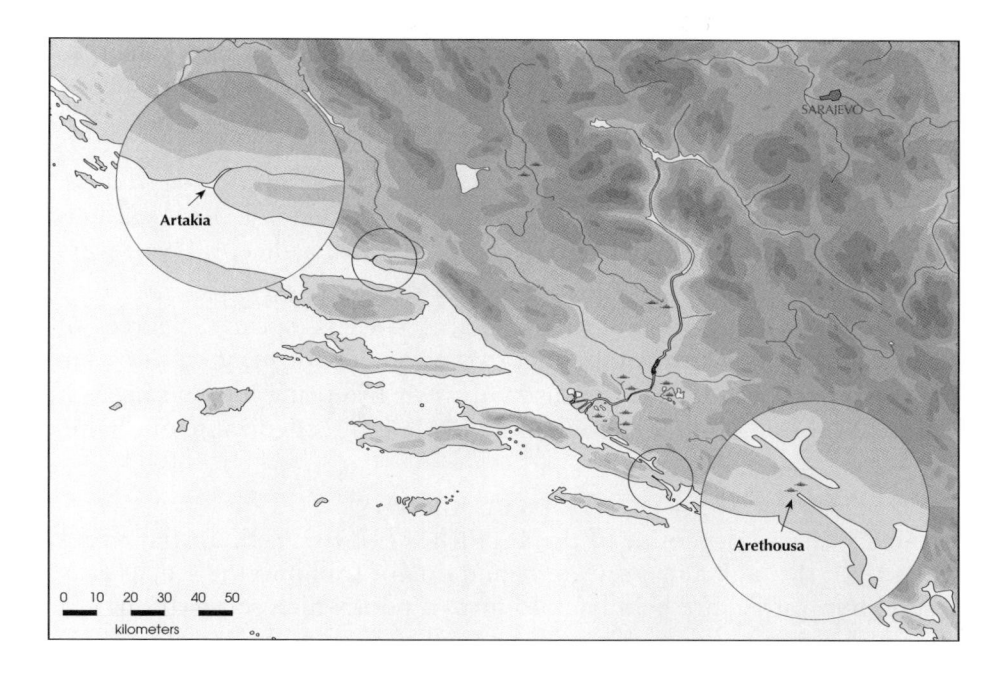

SPRINGS

Springs occur naturally, almost any place, for which reason the only two which are mentioned in the *Odyssey* should be notable for some spectacular or exceptional characteristic (a salt-marsh and a river-delta). The similarity of names and of geographical concepts might suggest that Arethousa could (or should) be adjusted to read "Arthousa" in keeping with the name of Artakia, or, vice versa, that Artakia might be adjusted to read "Aretakia" in keeping with the name of Arethousa. However, any such emendation (for the purpose of obtaining an etymological harmony) would prove false, for the simple reason that each possesses a different association of ideas.

SUPPLEMENTARY GEOGRAPHY

Arethousa ('Αρέθουσα), the salt pans of *Stanum*, Soline, Ston: it is here, at the head of **Phorkys** (Stonski Channel) where Odysseus at last enters in contact with reality (xiii, 397):

> "But come, I will make thee unknown to all mortals. I will shrivel the fair skin on thy supple limbs, and destroy the flaxen hair from off thy head, and clothe thee in a ragged garment, such that one would shudder to see a man clad therein. And I will dim thy two eyes that were before so beautiful, that thou mayest appear mean in the sight of all the wooers, and of thy wife, and of thy son, whom thou didst leave in thy halls. And for thyself, do thou go first of all to the swineherd who keeps

thy swine, and withal has a kindly heart towards thee, and loves thy son and constant Penelope. Thou wilt find him abiding by the swine, and they are feeding by the rock of Corax and the spring Arethusa, eating acorns to their heart's content and drinking the black water, things which cause the rich flesh of swine to wax fat."

The name of **Arethousa** is akin with that of the ARI(E)MOI (that is, the *Delmatai* or Dalmatians, occupants of the marshy SKAMANDROS delta whose name means "sheep"), as if, perhaps, a sheep's fleece were symbolic of marsh vegetation.

Athene presides over all humid places —wells, springs, sources of rivers, and a salt-pan would be no exception— and, so, it would seem fitting and proper that she disguise Odysseus by curing him in salt, as it were, and turning him into something like an unrecognizable old ham.

FICTITIOUS GEOGRAPHY

Artakia ('Ἀρτακίη), mouth of the SATNIOEIS (*Titius?* Cetina): the river's waters exit through a narrow gorge and do not spill into the sea, as elsewhere, but, rather, are held back to form a pool which seeps through a wide and elongated dam of small rounded stones and boulders (x, 103):

> Now when they had gone ashore, they went along a smooth road by which waggons were wont to bring wood down to the city from the high mountains. And before the city they met a maiden drawing water, the goodly daughter of Laestrygonian Antiphates, who had come down to the fair-flowing spring Artacia, from whence they were wont to bear water to the town.

See **Telepylos**, below, for a fuller description of this place.

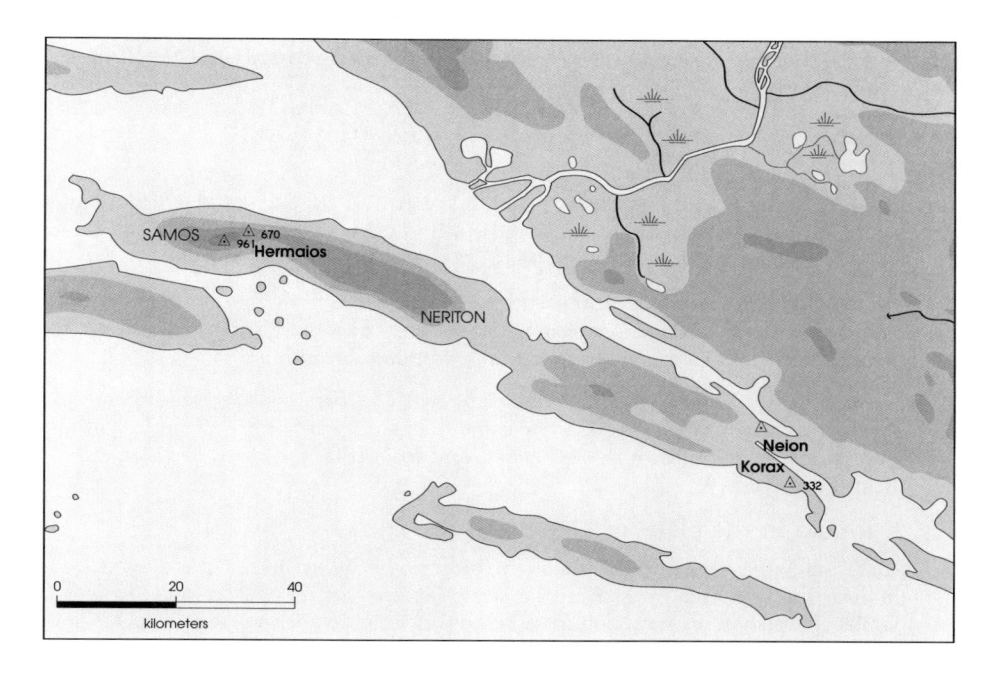

MOUNTAINS

The Balkan Peninsula is so called from the Turkish word "mountainous", and so it would seem that it is an apt successor to the term in the *Iliad*, "...the nether spurs of Ida". By contrast with the more ample treatment of mountains in the *Iliad*, the *Odyssey* is sparse, and concerned with only *one* mountain range, with details on it.

KNOWN GEOGRAPHY

NERITON (Νήριτον), Pelješac Peninsula: a long (65 kms.) and narrow peninsula running almost parallel with the coast (ix, 22; xiii, 351):

> But I dwell in clear-seen [ἐυδείελον] Ithaca, wherein is a mountain, Neriton, covered with waving forests, conspicuous from afar; and round it lie many isles hard by one another...

> "This is the harbour of Phorcys... and yonder is Mount Neriton, clothed with its forests".

SAMOS (Σάμος), Sveti Ilija/Zmijino Brdo (Monte Vípera), 961 mts.: the highest prominence of NERITON, situated towards its western end. There is confusion about its reading in the *Iliad*, since, conventionally, the name as that of an island relative to the Asia Minor Trojan mainland can be explained *only* by recourse to the expediency of antonomasia, thus "Samos wooded-Thracelike (XIII, 17), that is, "Samothrace", is not the Samos off the coast of Caria to the south. This confusion is still greater in the *Odyssey* (since there is no pressing need in the *Iliad* of relating ITHAKA *vis-à-vis* of SAMOS), thus,

1. SAMOS (Σάμος) becomes Same (Σάμη), an island (i, 246; xvi, 123, xix, 131; ix 24; xvi, 249):

> [Telemakhos]: "For all the princes who hold sway over the islands—Dulichium and Same and wooded Zacynthus—and those who lord it over rocky Ithaca, all these woo my mother and lay waste my house..."

> "But I [Odysseus] dwell in clear-seen Ithaca, wherein is a mountain, Neriton, covered with waving forests, conspicuous from afar; and round it lie many isles hard by one another, Dulichium, and Same, and wooded Zacynthus."

> [Telemakhos]: "From Dulichium there are two and fifty chosen youths, and six serving men attend them; from Same came four and twenty men; from Zacynthus there are twenty youths of the Achaeans; and from Ithaca itself twelve men, all of them the noblest..."

2. Ithaka in the place of LEKTON (iv, 671; iv, 845; xv, 29):

> "But come, give me [Antinous] a swift ship and twenty men, that I may watch in ambush for him as he passes in the strait between Ithaca [LEKTON] and rugged Samos. Thus shall his voyaging in search of his father come to a sorry end."

> There is a rocky isle in the midst of the sea, midway between Ithaca [LEKTON] and rugged Samos, Asteris, of no great size, but therein is a harbour where ships may lie, with an entrance on either side.

> [Athene]: "The best men of the wooers lie in wait for thee of set purpose in the strait between Ithaca [LEKTON] and rugged Samos, eager to slay thee before thou comest to thy native land."

3. The function of SAMOS misunderstood (xv, 361–000):

> With her [Ctimene, sister of Odysseus] was I [Eumaios] brought up, and the mother honoured me little less than her own children. But when we both reached the longed-for prime of youth they sent her to Same to wed, and got themselves countless bridal gifts, but as for me, my lady clad me in a cloak and tunic, right goodly raiment, and gave me sandals for my feet and sent me forth to the field; but in her heart she loved me the more.

That Ctimene was sent to Same (given the antecedents of *aristoi* in i, 246; xvi, 123, xix, 131) and Eumaios to the fields, reads oddly, out of place, since the inverse should be understood, that it was Eumaios who will have been sent to SAMOS where he might converse with **Harpyiai**, and Ctimene simply married off to whomever, from wherever.

4. Same replacing some unknown geonym which conflicted with an understanding of Ithaka situated at the mouth of the Gulf of Patras (xx, 288):

> There was among the wooers a man with his heart set on lawlessness—Ctesippus was his name, and in Same [read X] was his dwelling—who, trusting forsooth in his boundless wealth, wooed the wife of Odysseus, that had long been gone.

SUPPLEMENTARY GEOGRAPHY

The names of three additional prominences add to the already phallic associations of NERITON (*TABLE 5.0*).

Hermaios ("Ερμαιος), Čašnik: a hill on the outskirts of Ithaka (xvi, 471):

> "I [Eumaios] was now above the city, as I went on my way, where the hill of Hermaios is, where I saw a swift ship putting into the harbour...."

There are no natural sources of fresh water on NERITON other than seasonal (and short-lived) streams, for which reason ITHAKA will have required a fresh water supply from a reservoir, as described (xvii, 204 *et pas.*):

> But when, as they went along the rugged path, they were near the city, and had come to a well-wrought, fair-flowing fountain, wherefrom the townsfolk drew water —this Ithacus had made, and Neritus, and Polyctor, and around was a grove of poplars, that grow by the waters, circling it on all sides, and down the cold water flowed from the rock above, and on the top was built an altar to the nymphs where all passers-by made offerings— there Melantheus, son of Dolius met them as he was driving his she-goats, the best that were in all the herds, to make a feast for the wooers...

Such a reservoir exists on Čašnik, where three cisterns hewn from the limestone bedrock are said to have been filled, upon a time, one with gold, the second with silver, the third with snakes. The name is cognate with Latin *cattia*, > Spanish *cazo*, diminutive *cazuela*, "kitchen pot").

Korax (Κόραξ), Stari Grad: the farmstead of the swineherd Eumaios (xiii, 404):

> "And for thyself [says Athene to Odysseus], do thou go first of all to the swineherd who keeps thy swine, and withal has a kindly heart towards thee, and loves thy son and constant Penelope. Thou wilt find him abiding by the swine, and they are feeding by the rock of Corax and the spring Arethusa, eating acorns to their heart's content and drinking the black water, things which cause the rich flesh of swine to wax fat."

A closer description of the site is given when Odysseus approaches the place (xiv, 1, *et pas.*):

> But Odysseus went forth from the harbour by the rough path up over the woodland and through the heights to the place where Athene had shewed him that he should find the goodly swineherd, who cared for his substance above all the slaves that goodly Odysseus had gotten.
> He found him sitting in the forehall of his house, where his court was built high in a place of wide outlook, a great and goodly court with an open space around it. This the swineherd had himself built for the swine of his master, that was gone, without the knowledge of his mistress and the old man Laertes. With huge stones had he built it, and set on it a coping of thorn. Without he had driven stakes the whole length, this way and that, huge stakes, set close together, which he had made by splitting an oak to the black core; and within the court he had made twelve sties

close by one another, as beds for the swine, and in each one were penned fifty wallowing swine, females breeding; but the boars slept without. These were far fewer in numbers, for on them the godlike wooers feasted, and lessened them, for the swineherd ever sent in the best of all the fatted hogs, which numbered three hundred and sixty. By these ever slept four dogs, savage as wild beasts, which the swineherd had reared, a leader of men.

The name of **Korax** is close to that of KROKYLEIA (metathesis > Korčula), and while the traditional Greek meaning "Raven Rock" may well be, the Illyrian *kor-* conveys the antonyms "soft"("*cor*key"), and "hard", cf. κόρυς, "helmet", Spanish *coraza*, "shield".

Neion (Νήιον), Bartolomija, 228 mts.: the hill at the beginning of the Pelješac Peninsula, at the deep end of **Rheithron** (i; 185; iii; 81):

"My [Mentes'] ship lies yonder beside the fields away from the city, in the harbour of Rheithron, under woody Neion."

"We [says Telemakhos] have come from Ithaca that is below Neion (ὑπονηίου)..."

The sense of ὑπονηίου must, necessarily, convey the sense of "away, off to the west...".

V. THE ODYSSEY AND ITS FANTASTIC GEOGRAPHY

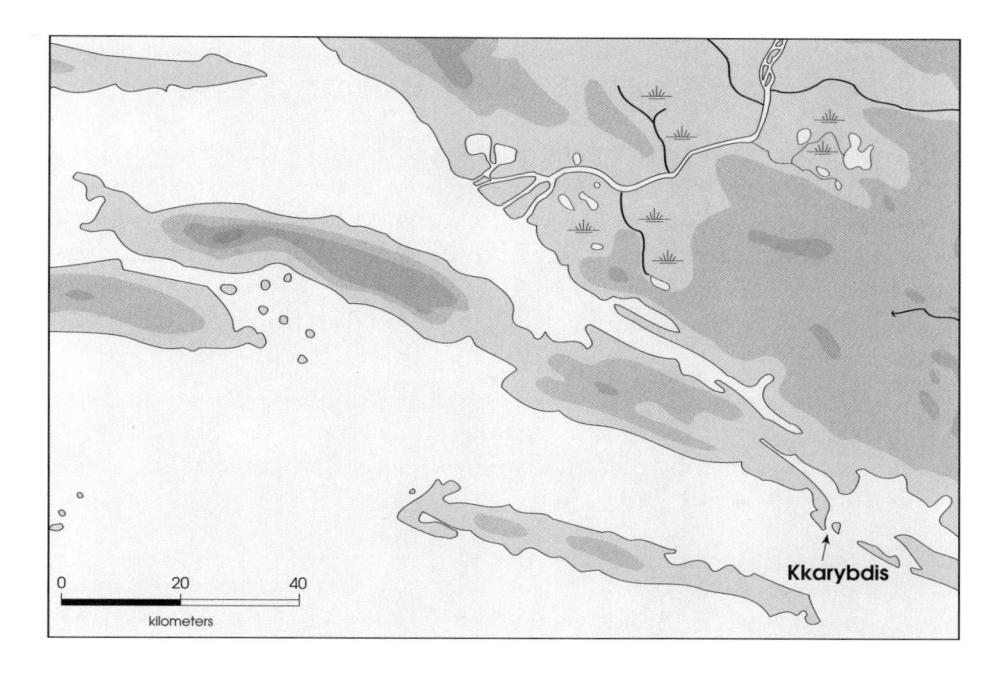

[Map with scale 0–40 kilometers, label "Kkarybdis"]

STRAIGHTS

Straights or narrows are, necessarily, part of the geography of an archipelago. Here, though Odysseus has already passed through several straights, the function of passing through one particular straight is indispensible to the structure and narrative line of the *Odyssey* (see VII, THE TWELVE MISADVENTURES OF ODYSSEUS).

FICTITIOUS GEOGRAPHY

Kharybdis (Χάρυβδις), Vratnik: narrows between NERITON and Olipa (xii, 101–000; xii, 234–000):

> [Kirke]: "'But the other cliff, thou wilt note, Odysseus, is lower—they are close to each other; thou couldst even shoot an arrow across—and on it is a great fig tree with rich foliage, but beneath this divine Charybdis sucks down the black water. Thrice a day she belches it forth, and thrice she sucks it down terribly. Mayest thou not be there when she sucks it down, for no one could save thee from ruin, no, not the Earth-shaker. Nay, draw very close to Scylla's cliff, and drive thy ship past quickly...'
>
> [Odysseus]: "We then sailed on up the narrow strait with wailing. For on one side lay Scylla and on the other divine Charybdis terribly sucked down the salt water of the sea. Verily whenever she belched it forth, like a cauldron on a great fire she would seethe and bubble in utter turmoil, and high over head the spray would fall on the tops of both the cliffs. But as often as she sucked down the salt water of the sea, within she could all be seen in utter turmoil, and round about the rock roared terribly, while beneath the earth appeared black with sand; and pale fear seized my

men... Scylla seized from out the hollow ship six of my comrades who were the best in strength and in might... To me they cried aloud, calling upon me by name for that last time in anguish of heart.

The description of **Kharybdis** belching forth and sucking down three times a day sounds like tides flowing in opposite directions through narrows barely below sea-level (but now submerged some 5 to 10 mts.). Thus, from the description of **Skylla** feeding on "dolphins and sea-dogs and whatever greater beast she may haply catch..." (xii, 88–000), these could become trapped among rocks and easily harpooned when the tides changed.

That **Kharybdis** was situated diametrically opposite **Leukas** suggests a similar diametrically opposite meaning, thus "dark" or "black". Now, if *khar-* > *phar-*, then by metathesis *phra-* > *vra-*, Serbian *vranac*, "red", + *ryb(d)-* > *rub-*, Latin *ruber* "red".

V. THE ODYSSEY AND ITS FANTASTIC GEOGRAPHY 159

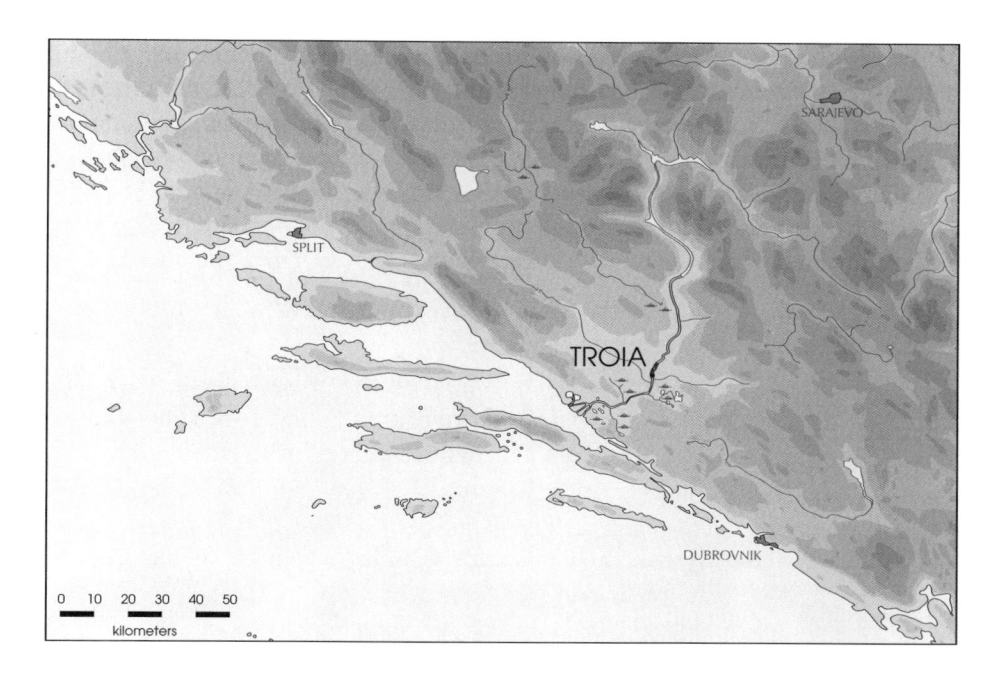

DISTRICTS

In the term DISTRICTS is to be understood the territorial extension of a general region, without any definite borders to speak of. Thus, the *Iliad* knows of a general region (TROIA) divided into both mainland and maritime districts. By contrast, the *Odyssey* seems only to have a memory of an ill fate that befell a land-locked political institution, and of its effects on a number of tribal societies now released into a spontaneous order of things.

KNOWN GEOGRAPHY

TROIA (Τροίη), (Troy), in the *Odyssey* the term is mentioned 36 times but ignores ASKANIA (the coast) and PHRYGIA (the islands). It is taken to mean the interior, the "land" of Troy (iv, 6; xiii, 248, xiii 315; xv, 153;

ALLUSIONS TO ILIOS		
i,	2:	the man who wandered after he had sacked the **sacred citadel** of Troy
iv,	146:	the warrior who left a child when Achaeans came **under the walls** of Troy
xiii,	388:	endue me with courage, even as when we loosed the **bright diadem** of Troy
xiv,	469:	when we made our ambush, and led it **beneath the walls** of Troy.

Table 5.15. ALLUSIONS TO ILIOS. The site intended cannot have been TROIA (Daorson), since, as a necropolis, its importance will have been lesser than that of ILIOS (Gabela).

xvii, 266; xxiv, 37), described as "broad", εὐρείη (i, 62; iv, 99; v, 307; xi, 499; xii, 189), wherein was to be found ILIOS, referred to elliptically.

Elsewhere, there are reminiscences of a foolish hubris *going to* Troy (i, 210; iii, 268; xiv, 229; xvi, 289; xvii, 314; xix, 8), and of the dismal *returns from* Troy (i, 327; iii, 257; iii, 276; ix, 259; xviii, 260; i, 355; v, 39; ix, 38; x, 40; x, 332; xi, 160; xiii, 137).

It is odd, indeed, that of the 36 references to TROIA, three are glaring interpolations (odd, because it brings the number of legitimate reference to 33, a magical number).

First, Menelaos informs Telemakhos of the misadventures on his homeward voyage from Troy in a convoluted story —it rings like a Greek fantasy, perhaps an effort at a would-be restoration of extensive lines which became lost?— about being blown off course to Egypt (iv, 481–490):

> "So he [Proteus] spoke, and my spirit was broken within me, for that he bade me go again over the misty deep to Aegyptus, a long and weary way. Yet even so I made answer, and said:
>
> "'All this will I perform, old man, even as thou dost bid. But come now, tell me this, and declare it truly. Did all the Achaeans return unscathed in their ships, all those whom Nestor and I left, as we set out from Troy? Or did any perish by a cruel death on board his ship, or in the arms of his friends, when he had wound up the skein of war...?'"

Elsewhere (iii, 169), Nestor talks about he and Menelaos having departed from LESBOS on their homeward journeys, but, oddly, only Menelaos was blown off course into waters that have no relevance with Homeric geography. If there is anything bizarre about Menelaos leaving from LESBOS —if Nestor's memory can be trusted— it is that nothing is known about Helen's response about visiting there with her estranged husband.

Second, is a statement by Odysseus himself in his conversation with diverse spirits of the Netherworld —an excellent place as any for an interpolation— about bringing the son of Akhilleus into the fray (xi, 504–000):

> "'Verily of noble Peleus have I heard naught, but as touching thy dear son, Neoptolemus, I will tell thee all the truth, as thou biddest me. I it was, myself, who brought him from Scyros in my shapely, hollow ship to join the host of the well-greaved Achaeans. And verily, as often as we took counsel around the city of Troy, he was ever the first to speak, and made no miss of words...'"

These words fall of their own weight, for Neoptolemos will scarcely have been eleven years of age at the funeral games of Hektor —the close of the *Iliad*— if, indeed, he had been born to Akhilleus at SKYROS

V. THE ODYSSEY AND ITS FANTASTIC GEOGRAPHY

in the first year of an AKHAIAN presence in Troy. Furthermore, Odysseus and his men departed the plains of war at the close of the *Iliad*, and he was not to be seen on the Trojan mainland (in **Nerikos**) again until after he made peace with Penelope, and, the following day, with his old father, Laertes, twenty one years later.

Third, is a tricky reference to Troy by Odysseus himself, disguised as Aethon, younger brother of Idomeneus of Crete, in a conversation with Penelope (xix, 185):

> "There it was that I saw Odysseus and gave him gifts of entertainment; for the force of the wind had brought him too to Crete, as he was making for the land of Troy, and drove him out of his course past Malea. So he anchored his ships at Amnisus, where is the cave of Eilithyia, in a difficult harbour, and hardly did he escape the storm..."

It seems unlikely Odysseus will have made a reference to himself as on his way to Troy, rather than ITHAKA, nor would a statement to this effect have made any sense at all to a Homeric audience, given the conventional understanding that Odysseus, on his *outward* voyage from Ithaka at the mouth of the Gulf of Patras, has stopped in Crete before joining the expeditionary forces in Troy, on the other side of Hellas, at the northwestern corner of Asia Minor.

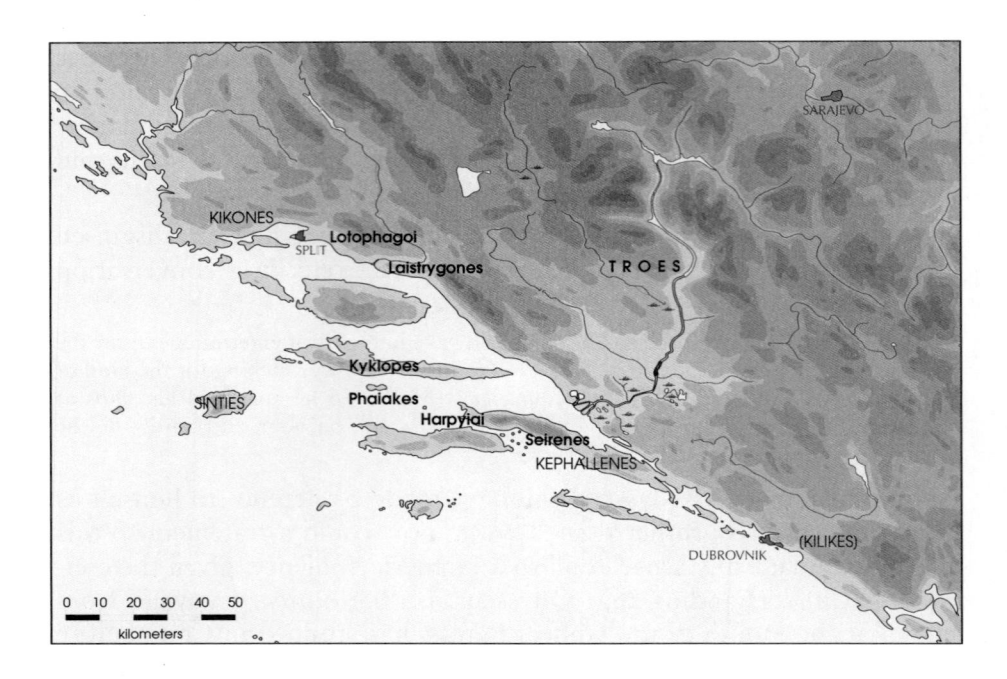

PEOPLES

The new social and political *status quo* omits the names of many peoples formerly confederated under the collective name of TROES divided into the landbound DARDANIOI and the maritime PHRYGES.

KNOWN GEOGRAPHY

The Kadmeio are mentioned in the visit of Odysseus to the Netherworld (xi, 276–000), but their name, properly the KADMEIONES, would seem like an erroneous correction of a folk who should otherwise read as KILIKES (which in an Asia Minor context does not make sense) and, to boot, does not fit symmetrically in a schema with other peoples mentioned in the *Odyssey* (choice A, below). See THEBES, further on.

TROES (Τρῶες), Trojans, the collective name for peoples from different tribes living under the political aegis of TROIA: the term occurs in the

A TROES:		B TROES:	
	KIKONES		KIKONES
	Kadmeioi	SINTIES	KEPHALLENES
SINTIES	KEPHALLENES		(KILIKES)

TABLE 5.17. GEONYMS OF PEOPLES. *Option B lends a better sense of schematic symmetry.*

text thirty times, a number which suggests an association with the lunar cycle. Specifically, it is a term of the past, a political reality no longer in existence, and Odysseus, with his fellow KEPHALLENES, were, properly, TROES or Trojans. However, after the Fall of Troy, Trojans become synonymous with the DARDANIOI, understood as nothing more than those land-locked folks of the interior (as distinguished from the PHRYGES, those of the seaboard and islands). This new perception of the Trojans is confirmed in a dialogue between Penelope and Eurymakhos (xviii, 261–000):

> "Verily, when he went forth and left his native land, he clasped my right hand by the wrist, and said: 'Wife, I deem not that the well-greaved Achaeans will all return from Troy safe and unscathed, for the Trojans, men say, are men of war, hurlers of the spear, and drawers of the bow, and drivers of swift horses...'"

Again, Odysseus himself confirms his mindset that Trojans are others, when he slays the suitors who have besieged his wife (xxii, 35–41):

> "Ye dogs, ye thought that I should never more come home from the land of the Trojans, seeing that ye wasted my house, and lay with the maidservants by force, and while yet I lived covertly wooed my wife, having no fear of the gods, who hold broad heaven, nor of the indignation of men, that is to be hereafter. Now over you one and all have the cords of destruction been made fast."

MAINLAND FOLK

KIKONES (Κίκονες), a northern peoples from the environs of Trogir and Split, inhabitants of **Ismaros** (*Tragurium*, Trogir?).

KEPHALLENES (Κεφαλλῆνες), occupants of NERITON (Pelješac Peninsula).

[KILIKES] (Κίλικες)], a southern peoples from the environs of PLAKOS (Mlini).

ISLAND FOLK

SINTIES (Σίντιες), inhabitants of LEMNOS (*Issa*, Viš): although integrated in the federation of diverse Trojan tribes, the SINTIES spoke a barbarous language (viii, 292–294), surely because the island's population was made up of merchants from abroad who took advantage of its unique geographical situation.

SUPPLEMENTARY GEOGRAPHY

Harpyiai ("Αρπυιαι), occupants of the region of Nakovana, on the western slopes of SAMOS: these folks, known to Telemakhos (i, 241), Eumaios (xiv, 371), and Penelope (xx, 61), have been depicted since early on as birds of prey with the head and breasts of a female, perched on clouds observing the passage of Odysseus through the **Planktai** tied to the mast of his ship (for which reason, perhaps, they have been associated with the surrealist adventures of Odysseus, though, in fact, he had naught to do with them).

Nothing is known about the **Harpyiai** or "Harpies" ("snatchers"), excepting that the foregoing icon betrays a fairly accurate historical memory of the scene, since this passage of Odysseus through the **Planktai** could not have been observed from anyplace else but from Nakovana. Greek lore learned from Hesiod (*Theogony*, 256–9) that the **Harpyiai** were the children of Thaumas, "magic", and cousins of Iris, the messenger.

The identity of the **Harpyiai**, hitherto grossly misunderstood, must be regarded as a name for that college of bards, perhaps established since earliest times, who created the various literary genres detected in the *Iliad* and *Odyssey*. Thus, the question about the dubious name of "Homer" in the authorship of these works is not *who* composed them —*anybody* can compose, as evinced by a plethora of interpolations in the texts, and, by those who, in later times, would imitate a "Homeric" style or manner of epic poetry— but, rather, the question to be addressed in the composition of these works is that of an *institutional framework* for the capturing, processing, storage, and retrieval of information.

There is much to be said about the **Harpyiai**, and the different states of their metamorphosis, locally and abroad, but this topic will divert us from the general purpose of this work, and it is best left for a proposed sequel, *The Songs of Harpies, literary genres in the Iliad and Odyssey*.

FICTITIOUS GEOGRAPHY

It is through the testimony of Odysseus —if at all credible— that one learns about two sets of fictitious folks, one occupying the islands, the other the seaboard, thus—

PHRYGIA (ISLANDS)

Kyklopes (Κύκλωπες), not-so-fictitious inhabitants of LEKTON (*Pharos/Lessina*, Hvar): a savage, unruly, cave-dwelling folk encountered by Odysseus (ix , 105 *et pas.*):

> "Thence we sailed on, grieved at heart, and we came to the land of the Cyclopes, an overweening and lawless folk, who, trusting in the immortal gods, plant nothing with their hands nor plough; but all these things spring up for them without sowing or ploughing, wheat, and barley, and vines, which bear the rich clusters of wine, and the rain of Zeus gives them increase. Neither assemblies for council have they, nor appointed laws, but they dwell on the peaks of lofty mountains in hollow caves, and each one is lawgiver to his children and his wives, and they reck noth-

V. THE ODYSSEY AND ITS FANTASTIC GEOGRAPHY

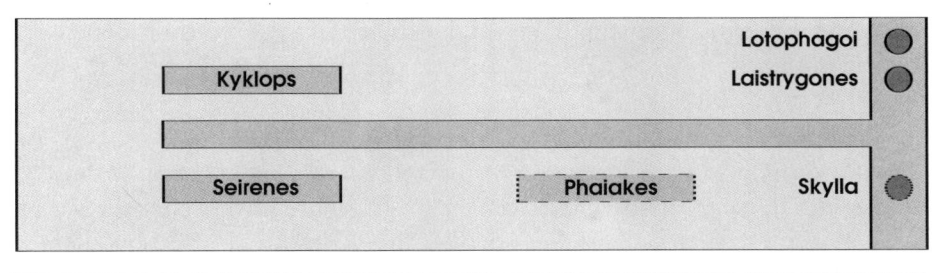

PHRYGIA (isalnds)				ASKANIA (seaboard)			
Kyklops	oyster	sing.	evil	good	plur.	people	**Lotophagoi**
Seirenes	seals	plur.	good	evil	plur.	ants	**Laistrygones**
Phaiakes	people	plur.	good	evil	sing.	crab	**Skylla**

TABLE 5. 18. FANTASTIC ENCOUNTERS. A Linnaean-like classification of subjects encountered is observed in their VALUE, LOCATION, HABITAT, KINGDOM, ORDER, GENDER, and NUMBER.

ing one of another... There a monstrous man was wont to sleep, who shepherded his flocks alone and afar, and mingled not with others, but lived apart, with his heart set on lawlessness. For he was fashioned a wondrous monster, and was not like a man that lives by bread, but like a wooded peak of lofty mountains, which stands out to view alone, apart from the rest.

"Speedily we came to the cave, nor did we find him within, but he was pasturing his fat flocks in the fields. So we entered the cave and gazed in wonder at all things there. The crates were laden with cheeses, and the pens were crowed with lambs and kids. Each kind was penned separately: by themselves the firstlings, by themselves the later lambs, and by themselves again the newly yeaned. And with whey were swimming all the well-wrought vessels, the milk-pails and the bowls into which he milked. Then my comrades spoke and besought me first of all to take of the cheeses and depart, and thereafter speedily to drive to the swift ship the kids and lambs from out the pens, and to sail over the salt water. But I did not listen to them—verily it would have been better far—to the end that I might see the man himself, and whether he would give me gifts of entertainment. Yet, as it fell, his appearing was not to prove a joy to my comrades.

"Then we kindled a fire and offered sacrifice, and ourselves, too, took of the cheeses and ate, and thus we sat in the cave and waited for him until he came back, herding his flocks. He bore a mighty weight of dry wood to serve him at supper time, and flung it down with a crash inside the cave, but we, seized with terror, shrank back into a recess of the cave. But he drove his fat flocks into the wide cavern—all those that he milked; but the males—the rams and the goats—he left without in the deep court. Then he lifted on high and set in place the great door stone, a mighty rock; two and twenty stout four wheeled waggons could not lift it from the ground, such a towering mass of rock he set in the doorway.

Odysseus and his men, held captive in the cave, finally seize the moment and drive a sharpened stake into the the single eye in the head of the slumbering monster. They make their escape, avoiding detection by the monster, clinging to the underside of rams released from the cave, and quickly sail away.

The name of the KYKLOPES is derived from Illyrian *kuk-* "cave" or "nest" (cognate with "cocoon" as well as Serbian *kuča*, "house", "dwelling"), + *lep-* also "cave" or "nest" (cognate with Lepenski Vir as well as Greek λεπίς, "husk", "shell"), thus, literally, "cave-dwellers". The Greek understanding of the name as "round face" (allusive of a single eye in the face) is anachronic.

Several caves situated on the southern shores of LEKTON have been found to have floor-beds packed with a thick layer of oyster shells, which, in a way, is reminiscent of the monster Polyphemus losing his one eye, gouged by Odysseus. Such a connection between the KYKLOPES and an ample supply of oysters, naturally prevalent in these waters and now of world-fame, invites further speculation that an excessive diet of such sea-food—oysters being especially rich in cholesterol—produced, along with the pleasure of eating them, the undesirable side-effects of a brutish mentality as well as acromegalia, a condition in which the bone structure acquires an abnormal thickness with an extra layer of tissue, not unlike a callus, making the body become unusually large and distorted.

Independently of a presumed connection between the KYKLOPES and oyster-beds abundant in the region, it should be noted that —for some hitherto unexplained reason— up until relatively recent times the inhabitants of the isle of Hvar have been known to be a stock of unusually tall people, so much so, that, by comparison with other tall folk, they towered over these.

Seirenes (Σειρῆνες), inhabitants of the **Planktai** (xii, 61): their singing beguiled all who heard them (xii; 158, *et pas.*):

> [Odysseus to his men]: "First she [Kirke] bade us avoid the voice of the wondrous Sirens, and their flowery meadow. Me alone she bade to listen to their voice; but do ye bind me with grievous bonds, that I may abide fast where I am, upright in the step of the mast, and let the ropes be made fast at the ends to the mast itself; and if I implore and bid you to loose me, then do ye tie me fast with yet more bonds."
> ..."Meanwhile the well-built ship speedily came to the isle of the two Sirens, for a fair and gentle wind bore her on. Then presently the wind ceased... But my comrades rose up and furled the sail and stowed it in the hollow ship, and thereafter sat at the oars and made the water white with their polished oars of fir. But I with my sharp sword cut into small bits a great round cake of wax, and kneaded it with my strong hands, and soon the wax grew warm, forced by the strong pressure and the rays of the lord Helios Hyperion. Then I anointed with this the ears of all my comrades in turn; and they bound me in the ship hand and foot, upright in the step of the mast, and made the ropes fast at the ends to the mast itself; and themselves sitting down smote the grey sea with their oars. But when we were as far distant as a

V. THE ODYSSEY AND ITS FANTASTIC GEOGRAPHY

> man can make himself heard when he shouts, driving swiftly on our way, the Sirens failed not to note the swift ship as it drew near, and they raised their clear-toned song: 'Come hither, as thou farest, renowned Odysseus, great glory of the Achaeans; stay thy ship that thou mayest listen to the voice of us two [?]. For never yet has any man rowed past this isle in his back ship until he has heard the sweet voice from our lips. Nay, he has joy of it, and goes his way a wiser man. For we know all the toils that in wide Troy the Argives and Trojans endured through the will of the gods, and we know all things that come to pass upon the fruitful earth.'
> ..."But when they had rowed past the Sirens, and we could no more hear their voice or their song, then straightway my trusty comrades took away the wax with which I had anointed their ears and loosed me from my bonds".

The **Seirenes** —said to be two, but this number is likely to be an interpolation— are likely to have been the Dalmatian seal, now extinct, that would seek out habitation on precisely such isles and rocks as the **Planktai**. That their song will have been deadly perhaps obeys to an infection (or rabies?) from the seal's bite, still, that Odysseus should have been bound to the mast of his vessel would seem to allude to sponge divers tied by the ankle to their boat as a precaution against diving too deeply, thus avoiding the charm of a ringing in the ears. Still, that Odysseus heard their song —his men did not— anticipates his own drowning, willy-nilly, in these waters, in which the tale is told about his woes and sufferings before he comes to and once again steps into reality, at **Arethousa**, at the end of **Phorkys**, where, properly, his misadventures end and a new phase of his life begins.

That the **Seirenes** sang of the Trojan War has an anachronic ring, and therefore that of an interpolation, for, presumably, they occupied the **Planktai** from even before, and were just as dangerous then, singing some other song. They seem, in later times, to have become seriously confused with the **Harpyiai** (about whose characteristics *nothing* is known from the text) such that iconography invariably lends both the **Harpyiai** and the **Seirenes** similar physical attributes as well as an ability of poetic composition.

Phaiakes (Φαίηκες): friendly, fairy-like inhabitants of **Skheria** (Sčedro) whom Odysseus encountered while drowning in the [IKAROPONTOS] (Korčulanski Channel).

ASKANIA (SEABOARD)

Lotophagoi (Λωτοφάγοι), an affable "lotus eating" folk from the environs of ENOPE [EPONE] (ix, 87):

> "But when we had tasted food and drink, I sent forth some of my comrades to go and learn who the men were, who here ate bread upon the earth; two men I chose, sending with them a third as a herald. So they went straightway and mingled with

the Lotus-eaters, and the Lotus-eaters did not plan death for my comrades, but gave them of the lotus to taste. And whosoever of them ate of the honey-sweet fruit of the lotus, had no longer any wish to bring back word or to return, but there they were fain to abide among the Lotus-eaters, feeding on the lotus, and forgetful of their homeward way. These men, therefore, I brought back perforce to the ships, weeping, and dragged them beneath the benches and bound them fast in the hollow ships; and I bade the rest of my trusty comrades to embark with speed on the swift ships, lest perchance anyone should eat of the lotus and forget his homeward way."

The lotus was probably wormwood, *Artemisia absinthium*, a hallucinogenic plant which grows well in sunny locations with poor and sandy soils, such as the length of the Dalmatian Coast.

Laistrygones (Λαιστρυγόνες), a hostile "ant-like" folk of **Telepylos**, the gorge of the SATNIOEIS. Their name is *à propos* of their habitat, an ant hill (see **Artakia**) as it were, at the narrow entrance to **Telepylos** (qv.) a deep tunnel (x; 80):

> [Odysseus]: "...we came to the lofty citadel of Lamus, even to Telepylus of the Laestrygonians, where herdsman calls to herdsman as he drives in his flock, and the other answers as he drives his forth... When we had come thither into the goodly harbour, about which on both sides a sheer cliff runs continuously, and projecting headlands opposite to one another stretch out at the mouth, and the entrance is narrow, then all the rest steered their curved ships in, and the ships were moored within the hollow harbour close together; for therein no wave ever swelled, great or small, but all about was a bright calm... So then I sent forth some of my comrades... two men I chose, and sent with them a third as a herald. Now when they had gone ashore, they went along a smooth road by which waggons were wont to bring wood down to the city from the mountains. And before the city they met a maiden drawing water, the goodly daughter of Laestrygonian Antiphates, who had come down to the fair-flowing spring Artacia, from whence they were wont to bear water to the town... And she showed them forthwith the high-roofed house of her father. Now when they had entered the glorious house, they found there his wife, huge as the peak of a mountain, and they were aghast at her. At once she called from the place of assembly the glorious Antiphates, her husband, and he devised for them woeful destruction. Straightway he seized one of my comrades and made ready his meal, but the other two sprang up and came in flight to the ships... They hurled at us from the cliffs with rocks huge as a man could lift, and at once there rose throughout the ships a dreadful din, alike from men that were dying and from ships that were being crushed. And spearing them like fishes they bore them home, a loathly meal..."

The true identity of these vicious folk who occupied the *struge*, or "funnel", of the Cetina gorge, is that of the otherwise peaceful LELEGES, a folk occupying the upper ground of the Biokovo Range. Thus, the men of Odysseus were pelted with stones hurled at them from on high (in a sense, the stones that made the pool of **Artakia**). That the wife of Antiphates was "...huge as the peak of a mountain", conforms to the unusually large and plump egg-bearing queen of an ant colony.

Skylla (Σκύλλη), a sea-monster occupying a cave at **Kharybdis** (xii, 80–000):

> And in the midst of the cliff is a dim cave, turned to the West, toward Erebus, even where you shall steer your hollow ship, glorious Odysseus. Not even a man of might could shoot an arrow from the hollow ship so as to reach into that vaulted cave. Therein dwells Scylla, yelping terribly. Her voice is indeed but as the voice of a new-born whelp, but she herself is an evil monster, nor would anyone be glad at sight of her, no, not though it were a god that met her. Verily she has twelve feet, all misshapen, and six necks, exceeding long, and on each one an awful head, and therein three rows of teeth, thick and close, and full of black death. Up to her middle she is hidden in the hollow cave, but she holds her head out beyond the dread chasm, and fishes there, eagerly searching around the rock for dolphins and sea-dogs and whatever greater beast she may haply catch, such creatures as deep-moaning Amphitrite rears in multitudes past counting.

The description of **Skylla** with twelve misshapen feet, six long necks ending in heads, and three rows of teeth, sounds like a garbled version of an original allegorical description, or, what is more likely, a broken-down perception —a deconstructed version— of that which was observed, as would happen under the influence of some psychotropic agent.[2] On a cue of a similarity with the **Laistrygones** (*TABLE 5.18*), and that **Skylla** lives half-in half-out of a cave, it is likely to be a crab, hence its name is cognate with σκύλλω, "to rend", "mangle". From this that "...three rows of teeth" are the mouth itself, and two claws with which it chews its food, as it were, "...six necks, exceeding long" being two pair of claws, as well as a pair of eyes (which pop up and down from their sockets), and, lastly, "...twelve feet, all misshapen" (that is, twelve extensions from a body) corresponding with four feet, one claw and one eye, on either side of the body. That it yelps, is not so. It hisses, when dropped into a pot of boiling water.

---

2. Presumably, all the fairy-like encounters of Odysseus occur while under the influence of Maro's wine, but, on a meditated view of the matter, the *only* fact which can be stated with certainty is that Odysseus has been with Kalypso a very long time —surely drugged with some brew?— and thus he gives a distorted account of realities in his past, even that of Maro's wine. A characteristic of some psychotropic agents is the blocking of the brains ability to integrate a set of concepts into an abstraction, thus, for instance, a hand is a set of fingers, a finger is three phalanges, a phalange is a nail, and so on, not unlike the desintegrated elements in the description of **Skylla**.

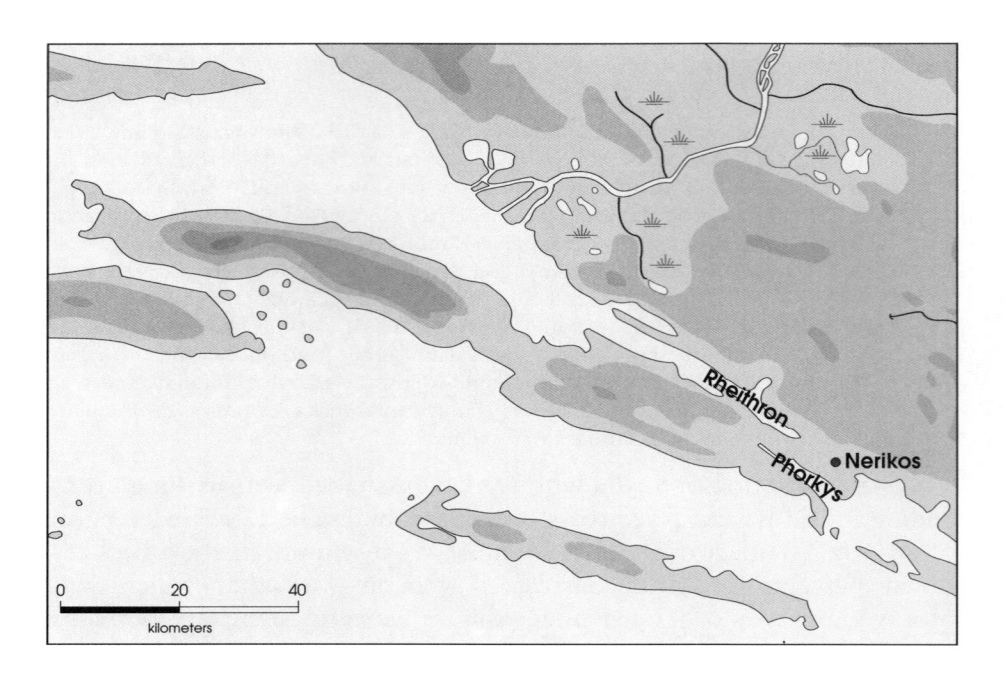

HARBOURS

Oddly, only two HARBOURS —which consist of a nameless port-town situated at the deep end of a fjord— are singled out from the profusely indented Trojan coastline (ASKANIA), although the concept is also applied, with a measure of the imagination, to a cove and a river gorge.

SUPPLEMENTARY GEOGRAPHY

Nerikos (Νήρικος), Djunta-Doli: a *vinograd* of intricate proportions situated on the border between the mainland and NERITON proper. Though the site is, properly, a town (not even a port-town, like other urban sites in Homeric Geography) its name is inspired on the natural accesses to the site, and is composed of the root *ner-* which conveys the murky, swamp-like aspect of the fjords **Phorkys** and **Rheithr(y)on** (from which the name of NERITON is likewise composed), + *-ik(os)*, "way" ("access to", cf. TRIKKA, *Triveum*), and cognate with Latin *ibo*, first person, future, of *ire*, "to go" (xxiv, 377):

> But Odysseus and his men, when they had gone down from the city, quickly came to the fair and well-ordered farm of Laertes, which he had won for himself in days past, and much had he toiled therefor. There was his house, and all about it ran the sheds in which ate, and sat, and slept the servants that were bondsmen, that did his pleasure but within it was an old Sicilian woman, who tended the old man with kindly care there at the farm, far from the city. Then Odysseus spoke to the servants and to his son, saying:

V. THE ODYSSEY AND ITS FANTASTIC GEOGRAPHY

> "Do you now go within the well-built house, and straightway slay for dinner the best of the swine; but I will make trial of my father, and see whether he will recognize me and know me by sight, or whether he will fail to know me, since I have been gone so long a time."
>
> So saying, he gave to the slaves his battle-gear. They thereafter went quickly to the house; but Odysseus drew near to the fruitful vineyard in his quest. Now he did not find Dolius as he went down into the great orchard, nor any of his slaves or of his sons, but as it chanced they had gone to gather stones for the vineyard wall, and the old man was their leader. But he found his father alone in the well-ordered vineyard, digging about a plant; and he was clothed in a foul tunic, patched and wretched, and about his shins he had bound stitched greaves of ox-hide to guard against scratches, and he wore gloves upon his hands because of the thorns, and on his head a goatskin cap; and he nursed his sorrow.

Phorkys (Φόρκυς), Stonski Channel: the long and narrow fjord on the southern coast of NERITON. It is here, at the deep end of this fjord, where Odysseus finally makes contact with reality after years of wanderings and misfortunes, and where he first steps on his native land (xiii; 96–000):

> There is in the land of Ithaca a certain harbour of Phorcys, the old man of the sea, and at its mouth two projecting headlands sheer to seaward, but sloping down on the side toward the harbour. These keep back the great waves raised by heavy winds without, but within the benched ships lie unmoored when they have reached the point of anchorage. At the head of the harbour is a long-leafed olive tree, and near it a pleasant, shadowy cave sacred to the nymphs that are called Naiads. Therein are mixing bowls and jars of stone, and there too the bees store honey. And in the cave are long looms of stone, at which the nymphs weave webs of purple dye, a wonder to behold; and therein are also ever-flowing springs. Two doors there are to the cave, one toward the North Wind, by which men go down, but that toward the South Wind is sacred, nor do men enter thereby; it is the way of the immortals.
>
> Here they rowed in, knowing the place of old; and the ship ran full half her length on the shore in her swift course, at such pace was she driven by the arms of the rowers. Then they stepped forth from the benched ship upon the land, and first they lifted Odysseus out of the hollow ship, with the linen sheet and bright rug as they were, and laid him down on the sand, still overpowered by sleep. And they lifted out the goods which the lordly Phaeacians had given him, as he set out for home, through the favour of great-hearted Athene. These they set all together by the trunk of the olive tree, out of the path, lest haply some before Odysseus awoke, might come upon them and spoil them. Then they themselves returned home again.

That **Phorkys** lay below **Korax**, the farmstead of Eumaios the swineherd, suggests it took its name from the Dalmatian "seal" (Latin *porcus*, "pig", Spanish *foca* "seal"), perhaps once a natural breeding ground for these creatures, now extinct.

Rheithron ('Ρεῖθρ[υ]ον), Mali Ston Canal: the long and narrow fjord, some 20 kms. deep by 2 kms. wide, formed by the length of the Pelješac peninsula lying aslant of the mainland coast (i; 185):

[Mentes]: "My ship lies yonder beside the fields away from the city [ITHAKA], in the harbour of Rheithron, under woody Neion."

The name of **Rheithron**, that is, **Rheithr[y]on**, would seem to convey the same geographical sense as that of ZANTHOS, "very flowery", but here that of a *flowing* brook (or underground streams) through swampy θρύον, "bull-rush vegetation".

FICTITIOUS GEOGRAPHY

Telepylos (Τηλέπυλος), gorge of the SATNIOEIS (*Titius*, Cetina): entrance into the gorge (PEDASOS) was controlled by a folk who in the *Iliad* are the LELEGES, but for Odysseus, whose capacity for perceiving realities has been altered by the special wine given him by Maron at **Ismaros** (ix, 197), they are **Laistrygones** (x, 80–132):

> So for six days we sailed, night and day alike, and on the seventh we came to the lofty citadel of Lamus, even to Telepylus of the Laestrygonians, where herdsman calls to herdsman as he drives in his flock, and the other answers as he drives his forth. There a man who never slept could have earned a double wage, one by herding cattle, and one by pasturing white sheep; for the outgoings of the night and of the day are close together. When we had come thither into the goodly harbour, about which on both sides a sheer cliff runs continuously, and projecting headlands opposite to one another stretch out at the mouth, and the entrance is narrow, then all the rest steered their curved ships in, and the ships were moored within the hollow harbour close together; for therein no wave ever swelled, great or small, but all about was a bright calm. But I alone moored my black ship outside, there on the border of the land, making the cables fast to the rock. Then I climbed to a rugged height, a point of outlook, and there took my stand; from thence no works of oxen or of men appeared; smoke alone we saw springing up from the land. So then I sent forth some of my comrades to go and learn who the men were, who here ate bread upon the earth—two men I chose, and sent with them a third as a herald. Now when they had gone ashore, they went along a smooth road by which waggons were wont to bring wood down to the city from the high mountains. And before the city they met a maiden drawing water, the goodly daughter of Laestrygonian Antiphates, who had come down to the fair-flowing spring Artacia, from whence they were wont to bear water to the town. So they came up to her and spoke to her, and asked her who was king of this folk, and who they were of whom he was lord. And she showed them forthwith the high-roofed house of her father. Now when they had entered the glorious house, they found there his wife, huge as the peak of a mountain, and they were aghast at her. At once she called from the place of assembly the glorious Antiphates, her husband, and he devised for them woeful destruction. Straightway he seized one of my comrades and made ready his meal, but the other two sprang up and came in flight to the ships. Then he raised a cry throughout the city, and as they heard it the mighty Laestrygonians came thronging from all sides, a host past counting, not like men but like the Giants. They hurled at us from the cliffs with rocks huge as a man could lift, and at once there rose throughout the ships a dreadful din, alike from men that were dying and from ships that were being crushed. And spearing them like fishes they bore them home, a loathly

meal. Now while they were slaying those within the deep harbour, I meanwhile drew my sharp sword from beside my thigh, and cut therewith the cables of my dark-prowed ship; and quickly calling to my comrades bade them fall to their oars, that we might escape from out our evil plight. And they all tossed the sea with their oar-blades in fear of death, and joyfully seaward, away from the beetling cliffs, my ship sped on; but all those other ships were lost together there.

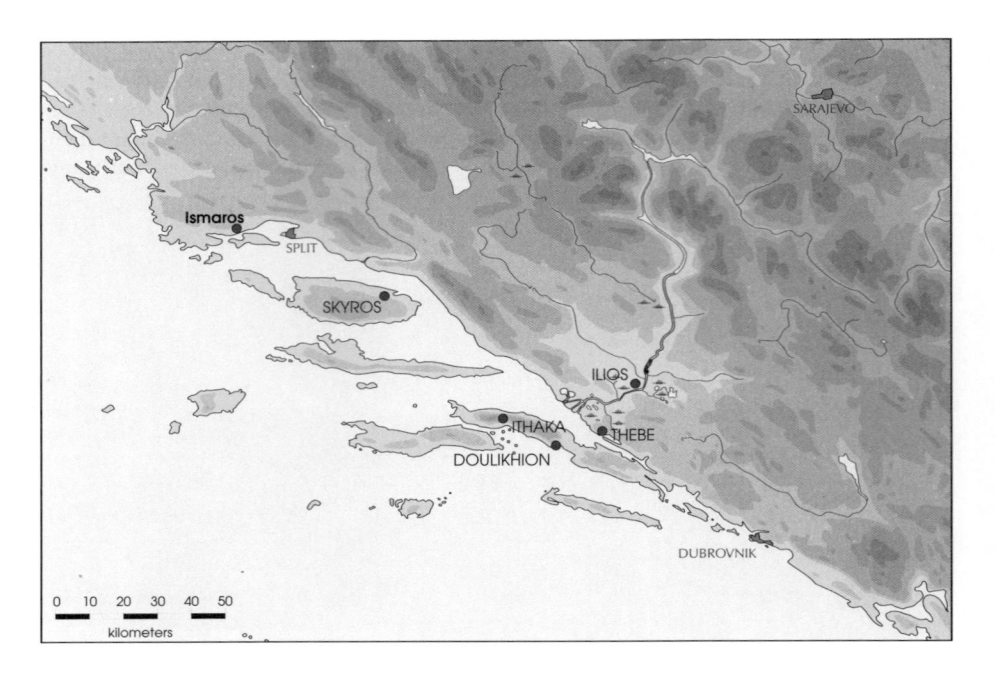

TOWNS

The two cities in Homer, *par excellance,* are ILIOS and ITHAKA: the one, destroyed in the *Iliad*; the other, rescued from destruction in the *Odyssey*. There are two other port-tows mentioned (as distinguished from "cities", which are at some distance from the sea), one in the present, still a vibrant social reality, the other already only a memory of a gallant past. Still a fifth urban concentration (to avoid using the terms city or port-town) is mentioned, but news about it comes from the testimony of Odysseus, and therefore its veracity is dubious.

KNOWN GEOGRAPHY

ITHAKA (Ἰθάκη), Donja Vručica: see VI. ITHAKA: PRELIMINARY NOTES.

DOULIKHION (Δουλίχιον), Trstenik: extensive *vinograd* situated at the western end of the Zuljana cove on the southern coast of NERITON. Of the set of sixteen port-towns mentioned in the *Iliad* (eight in ASKANIA, the seaboard, and eight in PHRYGIA, the islands), DOULIKHION is the only port-town to survive into the present, 52 young men plus 6 attendants that wooed Helen came from here (xvi, 247), THESPROTOI arrive here from southern Italy (xiv, 335, xix, 292), and it is here that Odysseus will come, seeking refuge, if necessary, like Meges did a generation before him. The only other port-town mentioned in the *Odyssey* is THEBE (below), albeit already in terms of the past, nevermore to be.

ILIOS ("Ἴλιος), Drijeva/Gabela: see II. ILIOS: A BRIEF SURVEY.

THEBE (Θήβη), Klek: the name occurs in an interpolated setting wholly out of geographical context as a city of Egypt (ix, 126), and, again, more extensively, in a reference to its foundation by Amphion and Zethos and its walls and seven gates (xi, 263–275), which reads anhistorically, since THEBE was founded by Kadmos, and hence occupied by his progeny, the KADMEIONES (qv., p. 00). Otherwise, the city was that of the blind seer Teiresias, with whom Odysseus spoke in his *Descent to the Netherworld* (x, 492; x, 565; xi, 90; xi, 165; xii, 267; xxiii, 323).

Skyros (Σκῦρος), Pušica: The reference is spurious, for it falls of its own weight, on two counts (xi, 504–515):

> "So he spoke, and I made answer and said: 'Verily of noble Peleus have I heard naught, but as touching thy dear son, Neoptolemus, I will tell thee all the truth, as thou biddest me. I it was, myself, who brought him from Scyros in my shapely, hollow ship to join the host of the well-greaved Achaeans. And verily, as often as we took counsel around the city of Troy, he was ever the first to speak, and made no miss of words; godlike Nestor and I alone surpassed him. But as often as we fought with the bronze on the Trojan plain, he would never remain behind in the throng or press of men, but would ever run forth far to the front, yielding to none in his might; and many men he slew in dread combat...'"

This reference to SKYROS occurs in the dialogue of Odysseus with the spirits of the Netherworld, an apt a place as any for the interpolation of well-wrought lines by some ambitious Homer-imitator, but their illegitimacy is self-evident for the following two reasons: first, there is the assumption that Akhilleus will have been on Skyros (in the Aegean), where Neoptolemos was born, some time *before* being discovered by Odysseus and taken to Troy (Asia Minor) to fight in the war, thus making Neoptolemos old enough —but just barely— to fight and kill men; second, Odysseus was not to be seen in Troy for twenty one years after the close of the *Iliad* with the funeral rites of Hector, two decades after the Fall of Troy.

FICTITIOUS GEOGRAPHY

Ismaros ("Ἴσμαρος), *Tragurion*, Trogir: a city of the KIKONES sacked by Odysseus and his men. It is the first of eleven subsequent places visited by Odysseus, where he loses contact with reality by "downing", so to speak, in a wine of certain magical properties (iv, 193, *et pas.*):

> "Then I bade the rest of my trusty comrades to remain there by the ship and to guard the ship, but I chose twelve of the best of my comrades and went my way. With me I had a goat-skin of the dark, sweet wine, which Maro, son of Euanthes, had given me, the priest of Apollo, the god who used to watch over Ismarus. And he had given it me because we had protected him with his child and wife out of rev-

erence; for he dwelt in a wooded grove of Phoebus Apollo. And he gave me splendid gifts: of well-wrought gold he gave me seven talents, and he gave me a mixing-bowl all of silver; and besides these, wine, wherewith he filled twelve jars in all, wine sweet and unmixed, a drink divine. Not one of his slaves nor of the maids in his halls knew thereof, but himself and his dear wife, and one house-dame only. And as often as they drank that honey-sweet red wine he would fill one cup and pour it into twenty measures of water, and a smell would rise from the mixing-bowl marvelously sweet; then verily would one not choose to hold back. With this wine I filled and took with me a great skin, and also provision in a scrip; for my proud spirit had a foreboding that presently a man would come to me clothed in great might, a savage man that knew naught of justice or of law.

The two component elements in the name of **Ismaros** are either synonymous, or have different meanings. Now, on the premise that *mar-* is cognate with Serbian *more*, "sea" (Gaelic *muir*, Latin *mare*), then *ism-* might likewise be some body of "water", perhaps as that of an artesian well, as perceived in the Biblical story of *Ism*ael (*Gen*. II, 2), surviving in the desert. The inference of an aqueous association of this root would seem supported by the Greek story of Hyllos, who was said to have fallen deep into a well, after which his name was given to the *Peninsula Hyllica* at the western end of the territory occupied by the KIKONES.

V. THE ODYSSEY AND ITS FANTASTIC GEOGRAPHY

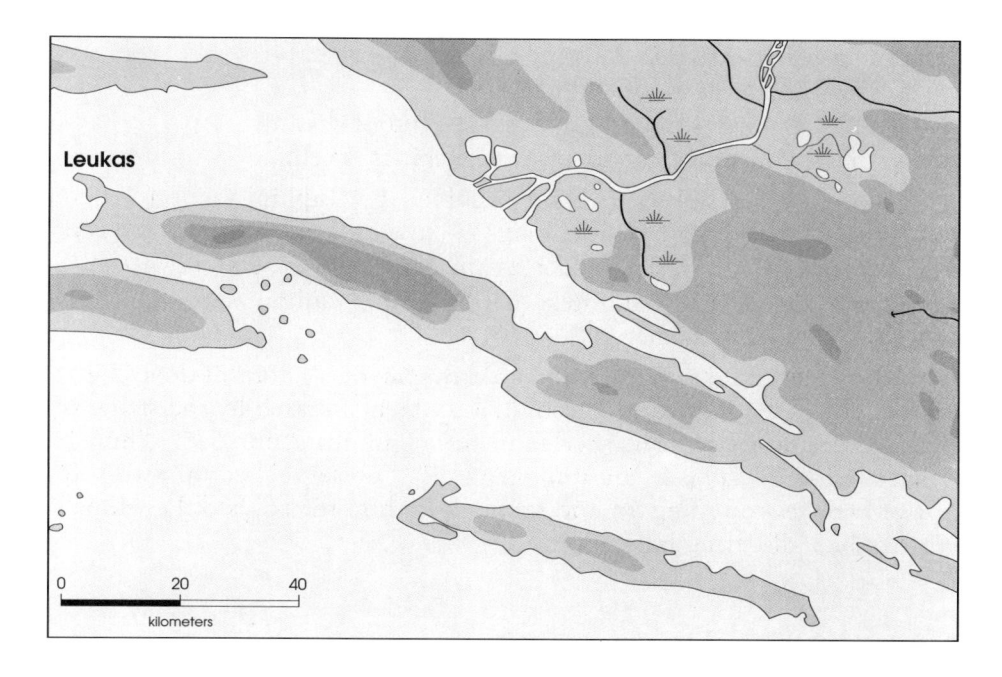

CAPES

CAPES are a natural reference to all maritime traffic, oftentimes bearing an association with light, as if tipped with some lighthouse device. Names of capes with variations of the root *luk-* abound in the Adriatic Archipelago.

SUPPLEMENTARY GEOGRAPHY

Leukas (Λευκάς), Lovište: the sheer white cliffs on the northern side of the western tip of NERITON (xxiv; 1, *et pas.*):

> Meanwhile Cyllenian Hermes called forth the spirits of the wooers. He held in his hands his wand, a fair wand of gold, wherewith he lulls to sleep the eyes of whom he will, while others again he wakens even out of slumber; with this he roused and led the spirits, and they followed gibbering. And as in the innermost recess of a wondrous cave bats flit about gibbering, when one has fallen from off the rock from the chain in which they cling to one another, so these went with him gibbering, and Hermes, the Helper, led them down the dank ways. Past the [2] streams of Oceanus they went, past the [1] rock Leucas, past the [3] gates of the sun and the land of dreams, and quickly came to the [4] mead of asphodel, where the spirits dwell, phantoms of men who have done with toils.

The itinerary of the fifty gibbering souls (otherwise understood in the context of islands —Ithaka— at the mouth of the Gulf of Patras) has been, perforce, altered to give it a reasonable geographical reading, but should stand, after the exit from the cave, as follows:

1. Past the rock LEUKAS
2. Past the streams of OKEANOS
3. Past the gates of the sun and the land of dreams
4. To the mead of asphodel, where spirits dwell...

This place is **Taphos** (Svetac) occupied by **Taphioi**, a non-Trojan folk notorious for their piratical acts (i, 105, 419; xiv, 452; xv, 427; xvi, 426), certainly an apt resting-place as any for fifty wastrels (see TABLE 5.6). The name of Svetac connotes the Spanish "campo santo", "holy ground", that is, a "cemetery".

An epithet of **Leukas** might be πολυτρήρωνος, "haunt of doves", the epithet of THISBE (*Leucera*, Lecco; II, 502), as insinuated by the string of fifty gibbering bats. The Serbian *lov* connotes "pursue", "hunt", "chase", and *loviste* is a "hunting-ground", "preserve", certainly *à propos* of Hermes rounding up and taking with him the souls of Penelope's wooers like gibbering bats.

CHAPTER VI

ITHAKA: PRELIMINARY NOTES

The site of ITHAKA occupies an area of some 40–50,000 mts², adjoining the hamlet of Donja Vručica, situated at the end of a narrow and fertile valley towards the western end of NERITON (Pelješac Peninsula), below the summit of Čašnik (667 mts). A succinct description of the surrounding countryside is given as follows (xiii, 248):

> [Athene]: "A fool art thou, stranger, or art come from far, if indeed thou askest of this land. Surely it is no wise so nameless, but full many know it, both all those who dwell toward the dawn and the sun, and all those that are behind toward the murky darkness. It is a rugged isle [land], not fit for driving horses, yet it is not utterly poor, though it be but narrow. Therein grows corn beyond measure, and the wine-grape as well, and the rain never fails it, nor the rich dew. It is a good land for pasturing goats and kine; there are trees of every sort, and in it also pools for watering that fail not the year through. Therefore, stranger, the name of Ithaca has reached even to the land of Troy, which, they say, is far from this land of Achaea."

A GENERAL DESCRIPTION OF ITHAKA

The general plan of a widely dispersed nuraghic-like *vinograd*, of massive proportions, could be said to be trisected by a forked road paved with large, polished cobble stones leading from the fields of Donja Vručica (*Map 6. 1.* ITHAKA): to the left, is the way down to a ravine, and to the right, likewise to the same ravine that enfolds, as it were, an elevation with a grid of narrow alleys and some 20 or 30 rooms, or so; the road to the left passes, on the left, another grid of rooms, and, on the right, a lesser side-street running parallel with a massive, fortress-like wall, broken approximately in the middle with a conical doorway; the road to the right passes, on the left, what appears to be the inside of a fortress, and, on the right, still other grids of alleys and rooms, some even as large as small plots of land.

ITHAKA might be thought of as an urban agglomeration, a city, as opposed to a religious site peopled only by an elite (xvii, 263):

> To him then, swineherd Eumaeus, didst thou make answer, and say: "Antinous, no fair words are these thou speakest, noble though thou art. Who, pray, of himself

ever seeks out and bids a stranger from abroad, unless it be one of those that are masters of some public craft, a prophet, or a healer of ills, or a builder, aye, or a divine minstrel, who gives delight with his song? For these men are bidden all over the boundless earth. Yet a beggar would no man bid to be burden to himself. But thou art ever harsh above all the wooers to the slaves of Odysseus, and most of all to me; yet I care not, so long as my lady, the constant Penelope, lives in the hall, and godlike Telemachus."

A DESCRIPTION OF THE PALACE OF ODYSSEUS
There is no history of ITHAKA, as there is of ILIOS, which was chosen to be configured according to a specific plan in succeeding generations. All that is known about ITHAKA is that it was founded, as Telemakhos recalls, by his paternal great-grandfather, Arkeisios (xvi, 113–000):

> [Telemakhos to Odysseus]: "Then verily, stranger, I will frankly tell thee all. Neither do the people at large bear me any grudge or hatred, nor have I cause to blame brothers, in whose fighting a man trusts, even if a great strife arise. For in this wise has the son of Cronos made our house to run in but a single line. As his only son did Arceisius beget Laertes, as his only son again did his father beget Odysseus, and Odysseus begot me as his only son, and left me in his halls, and had no joy of me. Therefore it is that foes past counting are now in the house...

Of Arkeisios not much is known, and the guess has been ventured, on a cue with the root *ark-* in his name, that he was one of the heroes that sailed with Jason on the *Argo*, after the Calydonian Boar Hunt, and that when they stopped here, on their way to Kolkhis, he decided to stay. All told, then, ITHAKA was not that old, albeit at this time there is no way of knowing whether Arkeisios did not settle on an older site.

Now, there is a difference between a general description of ITHAKA, how it lies, *vis-à-vis* with other points of reference, as well as how specific places are configured within the "city" itself, and the meticulous descriptions of the **Palace of Odysseus** given here and there throughout the text. The enormous difficulty of relating these descriptions with any part of the existing *vinograd* agglomeration of Donja Vručica —or with any other place in the Mediterranean Basin— is an apparently insurmountable problem, for these descriptions tend to be understood in their most external, or literal, sense. Thus, the criteria for establishing some sort of ground-plan for a number of diverse chambers, upstairs and downstairs (and in my lady's chamber...), store-rooms and halls, apparently all assembled around one grand courtyard, is, certainly, not any sort of plan as might have been developed by a Palladio of the Veneto nor a Gaudí of Barcelona, but, rather, inspired on a theoretical reconstruction of some lofty Mykenaian or Minoan palace. However, one plan is as valid and meritorious as any another, for, necessarily, they

VI. ITHAKA: PRELIMINARY NOTES

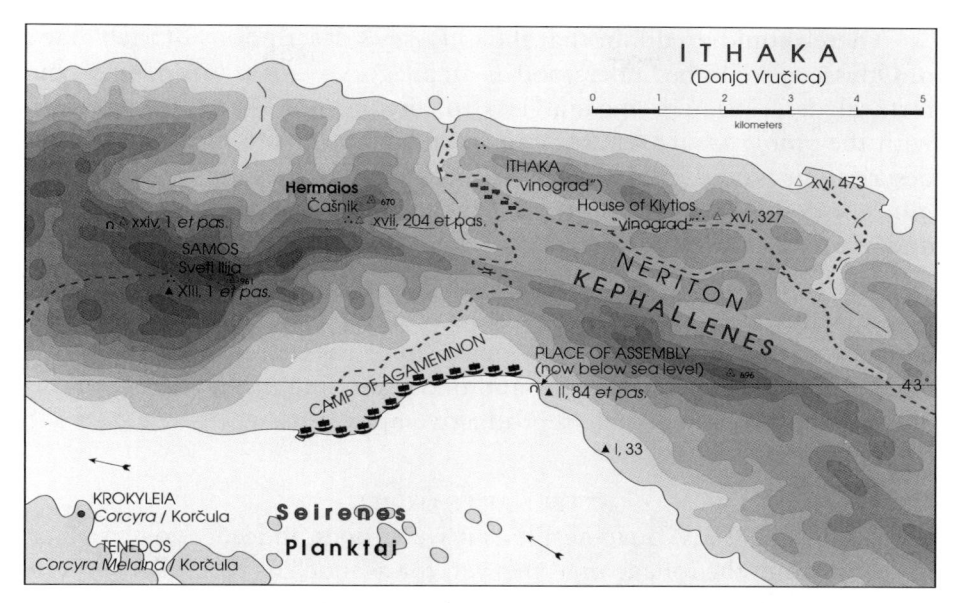

MAP 6.1. ITHAKA. *The Palace of Odysseus is a unit together with a complex of other units which, in toto, are to be regarded as a city. It was here that Odysseus, prime informant of the Odyssey, told his story, thus the inference the Odyssey was composed here.*

are figments of the imagination in the modern scholar's well-intended effort to capture some measure of archaeological reality (A. T. Murray, *The Odyssey*, II. The Loeb Classical Library, 1960, p. 346–7):

> The ὀρσοθύρη appears to have been a door, in the innermost part of the hall, higher in level than the floor of the great hall itself (hence the name "raised door"), and approached by a flight of steps (the ῥῶγες of line 143). This door may well have been invisible from where Odysseus stood, and it opened upon a "way" leading into a passage (λαύρη). This last need not be further defined. The palace embraced many smaller buildings besides the main hall, and there may have been many such passages between them. The obscure phrase ἀκρότατον δὲ παρ' οὐδὸν I understand thus: assuming that the ground rose slightly from the front of the palace to the rear, I assume further that the floor of the hall itself was levelled, so that the οὐδός (by which I understand the whole foundation upon which the walls rested), which was level with the threshold in front, was elevated to the ground level in the rear. Hence the fact that the ὀρσοθύρη, opening upon a "way" outside, was itself above the floor of the hall, and had to be reached by steps. That the οὐδός, or foundation wall, was not itself level, but followed the slope of the ground, seems to me to offer no difficulty.
>
> See the preceding note. Others understand the ῥῶγες to have been openings in the wall (one of which was the ὀρσοθύρη itself) whereby one could climb up. But it is certain that the store-room was on the ground floor. The word ῥῶγες is, I take it, to be connected with ῥήγνυμι, and to call the steps "break" in an ascent is surely natural enough; see Monro.

There should no doubt that the *Odyssey*'s descriptions of the **Palace of Odysseus** are to be understood as an allegory —for, *a priori*, an architectural description is meaningless to anyone not intimately familiar with the *vinograd* of ITHAKA, and, even so, an on-site reading of these descriptions would yield nothing— so, then, two questions arise: first, *a qui bon* descriptions in the text of what nobody may ever understand and are neither here nor there? and, second, an allegory of what?

The various units in the **Palace of Odysseus** seem to be connected, in some way or another, to one grand central hall, but, *how* they are connected —in a measure explaining *why* they are so connected— depends on a certain familiarity and understanding of the subject of the allegory, namely, the female reproductive apparatus.

EXTERNAL FEATURES:

1. MARRIAGE BED. A "love-nest", as it were, does, indeed, evoke a place of sorts within the foliage of a tree, yet, for as much as this folksy notion of romantic love is far removed in culture and time from an Odyssean context, it serves to draw a parallel between the description Odysseus gives of his cunningly-wrought marriage bed and its homology with the clitoris (xxiii, 174–204):

> [Penelope]: "Strange sir, I am neither in any wise proud, nor do I scorn thee, nor yet am I too greatly amazed, but right well do I know what manner of man thou wast, when thou wentest forth from Ithaca on thy long-oared ship. Yet come, Eurycleia, strew for him the stout bedstead outside the well-built bridal chamber which he made himself. Thither do ye bring for him the stout bedstead, and cast upon it bedding, fleeces and cloaks and bright coverlets."
>
> So she spoke, and made trial of her husband. But Odysseus, in a burst of anger, spoke to his true-hearted wife, and said: "Woman, truly this is bitter word that thou hast spoken. Who has set my bed elsewhere? Hard would it be for one, though never so skilled, unless a god himself should come and easily by his will set it in another place. But of men there is no mortal that lives, be he never so young and strong, who could easily pry it from its place, for a great token is wrought in the fashioned bed, and it was I that built it and none other. A bush of long-leafed olive was growing within the court, strong and vigorous, and in girth it was like a pillar. Round about this I built my chamber, till I had finished it, with close-set stones, and I roofed it over well, and added to it jointed doors, close-fitting.
>
> Thereafter I cut away the leafy branches of the long-leafed olive, and, trimming the trunk from the root, I smoothed it around with the adze well and cunningly, and made it straight to the line, thus fashioning the bed-post; and I bored it all with the augur. Beginning with this I hewed out my bed, till I had finished it, inlaying it with gold and silver and ivory, and I stretched on it a thong of ox-hide, bright with purple. Thus do I declare to thee this token; but I know not, woman, whether my bedstead is still fast in its place, or whether by now some man has cut from beneath the olive stump, and set the bedstead elsewhere."

VI. ITHAKA: PRELIMINARY NOTES

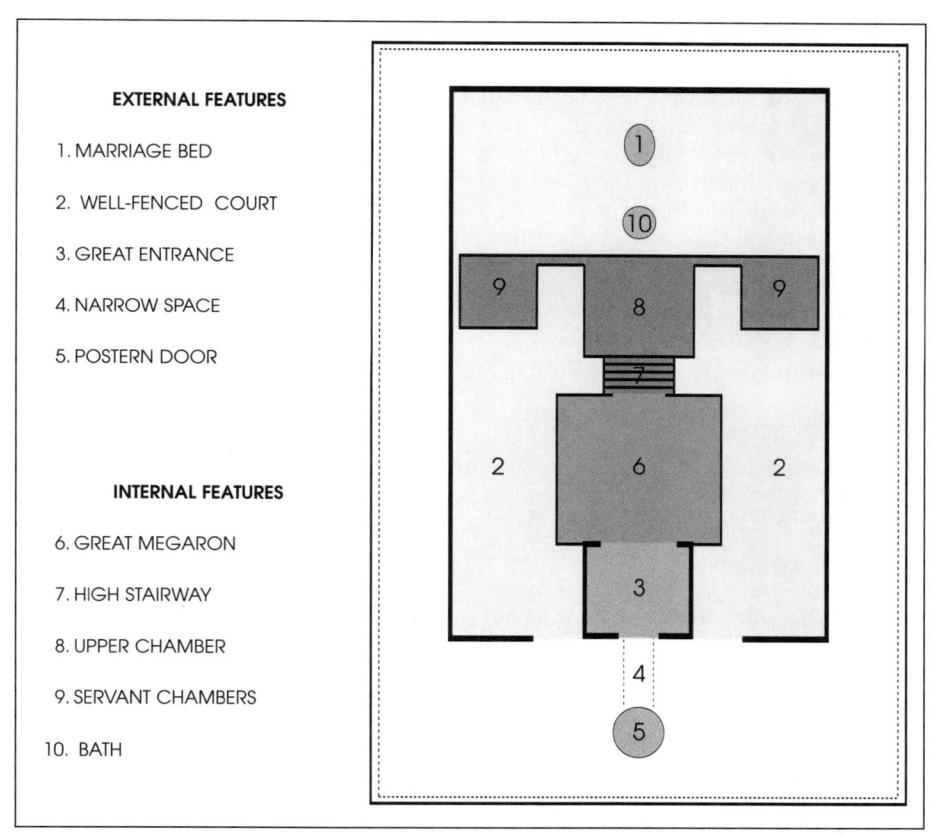

EXTERNAL FEATURES

1. MARRIAGE BED
2. WELL-FENCED COURT
3. GREAT ENTRANCE
4. NARROW SPACE
5. POSTERN DOOR

INTERNAL FEATURES

6. GREAT MEGARON
7. HIGH STAIRWAY
8. UPPER CHAMBER
9. SERVANT CHAMBERS
10. BATH

TABLE 6. 2. THE PALACE OF ODYSSEUS. The schematic representation of diverse rooms, and their relationship to each other, suggest the existence of a habitational unit of palacial proportions together with a complex of other units which comprised the city of ITHAKA.

That Odysseus "fashioned" their marriage bed in this or that way, seems *à propos* of newlyweds seeking to understand and adapt to each other. Penelope's fidelity, the preservation of her sexual integrity, is paramount to the exquisite beauty of the story —the requital of their unspent youth in old age (xxiii, 211-12)— yet of Odysseus, we know not of the women in his life. Alas.

2. WELL-FENCED COURT. All units of the palace enclosed by a wall homologous with the *labia majora* (xxii, 437):

> "Begin now to bear forth the dead bodies and bid the women help you, and thereafter cleanse the beautiful chairs and the tables with water and porous sponges. But when you have set all the house in order, lead the women forth from the well-built hall to a place between the dome and the goodly fence of the court, and there strike them down with your long swords, until you take away the life from them all, and

they forget the love which they had at the bidding of the wooers, when they lay with them in secret."

So he spoke, and the women came all in a throng, wailing terribly and shedding big tears. First they bore forth the bodies of the slain and set them down beneath the portico of the well-fenced court, propping them one against the other; and Odysseus himself gave them orders and hastened on the work, and they bore the bodies forth perforce. Then they cleansed the beautiful high seats and the tables with water and porous sponges. But Telemachus and the neatherd and the swineherd scraped with hoes the floor of the well-built house, and the women bore the scrapings forth and threw them out of doors.

3. GREAT ENTRANCE. Entrance, or "vestibule", to the interior of the palace, homologous with the vaginal opening (i, 106; 252):

There she found the proud wooers. They were taking their pleasure at draughts in front of the doors, sitting on the hides of oxen which they themselves had slain; and of the heralds and busy squires, some were mixing wine and water for them in bowls, others again were washing the tables with porous sponges and setting them forth, while still others were portioning out meats in abundance.

Then, stirred to anger, Pallas Athene spoke to him: "Out on it! Thou hast of a truth sore need of Odysseus that is gone, that he might put forth his hands upon the shameless wooers. Would that he might come now and take his stand at the outer gate of the house, with helmet and shield and two spears, such a man as he was when I first saw him in our house drinking and making merry, on his way back from Ephyre, from the house of Ilus, son of Mermerus..."

4. NARROW SPACE. A pathway leading from the GREAT ENTRANCE to the POSTERN DOOR, homologous with the *perineum* (xxii, 457, 465):

But when they had set in order all the hall, they led the women forth from the well-built hall to a place between the dome and the goodly fence of the court, and shut them up in a narrow space, whence it was in no wise possible to escape. Then wise Telemachus was the first to speak to the others...

So he spoke, and tied the cable of a dark-prowed ship to a great pillar and flung it round the dome, stretching it on high that none might reach the ground with her feet. And as when long-winged thrushes or doves fall into a snare that is set in a thicket, as they seek to reach their resting-place, and hateful is the bed that gives them welcome, even so the women held their heads in a row, and round the necks of all nooses were laid, that they might die most piteously. And they writhed a little while with their feet, but not long.

5. POSTERN DOOR. A back entrance, of sorts, homologous with the anal sphincter (xxii, 126):

Now there was in the well-built wall a certain postern door, and along the topmost level of the threshold of the well-built hall was a way into a passage, and well-fitting folding doors closed it. This postern Odysseus bade the goodly swineherd watch, taking his stand close by, for there was but a single way to reach it. Then Agelaus spoke among the wooers, and declared his word to all: "It may not be, Agelaus, fostered of Zeus, for terribly near is the fair door of the court, and the mouth of the passage is hard. One man could bar the way for all, so he were

VI. ITHAKA: PRELIMINARY NOTES   185

valiant. But come, let me bring you from the store-room arms to don, for it is within, methinks, and nowhere else that Odysseus and his glorious son have laid the arms."

INTERNAL FEATURES:
6. GREAT MEGARON (PLACE OF ASSEMBLY): Interior palace chamber adjacent to the GREAT ENTRANCE, homologous with the *vagina* (ii, 8; xxii, 108; xviii, 304):

And the heralds made the summons, and the Achaeans assembled full quickly. Now when they were assembled and met together, Telemachus went his way to the place of assembly, holding in his hand a spear of bronze—not alone, for along with him two swift hounds followed; and wondrous was the grace that Athene shed upon him, and all the people marvelled at him as he came. But he sat down in his father's seat, and the elders gave place.

So he spoke, and Telemachus hearkened to his dear father, and went his way to the store-chamber where the glorious arms were stored. Thence he took four shields and eight spears and four helmets of bronze, with thick plumes of horse-hair; and he bore them forth, and quickly came to his dear father. Then first of all he himself girded the bronze about his body, and even in like manner the two slaves put on them the beautiful armour, and took their stand on either side of Odysseus, the wise and crafty-minded.

But the wooers turned to dance and gladsome song, and made them merry, and waited for evening to come on. And as they made merry dark evening came upon them. Presently they set up three braziers in the hall to give them light, and round about them placed dry faggots, long since seasoned and hard, and newly split with the axe; and in the spaces between they set torches; and in turn the handmaids of Odysseus, of the steadfast heart, kindled the flame.

7. HIGH STAIRWAY. A set of steps leading from an UPPER CHAMBER OF PENELOPE to a lower GREAT HALL (PLACE OF ASSEMBLY), homologous with the *cervix* (i, 328; xxiii, 85):

And from her upper chamber the daughter of Icarius, wise Penelope, heard his wondrous song, and she went down the high stairway from her chamber, not alone, for two handmaids attended her. Now when the fair lady had come to the wooers, she stood by the doorpost of the well-built hall, holding before her face her shining veil; and a faithful handmaid stood on either side of her.

So saying, she went down from the upper chamber, and much her heart pondered whether she should stand aloof and question her dear husband, or whether she should go up to him, and clasp and kiss his head and hands. But when she had come in and had passed over the stone threshold, she sat down opposite Odysseus in the light of the fire beside the further wall; but he was sitting by a tall pillar, looking down, and waiting to see whether his noble wife would say aught to him, when her eyes beheld him.

8. UPPER CHAMBER OF PENELOPE: The innermost recess of the palace complex —indeed, the *raison d'être* of ITHAKA— homologous with the

uterus. Presumably, the description of this chamber is that of a female understanding of her innermost being (xxi, 1, 42):

> But the goddess, flashing-eyed Athene, put it into the heart of the daughter of Icarius, wise Penelope, to set before the wooers in the halls of Odysseus the bow and the gray iron, to be a contest and the beginning of death. She climbed the high stairway to her chamber, and took the bent key in her strong hand—a goodly key of bronze, and on it was a handle of ivory. And she went her way with her handmaidens to a store-room, far remote, where lay the treasures of her lord, bronze and gold and iron, wrought with toil. And there lay the back-bent bow and the quiver that held the arrows, and many arrows were in it...

> Now when the fair lady had come to the store-room, and had stepped upon the threshold of oak, which of old the carpenter had skillfully planed and made straight to the line—thereon had he also fitted door-posts, and set on them bright doors—straightway she quickly loosed the thong from the handle and thrust in the key, and with sure aim shot back the bolts. And as a bull bellows when grazing in a meadow, even so bellowed the fair doors, smitten by the key; and quickly they flew open before her. Then she stepped upon the high floor, where the chests stood in which fragrant raiment was stored, and stretched out her hand from thence and took from its peg the bow together with the bright case which surrounded it. And there she sat down and laid the case upon her knees and wept aloud, and took out the bow of her lord.

A would-be **High chamber of Telemakhos** has been interpolated by some ambitious scholar of the *Odyssey* who failed to understand the correspondence between a chamber and internal female reproductive organs, as evinced not only by an inappropriate chamber of a son, but also by falling short of an adequate description (i, 420):

> But Telemachus, where his chamber was built in the beautiful court, high, in a place of wide outlook, thither went to his bed, pondering many things in mind; and with him, bearing blazing torches, went true-hearted Eurycleia, daughter of Ops, son of Peisenor... He opened the doors of the well-built chamber, sat down on the bed, and took off his soft tunic and laid it in the wise old woman's hands. And she folded and smoothed the tunic and hung it on a peg beside the corded bedstead, and then went forth from the chamber, drawing the door to by its silver handle, and driving the bolt home with the thong. So there, the night through, wrapped in a fleece of wool, he pondered in his mind upon the journey which Athene had shewn him.

9. SERVANT CHAMBERS (OF EURYKLEIA AND EURYNOME). Chambers of attendant maidservants, adjoining the main UPPER CHAMBER OF PENELOPE, homologous with the ovaries (xxiii, 40):

> [Eurykleia]: "As for us women, we sat terror-stricken in the innermost part of our well-built chambers, and the close-fitting doors shut us in, until the hour when thy son Telemachus called me from the hall, for his father had sent him forth to call me. Then I found Odysseus standing among the bodies of the slain, and they, stretched all around him on the hard floor, lay one upon the other; the sight would have warmed thy heart with cheer".

10. BATH. This place, apparently privy to Penelope and Odysseus, is homologous with the female urinary *meatus* (iv, 758; xxiii, 152):

> She [Penelope] then bathed, and took clean raiment for her body, and went up to her upper chamber with her handmaids, and placing barley grains in a basket prayed to Athene...

> Meanwhile the housewife Eurynome bathed the great-hearted Odysseus in his house, and anointed him with oil, and cast about him a fair cloak and a tunic; and over his head Athene shed abundant beauty, making him taller to look upon and mightier, and from his head she made locks to flow in curls like the hyacinth flower.

ITHAKA, A LITERARY CENTER

That ITHAKA was a literary centre would seem best understood on two counts:

First, there had to be some knowledge about an AKHAIAN proposal of a massive DANAAN invasion on Troy, since such a proposal could only be successful *if* permission were granted by Odysseus, lord of NERITON (II, 631). That Odysseus was the correct candidate for —let us not call it "treason", but, rather, "a reason"— rhymes with his presence among kin in Tyrhenian waters (xix, 428 *et pas.*), and, so, eventually, an initial *pied-a-tère* was gained on the shores of Orebič (MAP 6. 1). Thus, a large number of a varied peoples from the length and breadth of the Italian Peninsula, assembled in the vicinity of ITHAKA for nine years, offered the unique opportunity —truly, one that would never again happen— of making a detailed census of who had come from where. This census will have been fashioned in the same manner as an earlier one, the *Catalogue of Trojan Forces* (II, 818–877), which contains only sparse information on local Trojan defensive forces, and thus is simply a catalogue of Trojan allies abroad, schematically distributed from north to south along the length and breadth of the Italian Peninsula. This *Catalogue of Trojan Allies* (or, alternately, *Catalogue of Trojan Forces [Abroad]*), probably worked in conjunction with some other body of information (perhaps a work on astronomy?) as some sort of accounting of the past. However, by the time the Danaan Invasions became a political reality, the *Catalogue of Trojan Allies* probably served as a model for the composition of a far larger and far more detailed census of peoples and their places of origin who were mingled with Trojan allies, the magnificent *Catalogue of Ships* (II, 494–756).

Second, that Odysseus will have been, without a doubt, the prime informant for the subject-matter of the *Odyssey*, and, further, that he tells of Demodokos in the Palace of Alkinoos (viii, 44 *et pas.*), can only have been inspired by empirical knowledge, thus the account about Phemios among the wooers of Penelope (i, 325; xxii, 330):

> For them the famous minstrel [Phemios] was singing, and they sat in silence listening; and he sang of the return of the Achaeans—the woeful return from Troy which Pallas Athene laid upon them. And from her upper chamber the daughter of Icarius, wise Penelope, heard his wondrous song...

> Now the son of Terpes, the minstrel, was still seeking to escape black fate, even Phemius, who sang perforce among the wooers. He stood with the clear-toned lyre in his hands near the postern door, and he was divided in mind whether he should slip out from the hall and sit down by the well-built altar of great Zeus, the God of the court, whereon Laertes and Odysseus had burned many thighs of oxen, or whether he should rush forward and clasp the knees of Odysseus in prayer. And as he pondered this seemed to him the better course, to clasp the knees of Odysseus, son of Laertes.

NAKOVANA: COMPOSITIONS OF THE ILIAD AND ODYSSEY

By the same token that an unavoidable inference is made about ITHAKA having been a literary centre, another, likewise unavoidable inference may be made about diverse places in the region of Nakovana, on the western slopes of SAMOS (Sveti Ilija/Monte Vípera), which cannot be separated from the compositions of the *Iliad* and *Odyssey*.

AN ASTRONOMIC OBSERVATION PLATFORM

There exists an observation platform, situated on the western slopes of SAMOS (Sveti Ilija/Monte Vípera), some 150 meters below the summit (961 meters above sea level), from where two equinox sunsets were recorded.₀

The one, a Spring Equinox sunset on March 21, *c*.1,100 BC, describes how the small constellation of Pleiades, "the Seven Banished Sisters" represents Hephaistos (in whose name is implicit "the seven banished ones"). The Pleiades are separated from the ecliptic (that is, the sun's "path" along the stars) by some five degrees, and thus, in the dusk, after sunset, the constellation which seems to have only one "foot", as it were, appears to fall directly on LEMNOS (*Issa*, Viš), which lies some five degrees north of where the sun will have sunk into the horizon (I, 590–4):

> "...Yea, on a time ere this, when I [Hephaistos] was fain to save thee [Hera}, he caught me by the foot and hurled me from the heavenly threshold; the whole day long was I borne headlong, and at set of sun I fell in Lemnos, and but little life was in me. There did the Sintian folk make haste to tend me for my fall."

The other, an Autumn Equinox sunset (XIII, 10, *et passim*), has already been described in the FOREWORD, p. 26.

VI. ITHAKA: PRELIMINARY NOTES

This platform appears to have been a hallowed site —indeed, perhaps the *most* sacred of all in TROIA— for here, a few minutes after sunrise of every Spring and Autumn Equinox, and *only* on these dates, the sun's disk —the brightest light in all the Unviverse— will appear briefly, for a minute, or so, to be perched on the very peak of SAMOS. So it is that the archetypal icon of Orpheus comes to mind, unbidden, also perched on a stone, lyre in hand, singing...[1] Historically, this mountain, a precinct of light, as it were, became *Veliki Triglav*, the Great Trinity of Svetovid ("He who sees all and is *seen* by all"), Perun and Svarog, and, in time, after Perun was Christianized, became known as Sveti Ilija, Saint Elijah, lord of thunder and lightning, who arose into heaven in flames.

WITNESSES OF AN ODYSSEAN SCENE

Scenes from the Misadventures of Odysseus represented in Greco-Italic iconography all seem to have been derived from the first-hand account given by Odysseus himself, all, with the exception of one, which comes from a source external to the *Odyssey*, namely, the scene of Odysseus tied to the mast of his vessel as it sails through the **Planktai**, being observed by one, sometimes two, winged creatures with female faces.

These creatures usually have been identified as the **Seirenes** —an easy inference... monsters observing a man tied to the mast of a vessel— albeit they should have obvious watery associations, they are distinctly airy beings. The correct inference, then, is that this scene will have been drawn from some historical memory crediting the **Harpyiai** with having sighted Odysseus from Nakavana, as he passed by silently on his predestined encounter with disaster at **Kharybdis** (Vratnik).

Nothing of substance is known of the **Harpyiai**, or "snatchers", other than they are thought to have been storm demons (hence Greek lore credited Iris, the messenger, as a cousin) albeit they were a people (see TABLE 5.2) who did *not* consort with Odysseus (which does not preclude his knowledge of them), and that they were known to Telemakhos (i, 241–000), Eumaios (xiv, 371–000), and Penelope (xx, 77–00).

Their icon is a representation of their totemic identity, the bat, thus, a winged creature with talons and breasts (since the bat is a mammal), and because it has breasts, the face of a female. Still, why is it that the **Harpyiai** were a bat-totem folk, and not, say, the local jackal, or the

---

1. Herein lies the origin of Apollo's place as a patron of the arts.

much sought after mountain-goat? or even snake, abundant in the region? Gibbering bats might, perhaps, be associated with the chirruping songs of the cicada, the totemic identity of Tros, father of Ilos, after whom the mountain Sveti Ilija is named...

Surely, a connection can be made between the souls of fifty suitors, led by Hermes to their resting place, like bats issuing in a string from a cave at sunset (xxiv, 1, *et pas.*), and the cleansed halls of ITHAKA, where **Harpyiai** might once again be welcomed?

CHAPTER VII

THE TWELVE MISADVENTURES OF ODYSSEUS

Odysseus is mentioned 126 times in the *Iliad*, third in place after Agamemnon (167) and Menelaos (134). With regard to the Trojan plight of fighting a massive invasion of Danaans, it is Odysseus who is the central figure, for, without his consent, Agamemnon could never have gained an indispensible *pied-à-terre* on Trojan soil. It is little wonder that Odysseus was so distinguished as to have been mentioned leading twelve vermillion-prowed ships (II, 631–637) from the south side of NERITON (PelješacPeninsula), around its western tip, to disembark on the north side, at the marshy delta of the SKAMANDROS (Neretva).

ULYSSES AND ODYSSEUS

It is common to confuse the name Ulysses with that of Odysseus, which is *not* the Latinization of Odysseus, but, rather, the name of an entirely different personage whose name is derived from an earlier Etruscan form, Flixes or Vlixes or Uluxe. Apparently, it was Lucius Livius Andronicus (*c.* 284 – *c.* 204 BC) who first equated the name of Odysseus with that of Ulixes in his *Odusia*, a rendering of the *Odyssey* into Latin. He also established (rather than "translated") the Roman counterparts of Greek gods and goddesses (Mousa, Camena; Athena, Minerva; Aphrodite, Venus; Poseidon, Neptune; and so on). This Flixes or Vlixes or Uluxeis is registered in the *Catalogue of Ships* (II, 653–670) under the name of Tlepolemos. He was exiled from his native EPHYRE (*Cortona*) in the heart of Etruria for the accidental (or some say premeditated) murder of his granduncle. He took with him a band of Rhodian followers, and they established colonies in LINDOS (Corsica), IALYSOS (Sardinia), and KAMEIROS (Sicily). The pathos in the story is not in the details about the woes that Vlixes *alias* Tlepolemos suffered, about which little is known, but, rather, in the harshness of justice, further heightened by the use of the term *rhodioi* (II, 653 *et pas.*), denoting "autochthonous". The root *rhod-* is cognate with Russian *rodina*, meaning "mother earth" and, indeed, *rod*, that which "wells up from the earth", whence *narodna*, "national", from whence the inference that his loyal followers were an innocent folk forcibly uprooted and banished from their native land. Silius Italicus (*c*. AD 26–102) claimed (*Punica*, III, 364) that Tlepolemos and a certain Lindos also settled the Balearics, in the Western Mediterranean[1].

Further doings of Tlepolemos in Tyrrhenian waters are adduced from a garbled version of the now non-existent *Telegonia* of the Epic Cycle, which brought the Heroic Age to a close. This work is ascribed to either a certain Eugammon of Cyrene or a Cinaethon of Lacedaemon, possibly of the 6th century BC. A summary is given by Proclus (412–485 AD) in his *Chrestomathia*, in which Telegonus, son of Odysseus by Circe, kills Odysseus (accidentally) and then marries Penelope, and, to even out the score, Telemachus, son of Odysseus and Penelope, marries Circe. The Thesprotians and the Brygi are brought into the fray, and it all reads ungeographically (H. G. Evelyn-White, *Hesiod, the Homeric Hymns and Homerica*, 1954). However, both Ovid (43 BC–AD 17) in his *Metamorphosis*, XIV, 246 ff, and his friend Hyginus, in his *Fabulae*, under "Telegonus", concur that Ulixes —not Odysseus— dallied with a certain sorceress Circe, at *Promontorium Circeum* (a hill riddled with caves infested with poisonous spiders), from whom Telegonus was born and who went on to be founder of *Tusculum*. It is to be assumed, of course, that Kirke is not the name of a person, but, rather, of a certain kind of sorceress, like a spider weaving a *circular* web, bound and drugged her victims... this must be so, because there is no way *Promontorium Circeum* in *Latium* can be understood as Odysseus coming to the Aiaian isle, νῆσόν τ' Αἰαίην (xii, 3)

THE HISTORICAL IDENTITY OF ODYSSEUS

Hitherto, Odysseus has only been a literary figure. When and where he steps into the reality of an historical personage, if at all, is impossible to say, unless his parallel —a conflictive individual of about the same period who departs from the established order— could be found in Hittite documentation[2]. Such an individual appears to have been a certain Madduwattas, whose name is made up of the Mittanian words *maddo-* "fat" (cognate with Greek μαζός, "breast") and -(*w*)*attas* "father" (cog-

---

1. Pausanias (x. 17. 5) would give a reverse account, that Iberians under Norax, son of Hermes, founded Nora, the most ancient town of Sardinia (LINDOS). There likewise exists the town of Nora on the isle of Formentera in the Balearics. The *nuraghe* (so called after Norax?) of Sardinia and Corsica resembles the *talayot* of Mallorca.
2. *Indictment of Madduwattas* by the Hittite king Arnuwandas IV, 1220–1190 BC.

nate with Greek ἄττα and Serbian *otac*, "father"), possibly a nickname meaning something on the order of "big father" as in the idea of "Fat Daddy". The identity of Madduwattas might well be that of Autolykos, grandfather of Odysseus (xix, 405 *et pa*s.):

> Then Autolycus answered her [Eurykleia], and said: "My daughter's husband and my daughter, give him whatsoever name I say. Lo, inasmuch as I am come hither as one that has been angered with many, both men and women, over the fruitful earth, therefore let the name by which the child is named be Odysseus [i.e., "Child of Wrath"][3].

Now, the presumed meaning of the name Autolykos seems somewhat artificial, albeit rationalized as follows (J. Russo, *Commentary on Homer's Odyssey* on xix, 394, 96):

> Αὐτόλυκον: Odysseus' maternal grandfather is significantly named: aÈto-lukow suggests 'the wolf himself' or 'the very wolf'. The brief portrait given in this passage shows a man impressive for his ability to come out on top of his dealings with others, who approaches such dealings always in an adversary manner. Autolykos is thus a prototype of Odysseus' personality seen in its most negative aspect.

Autolykos' conduct, by his own admission, is conflictive, and so his name could just as well be conveyed by that of Zalykos, "very wolf-like", rather than by an awkward use of αὐτο-. Perhaps, then, an inference can be made that the name of Autolykos is a late (Alexandrine?) editorial emendation of an original Autolipos, "fatness itself"[4].

THE EXILE OF ODYSSEUS

If, indeed, Troy was eventually sacked by the vast numerical superiority of invading Danaans, one might likewise contemplate that, perhaps, internal factors were also at work, namely a political and social weaknesses inherent in a Trojan hegemony, of foreign stock, established upon diverse autochthonous peoples. Thus, one of the ironies of the *Odyssey* is that Odysseus, fighting with his colleagues on the marshy plains of the SKAMANDROS (Neretva) delta-valley not more than some 90 kilometers from ITHAKA, could have returned on foot within a day, or two, or in

---

3. That Eurykleia has placed the infant on the knees ἐπί γούνασι (401) of its maternal grandfather is an act of legitimizing, of making "genuine", as it were, the infant Odysseus. This custom is mentioned in Milan Budimir's engaging collection of essays, *Ca balkanski istočnica* (*Balkan Sources*, Belgrade, 1969), how the custom, since time immemorial, is to place one's progeny on one's knees and so presented to society as one's *genuine* offspring. This is the underlying reason why early portraiture of the Virgin Mary depicts the Christ Child on her knees, presented to the world as a genuine Son of God.

4. A broader understanding of the connection of Autolykos/Autolipos with Madduwattas and the land(s) of Ardzawa associated with Zippasla and Apasos, would suggest that territories also held by the Var*dz*aei, an Illyrian folk of the Neretva delta, included SIPYLOS (Monti Sibillini) and PAISOS (*Asculum Picenum*, Ascoli), directly across the Adriatic Sea, on the Italian Peninsula.

half a day by crossing the HELLESPONTOS by boat, but he chose a self-imposed exile. It is not difficult to presume that the intrigues of Odysseus *polytropos* "of the many wiles" were a factor in the collapse of Troy, albeit his exile was voluntary, for the narrative line does not seem to suggest the contrary, even though he willfully elicited the wrath of Poseidon (who made his return all the more arduous). This exile became synonymous with the transference of a seat of power from ILIOS to ITHAKA, for the Trojan hinterland was left abandoned, and the number of cities which formerly made up a Trojan confederacy became reduced. The data which was, upon a time, collected on ILIOS during the Trojan War, later to be cast in the *Iliad*, now passed to ITHAKA for its custody, and, still later, the information offered up by Odysseus once returned to ITHAKA made him the prime informant of the *Odyssey*.

It could be said the *Odyssey* reflects the political apathy of a ruling class now domiciled in ITHAKA, for the Royal House of Troy has fled towards Pannonia, leaving no representative behind to reassemble the social wreckage, while foreign youths seek to gain local power through marriage with Penelope. Thus, after the return of the Danaan invaders to their dear native lands, who had come to Troy more for economic reasons than for the justice of returning Helen and the goods she and Paris had stolen, only fifty[5] courtesans remained, who would, all at once, in due course, find swift, unnatural deaths.

No Akhaiisms seem to be immediately detected in former Trojan lands, from which, the inference that Danaans were unable to colonize what already lay in depredation, and that perhaps the self-imposed exile of Odysseus might be understood as a proselytism in favour of a New Illyrian Order, a revolutionary movement (in the Burkian sense of drastic local changes which eventually transcend borders and effect similar changes abroad). However, what has been learned through the *Iliad*, and will be confirmed in the *Odyssey*, is that, quite independently of a Trojan War on account of the abduction of Helen, and to boot, the looting of the treasury, was the methodical preparation for substituting the age-old matriarchal society of Troy, represented by the alternate identities of the Mother Goddess as Eternal Virgin or Eternal Procreatrix, for the now (apparently) prevalent patriarchal society, represented by a new spectrum of imagery, specifically, in this venture against Troy, by the stag in whose antlers is borne a fiery sun-disk (see III. THE TROJAN WAR AND FALL OF TROY, p. 138; FIGURE 1 p. 269). Thus, Troy's fate had been

---

5. Fifty is a number used for progeny, thus Nereus and the fifty Nereids, Priam and his fifty sons. Here, fifty suitors is to be understood as all from a common class. It is not beyond credibility that fifty may represent "rabble", connoting a certain disdain.

sealed long before Helen was abducted, perhaps even before she was born. *Now* it will make geographical and historical sense *why* the modern names of the southernmost and northernmost islands of the Dalmatian Archipelago, Šipan in the south, and Brač in the north, have no linguistic or historic link with age-old Homeric geonyms, as do other neighbouring islands, for these are closely associated with a Danaan import, the stag (see *Map.* 7. 1). Henceforward, LESBOS would become *Brattia*, from Illyrian *brentos*, "stag", and AIGILIPS, *Elaphites*, "Deer Isles" (see I. THE ILIAD AND ITS TROJAN GEOGRAPHY, pp. 60, 64; also, V. THE ODYSSEY AND ITS FANTASTIC GEOGRAPHY, pp. 147, 150).

It seems obvious, then, that the Trojan Archipelago enclosed by ENOPE (*Epetium*, Stobrec) in the north, and KARDAMYLE (*Epidaurum*, Cavtat) in the south, which has passed from a Trojan dominion to an Achaiian possession, evinces the cruelty of Akhilleus in his conversation with the vanquished and tired old Priam (XXIV, 543, ff):

> And of thee, old sire, we hear that of old thou was blest; how of all that toward the sea Lesbos, the seat of Macar, encloseth, and Phrygia in the upland, and the boundless Hellespont, [truncated text] over all these folk, men say, thou, old sire, wast preeminent by reason of thy wealth and thy sons.

Was there, really, any need of apprising the old man of this fact?

It is now *c.* 1,100 BC. Two great ethnic groups coalesced into distinctive cultural identities: in the interior, a folk called by different names that would eventually become Serbs, and on the coast and islands, a folk comprised of several tribes that would eventually become Croats.

THE TRUTH ABOUT SKHERIA

The itinerary of the Misadventures of Odysseus is easy and schematically ordered: the first six places visited occur north of NERITON (Pelješac), the second six, south of it. Those that occur in the north have a clear parallel with those that occur in the south, which instantly shows that the *Descent to the Netherworld* is an independent episode, like a literary patch, skillfully woven into the narrative line at its midpoint. These Misadventures —fantastic as they seem— reflect some semblance of, or insinuate some acquaintance with, a factual truth regarding the habits and customs of different island folks of the Trojan Coast. Without the testimony of Odysseus, this information would have been lost to us.

Towards the end of the ninth year of captivity on the island of **Ogygia** (= ZAKYNTHOS, *Melita*, Mljet)[6], Odysseus has built a raft of

---

6. Calypso bids Odysseus leave the island in the eighth year (vii, 261), thus, in the ninth, he builds a raft and leaves. His absence of twenty years is corroborrated by his own words in xxiv, 322.

sorts at KILLA (Polače), situated at the northwestern end of the island facing the mainland. The feat is (deceptively) simple, to cross over the swift currents of the Mljetski Kanal, once again pass **Skylla** and **Kharybdis** (Olipa Straights), this time unscathed, enter **Phorkys** (Stonski Kanal), and, at the end of the narrow fjord, finally gain a foothold on NERITON (Pelješac).

Now, the question is whether Odysseus did, in fact, visit **Skheria** (Sčedro) after a near-fatal ordeal with a stormy sea, or, whether he simply began to drown as images of his life came into view? The answer must be that he was swept, like helpless flotsam and jetsam, into the treacherous waters of the [IKAROPONTOS] (Korčulanski Channel), in the midst of which **Skheria** was situated (*MAP 7. 1*).

Once, already, Odysseus had departed this island and sailed these waters, without incident, after having taken the young Chyseis back to her father, and returned to the camp the following day (I, 477):

> ... and as soon as early Dawn appeared, the rosyfingered, then they set sail for the wide camp of the Achaeans. And Apollo, that worketh afar, sent them a favouring wind, and they set up the mast and spread the white sail. So the wind filled the belly of the sail, and the dark wave sang loudly about the stem of the ship, as she went, and she sped over the wave, accomplishing her way. But when they were come to the wide camp of the Achaeans, they drew the black ship up on the shore, high upon the sands, and set in line the long props beneath, and themselves scattered among the huts and ships.

Compare the foregoing scene of Odysseus, proud, virile, master of his fate, captain of his soul, with the sad image of an aged vagabond, eighteen years later, frightened, hiding (v, 278):

> For seventeen days then he sailed over the sea, and on the eighteenth appeared the shadowy mountains of the land of the Phaeacians, where it lay nearest to him; and it shewed like unto a shield in the misty deep.

Later, when he arrives at **Skheria** (v, 388 *et pas*), the awesome figure of Orion comes to the fore, rising in the early evening with power and majesty from the horizon. If one can imagine being on the isle of **Skheria** (Sčedro), facing south, Orion would rise from the southeast, precisely from where Odysseus would be coming, and, almost reaching the safety of some small beach, as it were, yet, once passing the meridian, be pulled back out into the [IKAROPONTOS] (Korčulanski Channel) by mysterious forces, until at last, towards dawn, finding a resting place at the mouth of a river. A resemblance of Odysseus with Orion is inescapable, as well as the imagery of both associated with *ouron*, "urine" ("water") and *ouron*, "boundary", a place of rest at the mouth of a river. In the morning there arrives a young maiden on the scene. Who could she be? Her name is Nausikaa, her identity is Spica, in the constellation Virgo.

VII. THE TWELVE MISADVENTURES OF ODYSSEUS

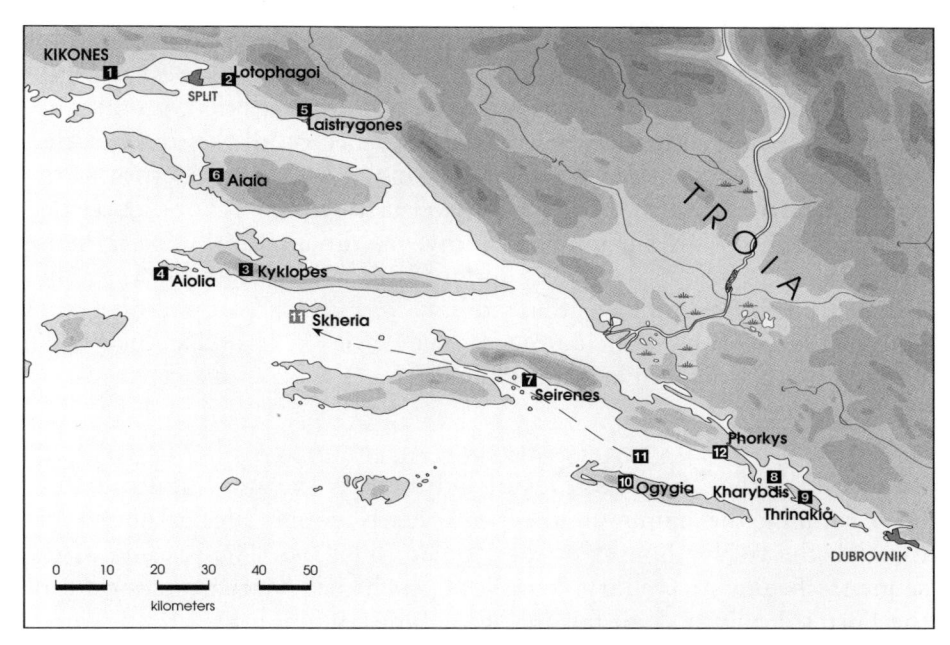

MAP 7.1. THE TWELVE MISADVENTURES OF ODYSSEUS. All episodes occur along the Trojan coast and islands, six north and six south of NERITON (Pelješac Peninsula). Of the six episodes in the north, three occur on the mainland, and three on the islands. If the same occurs with the six episodes in the south, then three occur on islands, two on the mainland (8 and 12), the third (11) being an interpretation of whether he touched "land" at the bottom of the sea, or came briefly on land at the shore of Nakovana.

	DEPARTURE FROM FIELDS OF WAR
KIKONES	Odysseus looses contact with reality
Lotophagoi	Odysseus in a place of rest and forgetfulness (the past)
Kyklopes	Odysseus is prisoner of a monster
Aiolia	Odysseus and his men commit a transgression
Laistrygones	Odysseus and his men are attacked
Aiaia	Odysseus in danger of a fatal seduction
	DESCENT TO THE NETHERWORLD
Seirenes	Odysseus in danger of a fatal seduction
Skylla	Odysseus and his men are attacked
Thrinakia	Odysseus and his men commit a transgression
Ogygia	Odysseus is prisoner of a nymph
Skheria	Odysseus in a place of peace and tranquility (the future)
Phorkys	Odysseus regains contact with reality
	ARRIVAL IN ITHAKA

TABLE 7.2. PARALLEL EPISODES. The first six misadventures represent Odysseus going down into the Netherworld, while the second six represent him coming up from it, thus, there are distinct parallels between both sets of episodes.

So it is that, as Odysseus drowns, he visits the Netherworld, as if his toes have touched the bottom of the sea, literally, the greatest depth of his woes, and at the very doors of death. Still, the external, literal sense of this episode, at the midpoint in the sequence of all the mishaps that would befall Odysseus, evinces a superficial allegory of a return to the womb of Mother Earth, perceived in a visit to **Kokytos** (Pópoli), nestled in the region of La Maiella massif. However, the internal, spiritual sense of an episode about drowning among the fishes of the sea, is that Odysseus has succumbed to that sublime *tour de force* of poetry, to that Song the Sirens sang, which already once before he had disdained while passing by the isles of **Planktai** (Planjak *et al.*).

A COURSE ALONG THE ECLIPTIC

The story of the Misadventures of Odysseus is the story about a solar hero running the gamut of the sun's yearly course along the ecliptic through the twelve houses of the Zodiac (*TABLE 7.4*). The reading of the sequence begins in January, with BULL, such that March, the month of the Spring Equinox, will fall in CRAB, June, the month of the Summer Solstice, in SCALES, September, the Autumn Equinox, in GOAT, and, finally, December, the Winter Solstice, in RAM, when the sun dies but is instantly reborn to begin a new cycle. This configuration does not represent an astronomical reality, as, otherwise, one would have to assume that the scheme begins at some date near 7,720 BC, which seems unlikely, since the composition of the *Odyssey* is sometime near 1,000 BC.

* * *

Now, the *Odyssey*, although a story about a solar hero running through the twelve houses of the Zodiac, is stretched to a period of twenty years (or units of time), but still parallels the *Iliad's* twelve years (or units of time). Thus, when the *Odyssey* opens, Odysseus has already experienced nine episodes, not unlike the *Iliad's* nine years of waiting until the appointed time. However, the *deus ex machina* of Odysseus leaving **Ogygia** on a raft, after a symbolic period of gestation, corresponds exactly with the *Iliad's* launching a definitive naval attack on the Trojan mainland (*TABLE 7. 5*).

There follows below a synopsis of each of the twelve Misadventures of Odysseus[7].

---

7. The parallels between the Misadventures of Odysseus and the *Epic of Gilgamesh* are so close as to imply that the final version of the *Epic of Gilgamesh*, occuring in twelve stations (which has a long and varied history before reaching this state) was the result of a direct contact between the authorships of both works. These parallels are best broached in a separate work at some later date.

VII. THE TWELVE MISADVENTURES OF ODYSSEUS

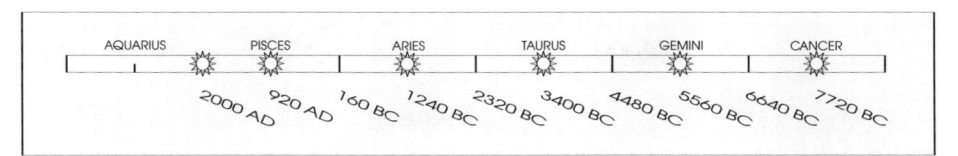

TABLE 7.3. PRECESSION OF THE EQUINOXES. The sun appears to slip backwards on the Ecliptic at the rate of 1° every 72 years, thus, the Equinoxes (the point where the Ecliptic crosses the Equator), have slipped out of ARIES long ago, and are now, literally, at "The Dawning of the Age of Aquarius". This phenomenon, though observed in antiquity, could not be explained until the advent of modern astronomy.

HOUSES OF THE ZODIAC

JANUARY	-	BULL	JULY	-	SCORPION
FEBRUARY	-	TWINS	AUGUST	-	BOWMAN
MARCH	-	**CRAB**	**SEPTEMBER**	-	**GOAT**
APRIL	-	LION	OCTOBER	-	WATERMAID
MAY	-	VIRGIN	NOVEMBER	-	FISH
JUNE	-	**SCALES**	**DECEMBER**	-	**RAM**

TABLE 7.4. TWELVE HOUSES OF THE ZODIAC. That CRAB corresponds with the Spring Equinox in March is a literary convention that associates the yearly rebirth of life with the amazing regenerative powers of the crab, which can grow back an eye, or claw, or limb it has lost. That 7,720 BC attests to the date of invention of this scheme (Table 7.3.) does not ring true.

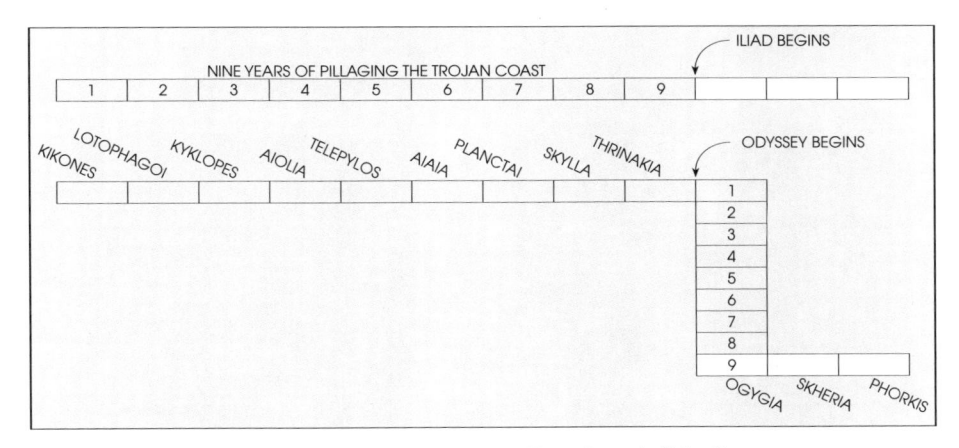

TABLE 7.5. TIME SPANS OF THE ILIAD AND ODYSSEY. The story-stuff in the MISADVENTURES OF ODYSSEUS occurs when Odysseus is drowning (that is, "visiting" among the **Phaiakes**) in the month of November, in the 19th year after leaving the fields of war. The number 19 has an inseparable association with the sea because it corresponds with the Metonic Cycle, which equals 235 lunations, after which the phases of the moon will occur on the same dates of the year, and therefore tides may be predicted.

EPISODE I: JANUARY – BULL

Ismaros (Kikones)

Odysseus and his men leave the scene of the Trojan War and come to **Ismaros** (*Tragurium*, Trogir), which they sack. They are drunken and rowdy, and behave shamelessly, until, at last, the KIKONES seek help from their neighbours, and finally are able to route Odysseus and his men from their midst. (However, Maro, whom Odysseus protected, has given Odysseus precious gifts and a skin of special wine).

COMMENTARY:

The BULL, while connoting a sense of untamed, disorderly conduct, as represented by Odysseus and his men, in fact, represents the domestication of animals and therefore of civilization. A synonym of civilization is not only the domestication of animals and the creation of urban communities, it is likewise concomitant with the concocting of inebriating drinks.

VII. THE TWELVE MISADVENTURES OF ODYSSEUS

EPISODE II: FEBRUARY – TWINS

Lotophagoi (ENOPE [EPONE])

After being buffeted by winds on the high seas, Odysseus and his men come to the land of the **Lotophagoi**, a gentle folk much given to eating the *lotus*, a fruit which brings on the narcotic effect of tranquility and abandonment of all preoccupations.

Odysseus, and some of his men who had not eaten of the lotus, are able to rescue those companions who had already succumbed to a state of lethargy, and they continue on their journey.

COMMENTARY:

The TWINS, it might be said, represent a congenial society (on a cue with the affection for each other exhibited by twins), and thus *à propos* of the narcotic effect of lotus (wormwood, *Artemisia absinthium*?).

That Odysseus and his men were buffeted by winds on the high seas is a clear indication they were still intoxicated by whatever they had ingested at **Ismaros** (ix, 198), for the **Lotophagoi** occupied the environs of ENOPE [EPONE], classical *Epetium* (cog. with *appetitum*, "appetite"), within a morning's walk from **Ismaros**.

EPIDODE III: MARCH – CRAB
(SPRING EQUINOX)

Kyklopes

Odysseus and his men reach the land of the **Kyklopes**, where they enter a cavern and wait for its owner. Polyphemos arrives, shutting them in by placing a huge stone at the entrance, and he eats two men.

The following day, Polyphemos has two more men for breakfast, and leaves the cavern with Odysseus and his men shut in it. A plan of escape is devised. That night, Polyphemus eats two more men and drinks excessively. Odysseus now blinds Polyphemus with an enormous stake, gouging the only eye from his head.

To escape the ranting Polyphemus, Odysseus and his men hang on to the underside of sheep exiting the cavern. Once on board his vessel, Odysseus shouts boastings to Polyphemus, who, furious, throws huge boulders at him which only serve to raise the waves and distance the vessel from that place.

COMMENTARY:

The CRAB is a symbol of concord and regeneration, and thus of life, as it were, since it is the only creature of the animal kingdom which has the ability of regenerating a lost claw, limb, or eye. The constellation CRAB has in its midst a nebula called *Praesepe*, hardly visible excepting on clear, moonless nights. This nebula, within the confines of the constellation, so to speak, perhaps corresponds with the one-eyed Polyphemus shut in within his cave, or perhaps, that single eye gouged from his face not unlike an oyster from its shell.

There seems to be no connection between the narrative line of this episode and the month of Spring, other than, perhaps, given the circumstances, the necessary preparation of some plan or other for the successful harvesting of crops later in the year.

EPISODE IV: APRIL – LION

Aiolia (Pakleni Isles)

Odysseus and his men arrive at **Aiolia**, the island of Aiolos, king of the winds. They are welcomed amicably, and feast in the palace of the king. Upon departing, Aiolos gives Odysseus a leathern pouch containing adverse winds, but advises him not to open it.

Once on the high sea, Odysseus falls asleep. His men, seizing on the opportunity, open the leathern pouch thinking it contained jewels, but inadvertently release the adverse winds. A strong wind then blows them back to **Aiolia**, and Odysseus asks Aiolos for his forgiveness and for his help, but Odysseus and his men are rebuffed and dispatched in anger for having been profane.

COMMENTARY:

The LION seems to have become a regal transformation of an otherwise mundane guardian of a door, a barking dog.

Aiolia (Pakleni Isles), situated at the entrance to the Bay of Hvar, resemble floating blobs of grease, for which reason they were (erroneously) identified with the Lipari Isles in the Tyrhennian Sea. These isles, uninhabitable and utterly bereft of vegetation, are nevertheless of an immense value as a natural breakwater at the mouth of the bay enclosing the port of PHARE (*Pharos*, Hvar), thus protecting all vessels anchored within from the most terrible storms.

That a leathern pouch contained adverse winds seems symbolic of a map with the four winds on it... or, perhaps the reverse, that a map of the region with the four winds on it (N. S. E. W.) was folded up and never used, and thus the return of Odysseus and his men to **Aiolia**, as if they themselves had released the adverse wind that blew them thence.

EPISODE V: MAY – VIRGIN

Laistrygones (Telepylos)

Odysseus and his men come to **Telepylos**, the mouth of a river lined with sheer cliffs, where the **Laistrygones** live. At the river's exit is the spring of **Artakia**, where the maiden daughter of the king has come to fetch water. She invites the men who have approached her into her father's palace, where they find the queen, who is of enormous proportions.

One of the men is cannibalized, and, as others flee the place, back to the ships, the **Laistrygones** pelt them with stones. Odysseus barely escapes in time.

COMMENTARY:

The VIRGIN —that is, the female sex— is synonymous with pregnancy, hence the name for this month, derived from that of Maia, the Great Goddess.

Telepylos, "deep port" aptly describes the gorge of the SATNIOEIS (*Titius*, Cetina), occupied by the **Laistrygones**, an "ant" people (see etymology, p. 166), hence the queen is large and grotesque. That the men of Odysseus were pelted with stones and rocks from on high is in keeping not only with the idea of an ant-hill —indeed, as the very word *struge*, "funnel", connotes— but also with the local topographic curiosity of countless rounded stones of all sizes, forming a sieve-like dam that holds back the waters of **Artakia**.

VII. THE TWELVE MISADVENTURES OF ODYSSEUS

EPISODE VI: JUNE – SCALES
(SUMMER SOLSTICE)

Aiaia

Odysseus and his men come to **Aiaia**, the isle of Kirke. Odysseus goes ashore and climbs to a height from where he sees the halls of Kirke. On his return to the ship a stag suddenly appears, which he kills and takes back for his men to feast on.

Odysseus sends men to Kirke, who receives them, feeds them food laced with poison, and they turn into swine. Odysseus is supplied by Hermes with *moly*, an antidote to the charms of Kirke, and eventually he obtains the release of his men, who rejoice.

Odysseus is sent away from **Aiaia** charged with the task of visiting the house of Hades, where he must consult with the spirit of Teiresias. To accomplish this task, he must cross the streams of OKEANOS.

COMMENTARY:

SCALES are symbolic of the division of the solar year into two equal periods of time at the mid-summer solstice.

The Stag of **Aiaia** (Illyrian *brentos*, "stag", whence *Brattia*, Brač) represents the new symbol of a light —the stag with antlers of fire— imposed upon a Trojan folk by invading AKHAIOI. It is killed defiantly by Odysseus, not unlike his men who would later kill and eat the kine of Helios on the isle of **Thrinakia**, AIGILIPS, which became the *Elaphites* or "Deer Isles".

DESCENT TO THE NETHERWORLD

Odysseus, following the instructions of Kirke (x, 508–512), sails with his men to the ends of the world (the Italian coast on the western horizon) and wends his way to **Kokytos** (Pópoli), nestled between the Gran Sasso d'Italia and la Maiella (MAP 7. 6). Here, he makes an offering and hordes of souls come forth like flies drawn by the smell of fresh blood.

At last, the soul of the seer Teiresias comes forth and advises Odysseus of the dangers that yet face him before arriving in ITHAKA, and of how he once again will establish his presence, but, all of this, without first the consent of Poseidon.

After Teiresias withdraws, Odysseus talks with the anxious souls of those wanting to know about how their loved ones still alive are faring. Among these are several who were famous during their lives. At last, sated, Odysseus escapes towards the sea with his men and returns to **Aiaia** (LESBOS, *Brattia*, Brač).

COMMENTARY:

The idea of Odysseus visiting with souls in the Netherworld is adapted from an independent literary genre, *Descent to the Netherworld*, neatly stitched into the midpoint of the Misadventures of Odysseus[8]. The Misadventures of Odysseus itself is woven with the *bildungromans* of a *Telemakhy*, as well as with a *Taking of Ithaka*, which, if not literary genres of their own, are distinct narrative units.

It seems as though a *Descent to the Netherworld* may have required the ingestion of a hallucinogenic agent, perhaps *moly*, which Odysseus had taken as a precaution against the charms of Kirke. However, this *Descent to the Netherworld* is not one as if entering the bowels of the earth through some cavern, or, symbolically, as Odysseus himself narrates, by digging a hole in the ground and calling forth spirits (cf. x, 516–520), but, rather, an allusion to that moment when one dies. Thus, symbolically, the *Descent to the Netherworld* represents the lowest point in the Misadventures of Odysseus, as if, as he drowns, he had sunk to the bottom of the sea, and his feet touched the very entrance to the Netherworld.

---

8. Such a descent is likewise ascribed to Orpheus (who went in search of Euridice), and whose name is inseparable from the format of a solar hero running through twelve houses of the Zodiac (albeit his presence in the environs of ITHAKA is implausible). See. pp 241–242.

VII. THE TWELVE MISADVENTURES OF ODYSSEUS

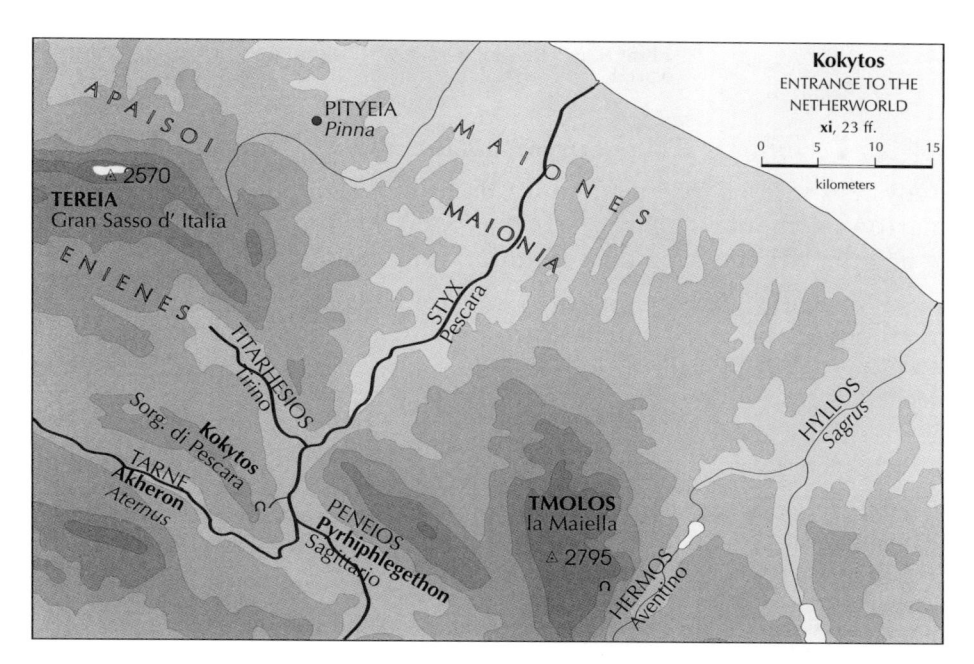

MAP 7.6. ENTRANCE TO THE NETHERWORLD. **Kokytos** > Pópoli is situated at the confluence of the TARNE/**Akheron** (Aternus) with the STYX (Sorgente di Pescara), also fed by waters of the PENEIOS/**Pyrhiphlegethon** (Saggitario). The STYX (Sorgente di Pescara) issues copiously from several underground sources at the base of a hill with remains of a building traced by heavy stone blocks. That the TARNE/**Akheron** (Aternus) forms a physical part of the Netherworld is seen in the linguistic equivalent of Aternus with Avernus, the Underworld (cf. abbas > attas). That the PENEIOS/**Pyrhiphlegethon** (Saggitario) likewise forms part of the Netherworld may have sparked the notion of a fiery hell by suggesting a connection between Charon and Perun (who are linguistically cognate). The environs of Pópoli are scented with an occasional sulphurous odour. The homology of the region with the female reproductive apparatus can hardly be missed.

EPISODE VII: JULY – SCORPION

Seirenes (Planktai)

Odysseus returns to **Aiaia** and learns from Kirke that he must pass the narrows without stopping where the rocky **Planktai** are to be found, and where the **Seirenes** sing their beautiful (but deadly) songs.

Odysseus plugs the ears of his men with wax, but, anxious to hear their songs, he has himself firmly tied to the mast. As they pass by Odysseus tries in vain to loosen his bonds, but, to no avail, and they pass through the **Planktai** without incident.

COMMENTARY:

The SCORPION, often found hidden under stones, connotes the sting of death not unlike the song of **Seirenes** on the rocks of **Planktai**.

That Odysseus was tied to a ship's mast, the same sort of expedient as his men having their ears plugged, suggests the profession of sponge-diving and having an ankle tied to a rope with which to be pulled back up to the surface in the event a ringing in the ears disorient the diver. Ironically, this very song the **Seirenes** sing that Odysseus claims he wished to avoid is the very song he is singing to his audience, as it were, in those very same waters where he is drowning.

EPISODE VIII: AUGUST – BOWMAN

Skylla (Kharybdis)

Odysseus and his men arrive at a perilous straight, flanked on one side by a smooth cliff, in the middle of which, facing the west, was a cave. Therein dwelt **Skylla**, an evil monster of horrid proportions, ever yelping and ever feeding on what the sea could offer. On the other flank, within an arrow's shot, was a fig-tree, and under it, **Kharybdis**, which three times a day sucked in water and belched it out in great spews. At its bottom, the rocks roared with a frightening sound.

As Odysseus and his men pass between the cliffs, **Skylla** snatches six men from the ship.

COMMENTARY:

The BOWMAN, an archer with deadly aim, would seem to recall the activity of **Skylla** fishing for whatever food might be found below, at **Kharybdis**. That **Skylla** lay within a cave on the western face of a sheer cliff, points to Marčuleti, at the very tip of NERITON, separated from the isle of Olipa by the Straight of Vratnik. Presumably, since the land mass of the Adriatic Coast has sunk below sea level (as witnessed by the periodic floodings that devastate Venice), Vratnik may have been a curious geological feature of incoming tides rushing in and then rushing back out in the opposite direction, three times a day.

EPISODE IX: SEPTEMBER – GOAT
(AUTUMN EQUINOX)

Thrinakia

Odysseus and his men arrive at **Thrinakia**, where the sacred kine of Helios Hyperion have been set to pasture. Regardless of the warning given him by Teiresias and Kirke not to touch this sacred cattle, and of his own warning to his men, some disobey and feast on the holy animals, and so incur the wrath of the gods.

As the men of Odysseus flee the island they are struck down by lightning, and Odysseus must once again pass through the straights of **Kharybdis**, which he exits, afloat on the remains of his destroyed vessel, rowing with his arms.

COMMENTARY:

GOAT is the month of the Autumn Equinox (thus, a sunset on this date seen from an observation platform on the western slopes of SAMOS (XIII, 17–000) appears to drop into AIGAI, a marine grotto not unlike the one at *Capri*). Here, the *thrinakia* is the three-legged sun-face that represents the sun's three positions on the meridian throughout the year. It is the symbol of the new world-order established by an AKHAIAN presence in Troy, albeit represented by the stag with fiery antlers, thus the kine of Helios Hyperion, and the name of **Thrinakia** (AIGILIPS), which became the *Elaphites*, or "Deer Isles".

The arrival at and departure from **Thrinakia** through **Kharybdis** could have been *easily avoided* by rounding the isle of Olipa on the East side, and points to a certain obduracy, but, *a quoi bon*, is elusive.

EPISODE X: OCTOBER – BARMAID

Ogygia

Odysseus arrives in **Ogygia** where he is taken in by Kalypso. He lives with her for seven years, but Hermes instructs her to set him free, and so in the eighth she bids him build a vessel on which he may return to ITHAKA, and, in the ninth, he says goodbye to her and departs on a flimsy raft.

COMMENTARY:

The BARMAID, a witch-like nymph familiar with the concoction of magical potions and brews, would seem to explain, if only partially, the functions of Kalypso and Kirke, both adept at nurturing in loving captivity those who came to them.

Once before, Odysseus had visited this island, ZAKYNTHOS (*Melita*, Mljet), when, in the early days before the onset of the Trojan War, he brought the maid Khryseis to her father Khryses. However, on this occasion, his lengthy stay of nine years, in addition to the nine episodes already transpired, is a contrivance to put him at sea (where his misadventures will become revealed) in the nineteenth year after leaving the Fields of War, a number associated with the sea and the prediction of tides which obeys to the Metonic Cycle, a period of 235 lunar months, after which the new and full moons return to the same days of the year. This cycle was the basis of the ancient Greek calendar and is still used for calculating movable feasts such as Easter.

EPISODE XI: NOVEMBER – FISH

Skheria

Odysseus is caught in a storm and his raft broken to pieces by the ceaseless turmoil of waves. He approaches **Skheria**, but then a mysterious force carries him back out, until, finally, towards dawn, nearly drowned, he reaches the safety of a beach and he sleeps. In the early morning Nausikaa discovers him and takes him to her father, King Alkinoos.

Odysseus is well-received in the beautiful Palace of Alkinoos, and during a banquet feast, in which there is much singing of poetry, he reveals his true identity and tells of his misadventures after the Fall of Troy.

Afterwards, Alkinoos sends Odysseus to ITHAKA with **Phaiakian** oarsmen on a boat laden with gifts.

COMMENTARY:

FISH coincides nicely with the watery events of this station.

The imagery of Odysseus approaching the safety of **Skheria**, and then being taken back out, before finally coming to rest on a beach at dawn, is that of the constellation Orion, rising from a watery bed and approaching **Skheria**, as it were, but upon reaching the meridian, continues moving along, until, at sunrise, he finally comes to rest. The appearance of Nausikaa on the scene corresponds with that of Spica in BARMAID (Virgo) on the meridian.

The description of the magnificent palace of Alkinoos is that of the Milky Way, with patches of black at one end, and the guardian dogs represented by Procyon and Sirius at the other end.

EPISODE XII: DECEMBER – RAM
WINTER SOLSTICE

Phorkis (Arethousa)

The **Phaiakes** have given gifts to Odysseus and sent him home on a swift ship. On the way, he falls fast asleep.

Odysseus awakens at the bottom of a fjord called **Phorkis**, where is the marsh of **Arethousa**. Frightened, he does not know what has happened, but, Athene, disguised, suddenly approaches him and tells him where he is. Together, they hide his gifts in a cave. Athene then transforms Odysseus into an old beggar and instructs him to search for Eumaios at his farm.

COMMENTARY:

RAM is the rebus for this station, for sheep are associated with all marshy places (as if fleece were symbolic of marsh vegetation). Thus the name of Aries seems imbedded in that of **Ar(i)ethousa** (Soline salt-pans), as much as in that of the ARI(E)MOI (occupants of the Neretva Delta).

The long and narrow fjord of **Phorkis** (Stonski Channel) extends beneath **Korax** (Grad), the pig-farm of Eumaios, and thus the easy inference that the name of **Phorkis** has some connection with a "sea *pig*", perhaps the Dalmatian seal (now extinct).

That Athena presides over all humid and marshy places, such that her presence at **Arethousa** is not surprising, for she even gave her name to the salt-pans of ATHENAI (*Taras/Tarentum*, Taranto). Thus, her transformation of Odysseus into an old man seems apt, as if he were cured in salt, like a ham.

This is the month of the winter solstice, when the sun, having run its gamut along the ecliptic, dies and is instantly reborn. Here end the Misadventures of Odysseus, and, upon establishing contact with reality once again, begin another series of lesser misfortunes in the process of recuperating his soul and his dominion of ITHAKA.

THE TAKING OF ITHAKA

The Misadventures of Odysseus have come to a close at **Arethousa** (Soline salt-pans), in the twentieth year after the funeral rites of Hector, precisely as Odysseus wends his way forth (xiv, 1):

> But Odysseus went forth from the harbour by the rough path up over the woodland and through the heights to the place where Athene had shewed him that he should find the goodly swineherd [Eumaios]...

Odysseus goes to **Korax** (Grad) where he finds Eumaios, who welcomes him kindly. Henceforward, Odysseus begins a journey westward along the length of NERITON towards ITHAKA in a process of spiritual regeneration as the seminal substance of his own soul, and, once again, at long last, becomes the lord of his dominions. This process is brought to a closure with the slaying of Penelope's fifty suitors. The structural elements of this event (TABLE 7.7) are identical with those in the stories of the bird-man *versus* bull-man ritual of Akhilleus *vs* Hector, Meleagros *vs* Giant Boar, Theseus *vs* Minotaur, and also present in such stories as that of Romulus and Remus, and Cain and Abel.

Classical scholarship has brought the end of the *Odyssey* up to the point where Odysseus and Penelope have finally become reunited (xxiii, 288–296)[7]:

> Thus they spoke to one another; and meanwhile Eurynome and the nurse made ready the bed of soft coverlets by the light of blazing torches. But when they had busily spread the stout-built bedstead, the old nurse went back to her chamber to lie down, and Eurynome, the maiden of the bed chamber, led them on their way to the couch with a torch in her hands; and when she had led them to the bridal chamber, she went back. And they then gladly came to the place of the couch that was theirs of old.

Still, they talk early in to the dawn, Odysseus recounting of his many experiences and woes, and, finally, when he and Penelope have spent their unspent youth, Athene (the planet Venus) brings Dawn from Okeanos (xxiii, 344–348).

It is here, precisely, with the new day, that the cycle of the Odyssey might have been brought to a full close (and not so drastically, earlier, at xxiii, 296, as Alexandrine editors proposed). Indeed, what seems superfluous, a needless appendage, for the story of Odysseus has already been told (or, alternately, the beginnings of a *third* Homeric epic, about which nothing has ever been suspected), is the rising of Odysseus from his marriage-bed in the early morning, and tracking his way back to

---

7. See a general summary of the complex arguments in Heubeck, Alfred; *A Commentary on Homer's Odyssey*, III. pp 342–353.

VII. THE TWELVE MISADVENTURES OF ODYSSEUS

	SLAYING OF THE SUITORS	
I:	ODYSSEUS ROAMS AT WILL	xiii – xvii
II.	PLANS FOR SLAUGHTERING WOOERS / TAUNTING	xviii
III.	THE PREPARATION OF ARMS	xix – xx
IV.	SEARCHING OUT (CHASE) OF WOOERS	xxi
V.	MERCILESS SLAUGHTER OF WOOERS	xxii
VI.	RETIREMENT TO ALCOVE WITH PENELOPE	xxiii

TABLE 7. 7. ODYSSEUS IN THE BIRD-MAN VS BULL-MAN RITUAL. *Odysseus, as a bird-man, goes through similar stages in the slaying of Penelope's suitors as Akhilleus did in the slaying of Hector (compare sequence of events with Table 3. 4. SIX STAGES OF A RITUAL).*

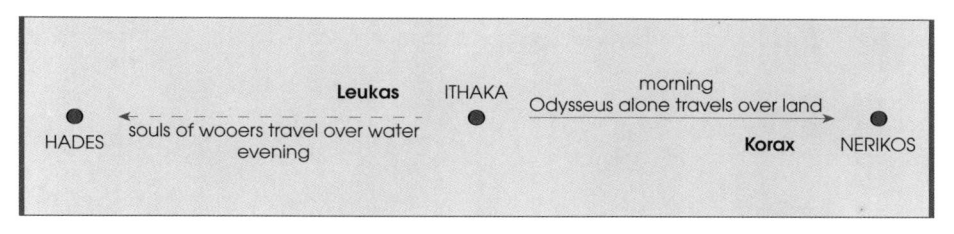

```
                              Leukas    ITHAKA        morning
                                                Odysseus alone travels over land
    ●      ← — — — — — — — —    ●                                              ●
  HADES    souls of wooers travel over water                        Korax    NERIKOS
                      evening
```

TABLE 7. 8. DEPARTURES FROM ITHAKA. **Leukas** *is to* ITHAKA, *what* **Korax** *is to* **Nerikos**. **Hades** *is probably* **Taphos** *("burial"), modern Svetac (akin with Spanish campo santo, "holy field", a reference to a cemetery). The orchard of Laertes at* **Nerikos** *is, perhaps, to be regarded as a kind of holy field as well.*

Korax, and beyond, stepping onto the Trojan mainland at NERIKOS to see his father, the old man Laertes.

To what purpose, this appendage, this would-be link to a third epic?

The life of Odysseus has been that of a treacherous individual, indeed, *polytropos,* "of many wiles". He betrayed Troy to the enemy by allowing Danaan forces to occupy the southern shores of NERITON until that appointed time, when, after pillaging and sacking the Trojan isles and coast during nine years, they would make a final naval assault on the SKAMANDROS delta-valley. But more than a *consent* in allowing the enemy to establish a *pied à terre* on Troy, was his *approval* of a patriarchal society represented by new symbols and tenets that eradicated a long-established matriarchal society. The new ethos thought it fitting and proper to make blood-offerings to Zeus, while Trojans viewed this act with horror (indeed, as the Slavic world abhors it today). Thus, Odysseus was like Akhilleus, by all counts, despicable, for he knew well that a matriarchal society to which he was born could not condone (let alone understand) the blasphemy of offering animal flesh to Zeus.

Indeed, Odysseus, has been a pillager and depredator, like the wastrel that was Akhilleus, the bird-man who takes, without asking, that fruit from the bull-man's orchard which is not his. He is nomadic, unsettled, and, by definition, uncivilized, he is the vagabond *par excellence*. By contrast, the bull-man possesses an orchard which he tends, thus he is static, settled, and, by all counts, civilized. Odysseus, in a gesture of that sublime quality of the humankind, *remorse*, is repentant of his misdeeds, goes to his father at NERIKOS as if to expiate his sins, and, so, once again, become a civilized man and care for those orchards given him by Laertes in his childhood.

CHAPTER VIII

PELASGIAN TROJANISM AND THE NEW ILLYRIANS

An association between Trojans and Illyrians can hardly be missed. Hitherto, these names have been thought of as those of two peoples, each dressed with distinctive cultural features, geographically separated by a distance of some 500 kilometers, though, in fact, they were the same folk who occupied the same place at the same time: so it was that from the AMAZONES (northernmost peoples) were eventually descended the Liburni, from the ARI(E)MOI (occupants of the SKAMANDROS/Neretva delta) the *Delmatae* or Dalmatians, from the KEPHALLENES (occupants of NERITON/Pelješac) the *Plerai* of the southern Dalmatian Coast, and the DARDANIOI (occupants of the Neretva valley) the Dardani who moved into the region of northeastern Albania and from whom modern Albanians now claim their predominantly Illyrian descent.

What, then, is the difference between the two terms?[1]

LEPENSKI VIR

Lepenski Vir, on the shores of the majestic Danube, downstream from Belgrade, shortly before the Iron Gates, is, to date, the site of the earliest indication of civilization in Europe —an urban organization, as opposed to a cave-dwelling habitat— dating from some 8,000 years BC. In the remains of this site are evinced, without possible hesitation, two unique features of humankind. First, an established methodology for the design and construction of human habitation which differed from the construction of, say, a bird's nest, which is the same year in year out, throughout the millenia, such that the general design could be altered, if so needed and desired. Second, an effort to understand the great mystery about the origins of man by the reduction of his creation to the fertilization of Mother Earth by the waters of the great Black Danube (nothing

---

1. The answers to diverse questions regarding the ethnogenesis of an Illyrian folk generally sit squarely on ill-framed premises (and consequently without adequate answers), for, surely, the ethnogenesis of a Danubian folk must not be mixed with that of an Adriatic folk, both of whose anthropological and archaeological characteristics are mistakenly called by a single term which did not come into existence until *after* the Fall of Troy.

"blue" about it) which flowed from the Black Forest to the Black Sea, from which emerged, symbolically, the superb Lepenski Vir boulders sculpted into the shapes of fish with humanoid faces.

These two distinctive features of the Lepenski Vir Culture would become intrinsic characteristics in the nature of Western Civilization. Surely, other aspects of this culture insured its survival, still, a fuller account about these amazing peoples belongs elsewhere. Here, all that need be established, is that the Great Danubian Basin became the umbilicus of civilization... the Lepenski Vir Culture flourished and became rooted in the Balkans for the following 5,000 years, or so.

VINČA

Vinča, also downstream from Belgrade, some 30 kilometers, or so, is the site where a Lepenski Vir people, now near 3,000 BC, or so, established two additional intellectual conquests that would remain fundamental characteristics of Western Civilization, to this day. First, it was discovered that a squiggle, *scratched* onto a brick or a stone, could represent a sound repeated exactly by all peoples, and so came about a method of writing *alphabetically* (as differenciated from a *syllabic* method of transmitting information used by other peoples based on a glyph to represent a syllable). Archaeological evidence —epigraphic material of *Vinčansko pismo*, "Vinča letters"— is abundant, the tally at this date now stands at over a thousand different inscribed objects. Second, Mother Earth acquired humanoid female characteristics, and eventually became known, far and wide throughout Eastern and Western Europe[2], as statuettes of different sizes, made of different materials, with the very odd feature that the head was always of an odd, unexplainable shape. Furthermore, at Vinča, the goddess developed something never before seen: she acquired letters on her buttocks (the relevance of which will not be fully appreciated until Hecabe offers a propitiatory robe to Athena).

PELASGIAN TROJANISM

That a Vinča folk eventually exported their letters to the Rasena (Etruscans), scattered throughout the Italic Peninsula, would seem to make sense. However, it was not these letters, exactly, that became what is now universally regarded as Etruscan script.

---

2. Marija Gimbutas (1921–1994) unequivocally became the doyenne in this field of research with her *The Language of the Goddess: Sacred Images and Symbols of Old Europe*. Introduction by Joseph Campbell. San Francisco: Harper and Row, 1989.

It was, perhaps, the fame abroad of these letters that motivated an inquisitive Dardanus to seek their origin, which brought him from GORTYNA (Rome) to the general area of *three* marshes, at the mouth of a river, a place aptly called TROIA. A thoretical reconstruction of what happened, of *how* and from *where* certain formative elements of Pelasgian identity arrived in TROIA and modified certain features of the Vinča Culture, looks much like the forerunner of a later Akhaian campaign. Thus, a primary emmigration from the central part of Italy's Tyrrhennian coast would eventually be followed up by the influence of two secondary cultural fountainheads emanating from Italy's northern and southern Adriatic coasts, respectively.

Now, Dardanus will have been a Pelasgian. This inference is drawn (on faint evidence, perhaps) from a relationship of the TROES with the PELASGOI, whose name is consigned in the list of *Trojan Forces* (II, 888–888), and thus a connection with Dardanus, founder of the Royal House of Troy. Still, what seems like an inseparable link between Dardanus and the PELASGOI is that Dardanus was descended from a certain Iapetus, one of the Titans (or Giants), who, in *Genesis*, is Japheth, son of Noah, himself descended from the evil Nephilim, a "mist people", or race of giants. This race of Titans/Nephilim, a tall, Nordic peoples (by contrast with a short, olive-skinned Mediterranean folk) seems to have been the PELASGOI, a name whose meaning "white" (*pel/bjel-*) + "edge", "coast line" (*ask-*, cf. ASKANIA, Ascanius), would place them at the edges of the melting polar ice cap (± 10,000 BC?) that caused prolonged heavy floodings over all Northern Europe[3].

So it was that Dardanus settled on a stratum of autochthonous social structures, and through his progeny were brought about novel changes (hence the idea of "Pelasgian Trojanism"). That this was so is evident in the foundation of TROIA (Daorson, the city) by Ilos, great-grandson of Dardanus (XX, 232), precisely on the site of an earlier necropolis[4]. Furthermore, an act of *transcendental* importance was that of giving Mother Earth a name, which became that of Athena, and of recognizing her double but inseparable characteristics as Eternal Procreatrix as well as Eternal Virgin. Athena became identified with the planet Venus, she

---

3. This hypothesis necessarily posits the presence of Cro Magnon man during the Middle and Late Pleistocene period, ± 45,000–10,000 BC, albeit the hisorical reality in the story-stuff of Titans-would-be-Nephilim would seem to be of a considerably later date, perhaps an historical memory dating from ± 8,000 BC.

4. It is the picture of Ilos, clad in a dappled dog-skin, on the wall of the Tomba dell'Orco II, in Tarquinia, which confirms that he followed a Dalmatian hound, and not a cow, to the fetid site where he founded TROIA. See II. ILIOS: A BRIEF SURVEY, p. 99.

who heralds the morning and closes the evening, and the rebus of her double characteristics —or double totemic identities— became the frog and the tortoise, whose earthly provinces were all humid or wet places, such as ponds, springs, marshes, wells, sources of rivers, and the like. Athena's rebus for Eternal Procreatrix as a frog was symbolic of all pubescent girls, and thus, to this day, in the Slavic world, *žaba*, "frog", is synonymous with young girls, thus, the saying "to be between *žaba i babe*, that is, between "froggies and grannies"[5]. Athena's other rebus for Eternal Virgin as a tortoise became a modernization of the Vinča Earth Goddess figurines, arms and legs truncated, with a beastly beaked head, and letters on her buttocks. Now, there is no quibbling with an argument that a double identity of the Earth Goddess in her rebus as a frog and as a tortoise may have been pre-Trojan, indeed, developments of the Vinča Culture itself, albeit, that she was given a name and a sanctuary on KALLIKOLONE, is a distinctly Trojan accomplishment. See II. ILIOS: A BRIEF SURVEY, pp 109–111.

Independently of the innovations of Pelasgian Trojanism established by the Dardanid line of descent, there also arrived from abroad a certain Kadmos, from the region of PAPHLAGONIA, at the mouth of the Po (see *Map 7. 1*), from whom were descended the KADMEIONES, occupants of THEBE (XX, 000).

Later Greek lore not only made Kadmos the father of Illyrus, eponymous ancestor of the Illyroi, but also credited him with the invention of "Greek letters" (those which an academic interpretation of the story would regard as an import of North Semitic script into Hellas). That Kadmos "invented" what has already been archaeologically established beyond doubt as an invention of Danubian-basin origins, the evidence being abundant, reads oddly... but there is a *caveat*... for the Vinča letters on the goddess figurines (*also* found incised on a rock on the Nakovana shore of Korčula Channel; see FIG. *7* and *8*, p. 272) are not the same as those that are likewise called "Vinča letters" which also spread throughout the Etruscan world[6]. What seems to have happened is that, *after* the arrival of Dardanus in Troy, a counter-migration of *teut*-Kres from the SKAMANDROS valley took the *early* Vinča letters abroad, to the region of KRETE, the environs of GORTYNA (*Palatinus, Roma Quadrata*).

---

5. Herein lies an understanding of Sappho's name, akin with Spanish *sapo*, "toad", as that of an ugly, deformed woman severely afflicted by goiter who sang exquisite verses about young girls.

6. One must call into evidence the work of Bilbija, S. Svetislav, *Staroevropski jezih i pismo Etruraca*. Chicago, Illinois, 1984, and Savli, J., Bor, M. and Tomazic, I. Veneti, *First Builders of European Community*. Canada, 1996, the first to address the question of reading Etruscan script and language as precursors of Cyrilic letters in a Slavic-based vocabulary.

VIII. PELASGIAN TROJANISM AND THE NEW ILLYRIANS 221

Map 7.1. ILLYRIAN TRIBES. Diverse tribes occupying the length of the Balkan coast are likely to have interacted with Pelasgian folks reckoned as Trojan Allies along the length of the Italian Peninsula, thus eventually acquring a "maritime" identity by contrast with those land-locked folks living along the length of the Danube.

Here (at *Tarquinia*, nearby), a certain Tages was said to have been the inventor of Etruscan letters, but the story is likely to be understood as though he simplified the Vinča letters. Tages will have traveled north, entered the Po valley, and gone down-river into the region TEGEA (environs of MANTINEIA, *Mantua*). Thus, he must be identical with Kadmos, said to have been the son of Agenor the Elder, founder of *Patavium*, Padova/Padua (not Agenor the Younger, a Trojan Elder who founded *Pardua*), a town too close in geographical proximity to Mantua for the names of Tages and Kadmos to have been those of two different celebrated personages. Furthermore, Kadmos had been sent to look for his lost sister Europa, who had been carried away to Rome by Minos, thus the provenance of Tages, from neighbouring Tarquinia.

In addition to the cultural ties between TROIA and PAPHLAGONIA, there also existed close connections between TROIA and APULIA (the Salentine Peninsula or "heel" of the Italian Boot, see *Map 7. 1*). Here, Erikhthonios ("wool of the earth", ie., the hairy tarantula), son of Dardanus (wasp-man), founded the city of ATHENAI (*Taras/Tarentum*, Taranto). However, whether Erikhthonius *came* to TROIA from ATHENAI to found the site of ILIOS that would house the Temple of Athena on KALLIKOLONE, or, the other way about, that, after founding the site of ILIOS where the Temple of Athena would be housed on KALLIKOLONE, Erikhthonios *left* TROIA and founded ATHENAI at the site of current Taranto, is an academic issue. The wasp and the tarantula are natural enemies (the wasp invariably worsting the tarantula), hence the totemic identity of Erikhthonios is incompatible with a descent from Dardanus, thus giving place to speculation whether Erikhthonios *arrived* in Troy from ATHENAI, or alternately was *expelled* from Troy to ATHENAI.

* * *

That Illyrians are a factor to conjure with in pondering causes and effects of a "Trojan War" —why not then an "Illyrian Revolt"?— can hardly be avoided, for the question arises about the basic differences between Trojans and Illyrians: was the authorship of the *Iliad* and *Odyssey* "Trojan" because of the subject matter? or "Illyrian" because of the anthropological context of their composition? It would seem that the first and most elementary distinction to be made between one term and the other is, that, while things Trojan pertained to a well-defined political and economic order that suddenly ceased to be, things Illyrian pertained to a number of different tribes widely distributed throughout the Balkan Peninsula (see footnote 1). In a certain way, Illyrism, a social fabric, as it were, was present in Trojanism, a political institution. Thus, when Trojanism fell apart, it was the disjointed social elements of ancestral Illyrism which acquired a new social and political guise.

Troy was self-centered and self-serving. What state is not? It was, to be sure, not only instrumental in the development of intellectual assets now common to our Western Civilization, it was also an economic factor in the evolution of a living-standard, at home and abroad, principally because of trade —the assuager of all ills— with, and between, peoples in distant lands. Idle talk among modern-day occupants of Gabela has suggested that in the name of Priam is to be found the modern Serbian *priateli*, "friend", and *priatno*, "*bon apetite*", yet, in the *Iliad*, any idea of a kindly old man, victimized by the cruelty of circumstances, reduced to piteous humility groveling for the body of Hektor before Akhilleus, the predator *par excellance*, must be weighed against the earlier description of a choleric old man in his treasure chamber, impatient with his children.

THE NEW ILLYRIANS

The Trojan War was *not* about Helen. The *Odyssey* makes this abundantly clear in the poignant words of Penelope who talks of her cousin's futile purpose in life (xxiii, 218):

> "Nay, even Argive Helen, daughter of Zeus, would not have lain in love with a man of another folk [ἀνδρὶ παρ' ἀλλοδαπῷ] had she known that the warlike sons of the Achaeans were to bring her home again to her dear native land."

The Trojan War, then, was about the supplanting of a matriarchal society by a patriarchal world-order. That political collapse of other states seemed to spread quickly throughout the Mediterranean Basin would seem to support this hypothesis, on the merits that a patriarchal world-order was far less complex as far as social issues were concerned, and, economically, far more agile.

That Troy ceased to exist, that is, that the workings of a political institution came to an end, is not to say that nothing of former Trojanism did not survive in a nascent society of the New Illyrians. However, *what*, precisely, it is that can be said about the New Illyrians, other than a misleading collective term for a number of widely dispersed tribal groups, must surely begin by isolating these from those groups which more-or-less remained within the geographical frame of what had been known as Troy. These New Illyrians, "orphaned Trojans", as it were, as distinguished from, say, the Amantini, or Autariates, or Scordisci, of the Danubian Basin, or any tribal group not linked directly with the Adriatic Coast, retained something of an earlier characteristic, namely, a distinct phallus-identity.

On this wise, perhaps the strongest argument for establishing a direct link between TROES and Illyrioi is a linguistic and symbolic link between ILIOS (Drijeva/Gabela) and the name of the Illyrii themselves: Ἴλιος could well be an emendation of an earlier (and correct transcription) of Ἴλλυς, where a letter, now lost, but equivalent with the Cyrillic Ь (lj), becomes λλ, with a phonemic value similar to that in French and the *elle* (eh-yeh) in Spanish (the letter between L and M)[7]; furthermore, the shape of ILIOS is, undeniably, that of a phallus, such that a presumption of some sort of association with an enormous phallus discovered relatively recently concealed in the recesses of a cave at Nakovana, on the western face of SAMOS (Sveti Ilija/Monte Vípera), can hardly be avoided.

The presumed original root *illu-* in the name of ILIOS is on a cue with the Hittite reference to Alaksandus of Wilusa, as well as with the name of Illuyankas, a snaky sort of storm-god, probably the equivalent of Typhoeus. *illu-* probably meant, simply, "phallus", indeed, as attested by the shape of ILIOS itself, and, by extension, became associated with "snake". Thus, the muddled Greek story about Illyrus, the would-be eponymous ancestor of the Illyrians, told of a snake becoming entwined around the body of the infant Illyrus which conferred upon him certain supernatural powers[8].

---

7. Linguistic support for such an inference is found in the phonetic transcription (as distinguished from a grammatic transliteration) of Ἁλίαρτος (conferred by its later names, *Bilitio*, *Bellinzona*), which is a geonym reflecting the same topographical condition as Ἑλλήσποντος and Ἕλλενες.

8. To this day the snake is respected along the Dalmatian Coast, such that it is considered improper to kill one (regardless of whether it is poisonous or not).

3. Homer

CHAPTER IX

THE MAKINGS OF HELLAS

The Fall of Troy and the appearance of the New Illyrians was only one of several dramatic events that troubled the Mediterranean basin: from what might be inferred from the *Odyssey*, the Akhaian Confederation no longer held the political unity evinced in the *Iliad*; the Hittite Empire, established in the centre of Anatolia, ceased to exist; even in more distant lands —in the Near East, external to any Homeric context— Egypt was invaded by foreign peoples. So it was that from the social and political chaos and its corresponding economic consequences on both the Italian and Balkan peninsulas there slowly emerged the reordering of new states, new territories, new ethnic groups, and new languages[1].

What is certain about the map of a would-be "pre-Homeric Greek world" of, say, ± 1,000 BC, is that, as any classical atlas will show, it is marked with the names of peoples and places mentioned in the *Iliad* and *Odyssey*[2], when, in point of fact, this map should be utterly barren of any such toponym and ethnicon (and furthermore, its onomastica, as refers to the Balkan mainland proper, should be consigned in a transcription of the non-Greek Linear B language of the Mykenaian Culture). The point, then, is that, necessarily, some process of migrations will have brought not only the names of peoples and places mentioned by Homer from their original locations throughout the Italian Peninsula, together with their corresponding local quasi-historical accounts, but also a new *lingua franca*.

The Greek intellectual world possessed only a scant and vague understanding of loose and disjointed facts about the formation of Archaic Hellas and the multiple sources of a Hellenic cultural identity.

---

1. One seeks a common cause for these presumably coetaneous sudden and violent upheavals in different and apparently unrelated parts of the world, and, for as much as perhaps there never was a common cause and these events were merely coincidental, then again perhaps some fortuitous cause such as some uncontrollable plague (for which there seems to be no record), or, maybe —and why not?— the sudden spread of tenets of a new patriarchal order might offer a partial answer.

2. Cf. *Barrington Atlas of the Greek and Roman World*, R. J. A. Talbert (ed.). Princeton and Oxford: Princeton Unviversity Press, 2000, pp 54–56, 58–61.

Isolated historical memories of this or that eventually became meaningless knowledges —facts either in the province of myth or simply "variant versions"— such that, by the time of Herodotus (*c*.490–*c*.425 BC), writing "four hundred years after Homer" (II, 53), a general understanding about the arrival of a Dorian folk into Hellas was hopelessly convoluted (*Histories*, I, 56):

> And inquiring he [Croesus] found that the Lacedemonians and the Athenians had the pre-eminence, the first of the Dorian and the others of the Ionian race. For these were the most eminent races in ancient time, the second being a Pelasgian and the first a Hellenic race: and the one never migrated from its place in any direction, while the other was very exceedingly given to wanderings; for in the reign of Deucalion this race dwelt in Pthiotis, and in the time of Doros the son of Hellen in the land lying below Ossa and Olympos, which is called Histiaiotis; and when it was driven from Histiaiotis by the sons of Cadmos, it dwelt in Pindos and was called Makednian; and thence it moved afterwards to Dryopis, and from Dryopis it came finally to Peloponnesus, and began to be called Dorian.

The earliest reference to a shift of onomastica from one location to another is to be found in the words of Odysseus to Penelope, in the twenty first year after his departure from the fields of battle (xix, 172):

> "There is a land called Crete, in the midst of the wine-dark sea, a fair, rich land, begirt with water, and therein are many men, past counting, and ninety cities. They have not all the same speech, but their tongues are mixed. There dwell Achaeans, there great-hearted native Cretans, there Cydonians, and Dorians of waving plumes, and goodly Pelasgians. Among their cities is the great city Cnosus, where Minos reigned when nine years old, he that held converse with great Zeus, and was father of my father, great-hearted Deucalion."

Penelope knew well where KRETE and its neighbouring towns were located[3], and, so, there is little need of apprising her of the facts (II, 645 *et pas.*):

> And the Cretans had as leader Idomeneus, famed for his spear, even they that held Cnosus and Gortys, famed for its walls, Lyctus and Miletus and Lycastus, white with chalk, and Phaestus and Rhytium, well-peopled cities; and all they beside that dwelt in Crete of the hundred cities.

Now, Odysseus, in the guise of Aethon, brother of Idomeneus, would appear to be lying to Penelope, but what he is saying is, simply, that a folk *has already emigrated* from mainland Italy to "a land called Crete, in the midst of the wine-dark sea... begirt with water..." (xix, 172), for which reason it only possesses ninety cities, and not one hundred, as formerly (II, 645). In this *double entente* on the location of

---

3. Penelope's cousins were the sisters Klytemnestra and Helen from neighbouring ARGOS, (*Cajeta*, Gaeta) to the southeast of KRETE (environs of Rome). It would seem as though she will have learned her weaving skills at SIDONIA (*Lanuvium*), where Klytemnestra and Helen also acquired their own.

IX. THE MAKINGS OF HELLAS

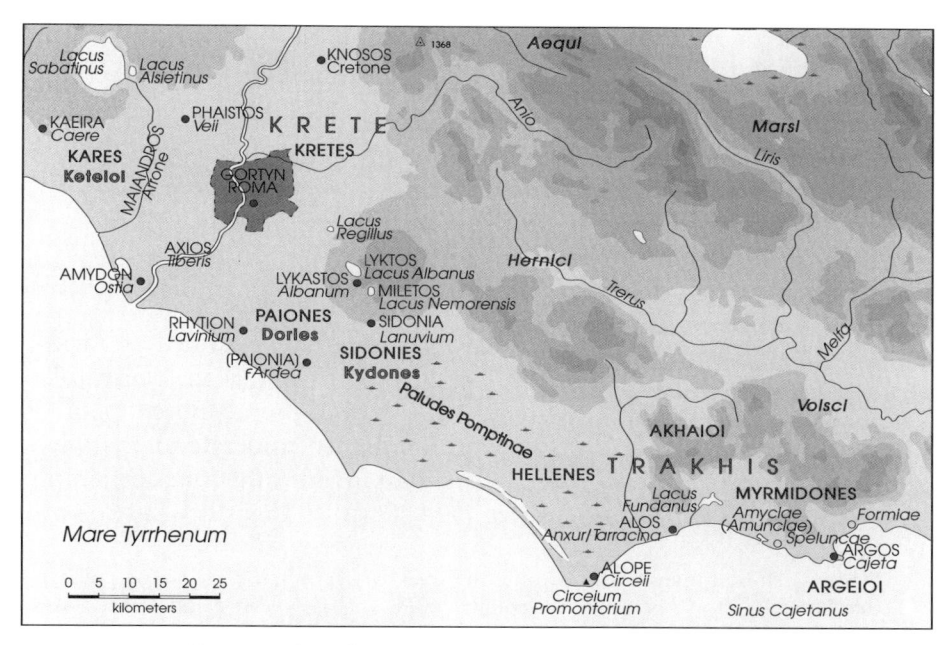

MAP 9.1. LATIUM. Geonyms from the ILIAD and the **Odyssey** are to found in the region. The districts of KRETE and TRAKHIS are each occupied by neighbouring groups of four peoples (a typical arrangement of Homeric geography), with the difference that those of KRETE are peoples with both a former and a latter identity.

KRETE is the *only* instance in Homeric Geography where there is an exception to the principle that, in the *Iliad*, the same geonym may be used for *two* different kinds of places (a district and an island), but in the *Odyssey,* the *same* geonym may not be used for two different kinds of places (KRETE the district, and Crete the island).[4]

Here, clearly, the rule is bent —willfully, one could say— from which the inference that a process of migrations from the Italian Peninsula into the Balkan Peninsula may have begun with the Trojan War itself, or immediately upon the return of diverse Danaan lords to their dear native lands, and that the authorship of the *Iliad* and *Odyssey* was aware of such a migratory movement and merely recorded a facet of what would subsequently become an important movement of peoples from one place to another.

---

4. That this is an obvious *faux pas* in Homeric Geography might, perhaps, suggest that this statement is, in fact, an interpolation. Still, that the passage is so skillfully braided into the narrative line, and that it *pointedly* states "ninety cities..." in disregard of the *Iliad's* earlier "*hecotonpolis*...", suggest the authorship of the *Iliad* and *Odyssey* has insinuated that the Homeric Canon —the story lines of both epics— has already gone well beyond the periphery of that mystical universe of Troy.

THE DORIAN COLONIZATIONS

Early on, not too long after the arrival of Dardanus in Troy, there arrived in the general environs of GORTYN (*Palatinus/Roma Quadrata*) "Teucrians" from Troy, or *teut-* "royal", *kretes* (a word of unknown meaning). These folks were ethnologically synonymous with SKAMANDROS-born Vardjaei, but became the PAIONES, a name which, in keeping with their heritage, was derived simply from *pai-*, "river" + *-ones*, a suffix denoting a social group, and who settled here and there in "deep-soiled" PAIONIA, (XXI, 157) but, specifically, at (ϝ)*Ardea* (MAP 9. 1.).

The "*teut*-Cretans"–*Vardjaei*–PAIONES river folk assumed an identity in the *Odyssey* as **Dories**. For some unknown reason, these folks embarked on what seems to have been a well-premeditated plan of expansionism, albeit the Greeks were unable to understand the whys and wherefores of peoples who, rather than invade and conquer, simply wished to settle in new territories (*The Oxford Classical Dictionary*, 1999):

> **Dorians, Dorian Invasion.** According to Greek Myth, it had been the will of Zeus that Heracles should rule over the country of Perseus at Mycenae and Tiryns. After Heracles' death, however, these cities came into the hands of the descendants of Pelops, and at the time of the Trojan War Agamemnon ruled at Mycenae. The Greeks believed as historical fact the legend that two generations after the Trojan War, c. 1100 BC, there was an invasion into Greece from the north by a new, Greek-speaking people known as Dorians (for the name see DORUS). They accompanied the sons of the hero Heracles (see AEGIMIUS), who were returning to the Peloponnese to claim their father's inheritance, first the city of Tiryns and then, by conquest, the whole Peloponnese. By this legend many historical facts were explained; first, how large parts of Greece were occupied by a (Greek) people who spoke in the Doric dialect. The close relationship between Doric and North-west Greek (see DIALECTS) supports the legend that the Dorians came from the north-west, from Epirus and south-west Macedonia, and advanced into Thessaly and Boeotia, and that some of them remained in the small district of central Greece known as Doris, whence they later advanced south (taking the name with them) through Delphi (where the priesthood remained by tradition Dorian in historical times), south-west to Naupactus, and thence into the Peloponnese. Corinth was, by tradition, one of their latest conquests. The fact that the Arcadian dialect remains closest to pre-Dorian Greek (see DIALECTS I) seems to indicate that the Dorian invaders failed to penetrate the remoter parts of Arcadia. Secondly, it was a peculiarity of Dorian states that every state was divided into the three tribes, Hylleis, Dymanes, and Pamphyli, a fact which suggests a strong sense of identity. Thirdly, the Dorians were apparently unknown at the time of the Trojan War (c. 1184 BC) and not mentioned by Homer, yet in later historical times they occupied the territory once held, according to Homer, by Agamemnon and the Achaeans, and in Argos and Sparta they ruled over a serf-like population of non-Dorian Greeks. The Dorian invasion may also account for a historical fact of which the Greeks themselves were scarcely aware, that the cities and civilization of Mycenaean Greece were destroyed in successive attacks in the twelfth century BC, to be succeeded by

IX. THE MAKINGS OF HELLAS

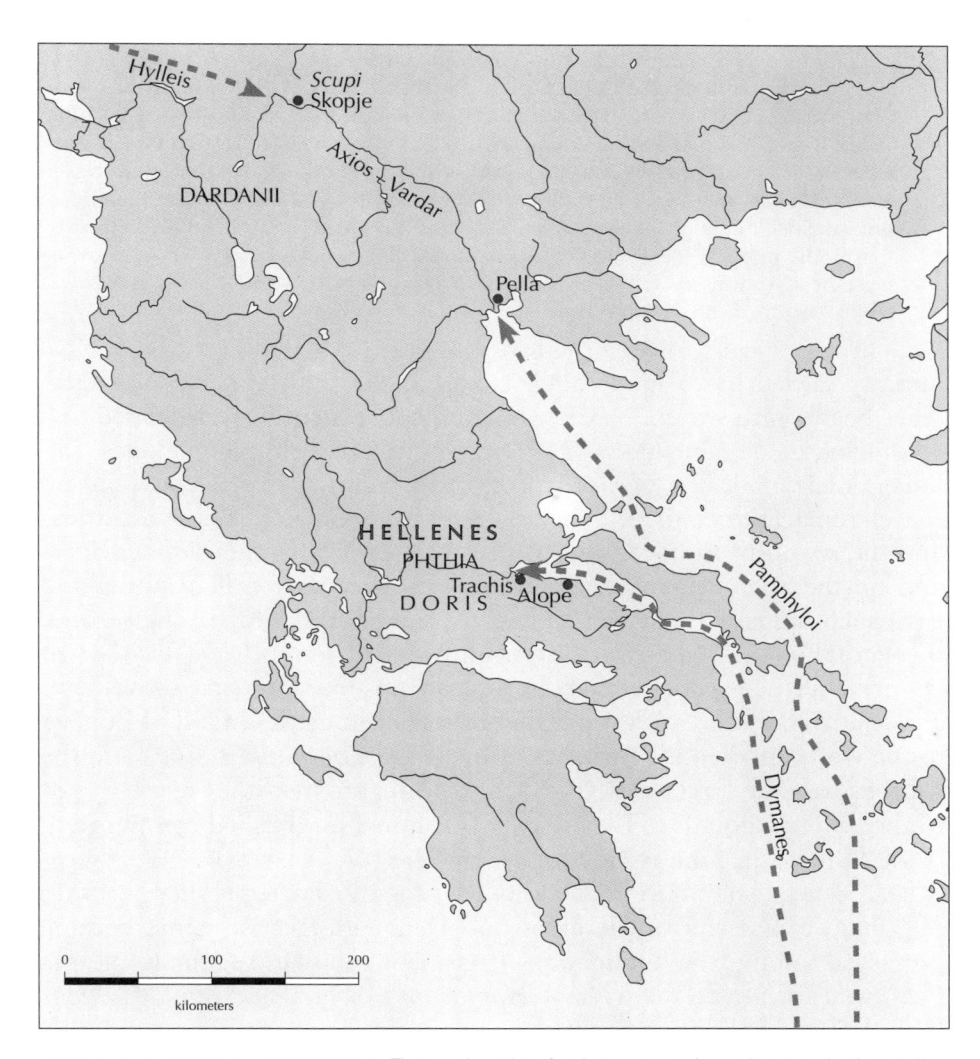

*MAP 9. 2. DORIAN COLONIZATIONS. Three singular features may be observed about the migration of a folk collectively called **Dories**: first, two attempts of reaching a destination situated up-river and in a westly direction; second, that the name of Hellas became established from that of the HELLENES (occupants of the Pomptine Marshes); third, that the names of the Hylos and the Dardanii are indelibly fixed in Albanian hisory. An ancillary observation worth noting (but somewhat off-topic), is that Albanian claims of an Illyrian descent are reasonable, but, still further, that it will have been an association of Hyllos with the AMAZONES that lies at the root of an Albanian custom still current where families may opt for the eldest female as a patriarchal figurehead (with its corresponding obligations and perquisites) when the male is wanting.*

migrations overseas to the coast of Asia Minor from c. 1050 to 950, and by poverty and deprivation in Greece itself. There is no archaeological evidence for the identity of the people who destroyed the Mycenaean culture, and no positive signs of an influx of new people. This makes sense if the invaders were of related Greek stock from the fringes of the Mycenaean world. It has also been argued that there was in fact no Dorian invasion, that different groups of Greeks had been present in Greece since the beginning of Mycenaean culture, and that the destructions were caused by spasmodic raids of local uprisings of a suppressed population. However, a strong sense of discontinuity following the destructions as well as the legends themselves tell in favour of the essential historicity of the Dorian invasion.

The historical reality of the foregoing article is that **Dories** will have initially settled in "a land called Crete, in the midst of the wine-dark sea... begirt with water..." (xix, 172), and subsequently spearheaded *two* colonizing movements (*Map 9.2.*). The first was that of the Dymanes (followers of Dymas, son of Dorus, son of Hellenus, son of Deucalion) up the channel (*Euboicus Sinus*) between the mainland (Boeotia–Attica) and the island of Euboea, and thence westward, into the *Malicus Sinus* and up the Spercheios river. This new territory they called Doris, and gave such names to new settlements as Trachis and Alope. The second, the Pamphyli (or "many tribes", followers of Pamphylos, brother of Dymas), seemed to be a correction of an unsuccessful first movement, and followed a more or less parallel course keeping the island of Euboea to the west, and headed further north, up the *Thermaikos Sinus* and the sources of the river AXIOS–Vardar that crosses the territory of Makedonia diagonally. Here, in new Dardania, established by migrating DARDANIOI, the many identities of the "*teut*-Cretans"–*Vardjaei*–PAIONES met their brethren, the Hylleis, so-called after Hyllos, brother of Makaria and son of Herakles and Deianeira, whose name became preserved along the Dalmatian Coast into historical times as the *Peninsula Hyllica* to the west of *Tragurium* (Trogir), and *Sinus Hyllicus* (Vela Luka), at the west end of *Corcyra Melaina* (Korčula).

So it is that **Dories**, leaving otherwise fertile and pleasing lands on the Italian Peninsula, settled in harsh and arid territories. The advantage had to be, perhaps, that of survival, or, simply, nothing more than that of an economic advantage obtained from the foundation of profitable communities abroad.

THE IONIAN MIGRATIONS

Towards 1,050 BC there seem to have occurred two phenomena, the one a natural catastrophe, the other a political crisis, which spurred the movement of a peoples known somewhat vaguely as Ionians, to places abroad (perhaps already known to them from commercial ties).

IX. THE MAKINGS OF HELLAS

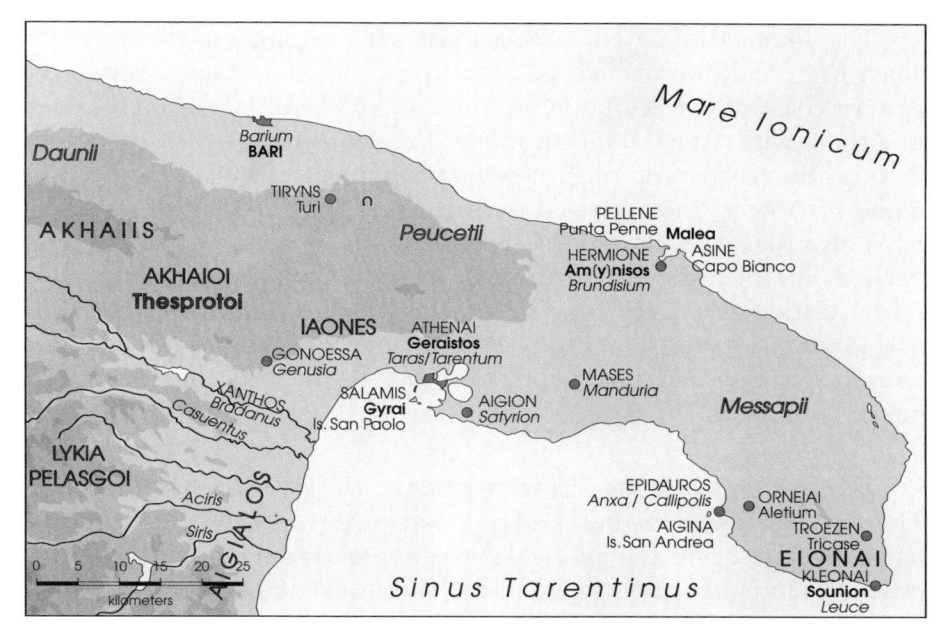

MAP 9. 3. OLD ATHENS. The site was founded by Erikhthonios, whose name means "wool of the earth". After cataclysmic events sank the trefoil-shaped salt-marsh below sea-level, the site became known as Taras or Tarentum, after which the wooly tarantula is so-called.

On the one hand, the sinking of the land mass below sea-level in the Ionian Gulf, or Gulf of Taranto, surely caused by cataclysmic earthquakes, produced the disappearance of ATHENAI (Map 9. 3.). A recollection of this event is registered in the *Odyssey* (iv, 499–511):

> "'Aias truly was lost amid his long-oared ships. Upon the great rocks of Gyrae Poseidon at first drove him, but saved him from the sea; and he would have escaped his doom, hated of Athene though he was, had he not uttered a boastful word in great blindness of heart. He declared that it was in spite of the gods that he had escaped the great gulf of the sea; and Poseidon heard his boastful speech, and straightway took his trident in his mighty hands, and smote the rock of Gyrae and clove it in sunder. And one part abode in its place, but the sundered part fell into the sea, even that on which Aias sat at the first when his heart was greatly blinded, and it bore him down into the boundless surging deep. So there he perished, when he had drunk the salt water.'"

On the other hand, the disappearance of ATHENAI precipitated not only a political crisis in regard to the line of succession of King Codrus (the last king of ATHENAI, who may have yielded to pressures from the Heraclidai in regard to the succession of Agamemnon in MYKENAI and of Diomedes in ARGOS), but also the urgent need of finding some other place for living.

The Ionians migrated, taking two main routes, one towards the coast of Asia Minor which became Ionia, and the other towards the eastern coast of the Peloponnese where a New Athens was established, in Attica, with a new political model for the sharing of the monarchy among the aristocratic oligarchy every four years. In addition to the name of Athens, there arrived the names of Salamis, Aigina, and perhaps also that of Sounion (MAP 9. 2). The Ionian dialect seems to have been a sort of argot proper to Athens (as might occur in important ports) distinguished not only in its pronunciation, but also its lexical and idiomatic expressions, since the Ionians had been surrounded by a Dorian-speaking Akhaian population (which in turn was a new language unto itself).

THE AKHAIOI AND NEW THESPROTIAN COLONIZATION
The once highly motivated and aggressive AKHAIOI, whom, it seems, had come into being as a political and economic union with the sole purpose of eventually vanquishing TROIA, simply evanesced after the Fall of Troy and become identified locally, in AKHAIIS (Calabria), with the **Thesprotoi** mentioned in the *Odyssey*.

Thus, at about the same time the IAONES from the general environs of ATHENAI (*Taras/Tarentum*, Taranto) were going abroad, the former-AKHAIOI-now-**Thesprotoi** also moved across the Straights of Otranto into the opposite coast where they established the name of Thesprotia in the region of Epirus, and that of Akhaiis in the northeastern Peloponnese, at the entrance to the Gulf of Corinth. With these former-AKHAIOI–now-**Thesprotoi** also arrived the names of AIGION (*Satyrion*, Sáturo) and HELIKE (the district comprised by AIGIALOS, ARGOS, and AKHAIIS), and at the end of the gulf, the celebrated name of KORINTHOS (*Sipontum*, Manfredonia) and perhaps also KLEONAI (*Leuce*, Sta. Maria di Leuca), to the south of Corinth.

* * *

So it was that only a *few* place names which occur early on as Homeric geonyms entered Hellas at different times *before* the arrival of the *Iliad* and *Odyssey*.

CHAPTER X

THE HELLENIZATION OF HOMER

A revised understanding of the *Iliad* and *Odyssey* —the reading of these works in a geographical and cultural context well beyond the periphery of the Hellenic World— necessarily addresses the question about their most likely place of composition, but also raises two other inescapable questions, namely: first, *how* did these works come into the Hellenic World? and, second, *how* did these works —dare I say it?— become the very quintessence of Graecity?

I. ILLYRIAN EXPANSIONS: THE WESTERN BALKAN COAST

Apparently, an Illyrian presence expanded southward from its original Trojan confines, mainly along the western Balkan Coast, but also across the Straights of Otranto, into the Salentine Peninsula (the "heel" of the Italian "boot"). However, it seems that a relationship had already been established between folks of this region and Troy, prior to the Trojan War, at that time when Tydeus (father of Diomedes) had married the daughter of Adrastus and joined Polynikes in the expedition of the Seven Against Thebes (IV, 376 ff).

Nevertheless, an inference of Illyrian maritime incursions southward along the western Balkan Coast is derived from the names of islands formerly in the dominion of Odysseus (II, 631–637) for the string of Ionian Islands off the coast of Epirus and at the mouth of the Gulf of Patras. These were *Corcyra* (Corfu), followed by Leucas, Cephalonia, Ithaki, and Zakinthos (Zante). Still, the gross misnomer of Cephalonia for that stretch of land upon a time occupied by KEPHALLENES would seem to suggest that the Ionian Islands did not receive an Odyssean identity, however inaccurate, until some time *after* the arrival and translation of the *Iliad* and *Odyssey* in Hellas.

By contrast with a presumed general "Illyrization" of the Ionian Sea was the emigration of a certain Trojanism, as evinced in the replica of "Troy", at *Bouthrotum*, in Epirus, directly opposite the northeastern promontory of *Corcyra* (Corfu), and by the site of *Olympia*, on the

Peloponnesus (perhaps founded earlier than the traditional date of the Olympic Games in 776 BC). However, for as much as the site at *Bouthrotum* may have been a Trojan revival effort, it was a crude one, bereft of a difference between a city called Ilion and a city called Troy. Olympia, the site was likely so-called after the principal sporting event, the foot race in the *stadium*, whose participants emulated the goings to and fro of the gods (that is, the planets) across the heavenly vault, for Olympos/Oulympos was "...conceived by Homer as the abode of the gods." (G. Autenrieth, *A Homeric Dictionary*)[1].

II. ILLYRIAN EXPANSIONS: TRANSBALKAN INCURSIONS

The DARDANIOI (occupants of the SKAMANDROS river-valley), together with Illyrian Hylleis from PHRYGIA (*DISTRICTS MAP*, p. 70), moved into the general area at the headwaters of the Axios/Vardar, whose banks were now occupied by ancestral kin, the Teukres–Vardaei–PAIONES –**Dories**. These folks, of different names but of a common stock, with new urban settlements both at *Scupi* (Skopje) as well as *Pella*, at the mouth of the Axios/Vardar, had reason to have historical memory of TROIA, as well as exact knowledge of the *omirones*[2] of NERITON (Pelješac) and their *Iliad* and *Odyssey*.

It was the *omirones*, and the natural conduit —or corridor— of a friendly kin occupying the length of a land route, that was the vehicle for the *physical* transference of the *Iliad* and *Odyssey* from the Adriatic into the North Aegean.

What the *omirones* pretended to do with their sublime compositions can only be an educated guess, but the idea of a revenue source ought not altogether be dismissed from the idea of establishing some sort of center at *Bouthrotum*, as at the *Bosphorus*, and, indeed, as at Olympia.

THE MISE EN SCENE AND TRANSLATION OF HOMER

The *omirones* at Pella —why not here?— became a fully bicultural and bilingual society. At this place, folks of two different ethnic backgrounds commingled, namely Slavs from the Balkan interior and a folk from the coast of Asia Minor and Aegean islands, and with them (perhaps in a second generation?) began the rough drafts of translations of the *Iliad*

---

1. To place Mount Olympos in Thessaly is a thorough misunderstanding of the name as that of the heavenly vault, indeed, the abode of gods and goddesses.

2. I owe this etymology to Mirko Ilijevski, in his *Antičkiot Makedonski* (*Makenonian Antiquity*), Skopje, 2003. He proposes ΟΜΗΡΟΣ < Οδ Μηρ (ομηρ), "from the world (abroad)".

X. THE HELLENIZATION OF HOMER

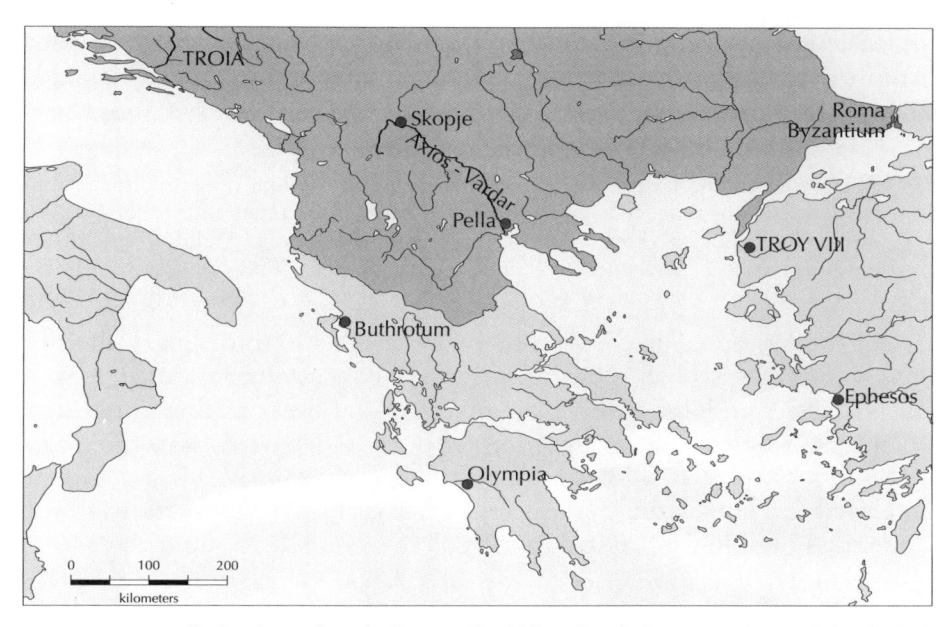

MAP 10. 1. PELLA. *Illyrian incursions to the south, skirting the Balkan coast, are detected at Buthrotum and as far south as Olympia, but it was the cultural corridor established along the length of the Axios–Vardar river that eventually exposed a Trojan Culture from Adriatic waters to a nascent Hellenic Culture in the North Aegean.*

and *Odyssey* into what would become an odd, somewhat unusual, "Homeric" Greek language.

Linguistic oddities about the Homeric poems are known to scholarship. Among these are the ϝ (digamma) and ϙ (koppa), as well as the puzzle about the obscure meaning of certain words, as mentioned by Aristotle (*Poetics*, 25.7):

> Other difficulties may be resolved by due regard to the usage of language. We may note a rare word, as in οὐρῆας μὲν πρῶτον, "the mules first [he killed]" (I, 50), where the poet perhaps employs οὐρῆας not in the sense of *mules*, but of *sentinels*[3].

Another example is the Graecizing of Trojan NICA, commonly but erroneously rendered as Νῖσα, NISA (*Nicaea*, Nice). Obviously, the "tz" sound of the Slavic letter C did not enter the Greek language.

Certainly, the idea of a translation of these most exquisite compositions from Language X[4] into the form we now possess them runs as

---

3. Indeed, Aristotle, regarded by some as a Macedonian Slav and not as a "Greek", must have understood the meaning of οὐρῆας as a "keep", "watch" (from which the modern Serbian *ura*, our "hour", "clock").

4. The name sought is, perhaps, simply, "Illyrian", in preference to "Trojan", a term which would seem to be erroneously distinguished from "Messapic" or "Venetic", or even from "Dalmatian" (ie., the ARI(E)MOI, occupants of the Neretva delta).

much counter-culture in a reverse direction as bringing them forward from their "original" Greek into a contemporary non-Greek language (Eva T. H. Brann, *The World of the Imagination, Sum and Substance*. 1991):

> Those who emphasize the timbre of language and its various other auditory qualities tend also to think that poetry and even prose is well-nigh untranslatable into any other language. Croce cites the translator's dilemma as "faithful ugliness or faithless beauty" (*Aesthetic* 1901), and Santayana asks "What could be better than Homer or worse than almost any translation of him?" (*The Sense of Beauty* 1896).

However, here, in considering whether this extraordinary literary feat was at all possible, is basically an issue concerning aesthetics as well as an issue —perhaps without an answer?— of how far this translation (or perhaps better said, adaptation) may have departed from the original. In any case, the following seems relevant (Glenn W. Most, "Violets in Crucibles: Translating, Traducing, Transmuting", Transactions of the American Philological Association, Vol 133, Num 2, Autumn 2003):

> The theory of translation on the one hand, balances precariously upon the high wire stretched tautly between two linguistic axioms, both of them unassailable, both of them evident upon reflection, and the two of them in appearance mutually exclusive: the absolute unattainability of exact synonymity, and the absolute certainty of universal translatability. However broadly or narrowly we understand the activity of translation —whether more universally (as the various meanings of the Greek term ἑρμηνεύω suggest and as most linguists have come to accept since Roman Jakobson's seminal article of 1959), as any transference of meaning whatsoever between one semiotic system and another, be it within one language ("intralingua"), between two languages ("interlingua"), or between two different symbolic codes ("intersemiotic"), or only as the everyday miracle of the communicative intercession performed by mediators operating between two different natural languages for the benefit of their linguistically less proficient fellows— it is both a datum of experience, and a postulate of theory, not only that there is not and cannot be any single term in one language for which a single precise equivalent, in any other language or for that matter in its own one, can ever be found, but also that there is not and cannot be any single term in one language for which no periphrastic equivalent at all, in its own language or for that matter in any other one, can ever be found. For on the one hand, the full significance of a word is not exhausted by its referent in the real world but also includes such other factors as the range of cultural associations connected with that word, with other related words, and with the referent, the connotations suggested by the way that word has been used in literary and in ordinary context within living cultural memory, and its particular phonic and metrical shape; so that for a single other term B to be exactly equivalent to some word A, B would have not only to designate the same referent as A but also to convey to readers or listeners precisely the same associations and connotations and to display the same material forms as A —in other words, B would have to be A, and the relation between them would be one not of synonymity but of identity, or at least of indiscernibility. On the other hand, a linguistic term for which no periphrastic equivalent could ever be found would amount to that

philosophical chimera, a private language: for the essential sociality of all semiotic systems means that there is no nuance of any utterance, however minute and evanescent, that cannot in the end be rendered precisely by some periphrasis, however lengthy, however detailed, however circumstantial: so that for some word A to be absolutely untranslatable into any form of discourse, it would have to be located entirely outside of the system of signification if its own language as of any other language, and would thus have to be equivalent to 0.

ANCILLARY KNOWLEDGE AND GREEK MYTH

One can imagine a second generation of *omirones* devoted to the arduous task of "reconstructing" the *Iliad* and *Odyssey* in a relatively new Greek language. The day-to-day speculations on how to render this or that passage —implying, of course, that the internal meaning of the passage was understood— necessarily produced a wealth of secondary material that was not part of the text itself, albeit just as fascinating. Metaphorically, the works were unwoven and rewoven, but the lint that spilled from them was likewise priceless. An example is the story told in later times about the death of Aias, who was said to have been buried alive in mud by Trojans for having desecrated the TEMPLE OF ATHENE, a sacred well on KALLIKOLONE, where her image, that is, her rebus, a tortoise, was kept. An apt death, it would seem[5].

This material, together with that fantastic lore about the past which would arrive in Hellas with new settlers from abroad, found its way into the writings of a novel caste of poets —perhaps inspired by the example of the *omirones* to lead a life devoted to letters?— and eventually became what is generally referred to as "Greek Myth".

It was under these circumstances, then, where a natural "Vardar corridor" crossed the foot-path of the *Via Egnatia* which led from the shores of Albania, through Macedonia into Thrace and the Bosphorus, that an intense literary life, of oracular dimensions, spawned another, ancient, mystical, pre-Trojan poet called Orpheus.

In the measure that trans-Balkan Illyrian incursions spread and established urban settlements, the overwhelming spiritual strength of Orpheus also spread, unrestrained, hither and thither and everywhither, as ideas are wont to do. So it was that Illyrism, that spiritual *haecity* of the TROES, which is easy to understand in a context of TROIA, quickly waned and was replaced by the vivid presence of Orpheus among folks

---

[5]. A broad spectrum of anecdotal material recounting a countless variety of events, hitherto nothing more than foppish literary gibberish, acquires a certain relevance when it is understood in a correct geographical circumstance. Still, much of it was invented without this understanding, and is utterly meaningless.

of different ethnicities and cultural backgrounds. His name is not too distant from that of the *omirones*, for a synonym of μηρ is *orbis*, "orb", "world", such that the name of "Homer", inseparable from the *composition* of the *Iliad* and *Odyssey*, and that of Orpheus, inseparable from the *format* of the *Iliad* and *Odyssey*, became archetypal images.

That Greek scholars reconstructed (or inferred) the early existence of an Orphic *Argonautica*, —to all intents and purposes a precursor of the *Odyssey*— is an historical puzzle to be solved. Still, be that as it may, this *Argonautica* could account, more or less, for the presence of Orpheus in Troy, yet he is never once mentioned nor alluded to in the *Iliad* or *Odyssey*.

SCHISM OF OMIRONES AND DISSEMINATION OF THE TEXTS

The premise that the *Iliad* and *Odyssey* were originally created in the Illyrian language, and then were brought from the Adriatic Sea into North Aegean shores, where they became translated into Greek, bears the inescapable need of positing a schism among a third generation *omirones* (that is, post-translation *omirones*).

Evidently, once the two epics had been translated, or "transformed", as it were, into an acceptable form in the Greek language, a serious difference of opinion arose among them, inevitably establishing two distinct groups of *omirones*, both of which moved out of Pella, for reasons unknown, and settled elsewhere. Only such a schism might account for the two irreconcilable circumstances about the texts, the one that the texts circulated openly, available to anyone, but *without* the necessary tutorial guidance to make them intelligible and workable texts, and the other, that they remained the zealously guarded property of a closed society.

One branch of *omirones* moved across the Aegean into the region of Ephesos, perhaps motivated by the prospect of finding financial reward. It was here that *omirones* became the Homeridai, an adequate *transliteration* of the name, albeit far from an adequate translation. Thus, the Greek meaning of their name was understood as "children of Homer", the possessors of the *Iliad* and *Odyssey*, and, from this, surely, the logical inference that their father had been "Homer", the author of these works. Ephesos lay at the mouth of the Caustrios (II, 461, spurious), and, surely, here, was a reminiscence of Troy, to judge from the nearby isle of Samos, and beyond it, the Icarian Sea. In time, the name of "Homer" became firmly entrenched in the region, with various presumed birthplaces such as Chios, Smyrna, Colophon, Miletos...

X. THE HELLENIZATION OF HOMER

By *c.* 800 BC, a fourth generation *omirones*-Homeridai had lost their intellectual grip on the *Iliad* and *Odyssey*. They were know-nothing would-be poets, irreparably separated from institutional instruction and guidance. Nevertheless, they remained self-evident works in an exquisite language, with superb rhetorical power and dramatic appeal. This was more than ample reason to insure their gradual fame, worldwide.

According to Plutarch (*c.* 46–127 AD), it was Lykourgos who was responsible for making the works known throughout Hellas, when he took copies of both epics to Sparta, where they became state property. The event is recorded in the *Lives*, "Lycurgus", IV, 3–4:

> From Crete, Lycurgus sailed to Asia, with the desire, as we are told, of comparing with the Cretan civilization, which was simple and severe, that of the Ionians, which was extravagant and luxurious, just as a physician compares with healthy bodies those which are unsound and sickly; he could then study the difference in their modes of life and forms of government. There too, as it would appear, he made his first acquaintance with the poems of Homer, which were preserved among the posterity of Creophylus; and when he saw that the political and disciplinary lessons contained in them were worthy of no less serious attention than the incentives to pleasure and license which they supplied, he eagerly copied and compiled them in order to take them home with him. For these epics already had a certain faint reputation among the Greeks, and a few were in possession of certain portions of them, as the poems were carried here and there by chance; but Lycurgus was the very first to make them really known.

Plutarch equates Homer with Ionia (that is, with the Homeridai in the environs of Ephesos). However, it may have been that Lykourgos went to Pella, where the *omirones* were already famous, and that in a bid for copies of the *Iliad* and *Odyssey*, he explained to the creators of these works regarding the destruction of the Trojan Culture that he wished to use them as a model for the education of a society which upon a time had been responsible for this act. One can understand that the request will have been offensive, and how it may have ignited disputes among the *omirones*, eventually leading to their leaving Pella, *en mase*.

So it was —whether at Pella or at Ephesos— that the *Iliad* and *Odyssey* fell to the province of scholars wholly wanting in even the most elementary training and guidance in the reading of these magical texts.

Another branch of *omirones* moved on, far beyond Ephesos, into the Near East, where they seem to have settled and transmitted a wealth of historical knowledges to a unique group of foreigners, more or less recently settled in the region, and who were in a process of developing Judaism.

Now, evidence of a contact between *omirones* and rabbis rests on far more than a set of coincidences between both groups. The most obvious are the use of the Phrygian cap and the *yarmulkeh* skullcap, the *guslar* and the cantor, and that the holy texts of both groups are rhymed. Beyond these external coincidences, is that the Deluge Story told in *Genesis*, prefaced by an account about the Nephilim, and purporting to give an explanation about the peopling of the earth and the division of languages, is long anticipated by an account of a line of descent in The Royal House of Troy. The *Iliad* impinges on *Genesis*. That the reverse may have happened, that the Biblical "Table of Nations" (the progeny of Noah, *Gen.* x, 1–5) was altered and became the "Royal House of Troy" (XX, 215–240), does not ring true, since this would require access to *Genesis*, which did not come into existence until long after the *Iliad* and *Odyssey* were being sung by the Homeridai.

* * *

It seems preposterous to assume there never existed an institutional framework for the creation of the *Iliad* and *Odyssey*, nor that any such framework abstained from tutorial instruction and guidance in the reading of these texts... The texts exist, but the institutional framework that created them does not, it vanished, long ago, impotent of self-propagation. The analogy, of course, is that the New Testament exists, but the context that gave it life, and the institutional framework that held it together, likewise vanished, long ago... If the syllogism is correct, then it must be presumed that the institutional framework that created the *Iliad* and *Odyssey* has, indeed, come to us, altered, renamed, dressed in some august guise and hitherto unrecognized.

CHAPTER XI

THE HOMERIZATION OF HELLAS

The foregoing scenario of a dychotomy between tutorial guidance of the *Iliad* and *Odyssey* by *omirones* and the dissemination of these works among a general public through the offices of Lykourgos, is, to be sure, an over-simplification of what, in any case, is an educated guess about how these works became known. However, what is certain is that the *Iliad* and *Odyssey* —in a word, "Homer"— became quickly entrenched in the soul of the Greek literary intelligentsia.

Greeks could relate to the *Iliad*, as if their ancestors had been those who, upon a time, had gone to war against Troy, which, in a measure, was true. The Dorian and Ionian migratory movements into the southern Balkan Peninsula soon after the Fall of Troy had brought with them a few place-names from the Italian Peninsula, followed by additional colonizations in the 10th and 9th centuries. Thus, the *Iliad* addressed, and confirmed, with no doubt about accuracy, vague hisorical memories of peoples in this or that new city-state. Oddly, it seemed that nothing Trojan was inherited by Hellas, and, in due course, everything which once had been Trojan became Hellenized.

However, by contrast with the *Iliad*, Greeks could not relate to the difficult, mysterious, maritime geography of the *Odyssey* with the same natural ease and confidence, simply because Trojan migratory movements were fundamentally of a territorial nature, wholly unrelated with a geography of a seaboard where some distant memory of Odysseus might have some credibility.[1]

Henceforward, the *Iliad* and *Odyssey* would become separate works, certainly, ascribed to the shimmering mirage of a common author, the name of one epic inspired on the siege on Ilios, the name of the other on a participant in the Trojan War. There was no *imagination* —what is more, *no* justification for it— that the name of the *Iliad* was

---

1. Imbros, Lemnos, Lesbos, and Tenedos are not Trojan exports, but, rather, identification of islands in the vicinity of the Troad made by Greeks with the foundation of Troy VIII.

taken from the goings to and fro between Danaans and Trojans on small, flat-bottomed boats, *harma* (understood as "chariots"), over the *swampy*, *muddy* Troic and Ileian Plains, and that the *Odyssey* was an extension of these naval engagements. The source material for these independent epics was truly puzzling, for, though a consensus endorsed a common authorship in the person of Homer, the *chorizontes* subscribed to a separatism in the story-stuff for the *Iliad*, rooted at the entrance to the Dardanelles in the northwestern corner of Asia Minor, while that of the *Odyssey* was spilled here and there throughout the Western Mediterranean.

In the same manner that the internal conceptual schemes for the geographical structures of each epic ceased to have a bearing on each other, there ceased to exist narrative points of contact between the two epics, which, precisely, had lent them their sublime literary stature. Thus, the Greeks never understood that *omirones* had seized on the unique opportunity of raising a detailed census of the diverse expeditionary forces sent against Troy brought together on the beaches of Orebič under the shadow of SAMOS (Sveti Ilija), and that this census was to be structured in the same manner as the one that already existed (perhaps for administrative purposes), namely, the *Catalogue of Trojan Allies* (to which information about local defensive forces was added).

THE CATALOGUE OF SHIPS (II, 494–759)

Two fundamental aspects of the *Catalogue of Ships* were, first, the reliable quality of information, and, second, the scientific methodology evinced in its classification of geonyms. Thus, the Greeks, from the very onset, wanting in institutional guidance or instruction for an adequate understanding of Homer, failed to understand what the *Catalogue of Ships* was about —since they *had no reason* for knowing— and that the geography of Troy conformed to the rigours of a structured format. They could easily accept that Troy had once been in Asia Minor, at the entrance to the Dardanelles. Furthermore, it seemed a reasonable assumption that most of the diverse communities which once had sent hostile forces against Troy were to be found in Hellas.

The *Catalogue of Ships* contained 200 geonyms, 50 of which corresponded with concepts of physical geography, and the remaining 150 with concepts of social geography, a neat ratio of 1:3. But this fact was meaningless, if at all perceptible, for at the very core of a difference between what the *Catalogue of Ships* said, and what the Greeks believed it said, was the implicit belief that Hellas had formerly possessed, as it

XI. THE HOMERIZATION OF HELLAS

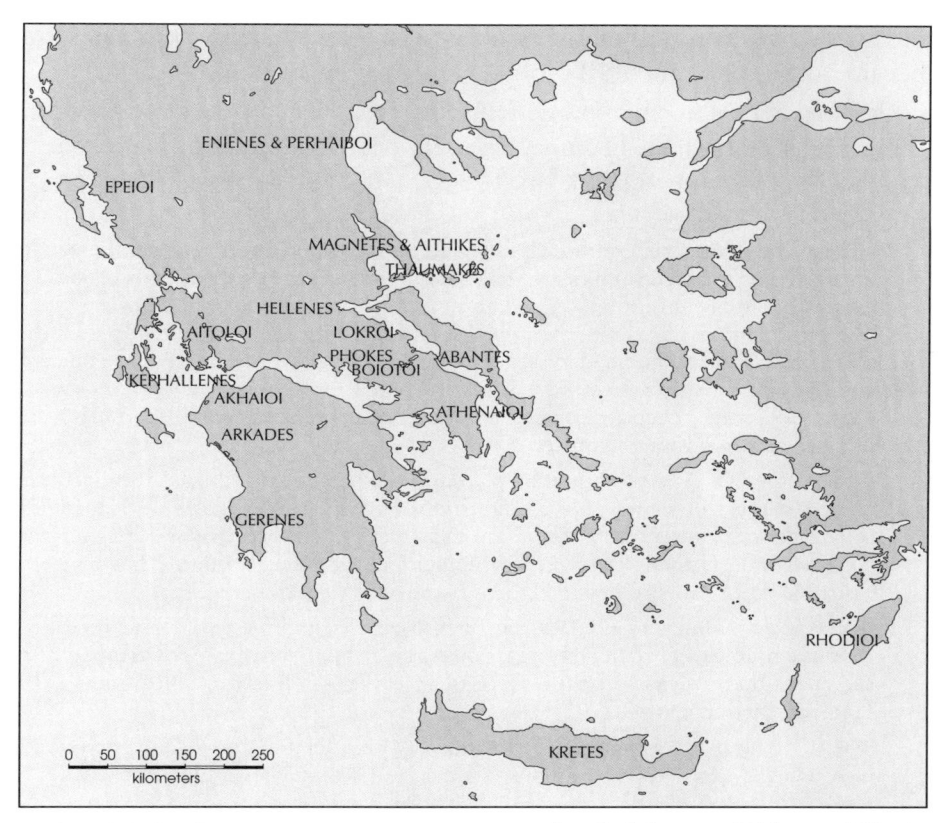

MAP 11. 1. PRESUMED PREHOMERIC CENSUS OF HELLAS. The Catalogue of Ships, *as hitherto understood, is laced with two insoluble problems: the first, it is a document recollecting a pre-Trojan status quo of diverse peoples with Mykenaian Linear B names transcribed into a language akin with the Homeric dialect, and, the second, that this document is an orderly and methodical census, which, obviously, it is not.*

now did, the names of peoples and places since time immemorial, and that Homer had simply collected and woven these, as well as grafted the *Catalogue of Ships* —surely, a composition from earlier times— into the narrative line of the *Iliad* (MAP 11. 1). Thus, difficulties with geographical realities lay with *all* attempts to rationalize what Homer was thought to have intended. The reverse argument, that Hellas did *not* acquire Homeric onomastica until *after* the composition of the *Iliad* could not be credibly sustained, since, simply, there was no need for any such hypothesis.

An example of difficulties with geographical realities is to be seen with the very first entry in the *Catalogue of Ships,* the BOIOTOI, a folk of the Piedmont (whose name is likely echoed in that of the *Boii*), who became the occupants of "Boiotia" (nonexistent in Homer).

Efforts to relate the 30 geonyms of the BOIOTOI (II, 494–510) with "Boiotia" seem to have become, indeed, hopelessly muddled (G. S. Kirk, *The Iliad: A Commentary*, I. pp. 168–69, 178–79, 190–91):

> The catalogue lists 29 Achaean[4] contingents covering most of the Greek world of Homer's time, or earlier; although it neglects the central Aegean islands, the whole of the Aegean coastline of western Asia Minor with large off-lying islands of Samos, Khios and Lesbos, also the Megarid and much of the Thessalian plain... The effect of the catalogue as a whole is somewhat daunting to most modern readers, or for all in fact who are not connoisseurs of ancient political geography; but ancient audiences and readers must have been fascinated in different ways by the documents's coverage, conciseness and virtuosity of expression, quite apart from its mythical and patriotic relevance.
>
> (i) That the BOEOTIANS should be placed at the head of the list, and be given the highest number of leaders, places and troops, is remarkable in view of their minor role in the rest of the poem. The usual explanation, which clearly deserves serious consideration, is that it is somehow connected with the expedition having been assembled at Aulis[5] in Boeotia before crossing the Aegean sea to Troy.
>
> According to Thucydides 1.12.3 the Boiotoi entered the region later to be called after them no earlier than sixty years after the Trojan war (for his afterthought to the effect that a group of them were there earlier is clearly a concession to the Homeric catalogue itself...
>
> 496–508 The 29 places named are as follows (with brief notes on location and finds, in which HSL refers to Hope Simpson-Lazenby, Giov to Giovannini, B to Buck):
>
> ETEONOS (497) Position unknown; in the Parasopia according to Strabo 9.408, though he assumed it had changed its name to Skarphe. Epithet πολύκνημον, 'many-spurred', suits many sites in Boeotia, but not for example those around Lake Kopais.
>
> THESPEIA (498) Presumably at or near the site of classical Thespiai, where some Mycenean pottery has been found (HSL 22).

---

4. Kirk and others err: the *Catalogue* lists not 29 but 28 contingents, since those from SALAMIS (557) properly belong listed in ¶6, with those from ATHENAI (546); furthermore, it is only by a considerable stretch of the imagination that the term "Achaean" can be taken to mean "those in the *Catalogue of Ships* who went against Troy", for the *Catalogue* itself evinces the names of 19 other folks in addition to that of the AKHAIOI (some of whom, albeit listed, did not send a contigent to Troy).

5. The tale is told there were *two* gatherings at Aulis (see Robert Graves, *The Greek Myths*, II. New York: George Braziller, Inc., 1959, pp. 278, 290.) such that the following inference may be drawn: that a *first* call for a gathering at AULIS (*Pedone*, Cuneo) went unanswered because of its inaccessability, from which failure, ever since, the custom became established in the Piedmont that, if anything ever went wrong for whatever the reason, it was certainly because the person to blame was a native of Cuneo; a *second* call was convened at DAULIS (*Rubra/Aulla*), located in the Apuan Hills upstream the *Macra*, which was attended by all, certainly because of the safe haven offered by the natural port facilities of what today is the naval base of La Spezia.

XI. THE HOMERIZATION OF HELLAS 247

GRAIA (498) Probably a kome of Oropos in the fifth century (cf. Thucydides 2.23.3; Giov 25); a possible Mycenaean site is mentioned by HSL 22, but B prefers the Dramesi site usually allotted to Hurie. According to Pausanias 9.20.2 the inhabitants of Tanagra (omitted by the catalogue) claimed that its early name was Graia; there is at least some phonetic similarity.

MUKALESSOS (498) Its ruins were known to Pausanias (9.19.4) and are probably to be identified with an ancient site near the modern village of Rhitsona; a little Mycenaean pottery has been found there, but the cemetery dates back to the mid-eighth century B.C. (HSL 22f)... Epithet εὐρύχορον, 'with broad dancing-floor(s)', which does not necessarily have a geographical implication.

HARMA (499) Was near Mukalessos, and its ruins were seen by Pausanias (9.19.4) and Strabo (9.404), who connect its name with Amphiaraos being engulfed by the earth with his chariot, ἅρμα, as he fled from Thebes. It is usually located at an ancient site (with Mycenaean and classical sherds, but no PG or G so far) commanding the pass on the road from Thebes to Khalkis. The lack of Dark Age and ninth-/ eighth-century pottery does not mean that knowledge of Harma must be Mycenaean in immediate origin, since the Amphiaraos connection might have been a long-standing one (and enabled an otherwise inconspicuous place called 'Harma' to have survived in the legendary tradition).

HARMA was not ever near Mukalessos, for, as its very name "assemblage" suggests (whence the Greek sense of "chariot"), it is the collective district-type name for the Western Alpine massif which incorporates MYKALESSOS (Pennine Alps) εὐρύχωρον, "with broad spaces", GRAIA (Graian Alps), THESPEIA (Cottian Alps), and ETEONOS (Maritime Alps).

Efforts to identify the *Catalogue of Ships* with a Greek geography have been as fruitless as bringing the starry cosmos into harmony with a Ptolemaic system. Still, the fact is that *some* Homeric onomastica became firmly established in Hellas —not just that which had arrived with immigrants, but also that which seemed to refer to this or that district— and, for as wide of the mark as these would-be Homeric place names may have been, this is not to say there is not some measure of logic in the assignation of some Homeric onomastica to a new context, as, for instance, in that of (new) Athens and the islands of (new) Salamis and (new) Aigina in the Saronic Gulf, and, at the end of the Attic promontory, (new) Sounion.

Still, one wonders, what shred of a hint might have placed Boeotia where it was thought to be, and not someplace else, maybe in the very center of the Peloponessus? Perhaps the reason is ancillary, as if the primary reason might have touched on the location of Delphi, near a late Bronze-Age site presumed to have been the PYTHO mentioned by Homer (IX, 405).

Such an identification of Delphi with PYTHO, then, —if the presumption is accurate— will have allowed for an inference about the location of "Phocis", and, of course, of its its immediate neighbour, "Boeotia". However, as artificial as such an identification may have been, some vague knowledge about the Homeric identity of PYTHO (*Portus Delphinus*, Portofino) is betrayed by the play on words in the beautiful (would-be Homeric) *Hymn to Pythian Apollo* (388–409):

> Then Phoebus Apollo pondered in his heart what men he should bring in to be his ministers in sacrifice and serve him in rocky Pytho. And while he considered this he became aware of a swift ship upon the wine-like sea in which were many men and goodly, Cretans from Cnossos ... These men were sailing in their black ship for traffic and for profit to sandy Pylos and to the men of Pylos. But Phoebus Apollo met them: in the open sea he sprang upon their swift ship, like a dolphin in shape, and lay there, a great and awesome monster, and none of them gave heed so as to understand but they sought to cast the dolphin overboard. But he kept shaking the black ship every way and making the timbers quiver. So they sat silent in their craft for fear, and did not loose the sheets throughout the black, hollow ship, nor lowered the sail of their dark-prowed vessel, but as they had set it first of all with oxhide ropes, so they kept sailing on; for a rushing south wind hurried on the swift ship from behind.

The Greek understanding of the name of Pytho was derived from πύθω, "rot, corrode", "become *putrid*", thus, here the dolphin in question is not the swift-swimming mammal that often accompanies vessels out at sea, but, rather, the fish by the same name which, when caught, goes from its natural wan aspect through a dazzling display of bright, iridescent colours as it dies, truly an amazing (and saddening) sight, after which this magic is lost forever and it becomes just another dead fish. However, a Homeric etymology for Πυθω πετρεσσαν, (IX, 405, above) calls for a root ϝιτ- "corniche", or even "horn" (as in Spanish *pitón*), as does indeed the corniche of (ϝ)Ιτον, today the Cilento, or the second element hidden in the name of NER(ϝ)ITON (Pelješac Peninsula).

ITON is mentioned in II, 695–710 (= ¶21), but here the *Catalogue* has fallen into some disarray, for ITON can hardly convey a sense of femininity to justify an epithet τε μητέρα μήλων, "the mother of flocks". Moreover, PHYL(L)AKE (*Agropoli*) and PURHASOS (*Paestum/Posidonia*) are ἀνθεμόεντα / Δήμητρος τέμενος "flowery, temenos of Demeter" respectively (695), but Demeter has substituted for "Poseidon", most likely to keep in harmony with a sense of vegetation in "flowery" PHYL(L)AKE (cognate with Latin *folium*, "leaf") and PTELEON (*Pyxus/Buxentum*) "couched in grass"(*Map 11.2.*).

Where could (new) Iton be? Anybody's guess would be accurate (G. S. Kirk, *The Iliad: A Commentary*, I. pp. 230–31 (on II, 695–710):

> 695–7 PHULAKE is shown by 700 (as well as by 13.696 = 15.335) to have been Protesilaos' home and therefore the capital. Its exact location is nevertheless unknown; Strabo 9.435 says it was near (Phthiotic) Thebes, and so in the north-west

XI. THE HOMERIZATION OF HELLAS 249

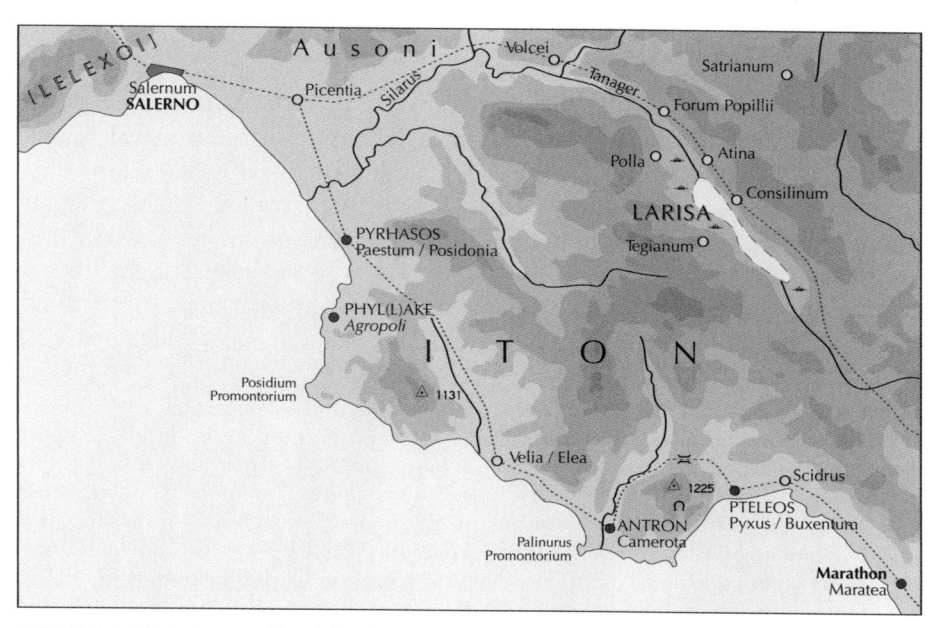

MAP 11.2. ITON CORNICHE. *The following entry in the Catalogue of Ships makes orderly geographical sense:* ¶21. *And they that held Phylace and flowery Pyrasus, the sanctuary of Demeter, and Iton, mother of flocks, and Antron, hard by the sea, and Pteleos, couched in grass, these again had as leader warlike Protesilaus, while yet he lived...*

PHYL(L)AKE	flowery
-PYRHASOS	-temenos of (Poseidon)
ITON	**mother of flocks**
-ANTRON	-hard by the sea
PTELEOS	couched in grass

corner of the Pagasitic gulf. 'Flowering' PURASOS was the later Demetrion, according to the same source, and is probably the mound-site above the harbour at Nea Ankhialos, where Myc and G sherds have been found (HSL 132). Strabo also says there was a grove of Demeter close by, which must be the Δήμητρος τέμενος of 696. ITON 'mother of flocks' has been provisionally placed 'in the foothills to the southwest of the Krokian plain' (HSL 133). ANTRON 'next the sea' was south of Pteleon and had an off-lying submarine reef known as 'Antron's donkey' according to Strabo 9.435; it is probably directly across the strait from Histiaia. 'Grassy' PTELEON — epithets come thick and fast here, and this one at least does not look particularly appropriate for another harbour site — lies on the hill called Gritsa at the head of Pteleon bay; the contents of tholos tombs there suggest continuous habitation from the Late Bronze into the Dark Ages (HSL 133). Thus Protesilaos' kingdom runs down the west side of the Pagasitic gulf to meet Akhilleus' along the northern shore of the Malian gulf to the south, and abuts Eumelos' kingdom centered on Pherai to the north. No particular date can be conjectured for the original source of the entry.

THE DISREPUTE OF HOMERIC ORTHODOXY

A collapse of Homeric orthodoxy was tantamount to a collapse of authority. Homer could be regarded as the source of serious mistakes in the province of historical thinking, and it was the fundamental inadequacy of Homer with the truth that Plato detested —not that Plato purported to possess it and Homer not, but, rather, somewhat the reverse, that Homer possessed it, whereas Plato merely *sought* to possess it— and thus a dichotomy between a presumed Nevernever Land of Poetry and the metaphysical World of Ideas of Philosophy *had* to be established (Sir John Edwin Sandys, *A History of Classical Scholarship*, I., 3rd ed., 1920, p. 31):

> But no apologetic interpretation of the Homeric mythology was of any avail to save Homer from being expelled with all the other poets from Plato's ideal Republic. Plato insists that the stories of gods and heroes told by Homer and Hesiod give a false representation of their nature[2]. The poet is a mere 'imitator', and 'we must inform him that there is no room for such as he in our State'[3]. 'The awe and love of Homer', of which Plato had been conscious from his childhood, 'makes the words falter on his lips; but the truth must be spoken'[4]. 'All the poets from Homer downwards, are only imitators; they copy images of virtue, but the truth they never reach'[5]. 'We are ready to admit that Homer is the greatest of poets.., but we must remain firm in our conviction that hymns to the gods and eulogies of famous men are the only poetry which ought to be admitted into our State'[6]. Homer's expulsion from Plato's Republic called forth a considerable controversial literature[7]. Athens, not withstanding this expulsion, continued to learn Homer by heart[8], and this ancient custom was continued far beyond the Athenian age.
>
> 2. Rep. 377 D–378 E. Hesiod is also clearly meant, though not mentioned, in Laws 886 B–C. 3. Rep. 398 A. 4. 595 B. 5. 600 E. 6. 607 A. 7. Sengebusch, Diss. i 119 (Mahaffy, Gr. Lit. i 33). 8. Xen. Symp. 3 §5.

CHAPTER XII

TROY VIII

The foundation of Troy VIII, ±700 BC, on the site of a former fortress that lay in shambles, where building materials were readily available, coincided not only with the economic viability of establishing a commercial station for servicing maritime trade into and out of the Aegean and Euxine seas, but also with the appearance of a story in mainland Hellas about a Trojan War. However, more than two-and-a-half millennia later, the archaeology of Hissarlik cannot show whether Troy VII, or the proceeding stratum of Troy VI, is the one that best corresponds with the period of a presumed Trojan War, besides there being a difficulty of relating all the descriptions of Ilios with places on either of these strata, as well as understanding a destruction by earthquake and not a war, as the post-Homeric legends would have it.

Another, entirely different scenario, is that Hissarlik VI collapsed and was replaced by Hissarlik VII, which was then destroyed by an earthquake, followed some time later, ±700 BC, by the foundation of a port-town called Troy, presumably by the same folk who also founded other cities called Troy[1] —or perhaps by some venturesome tyrant-entrepreneur who set out to establish a colony?— whose main purpose was to service maritime trade into and out of the Aegean and Euxine seas. One might assume that the foundation of Troy was an effort wholly *independent* of the appearance and sudden popularity of Homer for, the reverse argument, that the popularity of Homer was a prime or contributing factor in the establishment of a site called Troy, justified by serving as a commercial station, does not ring true for want of a pragmatic sense of economic reality.

Thus it was that soon, perhaps within the first decade of a new Troy's existence, the story about a Trojan War fought long ago in the surrounding countryside —a little this way of the Scamander, but not so

---

1. Presumably, these were folk from the same stock that established a duplicate Troy (Virgil, *Aen.* 4, 333) at *Buthrotum* (= "Bosphorus") in Albania, and went on to settle an Albania, in the Caucasus, the land today called Azerbajan.

far as the foothills of Ida— took a hold of an inquiring imagination. By now, a fourth or fifth generation Homeridai were, to all intents and purposes, know-nothing rhapsodes who could not teach a whit about the geographical intricacies of that beautiful microcosm called TROIA, a land now occupied by diverse Illyrian tribes, let alone the concepts of a basic structure of a "Trojan Geography".

An understanding of what Homer was saying began, certainly not with the beginning of the Misadventures of Odysseus in this region, but with an identification of the *Iliad's* Troy, or Ilios[2] —the odd duality of names has never been convincingly explained— and from here, outward, in concentric rings. With this identification was lost, instantly, the geographical concept that, in the *Iliad*, a place may not have two names, albeit the same name may be used for two different kinds of places, and the reverse idea in the *Odyssey*, that a place may have two different names, a former and a latter, albeit no two places may have the same name. Thus, *obviously*, it had to be Ilios which gave its name to the *Iliad* (in a way, not unlike Odysseus to the *Odyssey*[3]), yet Ilios, Priam's citadel, was called Troy, as was the land, perhaps in memory of Tros, one of the founders of Troy, rather than Dardania —a region within Troy— so called after Dardanus, grandfather of Tros and founder of the Royal House of Troy (XX, 215 *et pas.*). These were trivial issues, perhaps, but not without some historical value.

It might be assumed that the region's new acquisition of Homeric place names was a gradual process, dependent on a growing understanding of the *Iliad's* narrative line in this new context, and the inferences to the best explanation about an identification of this or that place mentioned in the text with this or that probable location. Noticeably, there seemed to be no local knowledge, or, let alone, memory of any town, river, plain, or mountain whose name was echoed in the *Iliad*, and, significantly, not even a generic toponym which might have lent some sort of hint about a forgotten past. As a result, what Homer had stated with clarity, and what Homer was thought to have intended, produced such crass mistakes in geographical thinking (and consequent historical implications) as to derive the name of Samothrace by antonomasia from "Samos wooded-Thracelike" (XIII, 12), or, the assumption that, by the same token the Phryges were the inhabitants of Phrygia (III,

---

2. The site was formerly believed to have been represented by the archaeological ruins at Bally Dag, considerably further inland, and in some measure affecting how the story might have been understood.

3. Οδυσσεια, "sufferings", whereas Οδυσσευς, "hateful", but also "man of suffering".

XII. TROY VIII

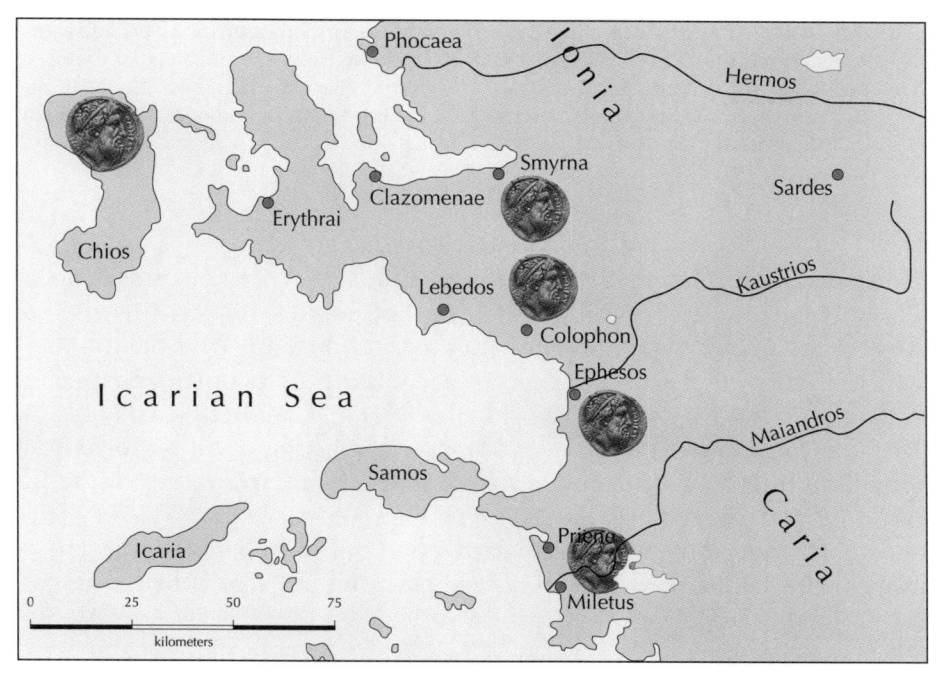

MAP 12.1. PLACES ASSOCIATED WITH "HOMER". Seven cities of antiquity claimed the birthplace of Homer, of which Smyrna, Chios, and Colophon were relatively nearby. Perhaps the historical reality of this perception is that the various authors of works comprising the "Epic Cycle" —of which the Iliad and Odyssey are believed to have formed a part— were the very Homeridai themselves.

184–5), the Mysoi (II, 858) were likewise the inhabitants of "Mysia", a nonexistent country in Homer.

Oddly, for as much as Troy —the Troad— became entrenched at the entrance to the Dardanelles, where not the faintest echo of the past was to be found, the name of Homer became established in the region around Ephesos (*MAP 12.1*), a considerable distance to the south, where a number of earlier migrations had brought toponyms and ethnicons from Italy's Tyrrhenian coast, upon a time known to the *Iliad*'s authorship. Here were to be found the names of the KARES from Caere (Κάειρα, IV, 142), along with Odyssean **Khios** (KRANAI), and that of MAIANDROS (Arrone) and MILETOS (*Lacus Nemorensis*, Lago de Nemi), which settled in Caria. Likewise, the names of the IAONES and LYKIOI (whence classical *Lucania* at the sole of the Italian Boot), who settled Ionian and Lycia, respectively.

It would be the ghost of "Homer", the Homeridai, who could not fail to interpolate beautiful lines relative to Ephesos (II, 459 *et pas.*):

And as the many tribes of winged fowl, wild geese or cranes or long-necked swans on the Asian mead by the streams of Caÿstrius, fly this way and that, glorying in their strength of wing, and with loud cries settle ever onwards, and the mead resoundeth; even so their many tribes poured forth from ships and huts into the plain of Scamander, and the earth echoed wondrously beneath the tread of men and horses.

A (NEW) TROJAN GEOGRAPHY

How was the *Catalogue Trojan of Forces* (II, 816–877) to be understood? There were only two aspects about it that could lend it any sense of coherence. First, by comparison with the *Catalogue of Ships* (II, 494–759) which gave a more or less general accounting of peoples and places throughout the Mykenaian World, the *Trojan Catalogue of Forces*, a Trojan reply to the *Catalogue of Ships*, was a listing of all political and economic interests, near and distant, vested in the powers residing at Ilios... or at Troy. Second, that *some* peoples and places were clearly recognizable, independently of any Troy-epic, but only because migratory movements had already taken a few place names from their original locations to a new context in Asia Minor.

However, the *Trojan Catalogue of Forces* was a deficient listing (G. S. Kirk, *The Iliad: A Commentary*, I, "Introduction to the Trojan catalogue", p. 248):

> This is a far sketchier list than that of the Achaeans, and displays only an erratic knowledge of western Asia Minor beyond the Troad, not only the hinterland, (which is largely ignored) but even the coast... Relatively few towns are mentioned and most of the entries are distinguished by tribal names; a relatively large number of natural features (rivers, mountains, a lake) occur, most of them on or near the coast.

A critical difference between what Homer was thought to say about Hellas, and what Homer was thought to say about Troy, is that, since, as regards Hellas, there were no *referents* against which to check for error, thus Pylos was PYLOS, Sparta was SPARTA, Argos was ARGOS, and Athens was ATHENS.[4] However, in the case of Trojan geographical data,

---

4. That the *Iliad's* authorship could give a more or less reasonable account of the geography of Hellas, although it was ignorant of —or incompetent with— a geography of Troy, seems not to ring the right way. However, the argument could be made that the *Catalogue of Ships*, was, after all, an earlier composition —a Mykenaian census?— interpolated in the narrative line and an ad hoc geography of a Troy-story assembled long after the facts. Still, that in Hellas there are no referents against which to check for error —that all seems to be in relatively sane order— whereas in the case of Troy a geographical setting is incompatible with geographical realities, does not necessarily endorse a hypothesis of a pre-Homeric *Catalogue of Ships*... rather, a disorderly geography of Troy will show that, a) either the *Iliad's* authorship knew not a whit about Trojan geography, or, alternately, b) that Troy was simply someplace else (hence the subtitle of this author's *Homer's Blind Audience* was, precisely, *an essay on the geographical prerequisites for the site of Ilios*). Hitherto, this second option has never been successfully explored (nor exploited).

PRIMARY (PERIPHERAL) GEOGRAPHICAL DATA ABOUT TROY
Information pertinent to the geographical context or environs of the Troad, but not a part of it, *per se:*

SEA	ISLANDS	DISTRICTS	PEOPLES
HELLESPONTOS	IMBROS	(MYSIA)	MYSOI
OKEANOS	LEMNOS	PHRYGIA	PHRYGES
	LESBOS		THRAIKES
	TENEDOS		
	SAMOTHRACE		

SECONDARY (STRUCTURAL) GEOGRAPHICAL DATA ABOUT TROY
Information about diverse features in the geographical configuration of the Troad (as distinguished from topographical props in the landscape):

RIVERS	MOUNTAINS	PROMONTORIES	PLACES
PRACTIOS	GARGAROS	LEKTON	BATIEIA
SATNIOEIS	IDA		PERGAMOS
SKAMANDROS	KALLIKOLONE		
SELLEIS	PLAKOS		
SIMOIS			
XANTHOS			

DISTRICTS	PEOPLES	TOWNS
DARDANIA	DARDANIOI	ABYDOS
HYPOPLAKIA	KIKONES	ARISBE
THYMBRA	KILIKES	KILLA
TROIA	LELEGES	ILIOS / TROIA
	TROES	KHRYSA
		LARISA
		LYRNESSOS
		PEDAIOS
		PEDASOS
		PERKOTE
		THEBE
		ZELEIA

TERTIARY (INCIDENTAL) GEOGRAPHICAL DATA ABOUT TROY
Descriptions of diverse topographical props in the landscape:

ii, 788	TOMB OF AISYETES
X 415	TOMB OF ILOS
X, 572	BATHS OF DIOMEDES
XXI, 553	BATHS OF AGENOR
XXII, 145	WOMEN'S WASHING TANKS

TABLE 12. 2. CLASSIFICATION OF TROJAN TOPONYMS AND ETHNICONS. Forty six names of peoples and places associated in diverse ways with Troy, rather than represent the physical and social characteristics of the land so-called, suggest an amalgamated complex (or sorts) of several social structures, viz., peoples living beyond the periphery of TROIA (ill-defined, as it is), as well as the islands off the Trojan coast as self-contained political units.

a number of referents indeed suggest a zany portrayal of a geographical scenario inconsistent with the sobriety of geographical realities. Thus, one can expect little more than the following wise opinion (J. M. Cook, *Troy, An Archaeological Survey*, p. 91):

> The difficulty with Homer is that of knowing what truth there is in his facts, figures and topographical clues. And this difficulty is so serious that on a strict view of the matter it could be said that to the modern topographer of the ancient Trojan Plain he is not a primary source. His value is an indirect one. In general, the ancient scholars who concerned themselves with Trojan topography regarded Homer as historically accurate and believed that anything that conflicted with his account must be false; and consequently the text of Homer is an essential control for the understanding of their arguments. But we cannot do more than recognize what the ancient scholars pointed out as the Homeric topographical features.

So it is that a new geography of Troy might be assembled, for the purpose of orderly thinking and clarity of understanding, with a set of geographical concepts made up of 46 place names (since more are simply not available) as shown in TABLE 12.1.

There is, to be sure, a difference between an early reader of the *Iliad* who assigned this or that location to this or that toponym or ethnicon listed in TABLE 12.1, and how the Troad in time came to be understood by a local population as well as an academic world in terms of a geography "preserved" in the *Iliad* (as well as utterly misunderstanding a geography that was *not* in the *Iliad* as patently Homeric, namely, the problem posed by the name of Samothrace and that of Samos, an island off the port of Ephesos well to the south of the Troad).

Since an obviously false presumption that some memory about various peoples and places survived in the environs of Troy into that period when the Homeric poems were first taking shape (presumed to have been *c.* 750 BC, albeit opinions vary), and that the authorship of these poems drew material from various sources (as did contemporary poets for their own works about the past), then, both ancient and modern scholars of Trojan geography must necessarily depart from the same *tabula raza*.

* * *

Once tutorial guidance of the *Iliad* and *Odyssey* became lost, only the technological achievements available to the modern investigator are capable of restoring Homeric Geography to a resemblance of its former elegance.

Postscript

Postscript

There remain not a few loose ends to tie up, surely to be addressed at another time in another place, but not before leaving the Gentle Reader with some basic idea about the general nature of a unique invention, Homeric Epic.

The identification of Troy with Hissarlik —how could this not be so?— is *precisely* what holds Homer firmly "gullivered" to Asia Minor, and because of this, impotent of yielding one iota from the vast body of historical information implicit in both the *Iliad* and the *Odyssey*. The impressive archaeology of Troy VII would seem to lend credence to the story of a Trojan War, and, since the texts also appear to tell a more or less cogent story, there has never been the need of "degullivering" Homer from the region to find what was never lost... excepting those inferences derived from trivial discrepancies between what was said about the geography of Troy and the existing realities of Asia Minor... or the difficulties of relating the events of a story-line, already complex as it is, with the local topography. Not the same is to be said about an identification of ILIOS with Drijeva/Gabela, linking the literacy of the *Iliad* and *Odyssey* with the land of Kadmos, indeed, of Vinča writing, the abundant archaeology of the region, the occurrence of still extant place-names, the exclusive use of the term ἀμπελόεσαν "vine-clad" for the *vinograds* to be found *only* in this area[1], the easy concordance of geographical descriptions with geographical realities, in sum, all bearing a distinct relevance to the narrative line of both epics.

Perhaps the *prime* objection to lifting Homer from his traditional Greek context (that is, to associate the composition of the *Iliad* and *Odyssey* beyond the periphery of the Hellenic world) is that, from early on, his Graecity was, to be sure, if not explicitly, at least implicitly,

---

1. III, 184, the land of PHRYGIA; IV, 152, 294, PEDASOS, (in the land of PHRYGIA); II, 561, an epithet for EPIDAURUS (cf. OCT) = *Anxa/Callipolis*, Gallipolis (see my *Atlas of Homeric Geography*, p. 47), albeit possibly an erroneous emmendation for an epithet like ἀμφίαλος "sea-girt", indeed an apt description, founded on a confusion with the name of KARDAMYLE, *Epidaurum* (ibid., p. 53).

unquestioned, for who would have reason to doubt it? and, *a quoi bon?* So, to question the validity of modern academic approaches to new understandings in the complexities of syntax and prosody of the *Iliad* and *Odyssey* as being out of cultural context, and therefore irrelevant, would seem as needless and pointless an exercise as, say, suggesting that since some important historical works of Shakespeare dealt with France, then one might legitimately presume him to have been a Frenchman by the name of Jacques Pierre. Shakespeare is in a sublime English language, and Homer is in an exquisite Greek. The very substance, the quintessence, in the objection to a would-be transference of Homer from his traditional context into a new one in the cultural periphery of the Hellenic world, is one that addresses not the *need* for doing so, nor its *feasibility*, but, rather, the *aesthetics of translation*: indeed, can translations ever be rendered into a more beautiful language than the original?

However, one grand mistake classical scholarship has made is the tacit assumption that Homer shared or obtained information from the same or similar sources as did Hesiod of Ascra (his age disputed with that of Homer), Arctinus of Miletos (?775 – ?744/1 BC), Cinaethon of Lacedaemon (?VI cent. BC), Stasinus of Cyprus or Hegesias of Salamis (presumed contemporaries of Homer), Lesches of Mytilene (?VII cent. BC), and so on. Thus, on many important facts and countless minor issues, these men of letters were often at odds with each other, and *departed* from Homer. Classical scholarship, ancient and modern, has failed to recognize that Homer had no Greek contemporaries, and so confuses their variant statements as just that —variants— rather than as a misunderstanding of what Homer long before them had stated with clarity. A random example of this departure from a "Homeric orthodoxy", so to speak, is what might be said about Ascra, Hesiod's own birthplace (*The Oxford Classical Dictionary*, 3rd. ed., 1999):

> Helicon, mountain in SW Boeotia sacred to the Muses. Running from Phocis to Thisbe in Boeotia, it stretched northwards to Lake Copais and southwards to the Corinthian Gulf. Its most famous feature is the Valley of the Muses, the site of Ascra, the unbeloved home of Hesiod...

About Helicon, Hesiod says the following (*Theogony*, 22–28):

> And one day they [the Muses] taught Hesiod glorious song while he was shepherding the lambs under holy Helicon (Ἑλικῶνος), and this word first the goddesses said to me—the Muses of Olympus, daughters of Zeus who holds the aegis:
> "Shepherds of the wilderness, wretched things of shame, mere bellies, we know how to speak many false things as though they were true; but we know, when we will, to utter true things."

The name of Ascra is, surely, native to the region, and why it became established there is anybody's guess. As for the name of Helicon, and its fanciful association with the Muses of Olympos, one must assume that Muses cannot be precluded from visiting a lesser mountain —or anywhere they wish, for that matter— but, if Hesiod was familiar with the pastures "...under holy Helicon", why, then, did he change lordly *kouroi* who drag a bellowing bull around HELIKONIOS (XX, 403) into famished "Shepherds of the wilderness, wretched things of shame..."?

αὐτὰρ ὁ θυμὸν ἄϊσθε καὶ ἤρυγεν, ὡς ὅτε ταῦρος
ἤρυγεν ἑλκόμενος Ἑλικώνιον ἀμφὶ ἄνακτα
κούρων ἑλκόντων· γάνυται δέ τε τοῖς ἐνοσίχθων·
ὣς ἄρα τόν γ' ἐρυγόντα λίπ' ὀστέα θυμὸς ἀγήνωρ·

But life [Hippodamas] breathed he up and bellowing forth, as a bull
bellowing forth drawn around Helikonios that lordly
kouroi have dragged, for in such rejoices the Earth Shaker,
even so his proud life left his bones;

The idea of this simile is "that which is brought forth from within" contained in the verb ἤρυγεν[2], accompanied not without considerable thundering, which is heightened by the fact that HELIKONIOS is to be identified with *Vesuvius*, at the base of which lived the KOURETES. In later times, these folk were thought to have been nature spirits, closely associated with a mountain goddess Rhea, whose name means "She who flows", allusive —how could it be missed?— of volcanic lava[3].

The wide chasm between Homer, his age and his culture, and that of those men of letters of a much later date who would embrace and seem to "converse" with him, as it were, necessarily establishes a *tabula raza* of a *presumed* inheritance of knowledges of Archaic Greece from the previous Mykenaian Culture. Thus, all information corresponding with the former Heroic Age that occurred abroad, and henceforward would be consigned to the blank blackboard of historical information by a new caste of poets and a new kind of poetry, abounds with geographical malapropisms and need be understood with this dichotomy in mind.

It is not possible to state, categorically, that the literary effervescence of city-state communities scattered here and there throughout Archaic Greece was only able to work with information brought from sources abroad, and was bereft of an ability to be adequately conversant with the historicity implicit in the works of one who was not from among them. Furthermore, it would seem unnatural that no memory or no knowledge of the former existence of Troy in lands now occupied by

---

2. From whence "eruption" and Spanish *eructo*, "a loud burp".
3. See the article on "Curetes" in the *The Oxford Classical Dictionary*, 3rd. ed., 1999, for their various other doings which became geographically confused, and in time, muddled.

Illyrian tribes ever existed, and, so, it might be presumed that those who knew the facts well, and were "dissenters" from mainstream wisdom, were few and silent. Moreover, all popular lore —"historical hearsay" as it were— captured in the nascent Greek world from both Danaan (non-Trojan) and Trojan sources alike, necessarily suffered alterations through some process of rationalization. Still, the results, muddled as they may be, are invaluable to bringing out the narrative luster of Homer, as in the case of what may be adduced about the KOURETES mentioned above.

ON THE NATURE OF HISTORICITY

There are two general understandings of the term "historicity" as it refers to the truth-content of an account. The first, as a noun, the term connotes the substance, or facts, *a priori*, of an historical account, namely, information which lends a sense of truthfulness and historical character to this or that account[4]. The second, as an adjective, the term denotes a qualitative substance, or value, *a posteriori*, of any account, regardless of its genre, and therefore any premise of truth-content must be sought from within the narration. Thus, there is a difference between those accounts where a fundamental core-issue of historicity is self-evident and uncontested, and those where a sense of credibility is unclear or wanting. One might compare, say, what could be said about the more or less self-evident historicity of the *Histories* of Herodotus (c. 484–c. 445 BC) with the historicity of the would-be Homeric *Frogmouse War*. While Herodotus, the so-called "Father of History" seems fairly knowledgeable about what was generally believed in his time of early migrations into Hellas (though he errs), he evinces inexperience with Homer (if not some distance with the genre of epic narrative). On the other hand, the *Frogmouse War* is a fable, a parody of the *Iliad* in a one-day war between the Frogs and the Mice which occupy the waters and banks of a river. Historically, it is the first account of its nature to make its debut,

---

4. The bibliography is ample: Wilhelm Hoffmann, *Von der Geschichtlichkeit des Denkens*, 1948. B. M. L. Delfgaauw, A. Boefraad, R. Kwant, *De historiciteit*, 1955. Emil L. Fackenheim, *Metaphysics and Historicity*, 1961 [The Aquinas Lecture, Marquette University, 1961]. August Brunner, *Geschichtlichkeit*, 1961. Gerhard Bauer, *"Geschichtlichkeit". Wage und Irrwege eines Begriffs*, 1963. Richard Schaeffler, *Die Struktur der Geschichtszeit*, 1963. Leonard von Renthe-Fink, *Geschichtlichkeit, Ihr terminologischer und begrifflicher Ursprung bei Hegel, Haym, Dilthey und Yorck*, 1964. H.-G. Gadamer, K. Löwith et al., *Truth and Historicity / Vérité et historicité*, 1972, ed. Hans-Georg Gadamer (Entretiens de Heidel-berg, 12/16-IX-1969). H.-G. Gadamer, W. Schultz et al., *Sein und Geschichtlichkeit*, 1974 ed. Ingeborg Schüssler and Wolfgang Janke (Homage to Karl-Heinz Volkmann-Schluck). C. Fynsk, *Thought and Historicity*, 1986.

a fairy-story most certainly from among that new caste of poets with a new kind of poetry, but its actors, frogs and mice, a water-snake, would-be gods, and crabs, are closer to the truth than the actors of the *Iliad*, all of whom *seemed* human, but conformed to their totemic identities and so responded not to the free will innate in mankind, but to climactic and seasonal phenomena. The Mice, no doubt, recall the Bebrykes, that horde of mice which attacked Skamandros early on in the history of Troy, and who are likely reflected in the name of ZKYNTHOS, *Melita*, Mljet, where the *kuna*, a badger-like creature roams wild. The frogs, *žaba*, are likewise reminiscent of the young maidens of LESBOS, *Brattia*, Brač, where only the idea of a tadpole can lend credence to the story about the head of Orpheus singing its way to this island. The hydra can be nothing less than the delicious eel of the Neretva estuary, and, certainly, the crabs which make a sudden *mise en scène* invites speculation about the arrival of Kadmos to these lands, and the peace he established between the warring tribes of Encheleis and Illyrians (Psd.-Apollodorus, 3. 39. 2). Along with the *Frogmouse War*, and of the same genre, are the *Fables* of Aesop, whose name is of the same kind as AESEPOS (Rama) and ASOPOS (Mala Neretva), the *marshy* sort of place where this story might have been set. If this understanding of the *Frogmouse War* makes any sense, then an inference that *someone* in the new world of literature was well aware of the former location of Troy is not unwarranted.

Now, the historicity of Herodotus is static, so to speak, for the facts of his work —the actors, the actions, the time, and the place— are taken at face value, whereas in the story about a would-be war between frogs and mice, each of the four component elements has its own "plasticity", each moulded in its own fashion. The actors, pre-Trojan tribes vying for territorial acquisition, the action, a war to vindicate a grievance, the time, sometime before the arrival of Dardanus and the Foundation of Troy, the place, the marshy delta of the SKAMANDROS (Neretva)... and the thought lingers, obtrusive, unwanted: *what* inspired the idea of creatures from the animal kingdom having a one-day *Iliad*? the answer has to be that the idea of the *Iliad's* participants behaving according to their totemic identities was brought around full circle to the notion of certain creatures of the animal world possessing anthropomorphic attributes.

A SENSE OF HOMERIC HISTORICITY

So, what about speculation on factual truth-content in the narrative lines of both the *Iliad* and *Odyssey*? What about the pragmatic realities in the causes and effects of such an enormous social upheaval, the politics, the economics, and corresponding ethnic and linguistic displacements?

An idea of Homeric factual truth-content is necessarily synonymous with an understanding of certain *behavioural qualities* —the theatrics and plasticity— in the four structural elements of the narrative lines, namely, the ACTORS and their PLACE, and their ACTIONS in their TIME. Now, since behavioural qualities require a measure of *control* (because they are the *qualitative* substance of two narrative lines), a moment of reflection will show that ACTORS act (hence the notion that peoples and places are inseparable and synonymous with history), and that an apparatus of geographical control is to ACTORS and their PLACE, what a scheme of time-control is to ACTIONS in their TIME (which are likewise inseparable, and likewise synonymous with history).

ACTORS

The central figure in the *Iliad* would seem to be Akhilleus; his counterpart in the *Odyssey* is, of course, Odysseus. Both personages withdraw from the objective of their purpose in the narrative line, Akhilleus from his dutiful part in the Trojan War, Odysseus from setting accounts straight in Ithaka. Akhilleus seems forever an airy being, while Odysseus relates as a profoundly chthonic being,[5] yet, oddly, both possess an association with ants, Akhilleus with his MYRMIDONES, his army of "ant men", and Odysseus with his father, Laertes, "ant man". Their respective natural habitats will have been places where, conceivably, men could enter caves, not unlike ants and their ant-tunnels, and so the authorship of the *Iliad* assigns Akhilleus to the district of TRAKHIS (*Latium*, Lazio) where names like *Speluncae, Formiae,* and *Minturnae* lend a credibility to MYRMIDONES occupying the region, and likewise connects Odysseus with the "orchards" of Laertes at **Nerikos** (Djunta Doli), where NERITON (Pelješac) joins the mainland, the region being riddled with caves.

That the participants in the Trojan War and the Misadventures of Odysseus readily mingle with gods and goddesses at once betrays their strange and super-natural character. In fact, these personages possess a totemic identity[5], and, as such, obey the natural forces of nature (for

---

5. The totemic identity of Odysseus may have been a small quadruped, a jackal, or fox, both natural to the Pelješac Peninsula (albeit this identity cannot be confirmed at the time of writing this), whence, presumably, an erroneous Greek editorial emendation —perhaps by some Alexandrine scholar— of Auto*lipos* to Auto*lykos*, grandfather of Odysseus, whose name seems to be reflected in Hittite documents as that of Madduwatas.

their ACTIONS are necessarily moderated by a scheme of time-control). As such, then, all personages, of the present and the past, possess a certain theatrical or histrionic function.

PLACE

The quintessence of Homeric Geography is the schematic balance and harmony of geographical information, which is as much as to say that all geographical information has been carefully selected (and consequently a narrative line made to suit the selected geography accordingly). As for the question about selected information suggesting not only incomplete information, and therefore also an undesirable bias, it is neither here nor there, since, again, this is because of the necessary control of qualitative substance, and, as it is, the information yielded by both narrative lines is of encyclopaedic proportions. For example, it really does not matter whether TROIA had more than sixteen port-towns, eight on the islands and eight on the mainland, eight of these in the north and eight in the south. Simply, what is important is that information be reigned in and contained in a geographical grammar, so to speak, such that it does not run away from one and become literary gibberish.

ACTIONS

The points of contact between a detailed account of a protracted war and the science-fiction story about a man lost at sea are that the one, the *Iliad*, is a story about diverse small naval engagements on flat-bottomed boats (*drijeva*, still in use today) between contending parties over eminently swampy and muddy terrain (hence the name of the *Iliad*), and the other, the *Odyssey*, about the varied episodes of a single naval experience (the drowning of Odysseus). That the participants of these events possess a totemic identity, and therefore a theatrical function, necessarily dramatizes their behaviour. A random example is the conduct of Helen, the "cause" of the Trojan War, a young woman confined to her quarters where she weaves a *peplos* with scenes of a Trojan War not yet in progress (III, 125–128). Now, Helen was an Argive (IV, 19), which is as much as to say that she came from the region of TRAKHIS (*Latium*, Lazio), possibly ARGOS (*Cajeta*, Gaeta), but ALOPE (*Circeii*) cannot be precluded, a hill with many caves, all abounding with spiders. Her parallel with Kirke would seem obvious, not so much because of the many men victimized on her account, but, rather, on certain prophetic abilities that both women shared, Helen with her *peplos*, Kirke with her forewarnings to Odysseus (xii, 37–134).

TIME

The *Iliad* sheds information on the remote past, such as the ARKADES "who knew not of boats..." (II, 603–614), and the *Odyssey* on a general *status quo* of the world, such as the new island of Krete "in the middle of the sea..." (xix, 172). Both narrative lines are compressed into periods of twelve, in a clear association with the twelve houses of the Zodiac (see *Table 7.5*). Thus, the *Iliad* gives a detailed account of the last three "years", that is, an ephemerides of celestial events in 36 lunar months (= periods of 29.5 days), while the *Odyssey* compresses the Misadventures of Odysseus into eighteen "years", nine of these wandering from place to place, and nine spent on the isle of **Ogygia**, such that his story (properly, up to that point where he finally awakens in the real world) occupies the space of twenty "years", takes ITHAKA in the twenty-first "year", that is, in the thirty-third "year" since the beginning of the Trojan War (when the various Danaan forces under Agamemnon and Menelaus first reached Troy).

A CONCLUSION

Ultimately, perhaps an age-old question must be asked, why do the *Iliad* and *Odyssey* address their particular subjects? Why is it that Hector, who had naught to do with the abduction of Helen, nor held any office greater than that of King Priam, was made to bear the political brunt of two wastrel brothers and the objective of the entire Trojan campaign? Why is it that Odysseus, a significant figure in the destruction of Troy, is made to wander like a vagabond in Trojan waters? At least, a partial answer must certainly lie in the direction that since the *Iliad* reflects the destruction of a matriarchal society by a new patriarchal world-order, then the *Odyssey*, perhaps, accounts for a measure of local proselytism on behalf of a new world-order... or, perhaps, relates the torment of a man overcome with remorse for the treachery of having abandoned his loyalty to a matriarchal society.

Still, the *Iliad* and *Odyssey* are not bereft of a particular spiritual touch of their creators, as evinced in the bird-man (Akhilleus) versus bull-man (Hektor) ritual of the *Iliad*, magnified in sheer horror by the added imagery on the Shield of Akhilleus —an exact picture of the place where Hektor will die— for this ritual represents the wanton depredation by a nomadic hunter-gatherer folk of the material and spiritual accomplishments of a civilized (ie., "domesticated") farmer-breeder folk, not unlike the unwanted pesky bird flying into the orchards of a zealous farmer. Thus, Alexandrine editors brought the story line of the *Odyssey* to an end when Odysseus is finally reconciled with Penelope (xxiii, 000-000), and scenes of the subsequent events in which Odysseus goes to Laertes, in his orchards, and identifies the trees given him in childhood, might be thought of as uncharacteristic of the *Odyssey's* verve and virility. In fact, this scene brings the *Odyssey* to an exquisite close, simply because, Odysseus, repentant —indeed, has he not already suffered enough?— *communes* with an orchard-man, a personage symbolic of civilization itself. Is this act not a bid for redemption?

* * *

The foregoing idea of a text —the *Iliad* and *Odyssey* as inseparable units— created by a college of literati domiciled in ITHAKA who lost control of their material after it was taken abroad and translated, is only an all-too-brief understanding of the local creative circumstances which, oddly, became reflected —like echoes of thunder of a distant storm— by a number of later events in far away lands. Somewhere along the line between the foundation of a Rome-Byzantium at the Bosphoros, perhaps by a faction of Illyrian Hylleis that split away from the would-be Dorianizing of Hellas (*Map 9.2, 10.1.*), and the eventual Greek possession of the *Iliad* and *Odyssey*, there arose, in the land that later would be called Thrace, a certain Orpheus, who has all the markings of some demiurge of SAMOS —indeed, his name would be linked with Samothrace— and who, by all counts, is the spiritual substance in the *Iliad* and *Odyssey*, yet, his presence in ITHAKA cannot be attested. The stories of his birth, his *Argonautica* and other works, cannot hold up to the idea of his presence in ITHAKA, and, moreover, he is anachronic...

The name of the very Homer himself remains as elusive as that of Orpheus. *If* some short progress has been made regarding the authorship of the *Iliad* and the *Odyssey,* it is that both names are now inextricable from each other, yet nothing more than archetypal images, abstractions from the reality of a personage. At best, it is the **Harpyiai** (Harpies), relegated to the region of Nakovana on the western slopes of SAMOS (Sveti Ilija), who must be brought into some sort of harmony with the authorsphip of Homeric Epic. These creatures were never storm-demons of any sort, as often thought, but, to judge from the fact that Penelope, Telemakhos, and Eumaeus knew them, a well-known folk with a purpose of their own. Their name, in the feminine plural, does not necessarily preclude the presence of men among them, and that later lore thought of them as fantastic creatures (whence the inference they were storm demons) perhaps obeys to some early teaching of tutorial guidance to the Homeric Epics about their *totemic identity*, namely, that of bats. Thus, the **Harpyiai** will have been associated with caves.

Still, there is a contradiction between a (presumed) college of literati domiciled in ITHAKA, and (known) **Harpyiai** relegated to the region of Nakovana on the western slopes of SAMOS (Sveti Ilija). How can these opposite positions be reconciled? Perhaps that Odysseus rid ITHAKA of fifty wastrel suitors, whose souls turned into bats on the evening of their deaths (xxiv, 1, *et pas.*), had a bearing on the **Harpyiai** also being present in ITHAKA. This would seem so, for ITHAKA, now cleansed of pesky suitors, could openly once again welcome **Harpyiai**.

Now, were the **Harpyiai** some autochthonous folk that became Trojanized? or were they of a descent from Dardanus? If, indeed, the **Harpyiai** are to be thought of as Dardanids, then, perhaps, some inference might be made about a long-standing social infrastructure that lay at the foundation of an institutional framework that created the *Iliad* and *Odyssey*.

So much, at this time, for these "Homeric Whispers".

FIGURE 1. SCYTHIAN GOLD STAG WITH ANTLERS OF FIRE. Early 6th century BC., from Kostromskaya, near the Kuban River. Hermitage Collection. The stag, also often depicted with a disk in its antlers, represents a new solar symbol of a new patriarchal world-order established in Troy by the invading AKHAIOI, a folk whose name seems not to have survived beyond a generation, but whose legacy became that of the Scythians.

FIGURE 2. MODERN VID, CLASSICAL NARONA. At the edge of northern banks of the TROIC (Glibuša) marshes drained by the Naro River. The two means of local transportation are shown (1967), the donkey and the flat-bottomed drijeva (the medieval name of Gabela).

FIGURE 3. ILIOS. Western face of walls around Stari Grad (of Turkish construction), with the site for the Palace Of Priam (Sanctuary of Apollo) on PERGAMOS, in the distance.

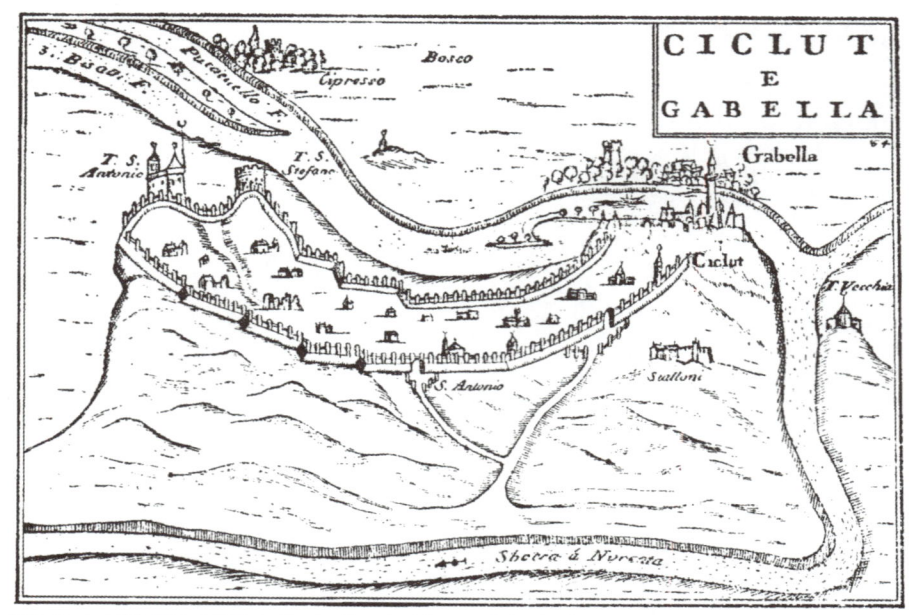

FIGURE 4. MODERN GABELA. Illustration in Mavro Orbini's Regni dei gli Slavi, 1661, showing a non-existent fortified perimeter of a hillock, as well as the garbbled name of Citluk, perhaps influenced by the mistaken idea that the Walls of Troy once surrounded the town (when only the Temple of Athena on KALLIKOLONE was enclosed by a wall).

FIGURE 5. TROIA. The walls of Daorson–Ošanici, perched on the edge of a plateau. The site functioned mostly as a necropolis, with little use as an urban settlement for want of water.

FIGURE 6. ITHAKA. Random picture of any one of the convoluted sets of walls in the "vinograd" of Donja Vručica, pierced at the end by an entrance (inset). That cobbled roads wind throughout the site, and some rooms show drainage ducts, betray it as the remains of an Illyrian settlement.

FIGURE 7. VINČA GODDEES. Figurine with writing around the buttocks and midriff, and head of her rebus, a tortoise. Approx. mid-3rd millennium BC, from R. Pešić, Vinčansko Pismo.
FIGURE 8. VINČA LETTERS. Incision in a rock on the shore below Nakovana, at the Western end of Pelješac Peninsula.

*FIGURE 9. FAMILIAR ICON. The **Harpyiai** observing the passage of Odysseus through the **Planktai**. Italian urn (n.d.), Berlin Museum. The **Harpyiai**, or "Harpies", are here depicted with a tambourine and a lyre, thus associating them with music and singing. Elsewhere, iconography of the **Seirenes**, occupants of the **Planktai** (Od., xx, 123–456), usually depicts them with physical attributes similar to those of the Harpies.*

Bibliography

CRITICAL TEXTS

MONRO, D. B. and ALLEN, T. W., *Homeri Opera*, 5 vols. Oxford Classical Texts. Oxford: Clarendon Press, 1963.

WEST, M. L., *HomerusIlias*, 2 vols. Bibliotheca Teubneriana. Stuttgart and Leipzig: 1998.

BILINGUAL TEXTS

MURRAY, A. T., *The Iliad*, 2 vols. Loeb Classical Library. London: William Heinemann Ltd., 1960.

MURRAY, A. T., *The Odyssey*, 2 vols. Loeb Classical Library. London: William Heinemann Ltd., 1956.

MAZON, P., *Introduction a L'Iliad & Homère Iliade*, 5 vols. Collection Des Universités de France. Paris: Société d'Edition "Les Belles Lettres", 1924.

BERARD, V., *L' Odyssée, "Poésie Homérique"*, 3 vols. Collection Des Universités de France. Paris: Société d'Edition "Les Belles Lettres", 1924.

HOMERIC COMMENTARIES

LEAF, W., *The Iliad*, 2 vols. London: Macmillan & Co., 1886.

KIRK, G. S., *The Iliad: A Commenatry*, vol. 1. Cambridge: Cambridge University Press, 1985.

KIRK, G. S., *The Iliad: A Commenatry*, vol. 2. Cambridge: Cambridge University Press, 1990.

HAINSWORTH, B., *The Iliad: A Commenatry*, vol. 3. Cambridge: Cambridge University Press, 1993.

JANKO, R., *The Iliad: A Commenatry*, vol. 4. Cambridge: Cambridge University Press, 1992.

EDWARDS, M. W., *The Iliad: A Commenatry*, vol. 5. Cambridge: Cambridge University Press, 1991.

RICHARDSON, N., *The Iliad: A Commenatry*, vol. 6. Cambridge: Cambridge University Press, 1993.

HEUBECK, A., WEST, S., and HAINSWORTH, J. B. *A Commentary on Homer's Odyssey*, vol. 1. Oxford: Clarendon Press: 1988.

HEUBECK, A. and HOEKSTRA, A. *A Commentary on Homer's Odyssey*, vol. 2. Oxford: Clarendon Press: 1989.

RUSSO, J., FERNANDEZ-GALIANO, M., and HEUBECK, A. *A Commentary on Homer's Odyssey*, vol. 3. Oxford: Clarendon Press: 1992.

STUDIES ON THE ILIAD

BOLLING, G. M., *The Athetized Lines of the Iliad*. Baltimore, Md: Linguistic Society of America, 1944.

PAGE, D. L., *History and the Homeric Iliad*. Berkeley and Los Angeles: University of California Press, 1959.

WADE-GERY, H. T., *The Poet of the Iliad*. Cambridge: Cambridge University Press, 1952.

WEST. M. L., *Studies in the Text and Transmission of the Iliad*. München, Leipzig: K. G. Saur, 2001.

WHITMAN, C. H., *Homer and the Heroic Tradition*. Cambridge, Massachusetts: Harvard University Press, 1958.

STUDIES ON THE ODYSSEY

FENIK, B., *Studies in the Odyssey*. Hermes Einzelschrift 30, Wiesbaden: 1974.

KOLAR, V., *Odisej luta Jadranom*. Beograd: Niro, 1984.

NORMAN, A., *Archery at the Dark of the Moon*. Berkeley and Los Angeles: 1975.

PAGE, D. L., *The Homeric Odyssey*. Oxford: Clarendon Press, 1966.

WORKS ON HOMER

BOLLING, G. M., *The External Evidence for Interpolation in Homer*. Oxford: The Clarendon Press, 1968.

KIRK, G. S., *The Songs of Homer*, Cambridge: 1962.

LORD, A. B., *The Singer of Tales*. Cambridge, Mass. 1960.

LORIMER, H. O., *Homer and the Monuments*. London 1950.

LUCE, J. V., *Homer and the Heroic Age*. London 1975.

NAGY, G., *The Best of the Achaeans: Concepts of the Hero in Archaic Greek Poetry*. Baltimore 1979.

NAGY, G., *Pindar's Homer: The Lyric Possession of an Epic Past*. Baltimore 1990.

PARRY, A. (ed.), *The Making of Homeric Verse: The Collected Papers of Milman Parry*. Oxford: 1971.

SIMPSON, R. H. and LAZENBY, J. F., *The Catalogue of Ships in Homer's Iliad*. Oxford: Oxford University Press, 1970.

WACE, A. J. B. and STUBBINGS, F. H. (eds.), *A Companion to Homer*. London: 1962.

WEBSTER, T. B. L., *From Mycenae to Homer, A Study in Early Greek Literature and Art*. London: Methuen and Co., 1958.

WOLF, F. A., *Prolegomena to Homer* [1795], translated with introduction and notes by A. Grafton, G. W. Most, and J. E. G. Zetzel. Princeton, 1985.

HOMERIC DIALECT

AUTENRIETH, G. (KEEP, R. P. trans.), *A Homeric Dictionary*. Norman: University of Oklakoma Press, 1979.

CUNLIFFE, R. J., *A Lexicon of the Homeric Dialect*. Norman: University of Oklahoma Press, 1980.

MONRO, D. B., *A Grammar of the Homeric Dialect*. Oxford 1891, repr. 1992.

LINGUISTICS

BILBIJA, S. S., *Staroevropski jezih i pismo Etruraca*. Chicago, Illinois: Institute of Etruscan Studies, 1984.

SAVLI, J., BOR, M. and TOMAZIC, I., *Veneti, First Builders of European Community*. Canada, British Columbia: Anton Skerbinc, 1996.

MALLORY, J. P., *In Search of the Indo-Europeans, Language, Archaeology and Myth*. New York: Thames and Hudson, 1989.

RENFREW, C., *Archaeology and Language, the puzzle of Indo-European origins*. New York: Cambridge University Press, 1988.

ATLASES

The Yugoslav Coast, Guide and Atlas. Zagreb: Yugoslav Lexicographical Institute, 1966.

HAMMOND, N. G. H. (ed.), *Atlas of the Greek and Roman World in Antiquity*. Park Ridge, New Jersey: Noyes Press, 1981.

ORTELIUS, A., *Theatrum Orbis Terrarum*. Antwerp, 1570.

TALBERT, R. J. A. (ed.), *Barrington Atlas of the Greek and Roman World*. Princeton and Oxford: Princeton University Press, 2000.

CARTOGRAPHY

Ostrovo Brač To Dubrovnik (H. O. 3958). Washington D. C.: U. S. Naval Oceanographic Office, rev. ed. 1969.

Stolac-Ošanici, gradina. [BASLER, Dj.], (Sarajevo): 1966.

GENERAL REFERENCES

Lexicon Homericum, 2 vols. (EBELING, H., ed). Hildesheim: Georg Olms Verlagsbuchhandlung, 1963.

The New Century Classical Handbook (AVERY, C. B., ed.). New York: Appleton-Century-Crofts, Inc., 1962.

The Oxford Classical Dictionary (CARY, M. et al. eds). Oxford: Clarendon Press, 1966.

The Oxford Companion to Classical Literature (HOWATSON, M. C. ed). Oxford & New York: Oxford University Press, 1989.

GENERAL LITERATURE

KUHN, T. S., *The Structure of Scientific Revolutions*. Chicago: The University of Chicago Press, 2nd ed., 1970.

PFEIFFER, R., *History of Classical Scholarship, from the beginnigs to the end of the Hellenistic Age*. Oxford: Clarendon Press, 1968.

NORTHERN BALKANIC (SLAVIC) STUDIES

Kulturna Istorija Bosne i Hercegovine, od najstarijih vremena do pada ovih zemalja pod osmansku vlast (POPADIĆ, M. ed.), Sarajevo: Veselin Masleša, 1966.

La vallée du fleuve Neretva depuis la prehistoire jusqu'au début du moyen âge (Réunion Scientifique, Metković, 1977). Split: Société Archéologique Croate, 1980.

Praistorija Jugoslavenskih Zemalja. Bronzano Doba, vol. 4. Sarajevo: Akademija Nauka i Umjetnosti Bosne i Hercegovine, Centar za balkanoloska ispitivanja, 1983.

The Neolithic of Serbia, Archaeological Research 1948–1988, (SREJOVIĆ, D. ed. and KOSTIĆ, V. trans.). Belgrade: University of Belgrade, Centre for Archaeological Research, 1988.

Les Illyriens at les Albanais, serie de conferences tenues du 21 mai au 4 juin 1986, (GARAŠANIN, M., ed.), Beograd: Academie Serbe des Sciences et des Arts, 1988.

APOLONJO, A. (ed.), *Čapljina, ilustrovani zbornik*. Čapljina: Turistički saves opštine Čapljina, 1989.

BUDIMIR, M., *Sa balkanskih istočnika*. Beograd: Srpska Knjizevna Zadruga, 1969.

CASSON, S., *Macedonia Thrace and Illyria*. Oxford University Press, 1926.

GIMBUTAS, M. (CAMPBELL, J. forwd.), *The Language of the Goddess*. New York: Harper and Row, 1989.

HORVATIĆ, D. (ZUBČEVIĆ, I. and KMAJSKI, V. trans.), *Croatia*. Zagreb, Turistkomerc, 1992.

MOSES KHORENATS'I (THOMPSON, R. W. trans.), *History of the Armenians*. Cambridge, Massachusetts: Harvard University Press, 1978.

MOVSĒS DASXURANÇI (DOWSETT, C. J. F. trans.), *The History of the Caucasian Albanians*. London: Oxford University Press, 1961.

SREJOCIĆ, D. (EDWARDS, L. F. trans.), *Europe's First Monumental Sculpture: New Discoveries at Lepenski Vir*. New York: Stein and Day, 1972.

STIPCEVIC, A. (CULIC BURTON, S. trans.), *The Illyrians, History and Culture*. Park Ridge, New Jersey: Noyes Press, 1977.

SOUTHERN BALKANIC (GREEK) STUDIES

Acta of the 2nd. International Colloquium on Aegean Prehistory, *The First Arrival of Indo-European Elements in Greece* (Athens, April/1971). Athens: Ministry of Culture and Science, General Directorate of Antiquities, 1972.

CHAMPION, T. et al., *Prehistoric Europe*. Orlando, Florida: Academic Press, Harcourt Brace Jovanovich, Publishers, 1984.

NILSSON, M. P., *The Mycenaean Origin of Greek Mythology*. Berkeley, California: University of California Press, 1932.

NILSSON, M. P., *Homer and Mycenae*. London: Methuen and Co., 1933.

PALMER, L. R., *The Interpretation of Mycenaean Greek Texts*. Oxford: Clarendon Press, 1969.

PALMER, L. R., *Mycenaeans and Minoans, Aegean Prehistory in the Light of the Linear B Tablets*. London: Faber and Faber Ltd., 1965.

SIMPSON, R. H., *Mycenaean Greece*. Park Ridge, New Jersey: Noyes Press, 1981.

FOREWORD

LEAF, W., *Troy, a study in Homeric geography*. London: Macmillan and Co., 1912.

COOK, J. M., The Troad, *An Archaeological and Topographical study*. Oxford: Clarendon Press, 1973.

I. THE ILIAD

ALFÖLDI, A., *Early Rome and the Latins*. Ann Arbor: University of Chicago Press, 1971.

BACHRACH, B. S. (ed. and trans.), *Liber Hisoriae Francorum*. Coronado Press: 1973.

FREDEGARIUS SCHOLASTICUS (KRUSCH, B., ed.) *Chronicon Francorum*. San Antonio: Scylax Press, 2006.

GALINSKY, G. K., *Aeneas, Sicily, and Rome*. Princeton, New Jersey: Princeton University Press, 1969.

GRAVES, R. and PATAI, R., *Hebrew Myths, the Book of Genesis*. Garden City, New York: Doubleday & Company, Inc., 1964.

GREGORY OF TOURS (THORPE, L. trans.), *The History of the Franks*. Penguin Classics, 1976.

HILD, J.-A., *La Légende d'Enée Avant Virgile*. Paris: Librairie E. Leroux, 1883.

JAMES, E., *The Franks*. Oxford: Basil Blackwell, Ltd., 1988.

LENGYEL, A. and RADAN, G. T. B. (eds.), *The Archaeology of Roman Pannonia*. University Press of Kentuky and Akadémia Kiadó, Budapest, 1980.

MAC DOUGAL, H. A., *Racial Myth In English History. Trojans, Teutons, and Anglo-Saxons*. Hanover, New Hampshire: University Press of New England, 1982.

PERRET, J., *Les Origines de la Legende de Rome*. Paris: Societe d'Editions "Les Belles Lettres", 1942.

RYDBERG, V. (ANDERSON, R. B. trans.), *Teutonic Mythology*. London: Swan Sonnenschein & Co., 1891.

SMOLJAN I., *Neretva*. Zagreb: printed for the author, 1970.

SOMMER, H. O., *The Recuyell of the Historyes of Troye*, 2 vols. The Strand, London: David Nutt, 1894.

SPEICER, A. E., *The Anchor Bible Genesis, Introduction, Translation and Notes*. Garden City, New York: Doubleday & Company, Inc., 1964.

WALLACE-HADRILL, J. M., *The Long-Haired Kings, and other studies in Frankish history*. London: Mehuen & Co. Ltd., 1962.

YOUNG, A. M., *Troy and Her Legend*. University of Pittsburgh Press, 1948.

2. THE ODYSSEY

BRYCE T., *The Kingdom of the Hittites*. Oxford: Clarendon Press, 1998.

GARDNER, J. and MAIER, J. (with HENSHAW, R. A.), *Gilgamesh, Translated from the Sîn-leqi-unninnî version*. New York: Alfred Knopf, 1984.

GEORGE, A., *The Epic of Gilgamesh, The Babylonian Epic Poem and Other Texts in Akkadian and Sumerian*. New York: Barnes and Noble, 1999.

HEIDEL, A., *The Gilgamesh Epic and Old Testament Parallels*. Chicago and London: University of Chicago Press, 1963.

HOFFNER JR, H. A., *Hittite Myths*. Ataĺnta, Georgia: Scholars Press, 1990.

MCQUEEN, J. G., *The Hittites, and their Contemporaries in Asia Minor*, Thames and Hudson, 2001.

POCOCK, L. G., *Odyssean Essays*. Oxford: Basil Blackwell, 1965.

TIGAY, J. H., *The Evolution of the Gilgamesh Epic*. Philadelphia: University of Pennsylvania Press, 1982.

TRACY, S, V., *The Story of the Odyssey*. Princeton, New Jersey: Princeton University Press, 1990.

WILKES, J. J., *Dalmatia*. Cambridge, Massachusetts: Harvard University Press, 1969.

YENER, K. A. and HOFFNER JR., H. A. (eds.), *Recent Developments in Hittite Archaeology and History, Papers in Memory of Hans G. Güterbock*. Winona Lake, Indiana: Eisenbrauns, 2002.

3. HOMER

Mycenaean Geography (Proceedings of the Cambridge Colloquium, September 1976, BINTLIFF, J. ed.). Cambridge: British Association for Mycenaean Studies, The University Library Press, 1977.

The Trojan War, its historicity and context (Papers of the First Greenbank Colloquium, Liverpool, 1981, FOXHALL, L. and DAVIES, J. eds.). University of Bristol, Bristol Classical Press, 1984.

BOARDMAN, J., *The Greeks Overseas, their early colonies and trade*. London: Thames and Hudson, 1988.

COLDSTREAM, J. N., *Geometric Greece*. London: Methuen and Co., Ltd., 1977.

FEHLING, D. (HOWIE, J. G. trans.), *Herodotus and His 'Sources'*. Leeds: Francis Cairns Publications, Ltd., 1989.

GORDON, C. H., *Homer and Bible, the origin and character of East Mediterranean literature*. Ventnor, N. J.: Ventnor Publishers, 1967.

HAMMOND, N. G. L., *A History of Macedonia, historical geography and prehistory*, vol. 1. Oxford: Clarendon Press, 1972.

JEFFEREY, L. H., *Archaic Grece, The City-States c. 700–500 B.C.* London: Methuen and Co., Ltd., 1976.

WARDEN, J. (ed.), *Orpheus, the Metamorphoses of a Myth*. Toronto: University of Roronto Press, 1982.

POSTSCRIPT

BUTTERFIELD, H., *The Origins of History*. New York: Basic Books, Inc., 1981.

FORNARA, C. W., *The Nature of History in Ancient Greece and Rome*. Los Angeles: University of California Press, 1983.

HSIAO-PENG LU, S., *From Historicity to Fictionality, The Chinese Poetics of Narrative*. Stanford, California: Stanford University Press, 1994.

SUGGESTED READING

Antiche Civilita: Europa. Milano: Fabbri Editori, 2000.

Gli Etruschi, Fuori D'Etruria. (CAMPOREALE, G. ed.). (Viterbo): Arsenale Editrice, 2001.

The Cambridge Companion to Homer (FOWLER, R. ed). Cambridge University Press, 2004.

BOYLE, D. and CROOT, V., *Troy: Homer's Iliad Retold*. New York: Barnes & Noble Books, *2004*.

BURGESS, J. S. *The Tradition of the Trojan War in Homer and the Epic Cycle*. Baltimore & London: The Johns Hopkins University Press, 2001.

DI MARIO, A., *Lingua Etrusca, La ricerca dei Tirreni attraverso la lingua*. Vasto: Edizioni Cnnarsa, 2002.

LATACZ, J. (WINDLE, K. and IRELAND, R., trans.), *Troy and Homer, Towards A Solution Of An Old Mystery*. Oxford & New York: Oxford University Press, 2004.

General Index

academia: 11.
Aineias: 74, 125–127.
aoidoi (*guslars*): 12.
Aesop's *Fables*: 263.
Agenor: 221.
AKHAIIS (district), Apulia: 124.
AKHAIOI (people), occupants of ACHAIIS: 113, 118, 124, 234.
Akhilleus: 85, 86, 264.
  at SKYROS: 55, 119.
  Shield of: 266.
Alexandrine editors: 266.
ALEION (district) Molise: 61.
ALOPE (town), *Circeii*: 265.
ALPHEIOS (river), *Padus*, Po: 113.
ambrosia: 52.
ampelóessan, "vine clad": 84, 259 fn.
AMYKLAI (town), *Patavium*, Padua: 94 fn.
Antenor: 94.
anthropomorphism: 263.
archaeology (definitive proof): 11, 12.
Archaic Greece: 261.
Argo: 83.
Argonautica: see *Odyssey*.
ARGOS (town), *Cajeta*, Gaeta: 113, 114, 254, 265.
ARGOS (district), environs of *Arpi/Argyrippa*, Fóggia: 113.
ARISBE (town), *Arretium*, Arezzo: 76.
ARKADES (people), a folk in environs of STYMPHALOS, *Lacus Benacus*, Lago di Garda: 119, 266.
Ascra: 260.
Asteris (island), Pločica: 141.
Athena: 120, 219–220.
ATHENAI (lagoon), *Taras/Tarentum*, Taranto: 222, 234.
ATHOS: Pedaso (Italy): 21.

autochthony: 74.
Autolykos (Autolipos): 193, 264 fn.
AULIS (town), *Pedone*, Cuneo: 114.

Basler, Djuro: 10.
Bebrykes: 263.
bird-man versus bull-man: 123.
Bouthrotum: 126.
Brut the Trojan: 129, 130–131.

CAPES—
  Leukas, Lovište: 177–178.
Catalogue of Ships: 43, 52, 114, 116–118, 120, 127, 191 244–247, 254.
Catalogue of Trojan Forces: 43, 219, 254.
Charlemagne: 129.
classical scholarship: 28, 260.
Curetes: 261 fn.

Dalmatian Agglomeration: 11.
Dalmatian Coast: 9.
Dalmatian hound: 99.
DANAAN DEFENSIVE WALL: 95–96, 121.
Danaans: 114, 119.
Dankovsky, Gregory: 10.
Danubian Basin: 74.
Dardanelles: 244, 253.
DARDANIAN GATE: 121.
Dardanus: 72, 74, 97–98.
DAULIS (town), *Rubra*, Aulla: 114.
Delmatae (*dalmeh*, "sheep"): 32, 50, 66, 217.
DISTRICTS (*Iliad*): 29–31, 70–73.
  ASKANIA, seaboard of Troy: 71.
  DARDANIA, SKAMANDROS delta-valley: 72, 95–95.
  HYPOPLAKIA, Jezero Kuti: 24, 73, 87, 93.
  PHRYGIA, Dalmatian Archipelago: 30, 61, 71.

THYMBRA, environs of Bačinsko
    Jezero: 72–73.
  TROIA, *Illyricum*: 52.
  ZELEIA, Jablanica Gorges: 66, 73.
DISTRICTS (*Odyssey*): 159–161.
  TROIA, *Illyricum*: 70, 159, 265.
Dorians (**Dories**): 228.
Dories, folk from environs of KRETE: 83,
    230–232.
drijeva: 265, 296 FIG. 2.

ENETOI (people), a folk in environs of
  Venice: 127–12, 132.
EPHYRE (town), *Cortona*: 191.
eponymy: 74, 98.
Erikhthonios: 98 fn, 222.

Fall of Troy: 114, 124, 227, 243.
Flixes: 191.
Fredegarius: 129.
Frogmouse War: 262, 263.

Ganymedes: 100, 125.
Genesis: 133.
Geoffrey of Monmouth: 130-131.
GORTYN (town), *Mons Palatinus*,
  Palatine Hill: 127, 219.
GRAIA (mountain), *Alpes Graiae*, Graean
  Alps: 248, 249.
Greek intelligentsia: 74.
Greek Myth: 239.
Gregory of Tours: 129
guslars (*aoidoi*): 12.
Gyrai (straight), entrance (SALAMIS), to
  ATHENAI: 111.

HALIARTOS (district), environs of *Bilitio*,
  Bellinzona: 99.
HARBOURS: 170–173.
  Nerikos, Djunta Doli: 170, 264.
  Phorkys, Stonski Kanal: 171, 213.
  Rheithron, Mali Ston Kanal: 171–172.
  Telepylos, delta of SATNIOEIS: 172.
HARMA (district), Western Alpine massif:
  249.
Harpies: (see **Harpyiai**).
Hektor: 123, 266.
Helen: 113, 265.
  parallel with Kirke: 265.
HELIKONIOS (mountain), *Vesuvius*: 261.
Helicon: 260–261.

Hellas: 227–234.
Hephaistos: 56, 116, 188.
Hera and Hypnos: 21–22, 120.
Herodotus: 228, 262, 263.
Heroic Age: 124, 261.
Hesiod: 260.
historicity: 262–263.
Homer: 243, 251, 252, 254.
  antiquity: 261.
  associations with Ephesos: 253.
  archetypal image: 12.
  college of bards: 9, 12.
  contemporaries: 260.
  geographical absurdities: 16, 17–40.
  geographical context: 9.
  Graecity: 11, 259.
  "gullivered": 259.
  historicity: 262–264.
  indistinguishable from Orpheus: 12, 69,
    240.
  language: 10.
  not primary source of geography: 15 fn.
  orthodoxy: 250, 260.
  schematic balance and harmony: 265.
  sources of information: 256, 260.
  time-lines: 266.
  transference to Hellas: 11, 260.
  translation: 236–239, 260.
Homeric Epic: 259, 267.
  component elements of: 264-266.
Homeric ethnological theory: 74.
Homeric Geography: 227, 265.
  of the *Iliad*: 43.
  of the *Odyssey*: 137.
Homeridai: 252, 253.
Hyllas: 83.
Hylleis: 267.

IAONES, a folk from environs of ATHENAI:
  253.
Ionians: 232–234.
Iliad: 9, 11, 40, 43, 122, 125, 194, 243.
Iliad and *Odyssey*—
  aesthetics of translation: 260.
  authorship: 118, 229.
  chorizontes: 244.
  cultural context: 9, 260.
  geographical realities: 15.
  geography unimportant: 9.
  inseparable units: 13, 122, 243–244, 267.

institutional framework of: 69.
language of: 46.
literacy: 259.
narrative deconstructionalism: 15.
narrative lines: 265, 266.
nomenclature: 252.
points of contact with each other: 114.
preservation and transmission: 12, 235.
tutorial guidance of: 243, 256.
ILIOS: see TOWNS (*Iliad*).
Ilos: 99, 133, 219 fn.
Illyrians: 222–224,
maritime expansion: 234
trans-Balkan expansions: 236.
ISLANDS (*Iliad*): 20–22.
AIGILIPS (archipelago), *Elaphites*, Lafota, Koločep, *et al.*: 59, 195.
EKHINAI (archipelago), *Lagosta*, Lastovo: 58–59.
IMBROS, Biševo: 21.
LEKTON, *Lessina/Pharos*, Hvar: 20–21, 55–56.
LEMNOS, *Issa*, Viš: 20, 55, 116.
LESBOS, *Brattia/Thauria*, Brač: 55, 119, 263, 195.
TENEDOS, *Corcyra Nigra*, Korčula: 57–58, 114, 115.
ZAKYNTHOS, *Melita*, Mljet: 37, 58.
ISLANDS (*Odyssey*): 143–150.
[LEKTON], *Lessina/Pharos*, Hvar: 55–56, 144.
LEMNOS, *Issa*, Viš: 144, 145.
LESBOS, *Brattia/Thauria*, Brač: 143, 146, 205.
TENEDOS, *Corcyra Nigra*, Korčula: 144.
ZAKYNTHOS (**Aiaia**), *Melite*, Mljet: 144.
Aiolia, Pakleni Isles: 149, 203
Asteris, Pločica: 145.
Ogygia, ZAKYNTHOS: 147–148, 211, 266.
Planktai, Planjak, *et al*. 150, 189.
Skheria, Sčedro: 149, 195–196, 212.
Thrinakia (archipelago), AIGILIPS, *Elaphites*, Lopud, Koločep , *et al*.: 148–149, 210.
Italian Peninsula: 243.
ITHAKA: see TOWNS (*Odyssey*).
ITON (district), Cilento: 116, 248–249.

Japheth (Iapetos): 97 fn. 219.
Kadmos, 78-79, 220, 221, 263.

KARES (people), inhabitants of *Caere*: 253.
Khios (island), KRANAI (*Aethalia/Ilva*, Elba): 113, 253.
Khryseis (Khryseid): 148.
Kirke: 146, 192.
Kokytos (river), Sorgente di Pescara: 198, 206–207.
KRETE (district), environs of GORTYN: 228–229.
KRISA (town), *Crixia*, Piana Crixia: 113.
kuna (marten): 37, 58, 263.
Kydones (people), a folk in environs of KRETE: 114.
Kyknos, father of Tenes: 71 fn.
KYTHERA (island), **Kythereia**, Palagruža: 141.

Laertes: 264, 267.
Lepenski Vir: 74, 217–218.
linguistics: 10, 11, 146, 148.
ethnicon synonyms and homonyms: 12.
Luković-Pjanović, Olga: 10.
lunar cycle: 20–21.
LYKIOI (people), inhabitants of LYKIA (*Lucania*): 253.
Lykourgos: 241, 243.

Madduwattas: 192–193, 265.
MAIANDROS (river), Arrone: 253.
MANTINEIA (town), *Mantua*, Mantova:
matriarchal society: 266.
MELIBOIA (lake), *Lacus Fucinus*, Lago di Celano: 115, 116.
METHONE (town), *Marruvium*, San Benedetto: 116.
Metonic Cycle: 52.
MILETOS (lake), *Lacus Nemorensis*, Lago di Nemi: 253.
Moscow: 132–133.
MOUNTAINS (*Iliad*): 26–28, 66–69.
BATIEIA, Kosjak: 67–68.
GARGAROS, Sveti Ilija and Sveti Jure (Biokovo): 67.
IDA, Biokovo Range: 21, 67.
KALLIKOLONE, Stari Grad (Gabela): 100, 101–102, 111, 220.
NERITON, Pelješac Peninsula: 66, 68, 114.
PERGAMOS, Avala and Djerzeles (Gabela): 69, 100.
SAMOS, Sveti Ilija/Monte Vípera: 26–27,

115.
   observatory (*vinograd*): 51, 56, 57, 68–69, 188–189.
   THROSMOS, high ground of marshy plains: 68.
MOUNTAINS (*Odyssey*): 153–156.
   NERITON, Pelješac Peninsula: 143, 145, 153
   SAMOS, Sveti Ilija/Monte Vípera: 153–154.
   Hermaios, Čašnik: 155
   Korax, Stari Grad (Pelješac): 155-156, 214–215.
   Neion, Bartolomija: 156.
MYKENAI (town), Monte d'Elio: 114.
Mykenaian Culture: 261.
   Linear B: 10, 227.
MYRMIDONES (people), inhabitants of TRAKHIS: 264.
MYSOI (people), a folk in environs of ABYDOS: 253.

Nakovana: 188, 267–268.
Narona (Vid): FIG. 2, 64, 296.
natural sciences, catastrophe: 14.
Nennius: 130.
North Semitic Script: 220.

Odysseus: 123, 146, 161, 191–194, 196, 216, 264.
Odyssey: 116, 118, 243, 244, 191, 194, 223.
   Argonautica, impossible precursor: 12, 240.
   dissatisfaction new world-order: 12.
   Misadventures of Odysseus: 191–216.
omirones (Homeridai): 13, 240–242.
oral transmission of poems: 13.
Orbini, Mavro: Citluk, 111, 270 FIG. 4.
Orion: 196.
Orpheus: 69, 189, 239, 263, 267.

palladium: 100.
pamjat (remembrance): 125.
Pannonia: 128–129, 130.
   origin of Franks: 129–130.
PAPHLAGONES (people), a folk of the Po delta: 113.
paradigm-shift: 16 fn.
patriarchy versus matriarchy: 11–12, 119, 123, 194.
Pelasgian Culture: 74, 113.

PELASGOI (people), a folk in LYKIA: 71, 219.
Pešič, Radivoje: 98 fn.
PEOPLES (*Iliad*): 32–35, 74–80.
   AMAZONES, northernmost Trojan folk: 61, 77.
   ARIMOI [ARIEMOI], a folk of the SKAMANDROS delta-valley: 32–35, 67, 79 , 217.
   DARDANIOI, landbound TROES: 71, 75, 98, 128, 132, 217.
   KADMEIOI, occupants of THEBE: 78.
   KEPHALLENES, occupants of NERITON: 79, 216.
   KIKONES [SIPONES], a northern Trojan folk: 77, 123.
   KILIKES, southernmost Trojan folk: 79.
   LELEGES: inhabitants of IDA: 78.
   LESBIDES, occupants of LESBOS: 76.
   PHRYGES, occupants of PHRYGIA: 71, 75, 76–77, 252.
   PYGMAIOI, would-be occupants of Neretva delta-valley: 32–33, 79–80.
   HELLESPONTOS: 33, 79–80.
   SINTIES, occupants of LEMNOS: 76, 116.
   SMINTHIES, a folk of ZAKYNTHOS: 37, 76.
   TROES, collective name for all Trojan tribes: 71, 75, 128.
PEOPLES (*Odyssey*): 162–169.
   KEPHALLENES, occupants of NERITON: 163.
   KIKONES, a northern Trojan folk: 163.
   [KILIKES], southernmost Trojan folk: 163.
   SINTIES, occupants of LEMNOS: 163.
   TROES, collective name for all Trojan tribes: 162-163.
   Harpyiai, a star-gazing(?) folk of NERITON: 163–164, 167, 189–190, 267–268, 272 FIG. 9.
      Dardanids (?), 268.
   Kyklopes, fictitious inhabitants of LEKTON: 164–166, 202.
   Laistrygones, fictitious inhabitants of PEDASOS: 168, 204.
   Lotophagoi, fictitious inhabitants of ENOPE: 167, 201.
   Phaiakes, inhabitants of SKHERIA: 149.
   Seirenes, fictitious occupants of the PLANKTAI: 166–167, 208, 272 FIG. 9.
   Skylla: and odd folk of NERITON: 168, 208.
phallus: 12, 100–102, 118.

GENERAL INDEX 285

Philoktetes: 57, 76, 115, 116.
phyla (two major): 75.
PLACES: 38–40, 92–96.
  ILEIAN PLAIN, Hutovo Blato: 94, 99, 121, 122.
  TROIC PLAIN, Glibuša: 64, 93–94, 99, 121, 122, 296 FIG. 2.
Plerai: 217.
Pliny (the Elder): 37.
PYLOS (town), Classis: 254.
PYTHO (promontory), Portus Delphinus, Portofino: 68, 248.
Protesilaos: 115, 116.

remorse: 266.
RIVERS (Iliad): 23–25, 60–65.
  AISEPOS, Rama: 63.
  ASOPOS, Mala Neretva: 24, 65, 73, 263.
  GRANIKOS, Ugrovača: 24, 63.
  HEPTAPOROS, Ostrovača: 24, 62.
  KARHESOS, Trebižat: 39, 64.
  RHESOS, Bregava: 39, 64.
  RHODIOS, Buna: 63.
  SANGARIOS, Krka: 61.
  SATNIOEIS, Titius, Cetina: 61.
  SIMOEIS, Krupa: 64.
  SKAMANDROS, Naro, Neretva: 24, 38, 62–65.
  XANTHOS [ZANTHOS], Norino: 24, 64.
Rome: 125.
Rome-Byzantium: 267.
Rumalia: 76.
RHYTION (town), Lavinium, Pratica de Mare: 126.

Sappho: 220.
SIDONIES (people), Kydones: qv.
Samos: 256.
Samothrace: 252, 267.
SEA (Iliad): 17–19, 49–53.
  AIGAI, Modra Spilja: 27, 51–52, 142.
  HELLESPONTOS, SKAMANDROS delta: 30, 50, 114, 119.
  [IKAROPONTOS], Korčulanski Channel: 50–51.
  OKEANOS, Mare Adriaticum: 52–53, 142.
SEA (Odyssey): 141–142.
  AIGAI, Modra Spilja: 142.
  HELLESPONTOS, SKAMANDROS delta: 142.
  [IKAROPONTOS], Korčulanski Channel: 142.

  OKEANOS, Mare Adriaticum: 142.
[SKAIA] (Gabela proper): 101.
Slavic dialect: 13.
Sminthian Apollo: 36.
SPARTA (district), environs of AMYKLAI: 114, 254.
SPRINGS: 151–152.
  Arethousa, Ston: 151-152.
  Artakia, mouth of SATNIOEIS: 152.
  spring at Telepylos: 206.
stag: 147, 194.
  New World-Order: 86.
  Scythian: 149 fn., 296 FIG. 1.
STRAIGHTS: 157–158.
  Kharybdis, Vratnik: 157–158, 168, 189.
Svetovid: 147.

Tages: 78, 221.
TEGEA (district), environs of MANTINEIA, Mantua: 78, 221.
TEMPLE OF ATHENA: 100, 109–111.
Tenes: 115 fn.
THEBE (town), Klek: 24.
Thesprotoi: 234.
Thrace: 267.
Titans: 219.
Tlepolemos: 191–192.
TOWNS (Iliad): 36–37, 81–91.
  AIPEIA, Milna: 82.
  ANTHEIA [ANTREIA], Vela Luka: 83.
  DOULIKHION, Zuljana: 59, 87.
  ENOPE [EPONE], Epetium, Strobreč: 84.
  HIRA, Bogomolje: 82.
  ILIOS, Drijeva, Gabela: 97–112, 118, 270 FIG. 3, 4.
    etymology: 99, 223.
    foundation of: 97–100.
    geographical prerequisites of site: 9, 15.
    location: 259.
    places on: 102–111.
  ITHAKA, Donja Vručica: 266, 271 FIG. 6.
  KARDAMYLE, Epidaurum, Cavtat: 87.
  KHRYSA, Sobra: 37, 84.
  KILLA, Polače: 37, 83, 86, 148.
  KROKYLEIA, Corcyra, Korčula: 83.
  LYRNESSOS, Ploče: 86.
  MAKAROS, Mucurrum, Makarska: 84.
  PEDASOS, Oneum, Omiš: 61, 84.
  PHARE, Pharos, Hvar: 82.
  PLAKOS, Mlini: 30, 73, 87.

SKYROS, Pučišća: 82, 119.
THEBE, Klek: 73, 86.
TROIA, Daorson: 88–91, 99, 219, 271, FIG. 5.
TOWNS (*Odyssey*): 174–176.
  DOULIKHION, Žuljana: 174.
  ILIOS, Drijeva, Gabela: see above.
  ITHAKA, Donja Vručica: 179–190.
    description: 179.
    history: 180.
    literary center: 187–188.
    Palace of Odysseus: 180–182.
      external features: 182–184.
      internal features: 184–187.
    taking of: 214–16.
  SKYROS (spurious): 138.
  THEBE, Klek: 175.
  Ismaros, *Tragurium*, Trogir: 175–176, 200.
TRAKHIS (district), *Latium*, Lazio: 264.
trinacria: 118, 148.
Trinovantum: 130.
tro- "three": 70 fn., 131.
Troad: 253.
Trojan Diaspora: 125–134.
Trojan Geography (*Iliad*): 43–96.
  concepts and paradigms: 44.
  etymologies: 46.
  general rule: 46.
  geonyms: 44–45.
  groups of information: 43.
  intact nomenclature: 46–47.
  orthography: 48 fn.
  textual corruption: 47–48.
Trojan Geography (*Odyssey*): 137–178.
  concepts and paradigms: 139.
  corruptions and emendations: 140.
  geonyms and general rule: 139.
  groups of information: 137–138.
  identifications: 140.

  ratios of concepts: 139.
Trojan Horse: 57, 122.
Trojan War: 113–124, 259.
  duration: 120.
  purpose of: 11, 31.
Troy—
  association with Hissarlik: 11.
  duality of names: 252.
  geographical discrepancies: 256, 259.
  legends: 129.
  memory of: 256, 261.
  new geography: 254–256.
Troy VII: 251–252, 259.

Ulysses (Odysseus): 191, 127 fn.
Upanishads: 69.

Vardea (ʄArdea): 230.
Vardjaei: 128, 132, 230.
Vesuvius: 261.
Vinča—
  Culture: 74, 218–219.
  figurines: 220, 272 FIG. 7.
Vinčasko pismo: 74, 79, 220–221, 272 FIG. 8.
vinograd: 259.
Virgil, *Aeneid*: 125, 126.
vell- (ʄelj-): 50.
vit- (ʄit-): 56.
Vlixes: 191.
Vučetić, Aristid S.: 140 fn.
vulva: 12.

WALLS OF ILIOS: 100, 108.
Warsaw: 132.

žaba (frog): 55, 220, 263.
ZAKYNTHOS (island), *Melita*, Mljet: 263.
Zodiac: 51, 120, 198–199, 200–213, 266.